Perfect Score. 33

Deduct .... —

Your Score .... —

Name _____

Date _____ Class _____

Checked by _____

UNIT A—Identifying Accounting Terms

DIRECTIONS: Select the one term in Column I that best fits each definition in Column II. Print the letter identifying your choice in the Answers column.

Column I	Column II	Answers	For Scoring
A. accounting	0. Each unit of ownership in a corporation	L	0. ✔
B. accounting records	1. The determination and control of costs of a business enterprise...	G	1.
C. accounting systems	2. Orderly records of a business' financial activities..........	B	2.
D. auditing	3. An owner of one or more shares of stock of a corporation...	M	3.
E. capital stock			
F. corporation	4. The independent reviewing and issuing of an opinion on the reliability of accounting records.........................	D	4.
G. cost accounting			
H. financial accounting	5. The analysis, measurement, and interpretation of financial accounting information.............................	I	5.
I. managerial accounting			
J. partnership	6. Planning, keeping, analyzing, and interpreting financial records..	A	6.
K. proprietorship			
L. share of stock			
M. stockholder			
N. tax accounting			

7. The recording of a business' financial activities and the periodic preparation of financial reports .... **H** | 7.

8. The preparation of tax returns as well as tax planning...................................... **N** | 8.

9. An organization with the legal rights of a person and which may be owned by many persons... **F** | 9.

10. Procedures which provide for financial information which will be helpful to management.. **C** | 10.

11. A business owned by one person .... **K** | 11.

12. A business in which two or more persons combine their assets and skills .... **J** | 12.

13. Total shares of ownership in a corporation.. **E** | 13.

D1450703

UNIT B—Identifying Accounting Concepts

DIRECTIONS: Select the one concept in Column I that best fits each statement in Column II. Print the letter of your choice in the Answers column.

				Answers	For Scoring

Column I

A. Accounting Period Cycle
B. Adequate Disclosure
C. Business Entity
D. Consistent Reporting
E. Going Concern
F. Historical Cost
G. Matching Expenses with Revenue
H. Materiality
I. Objective Evidence
J. Realization of Revenue
K. Unit of Measurement

Column II

#	Statement	Answers	For Scoring
0.	All business transactions are recorded in a common unit of measurement—the dollar	K	0. ✔
14.	Each transaction is described by a business document that proves the transaction did occur	I	14.
15.	In the preparation of financial statements, the same accounting concepts are applied in the same way in each accounting period	D	15.
16.	Revenue from business activities and expenses associated with earning that revenue are recorded in the same accounting period	G	16.
17.	The actual amount paid or received is the amount recorded in accounting records	F	17.
18.	A business' financial information is recorded and reported separately from the owner's personal financial information	C	18.
19.	Financial statements are prepared with the expectation that a business will remain in operation indefinitely	E	19.
20.	Changes in financial information are reported for a specific period of time in the form of financial statements	A	20.
21.	Financial statements should contain all information necessary for a reader to understand a business' financial condition	B	21.
22.	Business activities creating dollar amounts large enough to affect business decisions should be recorded and reported as separate items in accounting records and financial statements	H	22.
23.	Revenue from business transactions is recorded at the same time goods or services are sold	J	23.

UNIT C—Analyzing Information about Accounting Professions

DIRECTIONS: Place a check mark in the proper Answers column to show whether each of the following statements is true or false.

#	Statement	True	False	For Scoring
0.	Business owners and managers use financial information to evaluate current operations and plan future operations	✔		0. ✔
24.	The growth in the accounting profession is partially due to continual changes in federal tax reporting requirements	✔		24.
25.	The CMA certificate signifies professional status in public accounting		✔	25.
26.	Public accountants sell services to individuals, businesses, and governmental units or other not-for-profit organizations	✔		26.
27.	Financial accounting provides financial reports primarily for use by persons internal to the organization		✔	27.
28.	Cost accounting provides information for internal decision making concerning the costs of operating merchandising and manufacturing businesses	✔		28.
29.	An auditor examines the records which support the financial records of a business to assure that generally accepted accounting principles (GAAP) are being followed	✔		29.
30.	Limited liability is an advantage of a proprietorship		✔	30.
31.	Difficulty of establishment is a disadvantage of a partnership		✔	31.
32.	The Financial Accounting Standards Board (FASB) is responsible for the development of standards for financial accounting and reporting	✔		32.
33.	Administering and grading the uniform CPA examination is one of the primary roles of the FASB		✔	33.

Perfect Score. 50

Deduct .... __

Your Score .... __

Name _____

Date _____ Class _____

Checked by _____

STUDY
GUIDE
2

UNIT A—Identifying Accounting Terms

DIRECTIONS: Select the one term in Column I that best fits each definition in Column II. Print the letter identifying your choice in the Answers column.

Column I	Column II	Answers	For Scoring
A. account	0. An entry recorded in a credit column	K	0. ✔
B. account balance	1. A ledger that is summarized in a single general ledger account	AB	1.
C. accounting equation			
D. asset	2. The value of the owner's equity	F	2.
E. bank statement	3. A cash discount on purchases taken by a buyer	X	3.
F. capital	4. An account in a general ledger that summarizes all accounts in a subsidiary ledger	J	4.
G. cash discount			
H. contra account	5. An amount of cash kept on hand and used for making small payments	V	5.
I. contra balance			
J. controlling account	6. A business that purchases and sells goods	U	6.
K. credit	7. Anything of value that is owned	D	7.
L. debit	8. An amount owed by a business	T	8.
M. departmental accounting system	9. An entry recorded in a debit column	L	9.
N. double-entry accounting	10. A group of accounts	S	10.
	11. Recording both debit and credit parts of a transaction	N	11.
O. equities	12. A form for recording accounting information in chronological order	R	12.
P. general journal			
Q. general ledger	13. An account that reduces a related amount on financial statements	H	13.
R. journal			
S. ledger	14. A journal used to record only one kind of transaction	AA	14.
T. liability	15. A business paper from which information is obtained for a journal entry	Z	15.
U. merchandising business			
V. petty cash	16. The difference between the totals of amounts in an account's debit and credit columns	B	16.
W. posting			
X. purchases discount	17. Financial rights to the assets of a business	O	17.
Y. reconciling a bank statement	18. An account balance that is opposite the normal balance	I	18.
Z. source document	19. A journal with two amount columns to record transactions that cannot be recorded in a special journal	P	19.
AA. special journal			
AB. subsidiary ledger			

	Answers	For Scoring
20. Transferring information from journal entries to ledger accounts	W	20.
21. Bringing information on a bank statement and a checkbook into agreement	Y	21.
22. A deduction that a seller allows on an invoice amount to encourage prompt payment	G	22.
23. An accounting system showing accounting information for two or more departments	M	23.
24. A report of deposits, withdrawals, and bank balance sent to a depositor by a bank	E	24.
25. An equation showing the relationship among assets, liabilities, and capital	C	25.
26. A ledger that contains all accounts needed to prepare financial statements	Q	26.
27. An accounting form used to sort and summarize changes in a specific item	A	27.

UNIT B—Analyzing Accounting Principles, Concepts, and Procedures

DIRECTIONS: Place a check mark in the proper Answers column to show whether each of the following statements is true or false.

	Answers True	Answers False	For Scoring
0. Asset accounts have normal credit balances....................................		✔	0. ✔
28. Liability accounts have normal credit balances......................................	✔		28.
29. An owner's capital account has a normal credit balance..........................	✔		29.
30. Revenue accounts have normal debit balances.....................................		✔	30.
31. Cost accounts have normal debit balances...	✔		31.
32. Expense accounts have normal credit balances.....................................		✔	32.
33. Increases in asset accounts are recorded on the debit side........................	✔		33.
34. Increases in liability accounts are recorded on the debit side.....................		✔	34.
35. Decreases in revenue accounts are recorded on the credit side..................		✔	35.
36. Decreases in cost accounts are recorded on the credit side.......................	✔		36.
37. The accounting equation may be stated as assets = liabilities....................		✔	37.
38. Having a business paper supporting each journal entry is an application of the accounting concept Unit of Measurement......................................		✔	38.
39. Each business transaction causes a change in two or more account balances..	✔		39.
40. Increases in an account balance are recorded on the account's normal debit side		✔	40.
41. In a departmental accounting system, gross profit is figured for each department..	✔		41.
42. A departmental purchases journal should contain a Purchases Debit column for each department...	✔		42.
43. When a buyer returns merchandise for credit, the buyer issues a debit memorandum for the amount of the return..	✔		43.
44. Individual amounts in a purchases journal's Accounts Payable Credit column are posted at the end of each month..		✔	44.
45. Using a debit memorandum as the source document for a purchases returns and allowances transaction is an application of the accounting concept Objective Evidence	✔		45.
46. A purchases discount reduces the balance of the purchases account.............		✔	46.
47. Amounts in the General Debit and General Credit columns of a cash payments journal are posted individually...	✔		47.
48. When a bank statement is sent to a depositor by a bank, the depositor's canceled checks are normally included with the statement.........................	✔		48.
49. The entry to record a bank service charge is a credit to Petty Cash because the amount is small..		✔	49.
50. A depositor must deduct from the checkbook balance all bank charges listed on the bank statement	✔		50.

Journalizing and posting departmental purchases on
account and purchases returns and allowances

PURCHASES JOURNAL   PAGE 16

	DATE		ACCOUNT CREDITED	PURCH. NO.	POST. REF.	ACCOUNTS PAYABLE CREDIT (1)	PURCHASES DEBIT MEN'S SHOES (2)	PURCHASES DEBIT WOMEN'S SHOES (3)	
1	Aug. 19--	1	Bond Shoes	283	220	1 2 5 0 00		1 2 5 0 00	1
2		2	Catalina Shoes, Inc.	284	230	2 1 3 0 00		2 1 3 0 00	2
3		4	Artex Footwear	285	210	9 6 5 00	9 6 5 00		3
4		9	Delta Distributors	286	250	8 4 5 00	8 4 5 00		4
5		13	Gamex Shoes Unlimited	287	260	1 1 3 5 00	1 1 3 5 00		5
6		18	Sanz Shoes	288	280	2 6 8 00		2 6 8 00	6
7		24	Catalina Shoes, Inc.	289	230	8 9 3 00		8 9 3 00	7
8		27	Dade-Shoes, Inc.	290	240	1 0 4 5 00	1 0 4 5 00		8
9		30	Bond Shoes	291	220	1 3 6 0 00		1 3 6 0 00	9
10		31	Totals			9 8 9 1 00	3 9 9 0 00	5 9 0 1 00	10
11						(2105)	(5105-1)	(5105-2)	11
12									12

[1, 2, 4]

PURCHASES RETURNS AND ALLOWANCES JOURNAL   PAGE 7

	DATE		ACCOUNT DEBITED	DEBIT MEMO. NO.	POST. REF.	ACCOUNTS PAYABLE DEBIT (1)	PURCHASES RETURNS AND ALLOWANCES CREDIT MEN'S SHOES (2)	PURCHASES RETURNS AND ALLOWANCES CREDIT WOMEN'S SHOES (3)	
1	Aug. 19--	6	Dade-Shoes, Inc.	36	240	1 6 5 00	1 6 5 00		1
2		15	Bond Shoes	37	220	7 5 00		7 5 00	2
3		20	Artex Footwear	38	210	1 2 0 00	1 2 0 00		3
4		23	Perstel Shoes	39	270	5 5 00		5 5 00	4
5		31	Catalina Shoes, Inc.	40	230	1 4 0 00		1 4 0 00	5
6		31	Totals			5 5 5 00	2 8 5 00	2 7 0 00	6
7						(2105)	(5110-1)	(5110-2)	7
8									8
9									9
10									10
11									11
12									12

GENERAL LEDGER

ACCOUNT Accounts Payable   ACCOUNT NO. 2105

DATE		ITEM	POST. REF.	DEBIT	CREDIT	BALANCE	
						DEBIT	CREDIT
Aug.¹⁹	1	Balance	✓				2 1 7 0 00
	31		P16		9 8 9 1 00		12 0 6 1 00
	31		PR7	5 5 5 00			11 5 0 6 00

ACCOUNT Purchases — Men's Shoes   ACCOUNT NO. 5105-1

DATE		ITEM	POST. REF.	DEBIT	CREDIT	BALANCE	
						DEBIT	CREDIT
Aug.¹⁹	31		P16	3 9 9 0 00		3 9 9 0 00	

ACCOUNT Purchases — Women's Shoes   ACCOUNT NO. 5105-2

DATE		ITEM	POST. REF.	DEBIT	CREDIT	BALANCE	
						DEBIT	CREDIT
Aug.¹⁹	31		P16	5 9 0 1 00		5 9 0 1 00	

ACCOUNT Purchases Returns and Allowances — Men's Shoes   ACCOUNT NO. 5110-1

DATE		ITEM	POST. REF.	DEBIT	CREDIT	BALANCE	
						DEBIT	CREDIT
Aug.¹⁹	31		PR7		2 8 5 00		2 8 5 00

ACCOUNT Purchases Returns and Allowances — Women's Shoes   ACCOUNT NO. 5110-2

DATE		ITEM	POST. REF.	DEBIT	CREDIT	BALANCE	
						DEBIT	CREDIT
Aug.¹⁹	31		PR7		2 7 0 00		2 7 0 00

ACCOUNTS PAYABLE LEDGER

VENDOR Artex Footwear   **VENDOR NO.**   210

DATE		ITEM	POST. REF.	DEBIT	CREDIT	CREDIT BALANCE
19-- Aug.	1	Balance	✓			4 8 0 00
	4		P16		9 6 5 00	1 4 4 5 00
	20		PR7	1 2 0 00		1 3 2 5 00

VENDOR Bond Shoes   **VENDOR NO.**   220

DATE		ITEM	POST. REF.	DEBIT	CREDIT	CREDIT BALANCE
19-- Aug.	1		P16		1 2 5 0 00	1 2 5 0 00
	30		P16		1 3 6 0 00	2 6 1 0 00
	15		PR7	7 5 00		2 5 3 5 00

VENDOR Catalina Shoes, Inc.   **VENDOR NO.**   230

DATE		ITEM	POST. REF.	DEBIT	CREDIT	CREDIT BALANCE
19-- Aug.	1	Balance	✓			7 6 0 00
	2		P16		2 1 3 0 00	2 8 9 0 00
	24		P16		8 9 3 00	3 7 8 3 00
	31		PR7	1 4 0 00		3 6 4 3 00

VENDOR Dade-Shoes, Inc.   **VENDOR NO.**   240

DATE		ITEM	POST. REF.	DEBIT	CREDIT	CREDIT BALANCE
19-- Aug.	1	Balance	✓			5 7 0 00
	27		P16		1 0 4 5 00	1 6 1 5 00
	6		PR7	1 6 5 00		1 4 5 0 00

VENDOR Delta Distributors   **VENDOR NO.**   250

DATE		ITEM	POST. REF.	DEBIT	CREDIT	CREDIT BALANCE
19-- Aug.	9		P16		8 4 5 00	8 4 5 00

VENDOR Gamex Shoes Unlimited   **VENDOR NO.**   260

DATE		ITEM	POST. REF.	DEBIT	CREDIT	CREDIT BALANCE
19-- Aug.	13		P16		1 1 3 5 00	1 1 3 5 00

ACCOUNTS PAYABLE LEDGER

VENDOR Perstel Shoes   VENDOR NO.   270

DATE		ITEM	POST. REF.	DEBIT	CREDIT	CREDIT BALANCE
19-- Aug.	1	Balance	✔			3 6 0 00
	23		PR7	5 5 00		3 0 5 00

VENDOR Sanz Shoes   VENDOR NO.   280

DATE		ITEM	POST. REF.	DEBIT	CREDIT	CREDIT BALANCE
19-- Aug.	18		P16		2 6 8 00	2 6 8 00

Figuring purchases discounts and amounts due

1	2	3	4	5
Purch. No.	Purchase Amount	Discount Percent	Discount Amount	Amount Due
26	$1,340.00	2%	$26.80	$1,313.20
27	845.00	1%	8.45	836.55
28	1,560.00	2%	31.20	1,528.80
29	936.00	2%	18.72	917.28
30	1,475.00	1%	14.75	1,460.25
31	780.00	1%	7.80	772.20
32	295.00	2%	5.90	289.10
33	650.00	2%	13.00	637.00

Journalizing and posting departmental cash payments   [1–3]

CASH PAYMENTS JOURNAL

PAGE 15

| | | | | GENERAL | | ACCOUNTS PAYABLE DEBIT | PURCH. DISCOUNT CR. | | CASH CREDIT |
DATE	ACCOUNT TITLE	CK. NO.	POST. REF.	DEBIT	CREDIT		SKI CLOTHING	SKI EQUIPMENT	
				1	2	3	4	5	6
19-- Nov. 1	Rent Expense	303	6230	1500000					1500000
2	Miscellaneous Expense	304	6220	11000					11000
4	Webster Ski Apparel	305	240			88500	1770		86730
5	Advertising Expense	306	6105	8350					8350
8	Sportstown, Inc.	307	220			125000		1250	123750
10	Supplies	308	1130	8375					8375
13	Century Sportswear	309	210			96300	1926		94374
15	Miscellaneous Expense	310	6220	3350					3350
17	Supplies	311	1130	5200					5200
21	Supplies	312	1130	7900					20200
	Advertising Expense		6105	8340					
	Miscellaneous Expense		6220	3960					
23	United Skis	313	230			184000		3680	180320
27	United Skis	314	230			146000		2920	143080
30	Miscellaneous Expense	M26	6220	1430					1430
30	Credit Card Fee Expense	M27	6110	38820					38820
30	Totals			246725		639800	3696	7850	874979
				(✓)		(2105)	(5115-1)	(5115-2)	(1105)

GENERAL LEDGER

ACCOUNT Cash   ACCOUNT NO. 1105

DATE		ITEM	POST. REF.	DEBIT	CREDIT	BALANCE	
						DEBIT	CREDIT
19-- Nov.	1	Balance	✔			18 3 8 0 00	
	30		CP15		8 7 4 9 79	9 6 3 0 21	

ACCOUNT Petty Cash   ACCOUNT NO. 1110

DATE		ITEM	POST. REF.	DEBIT	CREDIT	BALANCE	
						DEBIT	CREDIT
19-- Nov.	1	Balance	✔			5 0 0 00	

ACCOUNT Supplies   ACCOUNT NO. 1130

DATE		ITEM	POST. REF.	DEBIT	CREDIT	BALANCE	
						DEBIT	CREDIT
19-- Nov.	1	Balance	✔			1 2 6 0 00	
	10		CP15	8 3 75		1 3 4 3 75	
	17		CP15	5 2 00		1 3 9 5 75	
	21		CP15	7 9 00		1 4 7 4 75	

ACCOUNT Accounts Payable   ACCOUNT NO. 2105

DATE		ITEM	POST. REF.	DEBIT	CREDIT	BALANCE	
						DEBIT	CREDIT
19-- Nov.	1	Balance	✔				6 3 9 8 00
	30		CP15	6 3 9 8 00			

ACCOUNT Purchases Discount — Ski Clothing   ACCOUNT NO. 5115-1

DATE		ITEM	POST. REF.	DEBIT	CREDIT	BALANCE	
						DEBIT	CREDIT
19-- Nov.	30		CP15		3 6 96		3 6 96

GENERAL LEDGER

ACCOUNT Purchases Discount—Ski Equipment   ACCOUNT NO. 5115-2

DATE	ITEM	POST. REF.	DEBIT	CREDIT	BALANCE DEBIT	BALANCE CREDIT
Nov. 30		CP15		7 8 50		7 8 50

ACCOUNT Advertising Expense   ACCOUNT NO. 6105

DATE	ITEM	POST. REF.	DEBIT	CREDIT	BALANCE DEBIT	BALANCE CREDIT
Nov. 5		CP15	8 3 50		8 3 50	
21		CP15	8 3 40		1 6 6 90	

ACCOUNT Credit Card Fee Expense   ACCOUNT NO. 6110

DATE	ITEM	POST. REF.	DEBIT	CREDIT	BALANCE DEBIT	BALANCE CREDIT
Nov. 30		CP15	3 8 8 20		3 8 8 20	

ACCOUNT Miscellaneous Expense   ACCOUNT NO. 6220

DATE	ITEM	POST. REF.	DEBIT	CREDIT	BALANCE DEBIT	BALANCE CREDIT
Nov. 2		CP15	1 1 0 00		1 1 0 00	
15		CP15	3 3 50		1 4 3 50	
21		CP15	3 9 60		1 8 3 10	
30		CP15	1 4 30		1 9 7 40	

ACCOUNT Rent Expense   ACCOUNT NO. 6230

DATE	ITEM	POST. REF.	DEBIT	CREDIT	BALANCE DEBIT	BALANCE CREDIT
Nov. 1		CP15	1 5 0 0 00		1 5 0 0 00	

ACCOUNTS PAYABLE LEDGER

VENDOR Century Sportswear   **VENDOR NO.** 210

DATE		ITEM	POST. REF.	DEBIT	CREDIT	CREDIT BALANCE
Nov.	3		P14		9 6 3 00	9 6 3 00
	13		CP15	9 6 3 00		————

VENDOR Sportstown, Inc.   **VENDOR NO.** 220

DATE		ITEM	POST. REF.	DEBIT	CREDIT	CREDIT BALANCE
Nov.	1	Balance	✔			1 2 5 0 00
	8		CP15	1 2 5 0 00		————

VENDOR United Skis   **VENDOR NO.** 230

DATE		ITEM	POST. REF.	DEBIT	CREDIT	CREDIT BALANCE
Nov.	13		P14		1 8 4 0 00	1 8 4 0 00
	17		P14		1 4 6 0 00	3 3 0 0 00
	23		CP15	1 8 4 0 00		1 4 6 0 00
	27		CP15	1 4 6 0 00		————

VENDOR Webster Ski Apparel   **VENDOR NO.** 240

DATE		ITEM	POST. REF.	DEBIT	CREDIT	CREDIT BALANCE
Nov.	1	Balance	✔			8 8 5 00
	4		CP15	8 8 5 00		————

Reconciling a bank statement

RECONCILIATION OF BANK STATEMENT

Date _10/28/--_

1. Enter CHECKBOOK BALANCE as shown on check stub.
2. Enter and add bank charges to obtain TOTAL BANK CHARGES.
3. Deduct TOTAL BANK CHARGES from CHECKBOOK BALANCE to obtain ADJUSTED CHECKBOOK BALANCE.
4. Enter BANK BALANCE as shown on bank statement.
5. Enter and add the amounts of any outstanding deposits recorded on the check stubs but not listed on the bank statement to obtain TOTAL OUTSTANDING DEPOSITS.
6. Add TOTAL OUTSTANDING DEPOSITS to BANK BALANCE to obtain TOTAL.
7. Sort all checks included in the statement numerically or by date issued.
   a. Check off on the check stubs of the checkbook each of the checks paid by the bank.
   b. Enter the check numbers and amounts of checks still outstanding.
   c. Add the outstanding checks to obtain TOTAL OUTSTANDING CHECKS.
8. Deduct TOTAL OUTSTANDING CHECKS from TOTAL to obtain ADJUSTED BANK BALANCE.
9. The ADJUSTED CHECKBOOK BALANCE and the ADJUSTED BANK BALANCE should agree, proving that both the checkbook balance and the bank balance are correct.

(1) CHECKBOOK BALANCE .... $ _38,860.00_

BANK CHARGES

Description	Amount	
Service Charge	11	80
Credit Card Charge	425	20

(2) DEDUCT TOTAL BANK CHARGES ... $ _437.00_

(3) ADJUSTED CHECKBOOK BALANCE . $ _38,423.00_

(4) BANK BALANCE .... $ _32,820.00_

OUTSTANDING DEPOSITS

Date	Amount	
10/27	6,152	75

(5) ADD TOTAL OUTSTANDING DEPOSITS .... $ _6,152.75_

(6) TOTAL .... $ _38,972.75_

OUTSTANDING CHECKS

CK. NO.	Amount	
361	89	50
362	460	25

(7) DEDUCT TOTAL OUTSTANDING CHECKS .... $ _549.75_

(8) ADJUSTED BANK BALANCE .... $ _38,423.00_

PURCHASES JOURNAL   PAGE 18

	DATE		ACCOUNT CREDITED	PURCH. NO.	POST. REF.	ACCOUNTS PAYABLE CREDIT (1)	PURCHASES DEBIT PAINT (2)	PURCHASES DEBIT WALLPAPER (3)	
1	Nov.	2	Julian Wallcovering	262		7 5 0 00		7 5 0 00	1
2		3	Trail-Color, Inc.	263		8 4 0 00	8 4 0 00		2
3		8	Zep Paint Co.	264		3 8 8 00	3 8 8 00		3
4		14	Famis, Inc.	265		5 5 0 00		5 5 0 00	4
5		18	Trail-Color, Inc.	266		1 1 2 0 00	1 1 2 0 00		5
6		23	Collazo Wallpaper	267		3 3 6 00		3 3 6 00	6
7		24	Astro Paint	268		7 2 6 40	7 2 6 40		7
8		30	Totals			4 7 1 0 40	3 0 7 4 40	1 6 3 6 00	8
9									9
10									10
11									11
12									12
13									13

[1, 2]

PURCHASES RETURNS AND ALLOWANCES JOURNAL   PAGE 6

	DATE		ACCOUNT DEBITED	DEBIT MEMO. NO.	POST. REF.	ACCOUNTS PAYABLE DEBIT (1)	PURCHASES RETURNS AND ALLOWANCES CREDIT PAINT (2)	PURCHASES RETURNS AND ALLOWANCES CREDIT WALLPAPER (3)	
1	Nov.	7	Trail-Color, Inc.	28		8 8 00	8 8 00		1
2		16	Collazo Wallpaper	29		1 2 2 50		1 2 2 50	2
3		18	Famis, Inc.	30		7 5 00		7 5 00	3
4		30	Totals			2 8 5 50	8 8 00	1 9 7 50	4
5									5
6									6
7									7
8									8
9									9
10									10
11									11
12									12
13									13

[1, 3, 4]

CASH PAYMENTS JOURNAL

PAGE 16

	DATE	ACCOUNT TITLE	CK. NO.	POST. REF.	GENERAL DEBIT	GENERAL CREDIT	ACCOUNTS PAYABLE DEBIT	PURCH. DISCOUNT CR. PAINT	PURCH. DISCOUNT CR. WALLPAPER	CASH CREDIT	
1	19-- Nov. 1	Rent Expense	273		1 3 5 0 00					1 3 5 0 00	1
2	1	Advertising Expense	274		8 2 50					8 2 50	2
3	3	Astro Paint	275				4 6 0 00	9 20		4 5 0 80	3
4	5	Julian Wallcovering	276				7 4 5 00		1 4 90	7 3 0 10	4
5	11	Supplies	277		8 2 50					8 2 50	5
6	14	Julian Wallcovering	278				7 5 0 00			7 5 0 00	6
7	17	Trail-Color, Inc.	279				7 5 2 00			7 5 2 00	7
8	18	Zep Paint Co.	280				3 8 8 00	7 76		3 8 0 24	8
9	21	Supplies	281		6 2 30					6 2 30	9
10	24	Famis, Inc.	282				4 7 5 00		9 50	4 6 5 50	10
11	26	Supplies	283		4 3 00					4 3 00	11
12	28	Trail-Color, Inc.	284				1 1 2 0 00	2 2 40		1 0 9 7 60	12
13	29	Supplies	285		4 7 10					2 0 1 00	13
14		Advertising Expense			6 2 50						14
15		Miscellaneous Expense			9 1 40						15
16	30	Miscellaneous Expense	M31		1 0 20					1 0 20	16
17	30	Credit Card Fee Expense	M32		3 9 2 80					3 9 2 80	17
18	30	Totals			2 2 2 4 30		4 6 9 0 00	3 9 36	2 4 40	6 8 5 0 54	18
19											19
20											20
21											21
22											22
23											23

RECONCILIATION OF BANK STATEMENT

Date _11/30/--_

1. Enter CHECKBOOK BALANCE as shown on check stub.
2. Enter and add bank charges to obtain TOTAL BANK CHARGES.
3. Deduct TOTAL BANK CHARGES from CHECKBOOK BALANCE to obtain ADJUSTED CHECKBOOK BALANCE.
4. Enter BANK BALANCE as shown on bank statement.
5. Enter and add the amounts of any outstanding deposits recorded on the check stubs but not listed on the bank statement to obtain TOTAL OUTSTANDING DEPOSITS.
6. Add TOTAL OUTSTANDING DEPOSITS to BANK BALANCE to obtain TOTAL.
7. Sort all checks included in the statement numerically or by date issued.
    a. Check off on the check stubs of the checkbook each of the checks paid by the bank.
    b. Enter the check numbers and amounts of checks still outstanding.
    c. Add the outstanding checks to obtain TOTAL OUTSTANDING CHECKS.
8. Deduct TOTAL OUTSTANDING CHECKS from TOTAL to obtain ADJUSTED BANK BALANCE.
9. The ADJUSTED CHECKBOOK BALANCE and the ADJUSTED BANK BALANCE should agree, proving that both the checkbook balance and the bank balance are correct.

(1) CHECKBOOK BALANCE .... $ _18,480.00_

BANK CHARGES

Description	Amount	
Service Charge	10	20
Credit Card Charge	392	80

(2) DEDUCT TOTAL BANK CHARGES ... $ _403.00_

(3) ADJUSTED CHECKBOOK BALANCE . $ _18,077.00_

(4) BANK BALANCE .... $ _16,378.00_

OUTSTANDING DEPOSITS

Date	Amount	
11/29	3,040	60

(5) ADD TOTAL OUTSTANDING DEPOSITS .... $ _3,040.60_

(6) TOTAL .... $ _19,418.60_

OUTSTANDING CHECKS

CK. NO.	Amount	
283	43	00
284	1,097	60
285	201	00

(7) DEDUCT TOTAL OUTSTANDING CHECKS .... $ _1,341.60_

(8) ADJUSTED BANK BALANCE .... $ _18,077.00_

Recording purchases at net amount and
using the account Discounts Lost

PURCHASES JOURNAL   PAGE 14

	DATE		ACCOUNT CREDITED	PURCH. NO.	POST. REF.	ACCOUNTS PAYABLE CREDIT (1)	PURCHASES DEBIT PAINT (2)	PURCHASES DEBIT WALLPAPER (3)	
1	19-- Nov.	2	Julian Wallcovering	262		7 3 5 00		7 3 5 00	1
2		3	Trail-Color, Inc.	263		8 2 3 20	8 2 3 20		2
3		8	Zep Paint Co.	264		3 8 0 24	3 8 0 24		3
4		14	Famis, Inc.	265		5 3 9 00		5 3 9 00	4
5		18	Trail-Color, Inc.	266		1 0 9 7 60	1 0 9 7 60		5
6		23	Collazo Wallpaper	267		3 2 9 28		3 2 9 28	6
7		24	Astro Paint	268		7 1 1 87	7 1 1 87		7
8		30	Totals			4 6 1 6 19	3 0 1 2 91	1 6 0 3 28	8
9									9
10									10
11									11
12									12

[1, 2]

PURCHASES RETURNS AND ALLOWANCES JOURNAL   PAGE 7

	DATE		ACCOUNT DEBITED	DEBIT MEMO. NO.	POST. REF.	ACCOUNTS PAYABLE DEBIT (1)	PURCHASES RETURNS AND ALLOWANCES CREDIT PAINT (2)	PURCHASES RETURNS AND ALLOWANCES CREDIT WALLPAPER (3)	
1	19-- Nov.	7	Trail-Color, Inc.	28		8 6 24	8 6 24		1
2		16	Collazo Wallpaper	29		1 2 0 05		1 2 0 05	2
3		18	Famis, Inc.	30		7 3 50		7 3 50	3
4		30	Totals			2 7 9 79	8 6 24	1 9 3 55	4
5									5
6									6
7									7
8									8
9									9
10									10
11									11
12									12

[1,2]

CASH PAYMENTS JOURNAL

DATE		ACCOUNT TITLE	CK. NO.	POST. REF.	GENERAL DEBIT	GENERAL CREDIT	ACCOUNTS PAYABLE DEBIT	CASH CREDIT	
19-- Nov.	1	Rent Expense	273		1 3 5 0 00			1 3 5 0 00	1
	1	Advertising Expense	274		8 2 50			8 2 50	2
	3	Astro Paint	275				4 5 0 80	4 5 0 80	3
	5	Julian Wallcovering	276				7 3 0 10	7 3 0 10	4
	11	Supplies	277		8 2 50			8 2 50	5
	14	Julian Wallcovering	278				7 3 5 00	7 5 0 00	6
		Discounts Lost			1 5 00				7
	17	Trail-Color, Inc.	279				7 3 6 96	7 5 2 00	8
		Discounts Lost			1 5 04				9
	18	Zep Paint Co.	280				3 8 0 24	3 8 0 24	10
	21	Supplies	281		6 2 30			6 2 30	11
	24	Famis, Inc.	282				4 6 5 50	4 6 5 50	12
	26	Supplies	283		4 3 00			4 3 00	13
	28	Trail-Color, Inc.	284				1 0 9 7 60	1 0 9 7 60	14
	29	Supplies	285		4 7 10			2 0 1 00	15
		Advertising Expense			6 2 50				16
		Miscellaneous Expense			9 1 40				17
	30	Miscellaneous Expense	M31		1 0 20			1 0 20	18
	30	Credit Card Fee Expense	M32		3 9 2 80			3 9 2 80	19
	30	Totals			2 2 5 4 34		4 5 9 6 20	6 8 5 0 54	20
									21
									22
									23
									24
									25

Name _____

Deduct .... __   Date _____ Class _____

Your Score .... __   Checked by _____

UNIT A—Analyzing Departmental Accounting Procedures

DIRECTIONS: Place a check mark in the proper Answers column to show whether each of the following statements is true or false.

	Answers		For Scoring
	True	**False**	
0. Records of departmental operating expenses are necessary to determine departmental gross profit from operations		✔	**0.** ✔
1. Preparing two copies of a sales invoice provides a copy for the customer and a copy for the business to use for journalizing the transaction	✔		**1.**
2. The details of each sales invoice are recorded on one line of a departmental sales journal	✔		**2.**
3. Each departmental sales journal entry is posted individually as a credit to the appropriate customer's account		✔	**3.**
4. After posting a line of a departmental sales journal, an account number is written in the journal's Post. Ref. column	✔		**4.**
5. The seller prepares a debit memorandum for a sales returns and allowances transaction		✔	**5.**
6. An account showing deductions from a sales account is known as a contra cost account		✔	**6.**
7. A departmental cash receipts journal contains a Cash Debit column for each department		✔	**7.**
8. A cash discount on sales is called a sales discount	✔		**8.**
9. Both the debit part and the credit part of a cash and credit card sales transaction are recorded in special amount columns in a departmental cash receipts journal	✔		**9.**
10. After each amount in a departmental cash receipts journal's General Credit column has been posted, a check mark is placed in the journal's Post. Ref. column		✔	**10.**
11. Each amount in a departmental cash receipts journal's Accounts Receivable Credit column is posted individually to the accounts receivable ledger	✔		**11.**
12. Each amount in a departmental cash receipts journal's Sales Credit columns is posted daily to the appropriate account in the general ledger		✔	**12.**
13. Each amount in a departmental cash receipts journal's Cash Debit column is posted individually to the debit side of the cash account		✔	**13.**
14. The total of each departmental cash receipts journal's Sales Credit column is posted to a general ledger account	✔		**14.**
15. Determining that the amount of cash on hand agrees with the accounting records is called proving cash	✔		**15.**

DIRECTIONS: For each item below, select the choice that best completes the sentence. Print the letter identifying your choice in the Answers column.

	Answers	For Scoring
0. The source document for recording a transaction in a departmental sales journal is **(A)** a cash register tape **(B)** a memorandum **(C)** a sales invoice **(D)** an adding machine tape	C	0. ✔
16. One item of information available through a departmental accounting system is the **(A)** net income or net loss for each department **(B)** gross profit for each department **(C)** administrative expenses for each department **(D)** total operating expenses for each department	B	16.
17. Supergolf's sales journal has **(A)** one debit column **(B)** two debit columns **(C)** three debit columns **(D)** no debit columns	A	17.
18. Supergolf's sales journal has **(A)** one credit column **(B)** two credit columns **(C)** three credit columns **(D)** four credit columns	C	18.
19. Recording all sales at the time of sale, regardless of when payment is made, is an application of the **(A)** Going Concern concept **(B)** Realization of Revenue concept **(C)** Matching Expenses with Revenue concept **(D)** Historical Cost concept	B	19.
20. Each amount in a departmental sales journal's Accounts Receivable Debit column is **(A)** posted daily **(B)** posted weekly **(C)** posted at the end of the month **(D)** not posted	A	20.
21. Completion of posting to a customer's account is indicated by placing in the departmental sales journal's Post. Ref. column **(A)** a check mark **(B)** a customer number **(C)** a page number **(D)** a sales number	B	21.
22. Each amount in a departmental sales journal's Accounts Receivable Debit column is **(A)** posted as a debit to a customer's account **(B)** posted as a credit to a customer's account **(C)** posted to a controlling account **(D)** not posted	A	22.
23. Completion of posting the total of any column of a departmental sales journal is shown by **(A)** placing a check mark under the total **(B)** writing a capital S under the total **(C)** writing a page number under the total **(D)** writing an account number under the total	D	23.
24. The account credited when a customer returns merchandise or is granted an allowance is **(A)** Accounts Payable **(B)** Sales Returns and Allowances **(C)** the appropriate departmental sales account **(D)** none of these	D	24.
25. The source document for a sales returns and allowances transaction is **(A)** a memorandum **(B)** a debit memorandum **(C)** a credit memorandum **(D)** none of these	C	25.
26. Each amount written in a sales returns and allowances journal's Accounts Receivable Credit column is **(A)** posted daily **(B)** posted weekly **(C)** posted monthly **(D)** not posted	A	26.
27. Completion of posting the total of any column of a departmental sales returns and allowances journal is shown by **(A)** writing the letters SR under the total **(B)** writing an account number under the total **(C)** placing a check mark under the total **(D)** none of these	B	27.
28. A departmentalized cash receipts journal has an amount column for each department for the general ledger account **(A)** Cash **(B)** Accounts Receivable **(C)** Sales **(D)** none of these	C	28.
29. The source document for recording cash and credit card sales in a departmental cash receipts journal is **(A)** an adding machine tape **(B)** a cash register tape **(C)** a sales invoice **(D)** a receipt	B	29.
30. An account showing a deduction from another general ledger account is known as a **(A)** minus account **(B)** negative account **(C)** contra account **(D)** counter account	C	30.

Journalizing and posting departmental sales on account
and sales returns and allowances

SALES JOURNAL

PAGE 9

	DATE	ACCOUNT DEBITED	SALE NO.	POST. REF.	ACCOUNTS RECEIVABLE DEBIT (1)	SALES TAX PAYABLE CREDIT (2)	SALES CREDIT WALLPAPER (3)	SALES CREDIT PAINT (4)	
1	19-- Sept. 1	Molly Dean	142	130	1 3 1 25	6 25	1 2 5 00		1
2	3	Judy O'Bryan	143	150	3 3 6 00	1 6 00		3 2 0 00	2
3	5	Bruce Byers	144	120	4 3 5 75	2 0 75		4 1 5 00	3
4	8	Molly Dean	145	130	9 2 40	4 40	8 8 00		4
5	15	Kathy Angell	146	110	1 4 1 75	6 75		1 3 5 00	5
6	20	Lyle Sanders	147	160	6 8 25	3 25	6 5 00		6
7	23	Jess Watts	148	170	1 0 2 90	4 90	9 8 00		7
8	27	Bruce Byers	149	120	1 5 2 25	7 25	1 4 5 00		8
9	29	Jefferson School District	150	140	2 6 5 00			2 6 5 00	9
10	30	Judy O'Bryan	151	150	4 0 4 25	1 9 25	3 8 5 00		10
11	30	Totals			2 1 2 9 80	8 8 80	9 0 6 00	1 1 3 5 00	11
12					(1115)	(2130)	(4105-1)	(4105-2)	12
13									13
14									14

[1, 2, 4]

SALES RETURNS AND ALLOWANCES JOURNAL

PAGE 6

	DATE	ACCOUNT CREDITED	CREDIT MEMO. NO.	POST. REF.	ACCOUNTS RECEIVABLE CREDIT (1)	SALES TAX PAYABLE DEBIT (2)	SALES RETURNS AND ALLOWANCES DEBIT WALLPAPER (3)	SALES RETURNS AND ALLOWANCES DEBIT PAINT (4)	
1	19-- Sept. 3	Molly Dean	24	130	3 1 50	1 50	3 0 00		1
2	12	Bruce Byers	25	120	7 8 75	3 75		7 5 00	2
3	17	Molly Dean	26	130	2 9 40	1 40	2 8 00		3
4	26	Lyle Sanders	27	160	2 4 15	1 15	2 3 00		4
5	30	Totals			1 6 3 80	7 80	8 1 00	7 5 00	5
6					(1115)	(2130)	(4110-1)	(4110-2)	6
7									7
8									8
9									9
10									10

GENERAL LEDGER

ACCOUNT Accounts Receivable ACCOUNT NO. 1115

DATE		ITEM	POST. REF.	DEBIT	CREDIT	BALANCE	
						DEBIT	CREDIT
Sept. 19--	1	Balance	✔			1 5 5 8 75	
	30		S9	2 1 2 9 80		3 6 8 8 55	
	30		SR6		1 6 3 80	3 5 2 4 75	

ACCOUNT Sales Tax Payable ACCOUNT NO. 2130

DATE		ITEM	POST. REF.	DEBIT	CREDIT	BALANCE	
						DEBIT	CREDIT
Sept. 19--	1	Balance	✔				1 2 3 20
	30		S9		8 8 80		2 1 2 00
	30		SR6	7 80			2 0 4 20

ACCOUNT Sales — Wallpaper ACCOUNT NO. 4105-1

DATE	ITEM	POST. REF.	DEBIT	CREDIT	BALANCE	
					DEBIT	CREDIT
Sept. 19-- 30		S9		9 0 6 00		9 0 6 00

ACCOUNT Sales — Paint ACCOUNT NO. 4105-2

DATE	ITEM	POST. REF.	DEBIT	CREDIT	BALANCE	
					DEBIT	CREDIT
Sept. 19-- 30		S9		1 1 3 5 00		1 1 3 5 00

ACCOUNT Sales Returns and Allowances — Wallpaper ACCOUNT NO. 4110-1

DATE	ITEM	POST. REF.	DEBIT	CREDIT	BALANCE	
					DEBIT	CREDIT
Sept. 19-- 30		SR6	8 1 00		8 1 00	

ACCOUNT Sales Returns and Allowances — Paint ACCOUNT NO. 4110-2

DATE	ITEM	POST. REF.	DEBIT	CREDIT	BALANCE	
					DEBIT	CREDIT
Sept. 19-- 30		SR6	7 5 00		7 5 00	

ACCOUNTS RECEIVABLE LEDGER

CUSTOMER Kathy Angell   **CUSTOMER NO.** 110

DATE		ITEM	POST. REF.	DEBIT	CREDIT	DEBIT BALANCE
Sept.	1	Balance	✔			2 9 9 25
	15		S9	1 4 1 75		4 4 1 00

CUSTOMER Bruce Byers   **CUSTOMER NO.** 120

DATE		ITEM	POST. REF.	DEBIT	CREDIT	DEBIT BALANCE
Sept.	1	Balance	✔			4 7 2 50
	5		S9	4 3 5 75		9 0 8 25
	27		S9	1 5 2 25		1 0 6 0 50
	12		SR6		7 8 75	9 8 1 75

CUSTOMER Molly Dean   **CUSTOMER NO.** 130

DATE		ITEM	POST. REF.	DEBIT	CREDIT	DEBIT BALANCE
Sept.	1		S9	1 3 1 25		1 3 1 25
	8		S9	9 2 40		2 2 3 65
	3		SR6		3 1 50	1 9 2 15
	17		SR6		2 9 40	1 6 2 75

CUSTOMER Jefferson School District   **CUSTOMER NO.** 140

DATE		ITEM	POST. REF.	DEBIT	CREDIT	DEBIT BALANCE
Sept.	1	Balance	✔			3 2 5 00
	29		S9	2 6 5 00		5 9 0 00

CUSTOMER Judy O'Bryan   **CUSTOMER NO.** 150

DATE		ITEM	POST. REF.	DEBIT	CREDIT	DEBIT BALANCE
Sept.	1	Balance	✔			2 7 3 00
	3		S9	3 3 6 00		6 0 9 00
	30		S9	4 0 4 25		1 0 1 3 25

ACCOUNTS RECEIVABLE LEDGER

CUSTOMER Lyle Sanders   CUSTOMER NO. 160

DATE		ITEM	POST. REF.	DEBIT	CREDIT	DEBIT BALANCE
Sept.¹⁹⁻⁻	20		S9	6 8 25		6 8 25
	26		SR6		2 4 15	4 4 10

CUSTOMER Jess Watts   CUSTOMER NO. 170

DATE		ITEM	POST. REF.	DEBIT	CREDIT	DEBIT BALANCE
Sept.¹⁹⁻⁻	1	Balance	✔			1 8 9 00
	23		S9	1 0 2 90		2 9 1 90

Figuring sales tax, sales discounts, and amounts due   *PROBLEM 3-2, p. 50*

1	2	3	4	5	6	7
Sales No.	Sales Amount	Sales Tax Amount	Amount Due Before Discount	Sales Discount Amount	Sales Tax Amount on Discount	Amount Due After Discount
83	$1,050.00	$52.50	$1,102.50	$21.00	$1.05	$1,080.45
84	930.00	46.50	976.50	18.60	.93	956.97
85	1,250.00	62.50	1,312.50	25.00	1.25	1,286.25
86	720.00	36.00	756.00	14.40	.72	740.88
87	380.00	19.00	399.00	7.60	.38	391.02
88	840.00	42.00	882.00	16.80	.84	864.36
89	1,160.00	58.00	1,218.00	23.20	1.16	1,193.64
90	280.00	14.00	294.00	5.60	.28	288.12

Journalizing and posting departmental cash receipts   [1–3, 5]

CASH RECEIPTS JOURNAL

PAGE 13

DATE	ACCOUNT TITLE	DOC. NO.	POST. REF.	GENERAL DEBIT	GENERAL CREDIT	ACCOUNTS RECEIVABLE CREDIT	SALES TAX PAYABLE DEBIT	SALES TAX PAYABLE CREDIT	SALES CREDIT BOOTS	SALES CREDIT COATS	SALES DISCOUNT DEBIT BOOTS	SALES DISCOUNT DEBIT COATS	CASH DEBIT
19-- Nov. 1	Mary Hyde	R87	130			9 03 00	86						8 84 94
2	Roger Cantrell	R88	120			2 73 00	26				5 20		2 67 54
5		T5	✓					3 87 50	3 62 0 00	4 13 0 00			8 13 7 50
8	Teri Miceli	R89	140			3 99 00	38					7 60	3 91 02
10	Gene Tate	R90	160			4 45 20	42				8 48		4 36 30
12		T12	✓					4 90 00	4 68 0 00	5 12 0 00			10 29 0 00
15	Greg Payne	R91	150			1 89 00	18				3 60		1 85 22
19		T19	✓					4 87 00	4 51 0 00	5 23 0 00			10 22 7 00
22	Peggy Allison	R92	110			2 81 40	27				5 36		2 75 77
25	Teri Miceli	R93	140			6 09 00	58					11 60	5 96 82
26		T26	✓					5 12 00	4 75 0 00	5 49 0 00			10 75 2 00
29	Greg Payne	R94	150			2 62 50	25				5 00		2 57 25
30		T30	✓					2 55 50	2 37 0 00	2 74 0 00			5 36 5 50
30	Totals					33 62 10	3 20	21 32 00	199 30 00	227 10 00	27 64	36 40	480 66 86
						(1115)	(2130)	(2130)	(4105-1)	(4105-2)	(4115-1)	(4115-2)	(1105)

GENERAL LEDGER

ACCOUNT Cash   ACCOUNT NO. 1105

DATE		ITEM	POST. REF.	DEBIT	CREDIT	BALANCE	
						DEBIT	CREDIT
Nov.	30	Balance	✓			5 5 3 0 00	
	30		CR13	48 0 6 6 86		53 5 9 6 86	

ACCOUNT Accounts Receivable   ACCOUNT NO. 1115

DATE		ITEM	POST. REF.	DEBIT	CREDIT	BALANCE	
						DEBIT	CREDIT
Nov.	1	Balance	✓			3 9 6 0 60	
	30		CR13		3 3 6 2 10	5 9 8 50	

ACCOUNT Sales Tax Payable   ACCOUNT NO. 2130

DATE		ITEM	POST. REF.	DEBIT	CREDIT	BALANCE	
						DEBIT	CREDIT
Nov.	1	Balance	✓				3 8 7 0 00
	30		CR13	3 20			3 8 6 6 80
	30		CR13		2 1 3 2 00		5 9 9 8 80

ACCOUNT Sales—Boots   ACCOUNT NO. 4105-1

DATE		ITEM	POST. REF.	DEBIT	CREDIT	BALANCE	
						DEBIT	CREDIT
Nov.	30		CR13		19 9 3 0 00		19 9 3 0 00

ACCOUNT Sales—Coats   ACCOUNT NO. 4105-2

DATE		ITEM	POST. REF.	DEBIT	CREDIT	BALANCE	
						DEBIT	CREDIT
Nov.	30		CR13		22 7 1 0 00		22 7 1 0 00

GENERAL LEDGER

ACCOUNT Sales Discount — Boots   ACCOUNT NO. 4115-1

DATE	ITEM	POST. REF.	DEBIT	CREDIT	BALANCE DEBIT	BALANCE CREDIT
Nov. 30		CR13	2 7 64		2 7 64	

ACCOUNT Sales Discount — Coats   ACCOUNT NO. 4115-2

DATE	ITEM	POST. REF.	DEBIT	CREDIT	BALANCE DEBIT	BALANCE CREDIT
Nov. 30		CR13	3 6 40		3 6 40	

[2]

ACCOUNTS RECEIVABLE LEDGER

CUSTOMER Peggy Allison   CUSTOMER NO. 110

DATE	ITEM	POST. REF.	DEBIT	CREDIT	DEBIT BALANCE
Nov. 1	Balance	✓			2 8 1 40
22		CR13		2 8 1 40	—

CUSTOMER Roger Cantrell   CUSTOMER NO. 120

DATE	ITEM	POST. REF.	DEBIT	CREDIT	DEBIT BALANCE
Nov. 1	Balance	✓			4 6 2 00
2		CR13		2 7 3 00	1 8 9 00

CUSTOMER Mary Hyde   CUSTOMER NO. 130

DATE	ITEM	POST. REF.	DEBIT	CREDIT	DEBIT BALANCE
Nov. 1	Balance	✓			9 0 3 00
1		CR13		9 0 3 00	—

ACCOUNTS RECEIVABLE LEDGER

CUSTOMER Teri Miceli   CUSTOMER NO.   140

DATE		ITEM	POST. REF.	DEBIT	CREDIT	DEBIT BALANCE
Nov.¹⁹⁻⁻	1	Balance	✓			1 0 0 8 00
	8		CR13		3 9 9 00	6 0 9 00
	25		CR13		6 0 9 00	——

CUSTOMER Greg Payne   CUSTOMER NO.   150

DATE		ITEM	POST. REF.	DEBIT	CREDIT	DEBIT BALANCE
Nov.¹⁹⁻⁻	1	Balance	✓			4 5 1 50
	15		CR13		1 8 9 00	2 6 2 50
	29		CR13		2 6 2 50	——

CUSTOMER Gene Tate   CUSTOMER NO.   160

DATE		ITEM	POST. REF.	DEBIT	CREDIT	DEBIT BALANCE
Nov.¹⁹⁻⁻	1	Balance	✓			8 5 4 70
	10		CR13		4 4 5 20	4 0 9 50

[4]

Prove Cash:

Cash on hand at beginning of month	$	43,840.00
Cash received during the month		48,066.86
Total	$	91,906.86
Cash paid during the month		38,310.00
Cash on hand at the end of the month	$	53,596.86

Journalizing departmental sales, sales returns and
allowances, and cash receipts

SALES JOURNAL
PAGE 10

	DATE		ACCOUNT DEBITED	SALE NO.	POST. REF.	ACCOUNTS RECEIVABLE DEBIT (1)	SALES TAX PAYABLE CREDIT (2)	SALES CREDIT CAMPING GEAR (3)	SALES CREDIT HIKING GEAR (4)	
1	19-- June	1	Steve Leny	134		588 00	28 00	560 00		1
2		3	Celia Perez	135		451 50	21 50	430 00		2
3		11	Paul DeBra	136		882 00	42 00	840 00		3
4		15	Linda Barr	137		449 40	21 40		428 00	4
5		17	Norma Howard	138		252 00	12 00	240 00		5
6		28	Alpine Schools	139		760 00			760 00	6
7		30	Totals			3382 90	124 90	2070 00	1188 00	7
8										8
9										9
10										10
11										11

[1, 2]

SALES RETURNS AND ALLOWANCES JOURNAL
PAGE 5

	DATE		ACCOUNT CREDITED	CREDIT MEMO. NO.	POST. REF.	ACCOUNTS RECEIVABLE CREDIT (1)	SALES TAX PAYABLE DEBIT (2)	SALES RETURNS AND ALLOWANCES DEBIT CAMPING GEAR (3)	SALES RETURNS AND ALLOWANCES DEBIT HIKING GEAR (4)	
1	19-- June	6	Celia Perez	28		96 60	4 60	92 00		1
2		21	Linda Barr	29		70 35	3 35		67 00	2
3		30	Totals			166 95	7 95	92 00	67 00	3
4										4
5										5
6										6
7										7
8										8
9										9
10										10
11										11

[1, 3, 5]

CASH RECEIPTS JOURNAL

PAGE 14

				GENERAL		ACCOUNTS RECEIVABLE CREDIT	SALES TAX PAYABLE		SALES CREDIT		SALES DISCOUNT DEBIT		CASH DEBIT
DATE	ACCOUNT TITLE	DOC. NO.	POST. REF.	DEBIT	CREDIT		DEBIT	CREDIT	CAMPING GEAR	HIKING GEAR	CAMPING GEAR	HIKING GEAR	
19-- June 4	William Hodges	R83				3 7 8 00	36					7 20	3 7 0 44
4	✓	T4						3 4 0 00	3 2 8 0 00	3 5 2 0 00			7 1 4 0 00
8	Norma Howard	R84				6 3 9 45	61				1 2 18		6 2 6 66
9	Celia Perez	R85				4 1 8 95	40					7 98	4 1 0 57
11	Steve Leny	R86				5 8 8 00	56				1 1 20		5 7 6 24
11	✓	T11						4 8 7 50	4 7 2 0 00	5 0 3 0 00			10 2 3 7 50
13	Celia Perez	R87				3 5 4 90	34				6 76		3 4 7 80
18	✓	T18						5 0 5 50	5 1 3 0 00	4 9 8 0 00			10 6 1 5 50
21	Paul DeBra	R88				8 8 2 00	84				1 6 80		8 6 4 36
25	Linda Barr	R89				3 7 9 05	36					7 22	3 7 1 47
25	✓	T25						4 8 3 00	4 7 5 0 00	4 9 1 0 00			10 1 4 3 00
27	Norma Howard	R90				2 5 2 00	24				4 80		2 4 6 96
30	✓	T30						2 5 4 50	2 4 8 0 00	2 6 1 0 00			5 3 4 4 50
30	Totals					3 8 9 2 35	3 71	2 0 7 0 50	20 3 6 0 00	21 0 5 0 00	5 1 74	2 2 40	4 7 2 9 5 00

[4]

Prove Cash:

Cash on hand at beginning of month	$ 36,940.00
Cash received during the month	47,295.00
Total	$ 84,235.00
Cash paid during the month	31,620.86
Cash on hand at the end of the month	$ 52,614.14

[1, 2]

Journalizing departmental sales, sales returns and allowances, and cash receipts

SALES JOURNAL
PAGE 13

	DATE		ACCOUNT DEBITED	SALE NO.	POST. REF.	ACCOUNTS RECEIVABLE DEBIT	SALES CREDIT	
							CAMPING GEAR	HIKING GEAR
1	19-- June	1	Steve Leny	134		5 6 0 00	5 6 0 00	
2		3	Celia Perez	135		4 3 0 00	4 3 0 00	
3		11	Paul DeBra	136		8 4 0 00	8 4 0 00	
4		15	Linda Barr	137		4 2 8 00		4 2 8 00
5		17	Norma Howard	138		2 4 0 00	2 4 0 00	
6		28	Alpine Schools	139		7 6 0 00		7 6 0 00
7		30	Totals			3 2 5 8 00	2 0 7 0 00	1 1 8 8 00

[1, 2]

SALES RETURNS AND ALLOWANCES JOURNAL
PAGE 4

	DATE		ACCOUNT CREDITED	CREDIT MEMO. NO.	POST. REF.	ACCOUNTS RECEIVABLE CREDIT	SALES RETURNS AND ALLOWANCES DEBIT	
							CAMPING GEAR	HIKING GEAR
1	19-- June	6	Celia Perez	28		9 2 00	9 2 00	
2		21	Linda Barr	29		6 7 00		6 7 00
3		30	Totals			1 5 9 00	9 2 00	6 7 00

[1, 2]

CASH RECEIPTS JOURNAL

PAGE 14

	DATE	ACCOUNT TITLE	DOC. NO.	POST. REF.	GENERAL DEBIT	GENERAL CREDIT	ACCOUNTS RECEIVABLE CREDIT	SALES CREDIT CAMPING GEAR	SALES CREDIT HIKING GEAR	SALES DISCOUNT DEBIT CAMPING GEAR	SALES DISCOUNT DEBIT HIKING GEAR	CASH DEBIT
1	June 4	William Hodges	R83				3 6 0 00				3 60	3 5 6 40
2	4	✓	T4					3 2 8 0 00	3 5 2 0 00			6 8 0 0 00
3	8	Norma Howard	R84				6 0 9 00			6 09		6 0 2 91
4	9	Celia Perez	R85				3 9 9 00				3 99	3 9 5 01
5	11	Steve Leny	R86				5 6 0 00			5 60		5 5 4 40
6	11	✓	T11					4 7 2 0 00	5 0 3 0 00			9 7 5 0 00
7	13	Celia Perez	R87				3 3 8 00			3 38		3 3 4 62
8	18	✓	T18					5 1 3 0 00	4 9 8 0 00			10 1 1 0 00
9	21	Paul DeBra	R88				8 4 0 00			8 40		8 3 1 60
10	25	Linda Barr	R89				3 6 1 00				3 61	3 5 7 39
11	25	✓	T25					4 7 5 0 00	4 9 1 0 00			9 6 6 0 00
12	27	Norma Howard	R90				2 4 0 00			2 40		2 3 7 60
13	30	✓	T30					2 4 8 0 00	2 6 1 0 00			5 0 9 0 00
14	30	Totals					3 7 0 7 00	20 3 6 0 00	21 0 5 0 00	2 5 87	11 20	45 0 7 9 93
15												
16												
17												
18												
19												
20												
21												
22												
23												
24												
25												

Perfect Score. 38

Deduct .... __

Your Score .... __

Name _____

Date _____ Class _____

Checked by _____

STUDY
GUIDE
4

UNIT A—Analyzing Departmental Payroll Procedures

DIRECTIONS: Place a check mark in the proper Answers column to show whether each of the following statements is true or false.

	Answers True	Answers False	For Scoring
0. Total operating expenses for most businesses include large payments for employee services and related taxes	✔		**0.** ✔
1. Reporting payroll expenses as separate items in accounting records and financial statements is an application of the Consistent Reporting concept.....		✔	**1.**
2. Employers are required to withhold certain payroll taxes from an employee's salary each pay period	✔		**2.**
3. Federal, state, and local governments specify the payroll information a business must keep and report...	✔		**3.**
4. Employee benefits are required by law		✔	**4.**
5. Benefit hours used are recorded on each employee's time card	✔		**5.**
6. Detailed information about an employee's benefits are recorded on a benefits record	✔		**6.**
7. A benefits authorization form is used to record and authorize employee benefits...	✔		**7.**
8. In a time clock system, a payroll time card is inserted in the time clock each time an employee arrives for work and leaves work	✔		**8.**
9. Information needed to complete an employee's earnings record is obtained from a time card		✔	**9.**
10. Income and social security are the two federal taxes deducted from earnings of each employee	✔		**10.**
11. A payroll register summarizes the payroll for one pay period	✔		**11.**
12. An employee's total earnings, marital status, and number of allowances claimed determine the federal income tax amount to be withheld from each employee's earnings	✔		**12.**
13. Congress sets the tax base and tax rate for FICA tax	✔		**13.**
14. In proving a payroll register's accuracy, the total of the Net Pay column is subtracted from the Total Deductions column		✔	**14.**
15. An employee's total earnings for a quarter are summarized on one line of the employee's earnings record...		✔	**15.**
16. After a biweekly payroll register has been completed, a check for the total earnings indicated on the payroll register is written for each employee........		✔	**16.**
17. Unemployment taxes are used to pay workers cash benefits for limited periods of unemployment..	✔		**17.**
18. Both employers and employees are required to pay a federal unemployment tax		✔	**18.**
19. The source document for recording an employer's payroll taxes is a memorandum	✔		**19.**
20. The amount withheld from an employee's earnings for hospital insurance is a liability to the employer until paid to the insurance company	✔		**20.**

UNIT B—Identifying Accounting Terms

DIRECTIONS: Select the one term in Column I that best fits each definition in Column II. Print the letter identifying your choice in the Answers column.

Column I	*Column II*	Answers	For Scoring
A. automatic check deposit	**0.** Taxes based on the payroll of a business	G	0. ✔
	21. The money paid for an employee's services	H	21.
B. employee benefits	**22.** A business form on which all payroll information		
C. employee's earnings record	is recorded...	F	22.
	23. The procedure of depositing payroll checks directly to		
D. pay period	an employee's checking or savings account in a		
E. payroll	specified bank	A	23.
F. payroll register	**24.** The period covered by a salary payment	D	24.
G. payroll taxes	**25.** Payments to employees for nonworking hours and to		
H. salary	insurance and retirement programs........................	B	25.
I. withholding allowance	**26.** The total amount paid to all employees for a pay period .	E	26.
	27. A business form showing details of all items affecting		
	payments made to an employee	C	27.
	28. A deduction from total earnings for each person legally		
	supported by a taxpayer...................................	I	28.

UNIT C—Analyzing Payroll Accounting

DIRECTIONS: For each item below, select the choice that best completes the sentence. Print the letter identifying your choice in the Answers column.

	Answers	For Scoring
0. The payroll system used by individual businesses **(A)** may differ **(B)** is specified by the federal government **(C)** is specified by state government **(D)** none of these	A	0. ✔
29. Reporting payroll expenses as separate items in accounting records and financial statements is an application of the **(A)** Business Entity concept **(B)** Going Concern concept **(C)** Consistent Reporting concept **(D)** Materiality concept .	D	29.
30. When employees are paid a percentage of sales in addition to their regular salary, the earnings are often referred to as **(A)** salary **(B)** pensions **(C)** commissions **(D)** wages	C	30.
31. FICA tax is paid by **(A)** the employees **(B)** the employer **(C)** both A and B **(D)** none of these	C	31.
32. A tax which is not deducted from employees' pay is **(A)** FICA Tax **(B)** state income tax **(C)** federal unemployment tax **(D)** federal income tax	C	32.
33. A biweekly payroll system requires each year **(A)** 24 pay periods **(B)** 26 pay periods **(C)** 28 pay periods **(D)** 30 pay periods	B	33.
34. The amount due an individual for a pay period after deductions is referred to as **(A)** regular earnings **(B)** overtime **(C)** total earnings **(D)** none of these..	D	34.
35. The payroll bank account appears in the **(A)** general ledger **(B)** chart of accounts **(C)** both A and B **(D)** none of these......................................	D	35.
36. The two journal entries to record payroll data are entered in a **(A)** general journal **(B)** cash payments journal **(C)** general journal and cash payments journal **(D)** none of these	C	36.
37. If the amount owed for federal income tax and FICA tax withholdings is less than $500.00 a quarter, payment is due **(A)** at the end of the quarter **(B)** semi-annually **(C)** at the end of the year **(D)** none of these	A	37.
38. Federal and state unemployment taxes are usually paid by the **(A)** employee **(B)** employer **(C)** both employee and employer **(D)** none of these	B	38.

Preparing a benefits record

BENEFITS RECORD

EMPLOYEE NO. __14__   EMPLOYEE NAME __Rose M. Doyle__   DEPARTMENT __Women's Shoes__

DATE OF INITIAL EMPLOYMENT __November 1, 1986__   YEAR __19--__

	1	2	3	4	5	6	7	8	9	10	11	12
PAY PERIOD ENDED	VACATION TIME				SICK LEAVE TIME				PERSONAL LEAVE TIME			
	BEGIN. HOURS AVAIL.	HOURS EARNED	HOURS USED	ACC. HOURS AVAIL.	BEGIN. HOURS AVAIL.	HOURS EARNED	HOURS USED	ACC. HOURS AVAIL.	BEGIN. HOURS AVAIL.	HOURS EARNED	HOURS USED	ACC. HOURS AVAIL.
1 1-2	63	4	8	59	72	2	0	74	16	1	4	13
2 1-16	59	4	0	63	74	2	4	72	13	1	2	12
3 1-30	63	4	16	51	72	2	0	74	12	1	0	13
4 2-13	51	4	0	55	74	2	2	74	13	1	3	11
5												

Figuring employees' earnings

Employee Number	Hours Worked		Regular Rate	Earnings		Total Earnings
	Regular	Overtime		Regular	Overtime	
1	80	4	$7.50	$600.00	$45.00	$645.00
2	80	2	6.00	480.00	18.00	498.00
3	80	0	8.25	660.00	——	660.00
4	80	3	7.00	560.00	31.50	591.50
5	80	1	8.50	680.00	12.75	692.75

Recording employee benefits and figuring earnings on time cards

BENEFITS AUTHORIZATION

EMPLOYEE NO. 3   EMPLOYEE Betty J. Acker

PAY PERIOD ENDED 3/12/--   DEPARTMENT Furniture

	HOURS AVAIL.	M	T	W	T	F	S	HOURS USED
VACATION	64			4			8	12
SICK LEAVE	46		4			4		4
PERSONAL LEAVE	13					2		2

Mary A. Brady   3/12/--
DEPARTMENT SUPERVISOR   DATE

MANAGER (only if needed)

BENEFITS AUTHORIZATION

EMPLOYEE NO. 8   EMPLOYEE Juan C. Perez

PAY PERIOD ENDED 3/12/--   DEPARTMENT Administrative

	HOURS AVAIL.	M	T	W	T	F	S	HOURS USED
VACATION	52	8						8
SICK LEAVE	32	4					8	12
PERSONAL LEAVE	17		2			1		3

Bonita Ott   3/12/--
MANAGER (only if needed)   DEPARTMENT SUPERVISOR   DATE

BENEFITS AUTHORIZATION

EMPLOYEE NO. 13   EMPLOYEE Maria L. Sotela

PAY PERIOD ENDED 3/12/--   DEPARTMENT Hardware

	HOURS AVAIL.	M	T	W	T	F	S	HOURS USED
VACATION	68				8	8	8	24
SICK LEAVE	47							0
PERSONAL LEAVE	20					4		4

Paul T. Burke   3/12/--
MANAGER (only if needed)   DEPARTMENT SUPERVISOR   DATE

BENEFITS RECORD

EMPLOYEE NO. __3__   EMPLOYEE NAME __Betty J. Acker__   DEPARTMENT __Furniture__

DATE OF INITIAL EMPLOYMENT __February 8, 1982__   YEAR __19--__

		1	2	3	4	5	6	7	8	9	10	11	12
PAY PERIOD ENDED		VACATION TIME				SICK LEAVE TIME				PERSONAL LEAVE TIME			
		BEGIN. HOURS AVAIL.	HOURS EARNED	HOURS USED	ACC. HOURS AVAIL.	BEGIN. HOURS AVAIL.	HOURS EARNED	HOURS USED	ACC. HOURS AVAIL.	BEGIN. HOURS AVAIL.	HOURS EARNED	HOURS USED	ACC. HOURS AVAIL.
6	3-12	64	4	12	56	46	2	4	44	13	1	2	12
7													

BENEFITS RECORD

EMPLOYEE NO. __8__   EMPLOYEE NAME __Juan C. Perez__   DEPARTMENT __Administrative__

DATE OF INITIAL EMPLOYMENT __July 16, 1984__   YEAR __19--__

		1	2	3	4	5	6	7	8	9	10	11	12
PAY PERIOD ENDED		VACATION TIME				SICK LEAVE TIME				PERSONAL LEAVE TIME			
		BEGIN. HOURS AVAIL.	HOURS EARNED	HOURS USED	ACC. HOURS AVAIL.	BEGIN. HOURS AVAIL.	HOURS EARNED	HOURS USED	ACC. HOURS AVAIL.	BEGIN. HOURS AVAIL.	HOURS EARNED	HOURS USED	ACC. HOURS AVAIL.
6	3-12	52	4	8	48	32	2	12	22	17	1	3	15
7													

BENEFITS RECORD

EMPLOYEE NO. __13__   EMPLOYEE NAME __Maria L. Sotela__   DEPARTMENT __Hardware__

DATE OF INITIAL EMPLOYMENT __March 11, 1983__   YEAR __19--__

		1	2	3	4	5	6	7	8	9	10	11	12
PAY PERIOD ENDED		VACATION TIME				SICK LEAVE TIME				PERSONAL LEAVE TIME			
		BEGIN. HOURS AVAIL.	HOURS EARNED	HOURS USED	ACC. HOURS AVAIL.	BEGIN. HOURS AVAIL.	HOURS EARNED	HOURS USED	ACC. HOURS AVAIL.	BEGIN. HOURS AVAIL.	HOURS EARNED	HOURS USED	ACC. HOURS AVAIL.
6	3-12	68	4	24	48	47	2	0	49	20	1	4	17
7													

[2-4] *The time cards prepared in this problem are needed to complete Problem 4-5.*

NAME Maria L. Sotela
DEPARTMENT Hardware
EMPLOYEE NO. 13
PAY PERIOD ENDED 3-12-19--

	MORNING		AFTERNOON		OVERTIME		HOURS		AMOUNT
	IN	OUT	IN	OUT	IN	OUT	REG	OT	
T	9:00	12:59	2:00	6:02	7:00	8:00	8	1	
M	9:01	1:00	2:00	6:01			8		
							V8		
							V8		
							V8		
T	9:00	1:03	2:00	6:00	7:00	9:30	8	2½	
W	8:58	1:00	2:01	6:01			8		
T	9:00	1:03					4P4		
F	9:00	1:00	2:02	6:03	7:00	8:00	8	1	
S	9:03	1:00	2:01	6:04			8		

	HOURS	RATE	AMOUNT
REGULAR	80	6.50	520.00
OVERTIME	4½	9.75	43.88
TOTAL HOURS	84½	TOTAL EARNINGS	563.88

NAME Juan C. Perez
DEPARTMENT Accounting
EMPLOYEE NO. 8
PAY PERIOD ENDED 3-12-19--

	MORNING		AFTERNOON		OVERTIME		HOURS		AMOUNT
	IN	OUT	IN	OUT	IN	OUT	REG	OT	
							V8		
T	9:00	12:01	1:00	6:00	7:00	8:30	8	1½	
W	8:59	12:00	12:58	4:00			6P2		
T	9:01	12:00	1:02	6:03	7:30	9:00	8	1½	
F	9:00	12:02	1:01	6:00			8		
							S8		
M			2:00	6:02			4S4		
	8:58	12:01	1:01	6:00			8		
T	9:01	12:00	1:00	6:00	7:00	8:00	8	1	
F	9:00	12:02	1:00	5:00			7P1		

	HOURS	RATE	AMOUNT
REGULAR	80	6.50	520.00
OVERTIME	4	9.75	39.00
TOTAL HOURS	84	TOTAL EARNINGS	559.00

NAME Betty J. Acker
DEPARTMENT Furniture
EMPLOYEE NO. 3
PAY PERIOD ENDED 3-12-19--

	MORNING		AFTERNOON		OVERTIME		HOURS		AMOUNT
	IN	OUT	IN	OUT	IN	OUT	REG	OT	
M	9:01	11:59	1:00	6:03			8		
T	9:00	12:01	1:00	6:00	7:00	9:00	8	2	
W	8:58	12:00	1:01	2:03			4V4		
T	9:02	12:01	1:00	6:00	7:30	9:00	8	1½	
F			2:00	6:01			4S4		
							8		
M	9:01	12:00	1:00	6:01			V8		
W	9:00	12:00	1:00	6:01	7:30	8:30	8	1	
T	9:01	12:00	1:01	6:00			8		
F	9:00	12:00	1:02	4:00			6P2		

	HOURS	RATE	AMOUNT
REGULAR	80	7.00	560.00
OVERTIME	4½	10.50	47.25
TOTAL HOURS	84½	TOTAL EARNINGS	607.25

Preparing departmental commissions records

The commissions records prepared in this problem are needed to complete Problem 4-5.

COMMISSIONS RECORD

Employee No. __9__   Employee Name __Mary A. Brady__

Commission __1%__   Month __February__   Year __19--__

Dept. __Furniture__   Regular Biweekly Salary __$540.00__

Sales

Sales on Account...	$	7,623.40
Cash and Credit Card Sales................................		12,936.20
Total Sales	$	20,559.60
Less: Sales Discounts.............. $ 138.40		
Sales Returns and Allowances 709.80	848.20	
Net Sales..	$	19,711.40
Commission on Net Sales................................	$	197.11

COMMISSIONS RECORD

Employee No. __14__   Employee Name __Paul T. Burke__

Commission __1%__   Month __February__   Year __19--__

Dept. __Hardware__   Regular Biweekly Salary __$520.00__

Sales

Sales on Account...	$	6,930.10
Cash and Credit Card Sales................................		14,730.60
Total Sales	$	21,660.70
Less: Sales Discounts.............. $ 122.70		
Sales Returns and Allowances 1,318.50	1,441.20	
Net Sales..	$	20,219.50
Commission on Net Sales................................	$	202.20

Completing a payroll register

PROBLEM 4-5, p. 75

The time cards prepared in Problem 4-3 and the commissions records prepared in Problem 4-4 are needed to complete this problem. The payroll register prepared in Problem 4-5 is needed to complete Problems 4-6 and 4-7.

PAYROLL REGISTER

PAY PERIOD ENDED March 12, 19--

	EMPL. NO.	EMPLOYEE'S NAME	MARITAL STATUS	NO. OF ALLOW- ANCES	TOTAL HOURS	EARNINGS REGULAR	EARNINGS OVERTIME	EARNINGS COMMIS- SION	EARNINGS TOTAL	
1	3	Acker, Betty J.	M	3	84½	560 00	47 25		607 25	1
2	9	Brady, Mary A.	S	1	—	540 00		197 11	737 11	2
3	14	Burke, Paul T.	M	2	—	520 00		202 20	722 20	3
4	8	Perez, Juan C.	M	2	84	520 00	39 00		559 00	4
5	13	Sotela, Maria L.	S	2	84½	520 00	43 88		563 88	5
6		*Totals*				2660 00	130 13	399 31	3189 44	6
7										7
8										8
9										9

Completing an employee's earnings record

PROBLEM 4-6, p. 75

The payroll register prepared in Problem 4-5 is needed to complete this problem.

EARNINGS RECORD FOR QUARTER ENDED March 31, 19--

EMPLOYEE NO. 3 NAME Betty J. Acker SOCIAL SECURITY NO. 013-62-1432

MARITAL STATUS M WITHHOLDING ALLOWANCES 3 HOURLY RATE $7.00 SALARY

DEPARTMENT Furniture POSITION Salesclerk

PAY PERIOD NO.	ENDED	TOTAL EARNINGS	DEDUCTIONS FEDERAL INCOME TAX	STATE INCOME TAX	FICA TAX	OTHER		TOTAL	NET PAY	ACCUMULATED EARNINGS
5	2-27	560 00	46 00	28 00	39 20	DH	1 9 3 / 40 20	135 80	424 20	3050 25
6	3-12	607 25	52 00	30 36	42 51	DH	1 9 3 / 40 20	147 47	459 78	3657 50

DATE OF PAYMENT March 19, 19--   **PAYROLL REGISTER**

	10	11	12	13	14	15	16		17	18	19	
	DEPARTMENT		ADMIN. SALARIES	DEDUCTIONS						PAID		
	FURNITURE	HARDWARE		FEDERAL INCOME TAX	STATE INCOME TAX	FICA TAX	OTHER		TOTAL	NET PAY	CK. NO.	
1	6 07 25			52 00	30 36	42 51	D H	1 3 9 40 3 20	1 47 47	4 59 78		1
2	7 37 11			1 10 00	36 86	51 60	D H	1 3 9 40 3 20	2 21 06	5 16 05		2
3		7 22 20		79 00	36 11	50 55	D H	1 3 9 40 3 20	1 88 26	5 33 94		3
4			5 59 00	49 00	27 95	39 13	D H	1 3 9 40 3 20	1 38 68	4 20 32		4
5		5 63 88		66 00	28 19	39 47	D H	1 3 9 40 3 20	1 56 26	4 07 62		5
6	13 44 36	12 86 08	5 59 00	3 56 00	1 59 47	2 23 26	D H	4 6 6 00 7 00	8 51 73	23 33 71		6
7												7
8												8
9												9

PROBLEM 4-6, continued

EARNINGS RECORD FOR QUARTER ENDED March 31, 19--

EMPLOYEE NO. 9   NAME Mary A. Brady   SOCIAL SECURITY NO. 311-32-1620

MARITAL STATUS S   WITHHOLDING ALLOWANCES 1   HOURLY RATE _____   SALARY $540.00

DEPARTMENT Furniture   POSITION Supervisor

	1	2	3	4	5	6	7		8	9	10	
	PAY PERIOD		TOTAL EARNINGS	DEDUCTIONS						NET PAY	ACCUMULATED EARNINGS	
	NO.	ENDED		FEDERAL INCOME TAX	STATE INCOME TAX	FICA TAX	OTHER		TOTAL			
	5	2-27	5 40 00	70 00	27 00	37 80	D H	1 3 9 40 3 20	1 57 40	3 82 60	31 65 20	
	6	3-12	7 37 11	1 10 00	36 86	51 60	D H	1 3 9 40 3 20	2 21 06	5 16 05	39 02 31	

EARNINGS RECORD FOR QUARTER ENDED March 31, 19--

EMPLOYEE NO. 14   NAME Paul T. Burke   SOCIAL SECURITY NO. 192-40-2162

MARITAL STATUS M   WITHHOLDING ALLOWANCES 2   HOURLY RATE _____   SALARY $520.00

DEPARTMENT Hardware   POSITION Supervisor

1	2	3	4	5	6	7	8	9	10
PAY PERIOD		TOTAL EARNINGS	DEDUCTIONS					NET PAY	ACCUMULATED EARNINGS
NO.	ENDED		FEDERAL INCOME TAX	STATE INCOME TAX	FICA TAX	OTHER	TOTAL		
5	2-27	520 00	46 00	26 00	36 40	D H 13 93 40 20	131 00	389 00	3094 30
6	3-12	722 20	79 00	36 11	50 55	D H 13 93 40 20	188 26	533 94	3816 50

EARNINGS RECORD FOR QUARTER ENDED March 31, 19--

EMPLOYEE NO. 8   NAME Juan C. Perez   SOCIAL SECURITY NO. 181-48-0482

MARITAL STATUS M   WITHHOLDING ALLOWANCES 2   HOURLY RATE $6.50   SALARY _____

DEPARTMENT Administrative   POSITION Clerk

1	2	3	4	5	6	7	8	9	10
PAY PERIOD		TOTAL EARNINGS	DEDUCTIONS					NET PAY	ACCUMULATED EARNINGS
NO.	ENDED		FEDERAL INCOME TAX	STATE INCOME TAX	FICA TAX	OTHER	TOTAL		
5	2-27	520 00	46 00	26 00	36 40	D H 13 93 40 20	131 00	389 00	2784 10
6	3-12	559 00	49 00	27 95	39 13	D H 13 93 40 20	138 68	420 32	3343 10

EARNINGS RECORD FOR QUARTER ENDED March 31, 19--

EMPLOYEE NO. 13   NAME Maria L. Sotela   SOCIAL SECURITY NO. 214-36-1832

MARITAL STATUS S   WITHHOLDING ALLOWANCES 2   HOURLY RATE $6.50   SALARY _____

DEPARTMENT Hardware   POSITION Salesclerk

1	2	3	4	5	6	7	8	9	10
PAY PERIOD		TOTAL EARNINGS	DEDUCTIONS					NET PAY	ACCUMULATED EARNINGS
NO.	ENDED		FEDERAL INCOME TAX	STATE INCOME TAX	FICA TAX	OTHER	TOTAL		
5	2-27	520 00	59 00	26 00	36 40	D H 13 93 40 20	144 00	376 00	2676 90
6	3-12	563 88	66 00	28 19	39 47	D H 13 93 40 20	156 26	407 62	3240 78

Paying a departmental payroll [1]

The payroll register prepared in Problem 4-5 is needed to complete this problem.

CASH PAYMENTS JOURNAL

PAGE 15

| | | | | GENERAL | | ACCOUNTS PAYABLE DEBIT | PURCH. DISCOUNT CR. | | CASH CREDIT | |
DATE	ACCOUNT TITLE	CK. NO.	POST. REF.	DEBIT	CREDIT		FURNITURE	HARDWARE		
19-- Mar. 19	Salary Expense—Furniture	463		1 3 4 4 36					2 3 3 7 71	1
	Salary Expense—Hardware			1 2 8 6 08						2
	Salary Expense—Administrative			5 5 9 00						3
	Employ. Inc. Tax Payable—Federal				3 5 6 00					4
	Employ. Inc. Tax Payable—State				1 5 9 47					5
	FICA Tax Payable				2 2 3 26					6
	Dental Insurance Payable				4 7 00					7
	Hospital Insurance Payable				6 6 00					8
										9

[2]

GENERAL JOURNAL

PAGE 8

DATE	ACCOUNT TITLE	POST. REF.	DEBIT	CREDIT	
19-- Mar. 19	Payroll Taxes Expense		4 2 1 01		1
	FICA Tax Payable			2 2 3 26	2
	Unemploy. Tax Payable—Federal			2 5 52	3
	Unemploy. Tax Payable—State			1 7 2 23	4
	M41				5
					6

Figuring and paying payroll taxes liabilities
[1]

CASH PAYMENTS JOURNAL

PAGE 11

	DATE	ACCOUNT TITLE	CK. NO.	POST. REF.	GENERAL DEBIT	GENERAL CREDIT	ACCOUNTS PAYABLE DEBIT	PURCH. DISCOUNT CR. FURNITURE	PURCH. DISCOUNT CR. HARDWARE	CASH CREDIT	
1	19-- Apr. 15	Employ. Income Tax Payable—Federal	462		993 88					2251 92	1
2		FICA Tax Payable			1258 04						2
3											3
4											4
5											5
6											6
7											7
8											8

[2, 3]

CASH PAYMENTS JOURNAL

PAGE 13

	DATE	ACCOUNT TITLE	CK. NO.	POST. REF.	GENERAL DEBIT	GENERAL CREDIT	ACCOUNTS PAYABLE DEBIT	PURCH. DISCOUNT CR. FURNITURE	PURCH. DISCOUNT CR. HARDWARE	CASH CREDIT	
1	19-- Apr. 30	Unemploy. Tax Payable—Federal	515		215 70					215 70	1
2	30	Unemploy. Tax Payable—State	516		1455 96					1455 96	2
3											3
4											4
5											5
6											6
7											7
8											8

Completing payroll records; paying payroll; and recording taxes

BENEFITS AUTHORIZATION

EMPLOYEE NO. __3__   EMPLOYEE __Keith R. Ellis__

PAY PERIOD ENDED __2/13/--__   DEPARTMENT __Tapes__

	HOURS AVAIL.	M	T	W	T	F	S	M	T	W	T	F	S	HOURS USED
VACATION	78	8												8
SICK LEAVE	52					5								5
PERSONAL LEAVE	18												3	3

__Celso Ochoa__   __2/13/--__
MANAGER (only if needed)   DEPARTMENT SUPERVISOR   DATE

BENEFITS AUTHORIZATION

EMPLOYEE NO. __1__   EMPLOYEE __Edna S. Kinchen__

PAY PERIOD ENDED __2/13/--__   DEPARTMENT __Records__

	HOURS AVAIL.	M	T	W	T	F	S	HOURS USED
VACATION	62					4		4
SICK LEAVE	43	5						5
PERSONAL LEAVE	20					5		5

__Doris Baker__   __2/13/--__
MANAGER (only if needed)   DEPARTMENT SUPERVISOR   DATE

BENEFITS AUTHORIZATION

EMPLOYEE NO. __2__   EMPLOYEE __Doris M. Baker__

PAY PERIOD ENDED __2/13/--__   DEPARTMENT __Records__

	HOURS AVAIL.	M	T	W	T	F	S	HOURS USED
VACATION	86					4		4
SICK LEAVE	72		8					8
PERSONAL LEAVE	22							0

__Maria Lucio__   __2/13/--__
MANAGER (only if needed)   DEPARTMENT SUPERVISOR   DATE

BENEFITS AUTHORIZATION

EMPLOYEE NO. ___5___ EMPLOYEE __Patsy A. Quist__ DEPARTMENT __Records__

PAY PERIOD ENDED __2/13/--__

	HOURS AVAIL.	M	T	W	T	F	S	M	T	W	T	F	S	HOURS USED
VACATION	38												8	8
SICK LEAVE	72											4		4
PERSONAL LEAVE	18										2			2

__Doris Baker__
DEPARTMENT SUPERVISOR   2/13/-- DATE

_____
MANAGER (only if needed)

BENEFITS AUTHORIZATION

EMPLOYEE NO. ___4___ EMPLOYEE __Celso T. Ochoa__ DEPARTMENT __Tapes__

PAY PERIOD ENDED __2/13/--__

	HOURS AVAIL.	M	T	W	T	F	S	M	T	W	T	F	S	HOURS USED
VACATION	86						8	8	8					24
SICK LEAVE	52											4		4
PERSONAL LEAVE	16					3						3		3

__Maria Lucio__
MANAGER (only if needed)   DEPARTMENT SUPERVISOR   2/13/-- DATE

BENEFITS AUTHORIZATION

EMPLOYEE NO. ___6___ EMPLOYEE __Juan E. Tovar__ DEPARTMENT __Administrative__

PAY PERIOD ENDED __2/13/--__

	HOURS AVAIL.	M	T	W	T	F	S	M	T	W	T	F	S	HOURS USED
VACATION	56	8												8
SICK LEAVE	52											4		4
PERSONAL LEAVE	22					3						3		3

__Maria Lucio__
MANAGER (only if needed)   DEPARTMENT SUPERVISOR   2/13/-- DATE

BENEFITS RECORD

EMPLOYEE NO. __2__   EMPLOYEE NAME __Doris M. Baker__   DEPARTMENT __Records__

DATE OF INITIAL EMPLOYMENT __February 19, 1985__   YEAR __19--__

		1	2	3	4	5	6	7	8	9	10	11	12
PAY PERIOD ENDED		VACATION TIME				SICK LEAVE TIME				PERSONAL LEAVE TIME			
		BEGIN. HOURS AVAIL.	HOURS EARNED	HOURS USED	ACC. HOURS AVAIL.	BEGIN. HOURS AVAIL.	HOURS EARNED	HOURS USED	ACC. HOURS AVAIL.	BEGIN. HOURS AVAIL.	HOURS EARNED	HOURS USED	ACC. HOURS AVAIL.
4	2-13	86	4	4	86	72	2	8	66	22	1	0	23
5													

BENEFITS RECORD

EMPLOYEE NO. __3__   EMPLOYEE NAME __Keith R. Ellis__   DEPARTMENT __Tapes__

DATE OF INITIAL EMPLOYMENT __November 7, 1984__   YEAR __19--__

		1	2	3	4	5	6	7	8	9	10	11	12
PAY PERIOD ENDED		VACATION TIME				SICK LEAVE TIME				PERSONAL LEAVE TIME			
		BEGIN. HOURS AVAIL.	HOURS EARNED	HOURS USED	ACC. HOURS AVAIL.	BEGIN. HOURS AVAIL.	HOURS EARNED	HOURS USED	ACC. HOURS AVAIL.	BEGIN. HOURS AVAIL.	HOURS EARNED	HOURS USED	ACC. HOURS AVAIL.
4	2-13	78	4	8	74	52	2	5	49	18	1	3	16
5													

BENEFITS RECORD

EMPLOYEE NO. __1__   EMPLOYEE NAME __Edna S. Kinchen__   DEPARTMENT __Records__

DATE OF INITIAL EMPLOYMENT __April 16, 1984__   YEAR __19--__

		1	2	3	4	5	6	7	8	9	10	11	12
PAY PERIOD ENDED		VACATION TIME				SICK LEAVE TIME				PERSONAL LEAVE TIME			
		BEGIN. HOURS AVAIL.	HOURS EARNED	HOURS USED	ACC. HOURS AVAIL.	BEGIN. HOURS AVAIL.	HOURS EARNED	HOURS USED	ACC. HOURS AVAIL.	BEGIN. HOURS AVAIL.	HOURS EARNED	HOURS USED	ACC. HOURS AVAIL.
4	2-13	62	4	4	62	43	2	5	40	20	1	5	16
5													

BENEFITS RECORD

EMPLOYEE NO. _4_ EMPLOYEE NAME _Celso T. Ochoa_ DEPARTMENT _Tapes_

DATE OF INITIAL EMPLOYMENT _June 3, 1985_ YEAR _19--_

	1	2	3	4	5	6	7	8	9	10	11	12
PAY PERIOD ENDED	VACATION TIME				SICK LEAVE TIME				PERSONAL LEAVE TIME			
	BEGIN. HOURS AVAIL.	HOURS EARNED	HOURS USED	ACC. HOURS AVAIL.	BEGIN. HOURS AVAIL.	HOURS EARNED	HOURS USED	ACC. HOURS AVAIL.	BEGIN. HOURS AVAIL.	HOURS EARNED	HOURS USED	ACC. HOURS AVAIL.
4 2-13	86	4	24	66	52	2	4	50	16	1	3	14
5												

BENEFITS RECORD

EMPLOYEE NO. _5_ EMPLOYEE NAME _Patsy A. Quist_ DEPARTMENT _Records_

DATE OF INITIAL EMPLOYMENT _July 9, 1985_ YEAR _19--_

	1	2	3	4	5	6	7	8	9	10	11	12
PAY PERIOD ENDED	VACATION TIME				SICK LEAVE TIME				PERSONAL LEAVE TIME			
	BEGIN. HOURS AVAIL.	HOURS EARNED	HOURS USED	ACC. HOURS AVAIL.	BEGIN. HOURS AVAIL.	HOURS EARNED	HOURS USED	ACC. HOURS AVAIL.	BEGIN. HOURS AVAIL.	HOURS EARNED	HOURS USED	ACC. HOURS AVAIL.
4 2-13	38	4	8	34	72	2	4	70	18	1	2	17
5												

BENEFITS RECORD

EMPLOYEE NO. _6_ EMPLOYEE NAME _Juan E. Tovar_ DEPARTMENT _Administrative_

DATE OF INITIAL EMPLOYMENT _August 3, 1985_ YEAR _19--_

	1	2	3	4	5	6	7	8	9	10	11	12
PAY PERIOD ENDED	VACATION TIME				SICK LEAVE TIME				PERSONAL LEAVE TIME			
	BEGIN. HOURS AVAIL.	HOURS EARNED	HOURS USED	ACC. HOURS AVAIL.	BEGIN. HOURS AVAIL.	HOURS EARNED	HOURS USED	ACC. HOURS AVAIL.	BEGIN. HOURS AVAIL.	HOURS EARNED	HOURS USED	ACC. HOURS AVAIL.
4 2-13	56	4	8	52	52	2	4	50	22	1	3	20
5												

Left Card

NAME **Keith R. Ellis**

DEPARTMENT **Tapes**

EMPLOYEE NO. **3**

PAY PERIOD ENDED **2-13-19--**

MORNING		AFTERNOON		OVERTIME		HOURS	
IN	OUT	IN	OUT	IN	OUT	REG	OT
						V8	
9:00	12:01	1:00	6:00	7:00	8:30	8	1½
8:58	12:00	1:01	6:03			8	
9:02	12:01					3S5	
9:00	12:00	1:00	6:01			8	
		1:00	6:01			5P3	
9:00	12:03	1:01	6:00			8	
9:00	12:00	1:00	6:01	7:00	8:00	8	1
9:01	12:00	1:01	6:00			8	
9:00	12:00	1:02	6:00			8	

	HOURS	RATE	AMOUNT
REGULAR	80	7.00	560.00
OVERTIME	2½	10.50	26.25
TOTAL HOURS	82½	TOTAL EARNINGS	586.25

Right Card

NAME **Edna S. Kinchen**

DEPARTMENT **Records**

EMPLOYEE NO. **1**

PAY PERIOD ENDED **2-13-19--**

MORNING		AFTERNOON		OVERTIME		HOURS	
IN	OUT	IN	OUT	IN	OUT	REG	OT
8:58	11:58	1:00	6:00	7:00	8:30	8	1½
9:00	12:01					3P5	
8:59	12:00	12:58	6:00			8	
9:01	12:00	1:02	6:03			8	
		2:01	6:00			4V4	
8:58	12:01	1:00	6:01			8	
9:00	12:00	1:00	6:02			8	
8:58	12:01	1:01	6:00			8	
9:01	12:00	1:00	6:00	7:00	8:30	8	1½
9:00	12:02					3S5	

	HOURS	RATE	AMOUNT
REGULAR	80	7.50	600.00
OVERTIME	3	11.25	33.75
TOTAL HOURS	83	TOTAL EARNINGS	633.75

NAME __Patsy A. Quist__

DEPARTMENT __Records__

EMPLOYEE NO. __5__

PAY PERIOD ENDED __2-13-19----__

MORNING		AFTERNOON		OVERTIME		HOURS	
IN	OUT	IN	OUT	IN	OUT	REG	OT
⊢ 9:00	⊢12:59	⊢ 2:00	⊢ 6:02	⊢ 7:00	⊢ 8:30	8	1½
		≳ 2:00	≳ 6:01			4S4	
⊢ 8:58	⊢ 1:00	⊢ 2:01	⊢ 6:00			8	
ᴸ 9:01	ᴸ 1:02	ᴸ 2:00	ᴸ 6:03			8	
ഗ 9:00	ഗ 1:00	ഗ 2:01	ഗ 6:00			8	
⊢ 9:00	⊢ 1:03	⊢ 2:00	⊢ 6:00	⊢ 7:30	⊢ 9:30	8	2
≳ 8:58	≳ 1:00	≳ 2:01	≳ 6:01			8	
⊢ 9:00	⊢ 1:03	⊢ 2:00	⊢ 4:00			6P2	
ᴸ 9:00	ᴸ 1:00	ᴸ 2:02	ᴸ 6:03			8	
						V8	

	HOURS	RATE	AMOUNT
REGULAR	80	6.50	520.00
OVERTIME	3½	9.75	34.13
TOTAL HOURS	83½	TOTAL EARNINGS	554.13

NAME __Juan E. Tovar__

DEPARTMENT __Accounting__

EMPLOYEE NO. __6__

PAY PERIOD ENDED __2-13-19----__

MORNING		AFTERNOON		OVERTIME		HOURS	
IN	OUT	IN	OUT	IN	OUT	REG	OT
						V8	
⊢ 9:00	⊢12:01	⊢ 1:00	⊢ 6:00	⊢ 7:00	⊢ 8:30	8	1½
≳ 8:58	≳12:00	≳ 1:01	≳ 6:03			8	
⊢ 9:02	⊢12:01	⊢ 1:00	⊢ 6:00	⊢ 7:30	⊢ 8:30	8	1
ᴸ 9:00	ᴸ12:00	ᴸ 1:00	ᴸ 3:01			5P3	
≳ 9:01	≳12:00	≳ 1:00	≳ 6:01			8	
⊢ 9:00	⊢12:03	⊢ 1:01	⊢ 6:00			8	
≳ 9:00	≳12:00	≳ 1:00	≳ 6:01	≳ 7:30	≳ 9:00	8	1½
⊢ 9:01	⊢12:00	⊢ 1:01	⊢ 2:00			4S4	
ᴸ 9:00	ᴸ12:00	ᴸ 1:02	ᴸ 6:00			8	

	HOURS	RATE	AMOUNT
REGULAR	80	6.50	520.00
OVERTIME	4	9.75	39.00
TOTAL HOURS	84	TOTAL EARNINGS	559.00

COMMISSIONS RECORD

Employee No. _____2_____   Employee Name __Doris M. Baker__

Commission __1%__   Month __January__   Year __19--__

Dept. __Records__   Regular Biweekly Salary __$600.00__

Sales

Sales on Account..............................	$	*5,334.60*
Cash and Credit Card Sales...................		*7,922.10*
Total Sales....................................	$	*13,256.70*
Less: Sales Discounts.............. $ *92.40*		
Sales Returns and Allowances *312.20*	*404.60*	
Net Sales.....................................	$	*12,852.10*
Commission on Net Sales.....................	$	*128.52*

COMMISSIONS RECORD

Employee No. _____4_____   Employee Name __Celso T. Ochoa__

Commission __1%__   Month __January__   Year __19--__

Dept. __Tapes__   Regular Biweekly Salary __$600.00__

Sales

Sales on Account..............................	$	*5,668.90*
Cash and Credit Card Sales...................		*8,375.30*
Total Sales....................................	$	*14,044.20*
Less: Sales Discounts.............. $ *101.70*		
Sales Returns and Allowances *288.60*	*390.30*	
Net Sales.....................................	$	*13,653.90*
Commission on Net Sales.....................	$	*136.54*

PAYROLL REGISTER

PAY PERIOD ENDED February 13, 19--

	EMPL. NO.	EMPLOYEE'S NAME	MARITAL STATUS	NO. OF ALLOW-ANCES	TOTAL HOURS	EARNINGS			
						REGULAR	OVERTIME	COMMIS-SION	TOTAL
1	2	Baker, Doris M.	M	3	—	600 00		128 52	728 52
2	3	Ellis, Keith R.	S	2	82½	560 00	26 25		586 25
3	1	Kinchen, Edna S.	S	1	83	600 00	33 75		633 75
4	4	Ochoa, Celso T.	M	2	—	600 00		136 54	736 54
5	5	Quist, Patsy A.	M	2	83½	520 00	34 13		554 13
6	6	Tovar, Juan E.	S	1	84	520 00	39 00		559 00
7		*Totals*				3400 00	133 13	265 06	3798 19
8									

[6]

EARNINGS RECORD FOR QUARTER ENDED March 31, 19--

EMPLOYEE NO. 2 NAME Doris M. Baker SOCIAL SECURITY NO. 212-60-3120

MARITAL STATUS M WITHHOLDING ALLOWANCES 3 HOURLY RATE SALARY $600.00

DEPARTMENT Records POSITION Supervisor

PAY PERIOD		TOTAL EARNINGS	DEDUCTIONS						NET PAY	ACCUMULATED EARNINGS
NO.	ENDED		FEDERAL INCOME TAX	STATE INCOME TAX	FICA TAX	OTHER		TOTAL		
3	1-30	600 00	52 00	30 00	42 00	L H	14	8 20 4 80	147 00	453 00	1938 40
4	2-13	728 52	71 00	36 43	51 00	L H	14	8 20 4 80	181 43	547 09	2666 92

EARNINGS RECORD FOR QUARTER ENDED March 31, 19--

EMPLOYEE NO. 3 NAME Keith R. Ellis SOCIAL SECURITY NO. 162-04-1612

MARITAL STATUS S WITHHOLDING ALLOWANCES 2 HOURLY RATE $7.00 SALARY

DEPARTMENT Tapes POSITION Salesclerk

PAY PERIOD		TOTAL EARNINGS	DEDUCTIONS						NET PAY	ACCUMULATED EARNINGS
NO.	ENDED		FEDERAL INCOME TAX	STATE INCOME TAX	FICA TAX	OTHER		TOTAL		
3	1-30	560 00	66 00	28 00	39 20	L H	14	8 20 4 80	156 20	403 80	1722 00
4	2-13	586 25	70 00	29 31	41 04	L H	14	8 20 4 80	163 35	422 90	2308 25

[5]

PAYROLL REGISTER

DATE OF PAYMENT February 20, 19--

	10	11	12	13	14	15	16	17	18	19
	DEPARTMENT		ADMIN. SALARIES	DEDUCTIONS					PAID	
	RECORDS	TAPES		FEDERAL INCOME TAX	STATE INCOME TAX	FICA TAX	OTHER	TOTAL	NET PAY	CK. NO.
1	728 52			71 00	36 43	51 00	L 1 4 / H 8 20 80	181 43	547 09		1
2		586 25		70 00	29 31	41 04	L 1 4 / H 8 20 80	163 35	422 90		2
3	633 75			87 00	31 69	44 36	L 1 4 / H 8 20 80	186 05	447 70		3
4		736 54		79 00	36 83	51 56	L 1 4 / H 8 20 80	190 39	546 15		4
5	554 13			49 00	27 71	38 79	L 1 4 / H 8 20 80	138 50	415 63		5
6			559 00	70 00	27 95	39 13	L 1 4 / H 8 20 80	160 08	398 92		6
7	1 916 40	1 322 79	559 00	426 00	189 92	265 88	L 8 8 / H 4 9 20 80	1 019 80	2 778 39		7
8											8

[6]

EARNINGS RECORD FOR QUARTER ENDED _March 31, 19--_

EMPLOYEE NO. ___1___ NAME _Edna S. Kinchen_ SOCIAL SECURITY NO. _213-30-9403_

MARITAL STATUS _S_ WITHHOLDING ALLOWANCES _1_ HOURLY RATE _$7.50_ SALARY _____

DEPARTMENT _Records_ POSITION _Salesclerk_

1	2	3	4	5	6	7	8	9	10
PAY PERIOD		TOTAL EARNINGS	DEDUCTIONS					NET PAY	ACCUMULATED EARNINGS
NO.	ENDED		FEDERAL INCOME TAX	STATE INCOME TAX	FICA TAX	OTHER	TOTAL		
3	1-30	600 00	82 00	30 00	42 00	L 1 4 / H 8 20 80	177 00	423 00	1 833 75
4	2-13	633 75	87 00	31 69	44 36	L 1 4 / H 8 20 80	186 05	447 70	2 467 50

EARNINGS RECORD FOR QUARTER ENDED _March 31, 19--_

EMPLOYEE NO. ___4___ NAME _Celso T. Ochoa_ SOCIAL SECURITY NO. _265-14-3810_

MARITAL STATUS _M_ WITHHOLDING ALLOWANCES _2_ HOURLY RATE _____ SALARY _$600.00_

DEPARTMENT _Tapes_ POSITION _Supervisor_

1	2	3	4	5	6	7	8	9	10
PAY PERIOD		TOTAL EARNINGS	DEDUCTIONS					NET PAY	ACCUMULATED EARNINGS
NO.	ENDED		FEDERAL INCOME TAX	STATE INCOME TAX	FICA TAX	OTHER	TOTAL		
3	1-30	600 00	58 00	30 00	42 00	L 1 4 / H 8 20 80	153 00	447 00	1 943 15
4	2-13	736 54	79 00	36 83	51 56	L 1 4 / H 8 20 80	190 39	546 15	2 679 69

EARNINGS RECORD FOR QUARTER ENDED March 31, 19--

EMPLOYEE NO. 5 NAME Patsy A. Quist SOCIAL SECURITY NO. 196-36-4402

MARITAL STATUS M WITHHOLDING ALLOWANCES 2 HOURLY RATE $6.50 SALARY

DEPARTMENT Records POSITION Salesclerk

1	2	3	4	5	6	7	8	9	10
PAY PERIOD		TOTAL EARNINGS	DEDUCTIONS					NET PAY	ACCUMULATED EARNINGS
NO.	ENDED		FEDERAL INCOME TAX	STATE INCOME TAX	FICA TAX	OTHER	TOTAL		
3	1-30	520 00	46 00	26 00	36 40	L H 14 8 4 20 80	131 40	388 60	1 599 00
4	2-13	554 13	49 00	27 71	38 79	L H 14 8 4 20 80	138 50	415 63	2 153 13

EARNINGS RECORD FOR QUARTER ENDED March 31, 19--

EMPLOYEE NO. 6 NAME Juan E. Tovar SOCIAL SECURITY NO. 262-36-3136

MARITAL STATUS S WITHHOLDING ALLOWANCES 1 HOURLY RATE $6.50 SALARY

DEPARTMENT Administrative POSITION Clerk

1	2	3	4	5	6	7	8	9	10
PAY PERIOD		TOTAL EARNINGS	DEDUCTIONS					NET PAY	ACCUMULATED EARNINGS
NO.	ENDED		FEDERAL INCOME TAX	STATE INCOME TAX	FICA TAX	OTHER	TOTAL		
3	1-30	520 00	66 00	26 00	36 40	L H 14 8 4 20 80	151 40	368 60	1 608 75
4	2-13	559 00	70 00	27 95	39 13	L H 14 8 4 20 80	160 08	398 92	2 167 75

[7]

CASH PAYMENTS JOURNAL

PAGE 9

DATE		ACCOUNT TITLE	CK. NO.	POST. REF.	GENERAL DEBIT (1)	GENERAL CREDIT (2)	ACCOUNTS PAYABLE DEBIT (3)	PURCH. DISCOUNT CR. RECORDS (4)	PURCH. DISCOUNT CR. TAPES (5)	CASH CREDIT (6)	
19-- Feb.	20	Salary Expense—Records	143		1 9 1 6 40					2 7 7 8 39	1
		Salary Expense—Tapes			1 3 2 2 79						2
		Salary Expense—Administrative			5 5 9 00						3
		Employ. Inc. Tax Payable—Federal				4 2 6 00					4
		Employ. Inc. Tax Payable—State				1 8 9 92					5
		FICA Tax Payable				2 6 5 88					6
		Life Insurance Payable				4 9 20					7
		Hospital Insurance Payable				8 8 80					8
											9

[8]

GENERAL JOURNAL

PAGE 5

DATE		ACCOUNT TITLE	POST. REF.	DEBIT	CREDIT	
19-- Feb.	20	Payroll Taxes Expense		5 0 1 36		1
		FICA Tax Payable			2 6 5 87	2
		Unemploy. Tax Payable—Federal			3 0 39	3
		Unemploy. Tax Payable—State			2 0 5 10	4
		M14				5

BENEFITS RECORD

EMPLOYEE NO. **7**   EMPLOYEE NAME **Alice K. Dotson**   DEPARTMENT **Women's Wear**

DATE OF INITIAL EMPLOYMENT **June 5, 1985**   YEAR **19--**

	1	2	3	4	5	6	7	8	9	10	11	12
PAY PERIOD ENDED	VACATION TIME				SICK LEAVE TIME				PERSONAL LEAVE TIME			
	BEGIN. HOURS AVAIL.	HOURS EARNED	HOURS USED	ACC. HOURS AVAIL.	BEGIN. HOURS AVAIL.	HOURS EARNED	HOURS USED	ACC. HOURS AVAIL.	BEGIN. HOURS AVAIL.	HOURS EARNED	HOURS USED	ACC. HOURS AVAIL.
1 1-15	35⅓	3⅓	0	38⅔	28⅔	1⅔	4	26⅓	18	1	2	17
2 1-31	38⅔	3⅓	4	38	26⅓	1⅔	0	28	17	1	3	15
3 2-15	38	3⅓	8	33⅓	28	1⅔	8	21⅔	15	1	0	16
4 2-29	33⅓	3⅓	0	36⅔	21⅔	1⅔	0	23⅓	16	1	2	15
5												
6												
7												
8												
9												
10												
11												
12												
13												

Perfect Score. 50

Deduct .... —

Your Score .... —

Name _____

Date _____ Class _____

Checked by _____

STUDY GUIDE 5

UNIT A—Identifying Accounting Terms

DIRECTIONS: Select the one term in Column I that best fits each definition in Column II. Print the letter identifying your choice in the Answers column.

Column I	*Column II*	Answers	For Scoring
A. accounting cycle	**0.** A proof of the equality of debits and credits in a general ledger..	U	0. ✔
B. adjusting entries	**1.** Assets which will be used for a number of years in the operation of a business............................	N	1.
C. balance sheet	**2.** A listing of vendor accounts, account balances, and total amount due all vendors.................	R	2.
D. closing entries	**3.** Journal entries used to prepare temporary capital accounts for a new fiscal period.................	D	3.
E. component percentage	**4.** The series of accounting activities included in recording financial information for a fiscal period	A	4.
F. departmental statement of gross profit	**5.** A listing of customer accounts, account balances, and total amount due from all customers	S	5.
G. depreciation	**6.** Estimating inventory by using previous years' percentage of gross profit on operations..................	I	6.
H. fiscal period	**7.** A statement prepared at the end of a fiscal period, showing the gross profit for each department..............	F	7.
I. gross profit method of estimating an inventory	**8.** A columnar accounting form on which the financial condition of a business is summarized	V	8.
J. income statement	**9.** Merchandise inventory determined by counting, weighing, or measuring items of merchandise on hand..	L	9.
K. interim departmental statement of gross profit	**10.** The percentage relationship between one financial statement item and the total that includes that item.......	E	10.
L. periodic inventory	**11.** A statement showing gross profit for each department for a portion of a fiscal period...............................	K	11.
M. perpetual inventory	**12.** A financial statement showing the revenue and expenses for a fiscal period	J	12.
N. plant assets	**13.** An amount earned by a corporation and not yet distributed to stockholders...................................	Q	13.
O. post-closing trial balance	**14.** Journal entries made to bring general ledger accounts up to date..	B	14.
P. ratio	**15.** A financial statement that shows changes in a corporation's ownership for a fiscal period................	T	15.
Q. retained earnings			
R. schedule of accounts payable	**16.** Merchandise inventory determined by keeping a continuous record of increases, decreases, and balance on hand	M	16.
S. schedule of accounts receivable	**17.** A financial statement that reports assets, liabilities, and stockholders' equity on a specific date................	C	17.
T. statement of stockholders' equity	**18.** The portion of a plant asset's cost transferred to an expense account in each fiscal period during a plant asset's useful life	G	18.
U. trial balance	**19.** A trial balance prepared after closing entries are posted..........	O	19.
V. work sheet	**20.** A comparison between two numbers showing how many times one number exceeds the other	P	20.
	21. The length of time for which a business analyzes financial information................	H	21.

UNIT B—Analyzing Departmental Adjusting and Closing Entries

DIRECTIONS: For each transaction below, print in the proper Answers column the identifying letters of the accounts to be debited and credited.

Account

A. Accum. Depr.—Equipment
B. Allow. for Uncoll. Accounts
C. Bad Debts Expense
D. departmental contra cost accounts
E. departmental contra sales accounts
F. departmental cost accounts
G. departmental income summary accounts
H. departmental merchandise inventory accounts
I. departmental sales accounts
J. Depr. Expense—Equipment
K. expense accounts
L. Income Summary—General
M. Insurance Expense
N. Prepaid Insurance
O. Retained Earnings
P. Supplies
Q. Supplies Expense

Transactions

	Transactions	Answers Debit	Answers Credit	For Scoring Debit	For Scoring Credit
0–0.	Adjust Supplies	Q	P	0. ✔	0. ✔
22–23.	Adjust Bad Debts Expense	C	B	22.	23.
24–25.	Adjust Prepaid Insurance	M	N	24.	25.
26–27.	Adjust ending merchandise inventory (increase)	H	G	26.	27.
28–29.	Adjust ending merchandise inventory (decrease)	G	H	28.	29.
30–31.	Adjust Depr. Expense—Equipment	J	A	30.	31.
32–33.	Close departmental income summary (credit balances), sales, and contra cost accounts	G,I,D	L	32.	33.
34–35.	Close departmental income summary (debit balances), contra sales, cost, and expense accounts	L	F,K G,E,	34.	35.
36–37.	Close Income Summary—General (net income)	L	O	36.	37.
38–39.	Close Income Summary—General (net loss)	O	L	38.	39.

UNIT C—Analyzing Financial Reporting Procedures for a Departmentalized Business

DIRECTIONS: Place a check mark in the proper Answers column to show whether each of the following statements is true or false.

	Answers True	Answers False	For Scoring
0. A common length of time for summarizing and reporting accounting information is one year	✔		0. ✔
40. An interim departmental statement of gross profit is usually prepared monthly	✔		40.
41. The ratio of total operating expenses to net sales shows the relationship between operating expenses and gross profit		✔	41.
42. Allowance for Uncollectible Accounts is debited in the adjustment for bad debts expense		✔	42.
43. Income Summary—General is used for adjusting the merchandise inventory account balances for a departmentalized business		✔	43.
44. Accumulated Depreciation—Office Equipment is a contra cost account		✔	44.
45. The annual departmental statement of gross profit uses an actual ending inventory determined by a periodic inventory	✔		45.
46. A departmentalized business has a separate income summary account for each department	✔		46.
47. The Income Summary—General account balance is equal to the net income (or net loss) for a fiscal period	✔		47.
48. Completing end-of-fiscal-period work is an application of the Accounting Period Cycle accounting concept	✔		48.
49. A departmentalized business does not prepare a post-closing trial balance		✔	49.
50. Recording expenses in the fiscal period in which the expenses contribute to earning revenue is an application of the Matching Expenses with Revenue accounting concept	✔		50.

Estimating ending merchandise inventory

ESTIMATED MERCHANDISE INVENTORY SHEET
Gross Profit Method

Department __*Men's Wear*_____ Date __*1/31/--*_____

1	Beginning inventory, January 1	$ *148,000.00*
2	Net purchases to date...	*14,300.00*
3	Merchandise available for sale.......................................	$ *162,300.00*
4	Net sales to date .... $ *49,200.00*	
5	Less estimated gross profit *22,140.00*	
	(Net sales × Estimated gross profit __*45*__ %)	
6	Estimated cost of merchandise sold...................................	*27,060.00*
7	Estimated ending inventory..	$ *135,240.00*

ESTIMATED MERCHANDISE INVENTORY SHEET
Gross Profit Method

Department __*Women's Wear*_____ Date __*1/31/--*_____

1	Beginning inventory, January 1	$ *153,000.00*
2	Net purchases to date...	*15,100.00*
3	Merchandise available for sale.......................................	$ *168,100.00*
4	Net sales to date .... $ *53,400.00*	
5	Less estimated gross profit *24,030.00*	
	(Net sales × Estimated gross profit __*45*__ %)	
6	Estimated cost of merchandise sold...................................	*29,370.00*
7	Estimated ending inventory..	$ *138,730.00*

Figuring percentage ratios of cost of merchandise sold and
gross profit on operations to net sales

PROBLEM 5-2, p. 105

1	2	3	4
Business	Component	Amount	Percentage Ratio
1	Total Net Sales Total Cost of Merchandise Sold Total Gross Profit on Operations	$100,000.00 60,000.00 40,000.00	100.0% 60.0% 40.0%
2	Total Net Sales Total Cost of Merchandise Sold Total Gross Profit on Operations	$150,000.00 80,000.00 70,000.00	100.0% 53.3% 46.7%
3	Total Net Sales Total Cost of Merchandise Sold Total Gross Profit on Operations	$130,000.00 60,000.00 70,000.00	100.0% 46.2% 53.8%
4	Total Net Sales Total Cost of Merchandise Sold Total Gross Profit on Operations	$180,000.00 100,000.00 80,000.00	100.0% 55.6% 44.4%
5	Total Net Sales Total Cost of Merchandise Sold Total Gross Profit on Operations	$160,000.00 85,000.00 75,000.00	100.0% 53.1% 46.9%
6	Total Net Sales Total Cost of Merchandise Sold Total Gross Profit on Operations	$220,000.00 115,000.00 105,000.00	100.0% 52.3% 47.7%

Preparing an interim departmental statement of gross profit;
figuring and recording percentage ratios

ESTIMATED MERCHANDISE INVENTORY SHEET
Gross Profit Method

Department __Cycles__ Date __3/31/--__

1	Beginning inventory, January 1..		$ 193,300.00
2	Net purchases to date..		29,200.00
3	Merchandise available for sale...		$ 222,500.00
4	Net sales to date	$ 97,200.00	
5	Less estimated gross profit	38,880.00	
	(Net sales × Estimated gross profit __40__ %)		
6	Estimated cost of merchandise sold..		58,320.00
7	Estimated ending inventory..		$ 164,180.00

ESTIMATED MERCHANDISE INVENTORY SHEET
Gross Profit Method

Department __Mopeds__ Date __3/31/--__

1	Beginning inventory, January 1..		$ 167,500.00
2	Net purchases to date..		24,840.00
3	Merchandise available for sale...		$ 192,340.00
4	Net sales to date	$ 93,800.00	
5	Less estimated gross profit	37,520.00	
	(Net sales × Estimated gross profit __40__ %)		
6	Estimated cost of merchandise sold..		56,280.00
7	Estimated ending inventory..		$ 136,060.00

[2]

Motor Sports

Interim Departmental Statement of Gross Profit

For Month Ended March 31, 19--

	CYCLES	% OF NET SALES	MOPEDS	% OF NET SALES	TOTAL	% OF NET SALES
Operating Revenue:						
Net Sales	36,500.00	100.0	34,600.00	100.0	71,100.00	100.0
Cost of Merchandise Sold:						
Est. Mdse. Inv., March 1	168,442.00		146,218.80		314,660.80	
Net Purchases	16,871.50		9,978.40		26,849.90	
Mdse. Available for Sale	185,313.50		156,197.20		341,510.70	
Less Est. End Inv., March 31	164,180.00		136,060.00		300,240.00	
Cost of Merchandise Sold	21,133.50	57.9	20,137.20	58.2	41,270.70	58.0
Gross Profit on Operations	15,366.50	42.1	14,462.80	41.8	29,829.30	42.0

Preparing subsidiary schedules

Gombosky's
Schedule of Accounts Payable
December 31, 19--

Acton, Inc.	2	3	5	0	40
Doyle Associates	1	6	2	0	30
Huertas Supply		9	3	6	80
J & M Enterprises	1	2	6	2	50
Tafoya Products		8	2	6	10
Veloz Associates	2	3	7	0	60
Total Accounts Payable	9	3	6	6	70

[2]

Gombosky's
Schedule of Accounts Receivable
December 31, 19--

Mary Barnas	1	2	1	0	20
Teresa Conroy		8	2	0	70
Paul DeYoung		7	2	6	10
John Klem	1	3	0	4	20
Irma Musgrove		6	1	9	60
Alex Vail	1	9	2	6	40
Total Accounts Receivable	6	6	0	7	20

Figuring and analyzing ratios of total operating expenses
to net sales

PROBLEM 5-5, p. 106
[1, 2]

1	2	3	4	5	6
Bus.	Net Sales	Total Operating Expenses	Performance Standard— Not more than:	Percentage Ratio	Performance Level
1	$150,000.00	$45,000.00	32.0%	30.0%	A
2	$130,300.00	$36,500.00	26.0%	28.0%	U
3	$175,500.00	$51,750.00	30.0%	29.5%	A
4	$145,600.00	$35,930.00	25.0%	24.7%	A
5	$185,300.00	$58,250.00	30.0%	31.4%	U
6	$165,900.00	$44,980.00	28.0%	27.1%	A

Figuring and analyzing percentage ratios of net income
to net sales

PROBLEM 5-6, p. 107
[1, 2]

1	2	3	4	5	6
Bus.	Net Sales	Net Income	Performance Standard— Not Less than:	Percentage Ratio	Performance Level
1	$145,200.00	$15,130.00	10.0%	10.4%	A
2	$193,100.00	$24,150.00	12.0%	12.5%	A
3	$161,750.00	$10,820.00	8.0%	6.7%	U
4	$138,920.00	$13,940.00	9.0%	10.0%	A
5	$174,600.00	$ 8,200.00	6.0%	4.7%	U
6	$159,820.00	$19,350.00	11.0%	12.1%	A

Completing end-of-fiscal-period work for a departmentalized business   [2]

Superior Floor Covering

Departmental Statement of Gross Profit

For Year Ended December 31, 19--

	CARPETING	% OF NET SALES	LINOLEUM	% OF NET SALES	TOTAL	% OF NET SALES
Operating Revenue:						
Net Sales	381,248.20	100.0	331,164.00	100.0	712,412.20	100.0
Cost of Merchandise Sold:						
Mdse. Inv., Jan. 1	178,960.30		160,380.40		339,340.70	
Net Purchases	193,120.80		187,930.60		381,051.40	
Mdse. Available for Sale	372,081.10		348,311.00		720,392.10	
Less End. Inv., Dec. 31	173,450.80		168,820.10		342,270.90	
Cost of Merchandise Sold	198,630.30	52.1	179,490.90	54.2	378,121.20	53.1
Gross Profit on Operations	182,617.90	47.9	151,673.10	45.8	334,291.00	46.9

[1]

Superior Floor Covering

Work Sheet

For Year Ended December 31, 19--

	TRIAL BALANCE		ADJUSTMENTS		INCOME STATEMENT		BALANCE SHEET	
ACCOUNT TITLE	DEBIT	CREDIT	DEBIT	CREDIT	DEBIT	CREDIT	DEBIT	CREDIT
1 Cash	37 4 1 0 68						37 4 1 0 68	
2 Petty Cash	5 0 0 00						5 0 0 00	
3 Accounts Receivable	21 9 4 8 60						21 9 4 8 60	
4 Allowance for Uncollectible Accts.		3 2 0 80		(a)2 2 5 9 10				2 5 7 9 90
5 Mdse. Inventory — Carpeting	178 9 6 0 30			(b)5 5 0 9 50			173 4 5 0 80	
6 Mdse. Inventory — Linoleum	160 3 8 0 40		(c)8 4 3 9 70				168 8 2 0 10	
7 Supplies — Office	10 9 4 0 00			(d)6 0 0 9 40			4 9 3 0 60	
8 Supplies — Store	9 6 2 0 60			(e)3 9 0 0 20			5 7 2 0 40	
9 Prepaid Insurance	8 8 0 0 00			(f)4 2 0 0 00			4 6 0 0 00	
10 Office Equipment	18 9 0 0 00						18 9 0 0 00	
11 Accum. Depr. — Office Equipment		8 8 4 0 00		(g)1 2 8 0 00				10 1 2 0 00
12 Store Equipment	21 6 0 0 00						21 6 0 0 00	
13 Accum. Depr. — Store Equipment		10 3 1 0 00		(h)2 8 0 0 00				13 1 1 0 00
14 Accounts Payable		29 9 8 0 30						29 9 8 0 30
15 Employ. Inc. Tax Pay. — Federal		1 3 2 0 40						1 3 2 0 40
16 Employ. Inc. Tax Pay. — State		8 6 0 10						8 6 0 10
17 Federal Income Tax Payable				(i)3 8 4 1 45				3 8 4 1 45
18 FICA Tax Payable		2 1 0 4 00						2 1 0 4 00
19 Sales Tax Payable		6 8 3 0 40						6 8 3 0 40
20 Unemploy. Tax Pay. — Federal		1 9 30						1 9 30
21 Unemploy. Tax Pay. — State		1 3 0 28						1 3 0 28
22 Hospital Ins. Prem. Payable		1 7 4 2 00						1 7 4 2 00
23 Life Ins. Prem. Payable		1 2 4 8 00						1 2 4 8 00
24 Capital Stock		200 0 0 0 00						200 0 0 0 00
25 Retained Earnings		125 6 7 5 00						125 6 7 5 00
26 Income Summary — Carpeting			(b)5 5 0 9 50		5 5 0 9 50			
27 Income Summary — Linoleum				(c)8 4 3 9 70		8 4 3 9 70		
28 Income Summary — General								

[1]

	ACCOUNT TITLE	TRIAL BALANCE DEBIT	TRIAL BALANCE CREDIT	ADJUSTMENTS DEBIT	ADJUSTMENTS CREDIT	INCOME STATEMENT DEBIT	INCOME STATEMENT CREDIT	BALANCE SHEET DEBIT	BALANCE SHEET CREDIT	
29	Sales—Carpeting		387 1 6 9 80				387 1 6 9 80			29
30	Sales—Linoleum		337 8 9 4 70				337 8 9 4 70			30
31	Sales Ret. & Allow.—Carpeting	2 3 1 0 80				2 3 1 0 80				31
32	Sales Ret. & Allow.—Linoleum	2 9 4 0 60				2 9 4 0 60				32
33	Sales Discount—Carpeting	3 6 1 0 80				3 6 1 0 80				33
34	Sales Discount—Linoleum	3 7 9 0 10				3 7 9 0 10				34
35	Purchases—Carpeting	202 2 1 1 90				202 2 1 1 90				35
36	Purchases—Linoleum	196 9 4 1 50				196 9 4 1 50				36
37	Purch. Ret. & Allow.—Carpeting		3 9 6 0 30				3 9 6 0 30			37
38	Purch. Ret. & Allow.—Linoleum		4 2 8 0 70				4 2 8 0 70			38
39	Purchases Discount—Carpeting		5 1 3 0 80				5 1 3 0 80			39
40	Purchases Discount—Linoleum		4 7 3 0 20				4 7 3 0 20			40
41	Advertising Expense	5 4 8 0 00				5 4 8 0 00				41
42	Credit Card Fee Expense	4 7 6 0 80				4 7 6 0 80				42
43	Depr. Exp.—Store Equipment			(h)2 8 0 0 00		2 8 0 0 00				43
44	Salary Expense—Carpeting	72 8 0 0 00				72 8 0 0 00				44
45	Salary Expense—Linoleum	76 3 0 0 00				76 3 0 0 00				45
46	Supplies Expense—Store			(e)3 9 0 0 20		3 9 0 0 20				46
47	Bad Debts Expense			(a)2 2 5 9 10		2 2 5 9 10				47
48	Depr. Exp.—Office Equipment			(g)1 2 8 0 00		1 2 8 0 00				48
49	Insurance Expense			(f)4 2 0 0 00		4 2 0 0 00				49
50	Miscellaneous Expense	4 6 3 0 00				4 6 3 0 00				50
51	Payroll Taxes Expense	18 3 4 0 00				18 3 4 0 00				51
52	Rent Expense	18 0 0 0 00				18 0 0 0 00				52
53	Salary Expense—Administrative	39 8 6 0 00				39 8 6 0 00				53
54	Supplies Expense—Office			(d)6 0 0 9 40		6 0 0 9 40				54
55	Federal Income Tax	11 5 1 0 00		(i)3 8 4 1 45		15 3 5 1 45				55
56		1132 5 4 7 08	1132 5 4 7 08	38 2 3 9 35	38 2 3 9 35	693 2 8 6 15	751 6 0 6 20	457 8 8 1 18	399 5 6 1 13	56
57	*Net Income after Federal Income Tax*					58 3 2 0 05			58 3 2 0 05	57
58						751 6 0 6 20	751 6 0 6 20	457 8 8 1 18	457 8 8 1 18	58
59										59

Superior Floor Covering

Income Statement

For Year Ended December 31, 19--

					% OF NET SALES
Operating Revenue:					
Sales:			725 0 6 4 50		
Less: Sales Returns & Allow.		5 2 5 1 40			
Sales Discount		7 4 0 0 90	12 6 5 2 30		
Net Sales				712 4 1 2 20	100.0
Cost of Merchandise Sold:					
Mdse. Inv., Jan. 1, 19--			339 3 4 0 70		
Purchases		399 1 5 3 40			
Less: Purch. Returns & Allow.	8 2 4 1 00				
Purchases Discount	9 8 6 1 00	18 1 0 2 00			
Net Purchases			381 0 5 1 40		
Total Cost of Mdse. Available			720 3 9 2 10		
Less Mdse. Inv., Dec. 31, 19--			342 2 7 0 90		
Cost of Merchandise Sold				378 1 2 1 20	53.1
Gross Profit on Operations				334 2 9 1 00	46.9
Operating Expenses:					
Selling Expenses:					
Advertising Expense		5 4 8 0 00			
Credit Card Fee Expense		4 7 6 0 80			
Depr. Exp. — Store Equipment		2 8 0 0 00			
Salary Expense — Carpeting		72 8 0 0 00			
Salary Expense — Linoleum		76 3 0 0 00			
Supplies Expense — Store		3 9 0 0 20			
Total Selling Expenses			166 0 4 1 00		
Administrative Expenses:					
Bad Debts Expense		2 2 5 9 10			
Depr. Exp. — Office Equipment		1 2 8 0 00			
Insurance Expense		4 2 0 0 00			
Miscellaneous Expense		4 6 3 0 00			
Payroll Taxes Expense		18 3 4 0 00			
Rent Expense		18 0 0 0 00			
Salary Expense — Administrative		39 8 6 0 00			

Continue this income statement on the next page.

Superior Floor Covering

Income Statement (continued)

For Year Ended December 31, 19--

					% OF NET SALES
Supplies Expense — Office			6 0 0 9 40		
Total Administrative Expenses				94 5 7 8 50	
Total Operating Expenses					260 6 1 9 50	36.6
Net Income before Fed. Inc. Tax					73 6 7 1 50	
Less Federal Income Tax					15 3 5 1 45	
Net Income after Fed. Inc. Tax					58 3 2 0 05	8.2

Superior Floor Covering

Statement of Stockholders' Equity

For Year Ended December 31, 19--

Capital Stock:													
$100.00 Per Share													
January 1, 19--, 2,000 Shares Issued	200	0	0	0	00								
Issued during 19--, None		—	0	—									
Balance, December 31, 19--, 2,000 Shares Issued						200	0	0	0	00			
Retained Earnings:													
January 1, 19--	125	6	7	5	00								
Plus Net Income for 19--	58	3	2	0	05								
Balance, December 31, 19--						183	9	9	5	05			
Total Stockholders' Equity, December 31, 19--						383	9	9	5	05			

Superior Floor Covering

Balance Sheet

December 31, 19--

Assets										
Current Assets:										
Cash						37 4 1 0 68				
Petty Cash						5 0 0 00				
Accounts Receivable	21 9 4 8 60									
Less Allowance for Uncollectible Accounts	2 5 7 9 90					19 3 6 8 70				
Merchandise Inventory — Carpeting						173 4 5 0 80				
Merchandise Inventory — Linoleum						168 8 2 0 10				
Supplies — Office						4 9 3 0 60				
Supplies — Store						5 7 2 0 40				
Prepaid Insurance						4 6 0 0 00				
Total Current Assets								414 8 0 1 28		
Plant Assets:										
Office Equipment	18 9 0 0 00									
Less Accum. Depr. — Office Equipment	10 1 2 0 00					8 7 8 0 00				
Store Equipment	21 6 0 0 00									
Less Accum. Depr. — Store Equipment	13 1 1 0 00					8 4 9 0 00				
Total Plant Assets								17 2 7 0 00		
Total Assets								432 0 7 1 28		
Liabilities										
Current Liabilities:										
Accounts Payable						29 9 8 0 30				
Employees Income Tax Payable — Federal						1 3 2 0 40				
Employees Income Tax Payable — State						8 6 0 10				
Federal Income Tax Payable						3 8 4 1 45				
FICA Tax Payable						2 1 0 4 00				
Sales Tax Payable						6 8 3 0 40				
Unemployment Tax Payable — Federal						1 9 30				
Unemployment Tax Payable — State						1 3 0 28				
Hospital Insurance Premiums Payable						1 7 4 2 00				
Life Insurance Premiums Payable						1 2 4 8 00				
Total Current Liabilities								48 0 7 6 23		

Continue this balance sheet on the next page.

Superior Floor Covering

Balance Sheet (continued)

December 31, 19--

Stockholders' Equity					
Capital Stock		200 0 0 0 00			
Retained Earnings		183 9 9 5 05			
Total Stockholders' Equity				383 9 9 5 05	
Total Liabilities & Stockholders' Equity				432 0 7 1 28	

GENERAL JOURNAL   PAGE 15

	DATE		ACCOUNT TITLE	POST. REF.	DEBIT	CREDIT	
1			*Adjusting Entries*				1
2	*19--* Dec.	31	Bad Debts Expense		2 2 5 9 10		2
3			Allowance for Uncollectible Accounts			2 2 5 9 10	3
4		31	Income Summary — Carpeting		5 5 0 9 50		4
5			Merchandise Inventory — Carpeting			5 5 0 9 50	5
6		31	Merchandise Inventory — Linoleum		8 4 3 9 70		6
7			Income Summary — Linoleum			8 4 3 9 70	7
8		31	Supplies Expense — Office		6 0 0 9 40		8
9			Supplies — Office			6 0 0 9 40	9
10		31	Supplies Expense — Store		3 9 0 0 20		10
11			Supplies — Store			3 9 0 0 20	11
12		31	Insurance Expense		4 2 0 0 00		12
13			Prepaid Insurance			4 2 0 0 00	13
14		31	Depreciation Expense — Office Equipment		1 2 8 0 00		14
15			Accum. Depreciation — Office Equip.			1 2 8 0 00	15
16		31	Depreciation Expense — Store Equipment		2 8 0 0 00		16
17			Accum. Depreciation — Store Equip.			2 8 0 0 00	17
18		31	Federal Income Tax		3 8 4 1 45		18
19			Federal Income Tax Payable			3 8 4 1 45	19
20			*Closing Entries*				20
21		31	Income Summary — Linoleum		8 4 3 9 70		21
22			Sales — Carpeting		387 1 6 9 80		22
23			Sales — Linoleum		337 8 9 4 70		23
24			Purchases Ret. & Allow. — Carpeting		3 9 6 0 30		24
25			Purchases Ret. & Allow. — Linoleum		4 2 8 0 70		25
26			Purchases Discount — Carpeting		5 1 3 0 80		26
27			Purchases Discount — Linoleum		4 7 3 0 20		27
28			Income Summary — General			751 6 0 6 20	28
29		31	Income Summary — General		693 2 8 6 15		29
30			Income Summary — Carpeting			5 5 0 9 50	30
31			Sales Returns and Allow. — Carpeting			2 3 1 0 80	31
32			Sales Returns and Allow. — Linoleum			2 9 4 0 60	32
33			Sales Discount — Carpeting			3 6 1 0 80	33

GENERAL JOURNAL

PAGE 16

	DATE		ACCOUNT TITLE	POST. REF.	DEBIT	CREDIT	
1	19-- Dec.	31	Sales Discount — Linoleum			3 7 9 0 10	1
2			Purchases — Carpeting			202 2 1 1 90	2
3			Purchases — Linoleum			196 9 4 1 50	3
4			Advertising Expense			5 4 8 0 00	4
5			Credit Card Fee Expense			4 7 6 0 80	5
6			Depr. Expense — Store Equipment			2 8 0 0 00	6
7			Salary Expense — Carpeting			72 8 0 0 00	7
8			Salary Expense — Linoleum			76 3 0 0 00	8
9			Supplies Expense — Store			3 9 0 0 20	9
10			Bad Debts Expense			2 2 5 9 10	10
11			Depr. Expense — Office Equipment			1 2 8 0 00	11
12			Insurance Expense			4 2 0 0 00	12
13			Miscellaneous Expense			4 6 3 0 00	13
14			Payroll Taxes Expense			18 3 4 0 00	14
15			Rent Expense			18 0 0 0 00	15
16			Salary Expense — Administrative			39 8 6 0 00	16
17			Supplies Expense — Office			6 0 0 9 40	17
18			Federal Income Tax			15 3 5 1 45	18
19		31	Income Summary — General		58 3 2 0 05		19
20			Retained Earnings			58 3 2 0 05	20
21							21
22							22
23							23
24							24
25							25
26							26
27							27
28							28
29							29
30							30
31							31
32							32
33							33

Completing end-of-fiscal-period work for a departmentalized business   [2]

Worley's

Departmental Statement of Gross Profit

For Year Ended December 31, 19--

	APPLIANCES	% OF NET SALES	FURNITURE	% OF NET SALES	TOTAL	% OF NET SALES
Operating Revenue:						
Net Sales	381,430.00	100.0	361,160.00	100.0	742,590.00	100.0
Cost of Merchandise Sold:						
Mdse. Inv., Jan. 1	220,180.00		247,240.00		467,420.00	
Net Purchases	193,486.00		180,508.00		373,994.00	
Mdse. Available for Sale	413,666.00		427,748.00		841,414.00	
Less End. Inv., Dec. 31	205,380.20		236,520.80		441,901.00	
Cost of Merchandise Sold	208,285.80	54.6	191,227.20	52.9	399,513.00	53.8
Gross Profit on Operations	173,144.20	45.4	169,932.80	47.1	343,077.00	46.2

Worley's

Work Sheet

For Year Ended December 31, 19--

	ACCOUNT TITLE	TRIAL BALANCE DEBIT	TRIAL BALANCE CREDIT	ADJUSTMENTS DEBIT	ADJUSTMENTS CREDIT	INCOME STATEMENT DEBIT	INCOME STATEMENT CREDIT	BALANCE SHEET DEBIT	BALANCE SHEET CREDIT	
1	Cash	40 5 6 0 40						40 5 6 0 40		1
2	Petty Cash	6 0 0 00						6 0 0 00		2
3	Accounts Receivable	27 3 6 4 20						27 3 6 4 20		3
4	Allowance for Uncollectible Accts.		4 6 0 80		(a) 1 9 7 0 40				2 4 3 1 20	4
5	Mdse. Inventory—Appliances	220 1 8 0 00			(b)14 7 9 9 80			205 3 8 0 20		5
6	Mdse. Inventory—Furniture	247 2 4 0 00			(c)10 7 1 9 20			236 5 2 0 80		6
7	Supplies—Office	12 1 4 0 00			(d) 8 4 2 9 70			3 7 1 0 30		7
8	Supplies—Store	9 4 8 3 60			(e) 5 2 6 3 10			4 2 2 0 50		8
9	Prepaid Insurance	8 5 5 0 00			(f) 4 7 5 0 00			3 8 0 0 00		9
10	Office Equipment	17 9 4 0 00						17 9 4 0 00		10
11	Accum. Depr.—Office Equipment		9 3 6 0 00		(g) 1 2 0 0 00				10 5 6 0 00	11
12	Store Equipment	22 8 6 0 00						22 8 6 0 00		12
13	Accum. Depr.—Store Equipment		11 4 3 0 00		(h) 2 6 0 0 00				14 0 3 0 00	13
14	Accounts Payable		32 7 4 0 00						32 7 4 0 00	14
15	Employ. Inc. Tax Pay.—Federal		1 3 4 0 90						1 3 4 0 90	15
16	Employ. Inc. Tax Pay.—State		9 3 0 60						9 3 0 60	16
17	Federal Income Tax Payable				(i) 4 1 9 3 00				4 1 9 3 00	17
18	FICA Tax Payable		2 3 6 0 00						2 3 6 0 00	18
19	Sales Tax Payable		7 2 4 0 30						7 2 4 0 30	19
20	Unemploy. Tax Pay.—Federal		2 2 40						2 2 40	20
21	Unemploy. Tax Pay.—State		1 5 1 20						1 5 1 20	21
22	Hospital Ins. Prem. Payable		2 2 6 0 00						2 2 6 0 00	22
23	Life Ins. Prem. Payable		1 2 8 0 00						1 2 8 0 00	23
24	Capital Stock		300 0 0 0 00						300 0 0 0 00	24
25	Retained Earnings		125 0 0 0 00						125 0 0 0 00	25
26	Income Summary—Appliances			(b)14 7 9 9 80		14 7 9 9 80				26
27	Income Summary—Furniture			(c)10 7 1 9 20		10 7 1 9 20				27
28	Income Summary—General									28

[1]

[1]

#	ACCOUNT TITLE	TRIAL BALANCE DEBIT	TRIAL BALANCE CREDIT	ADJUSTMENTS DEBIT	ADJUSTMENTS CREDIT	INCOME STATEMENT DEBIT	INCOME STATEMENT CREDIT	BALANCE SHEET DEBIT	BALANCE SHEET CREDIT
29	Sales — Appliances		386 9 3 0 30				386 9 3 0 30		
30	Sales — Furniture		366 8 0 0 80				366 8 0 0 80		
31	Sales Ret. & Allow. — Appliances	2 6 4 0 30				2 6 4 0 30			
32	Sales Ret. & Allow. — Furniture	3 2 1 0 00				3 2 1 0 00			
33	Sales Discount — Appliances	2 8 6 0 00				2 8 6 0 00			
34	Sales Discount — Furniture	2 4 3 0 80				2 4 3 0 80			
35	Purchases — Appliances	201 0 8 6 90				201 0 8 6 90			
36	Purchases — Furniture	188 0 9 8 00				188 0 9 8 00			
37	Purch. Ret. & Allow. — Appliances		4 2 1 0 80				4 2 1 0 80		
38	Purch. Ret. & Allow. — Furniture		3 9 6 0 00				3 9 6 0 00		
39	Purchases Discount — Appliances		3 3 9 0 10				3 3 9 0 10		
40	Purchases Discount — Furniture		3 6 3 0 00				3 6 3 0 00		
41	Advertising Expense	5 7 3 0 00				5 7 3 0 00			
42	Credit Card Fee Expense	5 1 6 0 00				5 1 6 0 00			
43	Depr. Exp. — Store Equipment			(h)2 6 0 0 00		2 6 0 0 00			
44	Salary Expense — Appliances	68 3 0 0 00				68 3 0 0 00			
45	Salary Expense — Furniture	72 5 0 0 00				72 5 0 0 00			
46	Supplies Expense — Store			(e)5 2 6 3 10		5 2 6 3 10			
47	Bad Debts Expense			(a)1 9 7 0 40		1 9 7 0 40			
48	Depr. Exp. — Office Equipment			(g)1 2 0 0 00		1 2 0 0 00			
49	Insurance Expense			(f)4 7 5 0 00		4 7 5 0 00			
50	Miscellaneous Expense	4 8 6 0 00				4 8 6 0 00			
51	Payroll Taxes Expense	25 6 0 4 00				25 6 0 4 00			
52	Rent Expense	21 6 0 0 00				21 6 0 0 00			
53	Salary Expense — Administrative	41 3 0 0 00				41 3 0 0 00			
54	Supplies Expense — Office			(d)8 4 2 9 70		8 4 2 9 70			
55	Federal Income Tax	11 2 0 0 00		(i)4 1 9 3 00		15 3 9 3 00			
56		1263 4 9 8 20	1263 4 9 8 20	53 9 2 5 20	53 9 2 5 20	710 5 0 5 20	768 9 2 2 00	562 9 5 6 40	504 5 3 9 60
57	*Net Income after Federal Income Tax*					58 4 1 6 80			58 4 1 6 80
58						768 9 2 2 00	768 9 2 2 00	562 9 5 6 40	562 9 5 6 40
59									

Worley's

Income Statement

For Year Ended December 31, 19--

							% OF NET SALES
Operating Revenue:							
Sales:				753 7 3 1 10			
Less: Sales Returns & Allow.		5 8 5 0 30					
Sales Discount		5 2 9 0 80	11 1 4 1 10				
Net Sales					742 5 9 0 00	100.0	
Cost of Merchandise Sold:							
Mdse. Inv., Jan. 1, 19--			467 4 2 0 00				
Purchases		389 1 8 4 90					
Less: Purch. Returns & Allow.	8 1 7 0 80						
Purchases Discount	7 0 2 0 10	15 1 9 0 90					
Net Purchases			373 9 9 4 00				
Total Cost of Mdse. Available			841 4 1 4 00				
Less Mdse. Inv., Dec. 31, 19--			441 9 0 1 00				
Cost of Merchandise Sold					399 5 1 3 00	53.8	
Gross Profit on Operations					343 0 7 7 00	46.2	
Operating Expenses:							
Selling Expenses:							
Advertising Expense		5 7 3 0 00					
Credit Card Fee Expense		5 1 6 0 00					
Depr. Exp.—Store Equipment		2 6 0 0 00					
Salary Expense—Appliances		68 3 0 0 00					
Salary Expense—Furniture		72 5 0 0 00					
Supplies Expense—Store		5 2 6 3 10					
Total Selling Expenses			159 5 5 3 10				
Administrative Expenses:							
Bad Debts Expense		1 9 7 0 40					
Depr. Exp.—Office Equipment		1 2 0 0 00					
Insurance Expense		4 7 5 0 00					
Miscellaneous Expense		4 8 6 0 00					
Payroll Taxes Expense		25 6 0 4 00					
Rent Expense		21 6 0 0 00					
Salary Expense—Administrative		41 3 0 0 00					

Continue this income statement on the next page

[3]

Worley's

Income Statement (continued)

For Year Ended December 31, 19--

											% OF NET SALES
Supplies Expense — Office		8 4 2 9 70									
Total Administrative Expenses			109 7 1 4 10								
Total Operating Expenses					269 2 6 7 20						36.3
Net Income before Fed. Inc. Tax					73 8 0 9 80						
Less Federal Income Tax					15 3 9 3 00						
Net Income after Fed. Inc. Tax					58 4 1 6 80						7.9

Worley's

Statement of Stockholders' Equity

For Year Ended December 31, 19--

Capital Stock:									
$200.00 Per Share									
January 1, 19--, 1,500 Shares Issued	300	0	0	0	00				
Issued during 19--, None		–	0	–					
Balance, December 31, 19--, 1,500 Shares Issued						300	0	0	0	00
Retained Earnings:									
January 1, 19--	125	0	0	0	00				
Plus Net Income for 19--	58	4	1	6	80				
Balance, December 31, 19--						183	4	1	6	80
Total Stockholders' Equity, December 31, 19--						483	4	1	6	80

Worley's

Balance Sheet

December 31, 19--

Assets			
Current Assets:			
Cash		40 5 6 0 40	
Petty Cash		6 0 0 00	
Accounts Receivable	27 3 6 4 20		
Less Allowance for Uncollectible Accounts	2 4 3 1 20	24 9 3 3 00	
Merchandise Inventory — Appliances		205 3 8 0 20	
Merchandise Inventory — Furniture		236 5 2 0 80	
Supplies — Office		3 7 1 0 30	
Supplies — Store		4 2 2 0 50	
Prepaid Insurance		3 8 0 0 00	
Total Current Assets			519 7 2 5 20
Plant Assets:			
Office Equipment	17 9 4 0 00		
Less Accum. Depr. — Office Equipment	10 5 6 0 00	7 3 8 0 00	
Store Equipment	22 8 6 0 00		
Less Accum. Depr. — Store Equipment	14 0 3 0 00	8 8 3 0 00	
Total Plant Assets			16 2 1 0 00
Total Assets			535 9 3 5 20
Liabilities			
Current Liabilities:			
Accounts Payable		32 7 4 0 00	
Employees Income Tax Payable — Federal		1 3 4 0 90	
Employees Income Tax Payable — State		9 3 0 60	
Federal Income Tax Payable		4 1 9 3 00	
FICA Tax Payable		2 3 6 0 00	
Sales Tax Payable		7 2 4 0 30	
Unemployment Tax Payable — Federal		2 2 40	
Unemployment Tax Payable — State		1 5 1 20	
Hospital Insurance Premiums Payable		2 2 6 0 00	
Life Insurance Premiums Payable		1 2 8 0 00	
Total Current Liabilities			52 5 1 8 40

Continue this balance sheet on the next page.

Worley's

Balance Sheet (continued)

December 31, 19--

Stockholders' Equity																
Capital Stock						300	0	0	0	00						
Retained Earnings						183	4	1	6	80						
Total Stockholders' Equity											483	4	1	6	80
Total Liabilities & Stockholders' Equity											535	9	3	5	20

GENERAL JOURNAL

PAGE 18

	DATE		ACCOUNT TITLE	POST. REF.	DEBIT	CREDIT	
1			*Adjusting Entries*				1
2	19-- Dec.	31	Bad Debts Expense		1 9 7 0 40		2
3			Allowance for Uncollectible Accounts			1 9 7 0 40	3
4		31	Income Summary — Appliances		14 7 9 9 80		4
5			Merchandise Inventory — Appliances			14 7 9 9 80	5
6		31	Income Summary — Furniture		10 7 1 9 20		6
7			Merchandise Inventory — Furniture			10 7 1 9 20	7
8		31	Supplies Expense — Office		8 4 2 9 70		8
9			Supplies — Office			8 4 2 9 70	9
10		31	Supplies Expense — Store		5 2 6 3 10		10
11			Supplies — Store			5 2 6 3 10	11
12		31	Insurance Expense		4 7 5 0 00		12
13			Prepaid Insurance			4 7 5 0 00	13
14		31	Depreciation Expense — Office Equipment		1 2 0 0 00		14
15			Accum. Depreciation — Office Equipment			1 2 0 0 00	15
16		31	Depreciation Expense — Store Equipment		2 6 0 0 00		16
17			Accum. Depreciation — Store Equipment			2 6 0 0 00	17
18		31	Federal Income Tax		4 1 9 3 00		18
19			Federal Income Tax Payable			4 1 9 3 00	19
20			*Closing Entries*				20
21	19-- Dec.	31	Sales — Appliances		386 9 3 0 30		21
22			Sales — Furniture		366 8 0 0 80		22
23			Purchases Returns and Allow. — Appliances		4 2 1 0 80		23
24			Purchases Returns and Allow. — Furniture		3 9 6 0 00		24
25			Purchases Discount — Appliances		3 3 9 0 10		25
26			Purchases Discount — Furniture		3 6 3 0 00		26
27			Income Summary — General			768 9 2 2 00	27
28		31	Income Summary — General		710 5 0 5 20		28
29			Income Summary — Appliances			14 7 9 9 80	29
30			Income Summary — Furniture			10 7 1 9 20	30
31			Sales Returns and Allow. — Appliances			2 6 4 0 30	31
32			Sales Returns and Allow. — Furniture			3 2 1 0 00	32
33			Sales Discount — Appliances			2 8 6 0 00	33

GENERAL JOURNAL

PAGE 19

	DATE		ACCOUNT TITLE	POST. REF.	DEBIT	CREDIT	
1	19-- Dec.	31	*Sales Discount — Furniture*			2 4 3 0 80	1
2			*Purchases — Appliances*			201 0 8 6 90	2
3			*Purchases — Furniture*			188 0 9 8 00	3
4			*Advertising Expense*			5 7 3 0 00	4
5			*Credit Card Fee Expense*			5 1 6 0 00	5
6			*Depreciation Expense — Store Equipment*			2 6 0 0 00	6
7			*Salary Expense — Appliances*			68 3 0 0 00	7
8			*Salary Expense — Furniture*			72 5 0 0 00	8
9			*Supplies Expense — Store*			5 2 6 3 10	9
10			*Bad Debts Expense*			1 9 7 0 40	10
11			*Depreciation Expense — Office Equipment*			1 2 0 0 00	11
12			*Insurance Expense*			4 7 5 0 00	12
13			*Miscellaneous Expense*			4 8 6 0 00	13
14			*Payroll Taxes Expense*			25 6 0 4 00	14
15			*Rent Expense*			21 6 0 0 00	15
16			*Salary Expense — Administrative*			41 3 0 0 00	16
17			*Supplies Expense — Office*			8 4 2 9 70	17
18			*Federal Income Tax*			15 3 9 3 00	18
19		31	*Income Summary — General*		58 4 1 6 80		19
20			*Retained Earnings*			58 4 1 6 80	20
21							21
22							22
23							23
24							24
25							25
26							26
27							27
28							28
29							29
30							30
31							31
32							32
33							33

Estimating value of merchandise destroyed by fire

ESTIMATED MERCHANDISE INVENTORY SHEET
Gross Profit Method

Department _*Meir's Sport Center*_____ Date _*March 13, 19--*_

1	Beginning inventory, January 1	$ _318,520.30_
2	Net purchases to date	_42,100.00_
3	Merchandise available for sale	$ _360,620.30_
4	Net sales to date .... $ _93,610.40_	
5	Less estimated gross profit .... _29,206.16_ (Net sales × Estimated gross profit $\frac{10}{40}$ %)	
6	Estimated cost of merchandise sold	_64,404.24_
7	Estimated ending inventory	$ _296,216.06_

Estimated gross profit during special January sale:
($27,460.00 × 10%) .... $ 2,746.00

Plus estimated gross profit on balance of sales:
($66,150.40 × 40%) 26,460.16
Total estimated gross profit $29,206.16

ESTIMATED MERCHANDISE INVENTORY SHEET
Gross Profit Method

Department _____ Date _____

1	Beginning inventory, January 1..	$_____
2	Net purchases to date..	_____
3	Merchandise available for sale...	$_____
4	Net sales to date .... $_____	
5	Less estimated gross profit .... _____	
	(Net sales × Estimated gross profit _____%)	
6	Estimated cost of merchandise sold..	_____
7	Estimated ending inventory...	$_____

ESTIMATED MERCHANDISE INVENTORY SHEET
Gross Profit Method

Department _____ Date _____

1	Beginning inventory, January 1..	$_____
2	Net purchases to date..	_____
3	Merchandise available for sale...	$_____
4	Net sales to date .... $_____	
5	Less estimated gross profit .... _____	
	(Net sales × Estimated gross profit _____%)	
6	Estimated cost of merchandise sold..	_____
7	Estimated ending inventory...	$_____

PROCESSING AND REPORTING DEPARTMENTALIZED ACCOUNTING DATA

ESTIMATED MERCHANDISE INVENTORY SHEET
Gross Profit Method

Department **Art Equipment**   Date **11/30/--**

1	Beginning inventory, January 1	$ 163,164.20
2	Net purchases to date	133,339.60
3	Merchandise available for sale	$ 296,503.80
4	Net sales to date	$ 213,679.55	
5	Less estimated gross profit .... (Net sales × Estimated gross profit _45_ %)	96,155.80	
6	Estimated cost of merchandise sold	117,523.75
7	Estimated ending inventory	$ 178,980.05

ESTIMATED MERCHANDISE INVENTORY SHEET
Gross Profit Method

Department **Art Supplies**   Date **11/30/--**

1	Beginning inventory, January 1	$ 146,840.30
2	Net purchases to date	129,949.20
3	Merchandise available for sale	$ 276,789.50
4	Net sales to date	$ 219,670.40	
5	Less estimated gross profit .... (Net sales × Estimated gross profit _45_ %)	98,851.68	
6	Estimated cost of merchandise sold	120,818.72
7	Estimated ending inventory	$ 155,970.78

Artistry, Inc.

Interim Departmental Statement of Gross Profit

For Month Ended November 30, 19--

	ART EQUIPMENT	% OF NET SALES	ART SUPPLIES	% OF NET SALES	TOTAL	% OF NET SALES
Operating Revenue:						
Net Sales	18,480.60	100.0	19,240.30	100.0	37,720.90	100.0
Cost of Merchandise Sold:						
Est. Mdse. Inv., Nov. 1	176,561.55		152,699.90		329,261.45	
Net Purchases	12,250.20		13,410.58		25,660.78	
Mdse. Available for Sale	188,811.75		166,110.48		354,922.23	
Less Est. End. Inv., Nov. 30	178,980.05		155,970.78		334,950.83	
Cost of Merchandise Sold	9,831.70	53.2	10,139.70	52.7	19,971.40	52.9
Gross Profit on Operations	8,648.90	46.8	9,100.60	47.3	17,749.50	47.1

[2]

SALES JOURNAL   PAGE 11

	DATE	ACCOUNT DEBITED	SALE NO.	POST. REF.	ACCOUNTS RECEIVABLE DEBIT (1)	SALES TAX PAYABLE CREDIT (2)	SALES CREDIT ART EQUIPMENT (3)	SALES CREDIT ART SUPPLIES (4)	
1	19-- Dec. 5	Milton Betka	97	120	924 00	44 00	880 00		1
2	13	Marie Akels	98	110	472 50	22 50		450 00	2
3	22	Reed Public Schools	99	190	4750 00			4750 00	3
4	23	Bruce Foltz	100	140	1806 00	86 00	1720 00		4
5	23	Janice Kemp	101	170	966 00	46 00		920 00	5
6	26	David Ling	102	180	567 00	27 00		540 00	6
7	28	David Ling	103	180	682 50	32 50	650 00		7
8	31	Gifford Public Schools	104	150	6200 00		6200 00		8
9	31	Totals			16368 00	258 00	9450 00	6660 00	9
10					(1115)	(2130)	(4105-1)	(4105-2)	10
11									11
12									12
13									13
14									14
15									15
16									16

SALES RETURNS AND ALLOWANCES JOURNAL   PAGE 5

	DATE	ACCOUNT CREDITED	CREDIT MEMO. NO.	POST. REF.	ACCOUNTS RECEIVABLE CREDIT (1)	SALES TAX PAYABLE DEBIT (2)	SALES RETURNS AND ALLOWANCES DEBIT ART EQUIPMENT (3)	SALES RETURNS AND ALLOWANCES DEBIT ART SUPPLIES (4)	
1	19-- Dec. 2	Gifford Public Schools	31	150	250 00			250 00	1
2	3	Barbara Judge	32	160	78 75	3 75	75 00		2
3	9	Milton Betka	33	120	105 00	5 00	100 00		3
4	31	Reed Public Schools	34	190	1500 00			1500 00	4
5	31	Totals			1933 75	8 75	175 00	1750 00	5
6					(1115)	(2130)	(4110-1)	(4110-2)	6
7									7
8									8
9									9
10									10
11									11

PURCHASES JOURNAL

PAGE 13

	DATE		ACCOUNT CREDITED	PURCH. NO.	POST. REF.	ACCOUNTS PAYABLE CREDIT (1)	PURCHASES DEBIT		
							ART EQUIPMENT (2)	ART SUPPLIES (3)	
1	19-- Dec.	2	Olympic Crafts, Inc.	115	260	1 9 3 3 00	1 9 3 3 00		1
2		22	Shapiro Art Supplies	116	270	1 6 4 7 00		1 6 4 7 00	2
3		22	Apcoa Art Supplies	117	210	1 2 7 8 50		1 2 7 8 50	3
4		24	CMB Distributors	118	220	1 5 0 0 00	1 5 0 0 00		4
5		27	Milano Art Equipment	119	250	2 5 4 0 50	2 5 4 0 50		5
6		27	Grandeau Products	120	230	3 2 4 0 00		3 2 4 0 00	6
7		31	Totals			12 1 3 9 00	5 9 7 3 50	6 1 6 5 50	7
8						(2105)	(5105-1)	(5105-2)	8
9									9

PURCHASES RETURNS AND ALLOWANCES JOURNAL

PAGE 5

	DATE		ACCOUNT DEBITED	DEBIT MEMO. NO.	POST. REF.	ACCOUNTS PAYABLE DEBIT (1)	PURCHASES RETURNS AND ALLOWANCES CREDIT		
							ART EQUIPMENT (2)	ART SUPPLIES (3)	
1	19-- Dec.	5	H & R Crafts	58	240	1 4 3 5 00	1 4 3 5 00		1
2		7	Olympic Crafts, Inc.	59	260	3 0 0 00	3 0 0 00		2
3		26	Apcoa Art Supplies	60	210	2 6 5 00		2 6 5 00	3
4		31	Totals			2 0 0 0 00	1 7 3 5 00	2 6 5 00	4
5						(2105)	(5110-1)	(5110-2)	5
6									6

[3]

GENERAL JOURNAL

PAGE 7

	DATE		ACCOUNT TITLE	POST. REF.	DEBIT	CREDIT	
1	19-- Dec.	1	Payroll Taxes Expense	6225	9 6 4 38		1
2			FICA Tax Payable	2125		8 0 2 40	2
3			Unemployment Tax Payable — Federal	2135		2 0 90	3
4			Unemployment Tax Payable — State	2140		1 4 1 08	4
5			M40				5
6							6

[3, 5, 8, 10]

CASH RECEIPTS JOURNAL

PAGE 15

	DATE	ACCOUNT TITLE	DOC. NO.	POST. REF.	GENERAL DEBIT	GENERAL CREDIT	ACCOUNTS RECEIVABLE CREDIT	SALES TAX PAYABLE DEBIT	SALES TAX PAYABLE CREDIT	SALES CREDIT ART EQUIP.	SALES CREDIT ART SUPPLIES	SALES DISCOUNT DEBIT ART EQUIP.	SALES DISCOUNT DEBIT ART SUPPLIES	CASH DEBIT
1	Dec. 3	✓	T3						178 33	1978 00	1588 50			3744 83
2	5	Teresa Davis	R139	130			504 00	48					9 60	493 92
3	8	Gifford Public Schools	R140	150			5990 20						119 80	5870 40
4	8	Barbara Judge	R141	160			183 75	18				3 50		180 07
5	8	Reed Public Schools	R142	190			9581 50					191 63		9389 87
6	10	✓	T10						354 83	3946 50	3150 00			7451 33
7	15	Milton Betka	R143	120			819 00	78				15 60		802 62
8	17	✓	T17						353 06	3820 60	3240 50			7414 16
9	23	Marie Akels	R144	110			472 50	45					9 00	463 05
10	24	✓	T24						379 03	4160 10	3420 50			7959 63
11	31	✓	T31						303 02	3580 40	2480 00			6363 42
12	31	Totals					17550 95	1 89	1568 27	17485 60	13879 50	210 73	138 40	50133 30
13							(1115)	(2130)	(2130)	(4105-1)	(4105-2)	(4115-1)	(4115-2)	(1105)

[3, 5, 8, 11]

CASH PAYMENTS JOURNAL

PAGE 14

	DATE	ACCOUNT TITLE	CK. NO.	POST. REF.	GENERAL DEBIT	GENERAL CREDIT	ACCOUNTS PAYABLE DEBIT	PURCH. DISCOUNT CR. ART EQUIPMENT	PURCH. DISCOUNT CR. ART SUPPLIES	CASH CREDIT	
1	19-- Dec. 1	Salary Expense—Art Equipment	340	6120-1	4 5 2 2 20					7 8 5 9 71	1
2		Salary Expense—Art Supplies		6120-2	4 3 1 0 40						2
3		Salary Expense—Administrative		6235	2 6 3 0 25						3
4		Employ. Inc. Tax Pay.—Federal		2110		1 2 8 3 60					4
5		Employ. Inc. Tax Pay.—State		2115		5 7 3 14					5
6		FICA Tax Payable		2125		8 0 2 40					6
7		Hospital Ins. Prem. Payable		2145		8 4 0 00					7
8		Life Insurance Prem. Payable		2150		1 0 4 00					8
9	1	Rent Expense	341	6230	1 2 0 0 00					1 2 0 0 00	9
10	2	Supplies—Office	342	1130	1 3 5 00					1 3 5 00	10
11	6	CMB Distributors	343	220			2 2 3 0 10	4 4 60		2 1 8 5 50	11
12	7	H & R Crafts	344	240			3 9 9 5 15	7 9 90		3 9 1 5 25	12
13	8	Milano Art Supply	345	250			5 6 5 40		11 31	5 5 4 09	13
14	9	Olympic Crafts, Inc.	346	260			4 9 2 0 20	9 8 40		4 8 2 1 80	14
15	12	Olympic Crafts, Inc.	347	260			1 6 3 3 00	3 2 66		1 6 0 0 34	15
16	15	Employ. Inc. Tax Pay.—Federal	348	2110	1 2 4 0 80					2 8 2 3 70	16
17		FICA Tax Payable		2125	1 5 8 2 90						17
18	15	Federal Income Tax	349	7105	1 2 5 0 00					1 2 5 0 00	18
19	24	Supplies—Store	350	1135	1 4 5 00					4 1 5 00	19
20		Advertising Expense		6105	1 6 0 00						20
21		Miscellaneous Expense		6220	1 1 0 00						21
22	30	Miscellaneous Expense	M41	6220	1 1 40					1 1 40	22
23	30	Credit Card Fee Expense	M42	6110	3 5 4 20					3 5 4 20	23
24	31	Totals			1 7 6 5 2 15	3 6 0 3 14	1 3 3 4 3 85	2 5 5 56	11 31	2 7 1 2 5 99	24
25					(✓)	(✓)	(2105)	(5115-1)	(5115-2)	(1105)	25

GENERAL LEDGER

ACCOUNT Cash   ACCOUNT NO. 1105

DATE		ITEM	POST. REF.	DEBIT	CREDIT	BALANCE	
						DEBIT	CREDIT
19-- Dec.	1	Balance	✔			38 3 4 0 60	
	31		CR15	50 1 3 3 30		88 4 7 3 90	
	31		CP14		27 1 2 5 99	61 3 4 7 91	

ACCOUNT Petty Cash   ACCOUNT NO. 1110

DATE		ITEM	POST. REF.	DEBIT	CREDIT	BALANCE	
						DEBIT	CREDIT
19-- Dec.	1	Balance	✔			5 0 0 00	

ACCOUNT Accounts Receivable   ACCOUNT NO. 1115

DATE		ITEM	POST. REF.	DEBIT	CREDIT	BALANCE	
						DEBIT	CREDIT
19-- Dec.	1	Balance	✔			16 5 8 8 20	
	31		S11	16 3 6 8 00		32 9 5 6 20	
	31		SR5		1 9 3 3 75	31 0 2 2 45	
	31		CR15		17 5 5 0 95	13 4 7 1 50	

ACCOUNT Allowance for Uncollectible Accounts   ACCOUNT NO. 1120

DATE		ITEM	POST. REF.	DEBIT	CREDIT	BALANCE	
						DEBIT	CREDIT
19-- Dec.	1	Balance	✔				3 4 0 20
	31		G8		9 2 0 00		1 2 6 0 20

ACCOUNT Merchandise Inventory—Art Equipment   ACCOUNT NO. 1125-1

DATE		ITEM	POST. REF.	DEBIT	CREDIT	BALANCE	
						DEBIT	CREDIT
19-- Jan.	1	Balance	✔			163 1 6 4 20	
Dec.	31		G8	11 3 0 5 05		174 4 6 9 25	

ACCOUNT Merchandise Inventory—Art Supplies   ACCOUNT NO. 1125-2

DATE		ITEM	POST. REF.	DEBIT	CREDIT	BALANCE	
						DEBIT	CREDIT
19-- Jan.	1	Balance	✔			146 8 4 0 30	
Dec.	31		G8	4 5 9 9 55		151 4 3 9 85	

GENERAL LEDGER

ACCOUNT Supplies — Office   ACCOUNT NO. 1130

DATE		ITEM	POST. REF.	DEBIT	CREDIT	BALANCE DEBIT	BALANCE CREDIT
19-- Dec.	1	Balance	✔			6 0 8 0 20	
	2		CP14	1 3 5 00		6 2 1 5 20	
	31		G8		1 5 8 0 20	4 6 3 5 00	

ACCOUNT Supplies — Store   ACCOUNT NO. 1135

DATE		ITEM	POST. REF.	DEBIT	CREDIT	BALANCE DEBIT	BALANCE CREDIT
19-- Dec.	1	Balance	✔			4 9 6 0 80	
	24		CP14	1 4 5 00		5 1 0 5 80	
	31		G8		1 1 4 5 80	3 9 6 0 00	

ACCOUNT Prepaid Insurance   ACCOUNT NO. 1140

DATE		ITEM	POST. REF.	DEBIT	CREDIT	BALANCE DEBIT	BALANCE CREDIT
19-- Dec.	1	Balance	✔			5 2 8 0 00	
	31		G8		8 8 0 00	4 4 0 0 00	

ACCOUNT Office Equipment   ACCOUNT NO. 1205

DATE		ITEM	POST. REF.	DEBIT	CREDIT	BALANCE DEBIT	BALANCE CREDIT
19-- Dec.	1	Balance	✔			19 2 1 0 00	

ACCOUNT Accumulated Depreciation — Office Equipment   ACCOUNT NO. 1210

DATE		ITEM	POST. REF.	DEBIT	CREDIT	BALANCE DEBIT	BALANCE CREDIT
19-- Dec.	1	Balance	✔				8 7 6 0 00
	31		G8		8 7 0 00		9 6 3 0 00

ACCOUNT Store Equipment   ACCOUNT NO. 1215

DATE		ITEM	POST. REF.	DEBIT	CREDIT	BALANCE DEBIT	BALANCE CREDIT
19-- Dec.	1	Balance	✔			21 4 3 0 00	

GENERAL LEDGER

ACCOUNT Accumulated Depreciation — Store Equipment   ACCOUNT NO. 1220

DATE		ITEM	POST. REF.	DEBIT	CREDIT	BALANCE	
						DEBIT	CREDIT
19-- Dec.	1	Balance	✔				13 6 2 0 00
	31		G8		9 4 0 00		14 5 6 0 00

ACCOUNT Accounts Payable   ACCOUNT NO. 2105

DATE		ITEM	POST. REF.	DEBIT	CREDIT	BALANCE	
						DEBIT	CREDIT
19-- Dec.	1	Balance	✔				13 1 4 5 85
	31		P13		12 1 3 9 00		25 2 8 4 85
	31		PR5	2 0 0 0 00			23 2 8 4 85
	31		CP14	13 3 4 3 85			9 9 4 1 00

ACCOUNT Employees Income Tax Payable — Federal   ACCOUNT NO. 2110

DATE		ITEM	POST. REF.	DEBIT	CREDIT	BALANCE	
						DEBIT	CREDIT
19-- Dec.	1	Balance	✔				1 2 4 0 80
	1		CP14		1 2 8 3 60		2 5 2 4 40
	15		CP14	1 2 4 0 80			1 2 8 3 60

ACCOUNT Employees Income Tax Payable — State   ACCOUNT NO. 2115

DATE		ITEM	POST. REF.	DEBIT	CREDIT	BALANCE	
						DEBIT	CREDIT
19-- Dec.	1	Balance	✔				5 6 5 40
	1		CP14		5 7 3 14		1 1 3 8 54

ACCOUNT Federal Income Tax Payable   ACCOUNT NO. 2120

DATE		ITEM	POST. REF.	DEBIT	CREDIT	BALANCE	
						DEBIT	CREDIT
19-- Dec.	31		G8		3 2 2 40		3 2 2 40

ACCOUNT FICA Tax Payable   ACCOUNT NO. 2125

DATE		ITEM	POST. REF.	DEBIT	CREDIT	BALANCE	
						DEBIT	CREDIT
19-- Dec.	1	Balance	✔				1 5 8 2 90
	1		G7		8 0 2 40		2 3 8 5 30
	1		CP14		8 0 2 40		3 1 8 7 70
	15		CP14	1 5 8 2 90			1 6 0 4 80

GENERAL LEDGER

ACCOUNT   Sales Tax Payable   ACCOUNT NO.   2130

DATE		ITEM	POST. REF.	DEBIT	CREDIT	BALANCE DEBIT	BALANCE CREDIT
19-- Dec.	1	Balance	✔				4 1 2 0 30
	31		S11		2 5 8 00		4 3 7 8 30
	31		SR5	8 75			4 3 6 9 55
	31		CR15	1 89			4 3 6 7 66
	31		CR15		1 5 6 8 27		5 9 3 5 93

ACCOUNT   Unemployment Tax Payable — Federal   ACCOUNT NO.   2135

DATE		ITEM	POST. REF.	DEBIT	CREDIT	BALANCE DEBIT	BALANCE CREDIT
19-- Dec.	1	Balance	✔				3 2 80
	1		G7		2 0 90		5 3 70

ACCOUNT   Unemployment Tax Payable — State   ACCOUNT NO.   2140

DATE		ITEM	POST. REF.	DEBIT	CREDIT	BALANCE DEBIT	BALANCE CREDIT
19-- Dec.	1	Balance	✔				2 2 1 40
	1		G7		1 4 1 08		3 6 2 48

ACCOUNT   Hospital Insurance Premiums Payable   ACCOUNT NO.   2145

DATE		ITEM	POST. REF.	DEBIT	CREDIT	BALANCE DEBIT	BALANCE CREDIT
19-- Dec.	1	Balance	✔				1 6 8 0 00
	1		CP14		8 4 0 00		2 5 2 0 00

ACCOUNT   Life Insurance Premiums Payable   ACCOUNT NO.   2150

DATE		ITEM	POST. REF.	DEBIT	CREDIT	BALANCE DEBIT	BALANCE CREDIT
19-- Dec.	1	Balance	✔				2 0 8 00
	1		CP14		1 0 4 00		3 1 2 00

ACCOUNT   Capital Stock   ACCOUNT NO.   3105

DATE		ITEM	POST. REF.	DEBIT	CREDIT	BALANCE DEBIT	BALANCE CREDIT
19-- Jan.	1	Balance	✔				300 0 0 0 00

GENERAL LEDGER

ACCOUNT Retained Earnings   ACCOUNT NO. 3110

DATE	ITEM	POST REF.	DEBIT	CREDIT	BALANCE DEBIT	BALANCE CREDIT
19-- Jan. 1	Balance	✔				77 5 2 5 70
Dec. 31		G9		28 4 1 3 16		105 9 3 8 86

ACCOUNT Income Summary — Art Equipment   ACCOUNT NO. 3115-1

DATE	ITEM	POST REF.	DEBIT	CREDIT	BALANCE DEBIT	BALANCE CREDIT
19-- Dec. 31		G8		11 3 0 5 05		11 3 0 5 05
31		G9	11 3 0 5 05			

ACCOUNT Income Summary — Art Supplies   ACCOUNT NO. 3115-2

DATE	ITEM	POST REF.	DEBIT	CREDIT	BALANCE DEBIT	BALANCE CREDIT
19-- Dec. 31		G8		4 5 9 9 55		4 5 9 9 55
31		G9	4 5 9 9 55			

ACCOUNT Income Summary — General   ACCOUNT NO. 3120

DATE	ITEM	POST REF.	DEBIT	CREDIT	BALANCE DEBIT	BALANCE CREDIT
19-- Dec. 31		G9		520 6 8 9 57		520 6 8 9 57
31		G9	492 2 7 6 41			28 4 1 3 16
31		G9	28 4 1 3 16			

ACCOUNT Sales — Art Equipment   ACCOUNT NO. 4105-1

DATE	ITEM	POST REF.	DEBIT	CREDIT	BALANCE DEBIT	BALANCE CREDIT
19-- Dec. 1	Balance	✔				216 9 2 0 30
31		S11		9 4 5 0 00		226 3 7 0 30
31		CR15		17 4 8 5 60		243 8 5 5 90
31		G9	243 8 5 5 90			

ACCOUNT Sales — Art Supplies   ACCOUNT NO. 4105-2

DATE	ITEM	POST REF.	DEBIT	CREDIT	BALANCE DEBIT	BALANCE CREDIT
19-- Dec. 1	Balance	✔				223 6 1 0 90
31		S11		6 6 6 0 00		230 2 7 0 90
31		CR15		13 8 7 9 50		244 1 5 0 40
31		G9	244 1 5 0 40			

GENERAL LEDGER

ACCOUNT Sales Returns and Allowances — Art Equipment   ACCOUNT NO. 4110-1

DATE		ITEM	POST. REF.	DEBIT	CREDIT	BALANCE DEBIT	BALANCE CREDIT
19-- Dec.	1	Balance	✔			1 7 6 0 00	
	31		SR5	1 7 5 00		1 9 3 5 00	
	31		G9		1 9 3 5 00	—	

ACCOUNT Sales Returns and Allowances — Art Supplies   ACCOUNT NO. 4110-2

DATE		ITEM	POST. REF.	DEBIT	CREDIT	BALANCE DEBIT	BALANCE CREDIT
19-- Dec.	1	Balance	✔			2 1 3 0 20	
	31		SR5	1 7 5 0 00		3 8 8 0 20	
	31		G9		3 8 8 0 20	—	

ACCOUNT Sales Discount — Art Equipment   ACCOUNT NO. 4115-1

DATE		ITEM	POST. REF.	DEBIT	CREDIT	BALANCE DEBIT	BALANCE CREDIT
19-- Dec.	1	Balance	✔			1 4 8 0 75	
	31		CR15	2 1 0 73		1 6 9 1 48	
	31		G9		1 6 9 1 48	—	

ACCOUNT Sales Discount — Art Supplies   ACCOUNT NO. 4115-2

DATE		ITEM	POST. REF.	DEBIT	CREDIT	BALANCE DEBIT	BALANCE CREDIT
19-- Dec.	1	Balance	✔			1 8 1 0 30	
	31		CR15	1 3 8 40		1 9 4 8 70	
	31		G9		1 9 4 8 70	—	

ACCOUNT Purchases — Art Equipment   ACCOUNT NO. 5105-1

DATE		ITEM	POST. REF.	DEBIT	CREDIT	BALANCE DEBIT	BALANCE CREDIT
19-- Dec.	1	Balance	✔			140 3 1 0 40	
	31		P13	5 9 7 3 50		146 2 8 3 90	
	31		G9		146 2 8 3 90	—	

ACCOUNT Purchases — Art Supplies   ACCOUNT NO. 5105-2

DATE		ITEM	POST. REF.	DEBIT	CREDIT	BALANCE DEBIT	BALANCE CREDIT
19-- Dec.	1	Balance	✔			137 4 9 0 20	
	31		P13	6 1 6 5 50		143 6 5 5 70	
	31		G9		143 6 5 5 70	—	

GENERAL LEDGER

ACCOUNT Purchases Returns and Allowances—Art Equipment   ACCOUNT NO. 5110-1

DATE		ITEM	POST. REF.	DEBIT	CREDIT	BALANCE DEBIT	BALANCE CREDIT
19-- Dec.	1	Balance	✔				3 8 1 0 00
	31		PR5		1 7 3 5 00		5 5 4 5 00
	31		G9	5 5 4 5 00		—	—

ACCOUNT Purchases Returns and Allowances—Art Supplies   ACCOUNT NO. 5110-2

DATE		ITEM	POST. REF.	DEBIT	CREDIT	BALANCE DEBIT	BALANCE CREDIT
19-- Dec.	1	Balance	✔				4 1 2 0 70
	31		PR5		2 6 5 00		4 3 8 5 70
	31		G9	4 3 8 5 70		—	—

ACCOUNT Purchases Discount—Art Equipment   ACCOUNT NO. 5115-1

DATE		ITEM	POST. REF.	DEBIT	CREDIT	BALANCE DEBIT	BALANCE CREDIT
19-- Dec.	1	Balance	✔				3 1 6 0 80
	31		CP14		2 5 5 56		3 4 1 6 36
	31		G9	3 4 1 6 36		—	—

ACCOUNT Purchases Discount—Art Supplies   ACCOUNT NO. 5115-2

DATE		ITEM	POST. REF.	DEBIT	CREDIT	BALANCE DEBIT	BALANCE CREDIT
19-- Dec.	1	Balance	✔				3 4 2 0 30
	31		CP14		1 1 31		3 4 3 1 61
	31		G9	3 4 3 1 61		—	—

ACCOUNT Advertising Expense   ACCOUNT NO. 6105

DATE		ITEM	POST. REF.	DEBIT	CREDIT	BALANCE DEBIT	BALANCE CREDIT
19-- Dec.	1	Balance	✔			4 9 7 0 20	
	24		CP14	1 6 0 00		5 1 3 0 20	
	30		G9		5 1 3 0 20	—	—

ACCOUNT Credit Card Fee Expense   ACCOUNT NO. 6110

DATE		ITEM	POST. REF.	DEBIT	CREDIT	BALANCE DEBIT	BALANCE CREDIT
19-- Dec.	1	Balance	✔			4 8 9 0 60	
	30		CP14	3 5 4 20		5 2 4 4 80	
	31		G9		5 2 4 4 80	—	—

GENERAL LEDGER

ACCOUNT Depreciation Expense — Store Equipment   ACCOUNT NO. 6115

DATE	ITEM	POST. REF.	DEBIT	CREDIT	BALANCE DEBIT	BALANCE CREDIT
19-- Dec. 31		G8	9 4 0 00		9 4 0 00	
31		G9		9 4 0 00		

ACCOUNT Salary Expense — Art Equipment   ACCOUNT NO. 6120-1

DATE	ITEM	POST. REF.	DEBIT	CREDIT	BALANCE DEBIT	BALANCE CREDIT
19-- Dec. 1	Balance	✔			49 5 0 0 00	
1		CP14	4 5 2 2 20		54 0 2 2 20	
31		G9		54 0 2 2 20		

ACCOUNT Salary Expense — Art Supplies   ACCOUNT NO. 6120-2

DATE	ITEM	POST. REF.	DEBIT	CREDIT	BALANCE DEBIT	BALANCE CREDIT
19-- Dec. 1	Balance	✔			46 2 0 0 00	
1		CP14	4 3 1 0 40		50 5 1 0 40	
31		G9		50 5 1 0 40		

ACCOUNT Supplies Expense — Store   ACCOUNT NO. 6125

DATE	ITEM	POST. REF.	DEBIT	CREDIT	BALANCE DEBIT	BALANCE CREDIT
19-- Dec. 31		G8	1 1 4 5 80		1 1 4 5 80	
31		G9		1 1 4 5 80		

ACCOUNT Bad Debts Expense   ACCOUNT NO. 6205

DATE	ITEM	POST. REF.	DEBIT	CREDIT	BALANCE DEBIT	BALANCE CREDIT
19-- Dec. 31		G8	9 2 0 00		9 2 0 00	
31		G9		9 2 0 00		

ACCOUNT Depreciation Expense — Office Equipment   ACCOUNT NO. 6210

DATE	ITEM	POST. REF.	DEBIT	CREDIT	BALANCE DEBIT	BALANCE CREDIT
19-- Dec. 31		G8	8 7 0 00		8 7 0 00	
31		G9		8 7 0 00		

ACCOUNT Insurance Expense   ACCOUNT NO. 6215

DATE	ITEM	POST. REF.	DEBIT	CREDIT	BALANCE DEBIT	BALANCE CREDIT
19-- Dec. 31		G8	8 8 0 00		8 8 0 00	
31		G9		8 8 0 00		

GENERAL LEDGER

ACCOUNT Miscellaneous Expense   ACCOUNT NO. 6220

DATE		ITEM	POST. REF.	DEBIT	CREDIT	BALANCE DEBIT	BALANCE CREDIT
19-- Dec.	1	Balance	✓			5 2 0 8 80	
	24		CP14	1 1 0 00		5 3 1 8 80	
	30		CP14	1 1 40		5 3 3 0 20	
	31		G9		5 3 3 0 20	—	—

ACCOUNT Payroll Taxes Expense   ACCOUNT NO. 6225

DATE		ITEM	POST. REF.	DEBIT	CREDIT	BALANCE DEBIT	BALANCE CREDIT
19-- Dec.	1	Balance	✓			14 3 9 0 60	
	1		G7	9 6 4 38		15 3 5 4 98	
	31		G9		15 3 5 4 98	—	—

ACCOUNT Rent Expense   ACCOUNT NO. 6230

DATE		ITEM	POST. REF.	DEBIT	CREDIT	BALANCE DEBIT	BALANCE CREDIT
19-- Dec.	1	Balance	✓			13 2 0 0 00	
	1		CP14	1 2 0 0 00		14 4 0 0 00	
	31		G9		14 4 0 0 00	—	—

ACCOUNT Salary Expense — Administrative   ACCOUNT NO. 6235

DATE		ITEM	POST. REF.	DEBIT	CREDIT	BALANCE DEBIT	BALANCE CREDIT
19-- Dec.	1	Balance	✓			28 6 0 0 00	
	1		CP14	2 6 3 0 25		31 2 3 0 25	
	31		G9		31 2 3 0 25	—	—

ACCOUNT Supplies Expense — Office   ACCOUNT NO. 6240

DATE		ITEM	POST. REF.	DEBIT	CREDIT	BALANCE DEBIT	BALANCE CREDIT
19-- Dec.	31		G8	1 5 8 0 20		1 5 8 0 20	
	31		G9		1 5 8 0 20	—	—

ACCOUNT Federal Income Tax   ACCOUNT NO. 7105

DATE		ITEM	POST. REF.	DEBIT	CREDIT	BALANCE DEBIT	BALANCE CREDIT
19-- Dec.	1	Balance	✓			3 7 5 0 00	
	15		CP14	1 2 5 0 00		5 0 0 0 00	
	31		G8	3 2 2 40		5 3 2 2 40	
	31		G9		5 3 2 2 40	—	—

ACCOUNTS RECEIVABLE LEDGER

CUSTOMER Marie Akels   CUSTOMER NO. 110

DATE		ITEM	POST. REF.	DEBIT	CREDIT	DEBIT BALANCE
19-- Dec.	13		S11	4 7 2 50		4 7 2 50
	23		CR15		4 7 2 50	—

CUSTOMER Milton Betka   CUSTOMER NO. 120

DATE		ITEM	POST. REF.	DEBIT	CREDIT	DEBIT BALANCE
19-- Dec.	5		S11	9 2 4 00		9 2 4 00
	9		SR5		1 0 5 00	8 1 9 00
	15		CR15		8 1 9 00	—

CUSTOMER Teresa Davis   CUSTOMER NO. 130

DATE		ITEM	POST. REF.	DEBIT	CREDIT	DEBIT BALANCE
19-- Dec.	1	Balance	✔			5 0 4 00
	5		CR15		5 0 4 00	—

CUSTOMER Bruce Foltz   CUSTOMER NO. 140

DATE		ITEM	POST. REF.	DEBIT	CREDIT	DEBIT BALANCE
19-- Dec.	23		S11	1 8 0 6 00		1 8 0 6 00

CUSTOMER Gifford Public Schools   CUSTOMER NO. 150

DATE		ITEM	POST. REF.	DEBIT	CREDIT	DEBIT BALANCE
19-- Dec.	1	Balance	✔			6 2 4 0 20
	2		SR5		2 5 0 00	5 9 9 0 20
	8		CR15		5 9 9 0 20	—
	31		S11	6 2 0 0 00		6 2 0 0 00

CUSTOMER Barbara Judge   CUSTOMER NO. 160

DATE		ITEM	POST. REF.	DEBIT	CREDIT	DEBIT BALANCE
19-- Dec.	1	Balance	✔			2 6 2 50
	3		SR5		7 8 75	1 8 3 75
	8		CR15		1 8 3 75	—

ACCOUNTS RECEIVABLE LEDGER

CUSTOMER   Janice Kemp   CUSTOMER NO.   170

DATE	ITEM	POST. REF.	DEBIT	CREDIT	DEBIT BALANCE
19-- Dec. 23		S11	9 6 6 00		9 6 6 00

CUSTOMER   David Ling   CUSTOMER NO.   180

DATE	ITEM	POST. REF.	DEBIT	CREDIT	DEBIT BALANCE
19-- Dec. 26		S11	5 6 7 00		5 6 7 00
28		S11	6 8 2 50		1 2 4 9 50

CUSTOMER   Reed Public Schools   CUSTOMER NO.   190

DATE	ITEM	POST. REF.	DEBIT	CREDIT	DEBIT BALANCE
19-- Dec. 1	Balance	✔			9 5 8 1 50
8		CR15		9 5 8 1 50	—
22		S11	4 7 5 0 00		4 7 5 0 00
31		SR5		1 5 0 0 00	3 2 5 0 00

[3, 5]

ACCOUNTS PAYABLE LEDGER

VENDOR   Apcoa Art Supplies   VENDOR NO.   210

DATE	ITEM	POST. REF.	DEBIT	CREDIT	CREDIT BALANCE
19-- Dec. 22		P13		1 2 7 8 50	1 2 7 8 50
26		PR5	2 6 5 00		1 0 1 3 50

VENDOR   CMB Distributors   VENDOR NO.   220

DATE	ITEM	POST. REF.	DEBIT	CREDIT	CREDIT BALANCE
19-- Dec. 1	Balance	✔			2 2 3 0 10
6		CP14	2 2 3 0 10		—
24		P13		1 5 0 0 00	1 5 0 0 00

ACCOUNTS PAYABLE LEDGER

VENDOR Grandeau Products   **VENDOR NO.** 230

DATE		ITEM	POST. REF.	DEBIT	CREDIT	CREDIT BALANCE
19-- Dec.	27		P13		3 2 4 0 00	3 2 4 0 00

VENDOR H & R Crafts   **VENDOR NO.** 240

DATE		ITEM	POST. REF.	DEBIT	CREDIT	CREDIT BALANCE
19-- Dec.	1	Balance	✔			5 4 3 0 15
	5		PR5	1 4 3 5 00		3 9 9 5 15
	7		CP14	3 9 9 5 15		

VENDOR Milano Art Supply   **VENDOR NO.** 250

DATE		ITEM	POST. REF.	DEBIT	CREDIT	CREDIT BALANCE
19-- Dec.	1	Balance	✔			5 6 5 40
	8		CP14	5 6 5 40		
	27		P13		2 5 4 0 50	2 5 4 0 50

VENDOR Olympic Crafts, Inc.   **VENDOR NO.** 260

DATE		ITEM	POST. REF.	DEBIT	CREDIT	CREDIT BALANCE
19-- Dec.	1	Balance	✔			4 9 2 0 20
	2		P13		1 9 3 3 00	6 8 5 3 20
	7		PR5	3 0 0 00		6 5 5 3 20
	9		CP14	4 9 2 0 20		1 6 3 3 00
	12		CP14	1 6 3 3 00		

VENDOR Shapiro Art Supplies   **VENDOR NO.** 270

DATE		ITEM	POST. REF.	DEBIT	CREDIT	CREDIT BALANCE
19-- Dec.	22		P13		1 6 4 7 00	1 6 4 7 00

[4]

RECONCILIATION OF BANK STATEMENT

Date *12/29/--*

1. Enter CHECKBOOK BALANCE as shown on check stub.
2. Enter and add bank charges to obtain TOTAL BANK CHARGES.
3. Deduct TOTAL BANK CHARGES from CHECKBOOK BALANCE to obtain ADJUSTED CHECKBOOK BALANCE.
4. Enter BANK BALANCE as shown on bank statement.
5. Enter and add the amounts of any outstanding deposits recorded on the check stubs but not listed on the bank statement to obtain TOTAL OUTSTANDING DEPOSITS.
6. Add TOTAL OUTSTANDING DEPOSITS to BANK BALANCE to obtain TOTAL.
7. Sort all checks included in the statement numerically or by date issued.
   a. Check off on the check stubs of the checkbook each of the checks paid by the bank.
   b. Enter the check numbers and amounts of checks still outstanding.
   c. Add the outstanding checks to obtain TOTAL OUTSTANDING CHECKS.
8. Deduct TOTAL OUTSTANDING CHECKS from TOTAL to obtain ADJUSTED BANK BALANCE.
9. The ADJUSTED CHECKBOOK BALANCE and the ADJUSTED BANK BALANCE should agree, proving that both the checkbook balance and the bank balance are correct.

(1) CHECKBOOK BALANCE .... $ *55,350.09*

BANK CHARGES

Description	Amount	
Service Charge	11	40
Credit Card Charge	*354*	*20*

(2) DEDUCT TOTAL BANK CHARGES ... $ _____ *365.60*

(3) ADJUSTED CHECKBOOK BALANCE . $ *54,984.49*

(4) BANK BALANCE .... $ *51,513.56*

OUTSTANDING DEPOSITS

Date	Amount	
12/29	*7,959*	*63*

(5) ADD TOTAL OUTSTANDING DEPOSITS .... $ *7,959.63*

(6) TOTAL .... $ *59,473.19*

OUTSTANDING CHECKS

CK. NO.	Amount	
348	*2,823*	*70*
349	*1,250*	*00*
350	*415*	*00*

(7) DEDUCT TOTAL OUTSTANDING CHECKS .... $ *4,488.70*

(8) ADJUSTED BANK BALANCE .... $ *54,984.49*

[9]

Prove Cash:

Beginning cash balance, December 1, 19--	$	*38,340.60*
Plus total cash received during the month		*50,133.30*
Total	$	*88,473.90*
Less total cash paid during the month		*27,125.99*
Equals total cash on hand, December 31, 19--	$	*61,347.91*

Artistry, Inc.

Schedule of Accounts Receivable

December 31, 19--

Bruce Foltz	1	8	0	6	00
Gifford Public Schools	6	2	0	0	00
Janice Kemp		9	6	6	00
David Ling	1	2	4	9	50
Reed Public Schools	3	2	5	0	00
Total Accounts Receivable	13	4	7	1	50

Artistry, Inc.

Schedule of Accounts Payable

December 31, 19--

Apcoa Art Supplies	1	0	1	3	50
CMB Distributors	1	5	0	0	00
Grandeau Products	3	2	4	0	00
Milano Art Supply	2	5	4	0	50
Shapiro Art Supplies	1	6	4	7	00
Total Accounts Payable	9	9	4	1	00

[15]

Artistry, Inc.

Departmental Statement of Gross Profit

For Year Ended December 31, 19--

	ART EQUIPMENT	% OF NET SALES	ART SUPPLIES	% OF NET SALES	TOTAL	% OF NET SALES
Operating Revenue:						
Net Sales	240,229.42	100.0	238,321.50	100.0	478,550.92	100.0
Cost of Merchandise Sold:						
Mdse. Inv., Jan. 1	163,164.20		146,840.30		310,004.50	
Net Purchases	137,322.54		135,838.39		273,160.93	
Mdse. Available for Sale	300,486.74		282,678.69		583,165.43	
Less End. Inv., Dec. 31	174,469.25		151,439.85		325,909.10	
Cost of Merchandise Sold	126,017.49	52.5	131,238.84	55.1	257,256.33	53.8
Gross Profit on Operations	114,211.93	47.5	107,082.66	44.9	221,294.59	46.2

[13, 14]

Artistry, Inc.

Work Sheet

For Year Ended December 31, 19--

	TRIAL BALANCE		ADJUSTMENTS		INCOME STATEMENT		BALANCE SHEET	
ACCOUNT TITLE	DEBIT	CREDIT	DEBIT	CREDIT	DEBIT	CREDIT	DEBIT	CREDIT
1 Cash	61347 91						61347 91	
2 Petty Cash	500 00						500 00	
3 Accounts Receivable	13471 50						13471 50	
4 Allowance for Uncollectible Accounts		340 20		(a) 920 00				1260 20
5 Mdse. Inv.—Art Equipment	163164 20		(b)11305 05				174469 25	
6 Mdse. Inv.—Art Supplies	146840 30		(c) 4599 55				151439 85	
7 Supplies—Office	6215 20			(d) 1580 20			4635 00	
8 Supplies—Store	5105 80			(e) 1145 80			3960 00	
9 Prepaid Insurance	5280 00			(f) 880 00			4400 00	
10 Office Equipment	19210 00						19210 00	
11 Accum. Depr.—Office Equipment		8760 00		(g) 870 00				9630 00
12 Store Equipment	21430 00						21430 00	
13 Accum. Depr.—Store Equipment		13620 00		(h) 940 00				14560 00
14 Accounts Payable		9941 00						9941 00
15 Employ. Inc. Tax Pay.—Fed.		1283 60						1283 60
16 Employ. Inc. Tax Pay.—State		1138 54						1138 54
17 Federal Income Tax Payable				(i) 32 40				32 40
18 FICA Tax Payable		1604 80						1604 80
19 Sales Tax Payable		5935 93						5935 93
20 Unemploy. Tax Pay.—Fed.		53 70						53 70
21 Unemploy. Tax Pay.—State		362 48						362 48
22 Hospital Ins. Prem. Payable		2520 00						2520 00
23 Life Ins. Prem. Payable		312 00						312 00
24 Capital Stock		300000 00						300000 00
25 Retained Earnings		77525 70						77525 70
26 Income Summary—Art Equip.				(b)11305 05		11305 05		
27 Income Summary—Art Supplies				(c) 4599 55		4599 55		
28 Income Summary—General								

[13, 14]

#	Account Title	Trial Balance Debit	Trial Balance Credit	Adjustments Debit	Adjustments Credit	Income Statement Debit	Income Statement Credit	Balance Sheet Debit	Balance Sheet Credit
29	Sales—Art Equipment		243 85 5 90				243 85 5 90		
30	Sales—Art Supplies		244 15 0 40				244 15 0 40		
31	Sales Ret. & Allow.—Art Equip.	1 93 5 00				1 93 5 00			
32	Sales Ret. & Allow.—Art Supp.	3 88 0 20				3 88 0 20			
33	Sales Discount—Art Equip.	1 69 1 48				1 69 1 48			
34	Sales Discount—Art Supplies	1 94 8 70				1 94 8 70			
35	Purchases—Art Equipment	146 28 3 90				146 28 3 90			
36	Purchases—Art Supplies	143 65 5 70				143 65 5 70			
37	Pur. Ret. & Allow.—Art Equip.		5 54 5 00				5 54 5 00		
38	Pur. Ret. & Allow.—Art Supp.		4 38 5 70				4 38 5 70		
39	Pur. Discount—Art Equip.		3 41 6 36				3 41 6 36		
40	Pur. Discount—Art Supplies		3 43 1 61				3 43 1 61		
41	Advertising Expense	5 13 0 20				5 13 0 20			
42	Credit Card Fee Expense	5 24 4 80				5 24 4 80			
43	Depr. Exp.—Store Equip.			(h) 9 40 0 00		9 40 0 00			
44	Salary Exp.—Art Equipment	54 02 2 20				54 02 2 20			
45	Salary Exp.—Art Supplies	50 51 0 40				50 51 0 40			
46	Supplies Expense—Store			(e) 1 14 5 80		1 14 5 80			
47	Bad Debts Expense			(a) 9 20 0 00		9 20 0 00			
48	Depr. Exp.—Office Equip.			(g) 8 70 0 00		8 70 0 00			
49	Insurance Expense			(f) 8 80 0 00		8 80 0 00			
50	Miscellaneous Expense	5 33 0 20				5 33 0 20			
51	Payroll Taxes Expense	15 35 4 98				15 35 4 98			
52	Rent Expense	14 40 0 00				14 40 0 00			
53	Salary Expense—Admin.	31 23 0 25				31 23 0 25			
54	Supplies Expense—Office			(d) 1 58 0 20		1 58 0 20			
55	Federal Income Tax	5 00 0 00		(i) 3 22 40		5 32 2 40			
56		928 18 2 92	928 18 2 92	22 56 3 00	22 56 3 00	492 27 6 41	520 68 9 57	454 86 3 51	426 45 0 35
57	Net Income after Fed. Income Tax					28 41 3 16			28 41 3 16
58						520 68 9 57	520 68 9 57	454 86 3 51	454 86 3 51

Artistry, Inc.

Income Statement

For Year Ended December 31, 19--

					% OF NET SALES
Operating Revenue:					
Sales:			488 0 0 6 30		
Less: Sales Ret. & Allow.		5 8 1 5 20			
Sales Discount		3 6 4 0 18	9 4 5 5 38		
Net Sales				478 5 5 0 92	100.0
Cost of Merchandise Sold:					
Mdse. Inv., Jan. 1, 19--			310 0 0 4 50		
Purchases		289 9 3 9 60			
Less: Pur. Returns & Allow.	9 9 3 0 70				
Purchases Discount	6 8 4 7 97	16 7 7 8 67			
Net Purchases			273 1 6 0 93		
Total Cost of Mdse. Available			583 1 6 5 43		
Less Mdse. Inv., Dec. 31, 19--			325 9 0 9 10		
Cost of Merchandise Sold				257 2 5 6 33	53.8
Gross Profit on Operations				221 2 9 4 59	46.2
Operating Expenses:					
Selling Expenses:					
Advertising Expense		5 1 3 0 20			
Credit Card Fee Expense		5 2 4 4 80			
Depr. Exp.—Store Equip.		9 4 0 00			
Salary Expense—Art Equip.		54 0 2 2 20			
Salary Expense—Art Supplies		50 5 1 0 40			
Supplies Expense—Store		1 1 4 5 80			
Total Selling Expenses			116 9 9 3 40		
Administrative Expenses:					
Bad Debts Expense		9 2 0 00			
Depr. Exp.—Office Equip.		8 7 0 00			
Insurance Expense		8 8 0 00			
Miscellaneous Expense		5 3 3 0 20			
Payroll Taxes Expense		15 3 5 4 98			
Rent Expense		14 4 0 0 00			
Salary Expense—Admin.		31 2 3 0 25			

Continue this income statement on the next page.

[16]

Artistry, Inc.

Income Statement (continued)

For Year Ended December 31, 19--

							% OF NET SALES
Supplies Exp. — Office			1 5 8 0 20				
Total Admin. Expenses				70 5 6 5 63			
Total Operating Expenses					187 5 5 9 03		39.2
Net Income before Fed. Inc. Tax					33 7 3 5 56		
Less Federal Income Tax					5 3 2 2 40		
Net Income after Fed. Inc. Tax					28 4 1 3 16		5.9

[17]

Artistry, Inc.

Statement of Stockholders' Equity

For Year Ended December 31, 19--

Capital Stock:		
$100.00 per Share		
January 1, 19--, 3,000 Shares Issued	300 0 0 0 00	
Issued during 19--, None	- 0 -	
Balance, December 31, 19--, 3,000 Shares Issued		300 0 0 0 00
Retained Earnings:		
January 1, 19--	77 5 2 5 70	
Plus Net Income for 19--	28 4 1 3 16	
Balance, December 31, 19--		105 9 3 8 86
Total Stockholders' Equity, December 31, 19--		405 9 3 8 86

Artistry, Inc.

Balance Sheet

December 31, 19--

Assets				
Current Assets:				
Cash		61 3 4 7 91		
Petty Cash		5 0 0 00		
Accounts Receivable	13 4 7 1 50			
Less Allowance for Uncollectible Accounts	1 2 6 0 20	12 2 1 1 30		
Merchandise Inventory—Art Equipment		174 4 6 9 25		
Merchandise Inventory—Art Supplies		151 4 3 9 85		
Supplies—Office		4 6 3 5 00		
Supplies—Store		3 9 6 0 00		
Prepaid Insurance		4 4 0 0 00		
Total Current Assets			412 9 6 3 31	
Plant Assets:				
Office Equipment	19 2 1 0 00			
Less Accum. Depr.—Office Equipment	9 6 3 0 00	9 5 8 0 00		
Store Equipment	21 4 3 0 00			
Less Accum. Depr.—Store Equipment	14 5 6 0 00	6 8 7 0 00		
Total Plant Assets			16 4 5 0 00	
Total Assets			429 4 1 3 31	
Liabilities				
Current Liabilities:				
Accounts Payable		9 9 4 1 00		
Employees Income Tax Payable—Federal		1 2 8 3 60		
Employees Income Tax Payable—State		1 1 3 8 54		
Federal Income Tax Payable		3 2 2 40		
FICA Tax Payable		1 6 0 4 80		
Sales Tax Payable		5 9 3 5 93		
Unemployment Tax Payable—Federal		5 3 70		
Unemployment Tax Payable—State		3 6 2 48		
Hospital Insurance Premiums Payable		2 5 2 0 00		
Life Insurance Premiums Payable		3 1 2 00		
Total Current Liabilities			23 4 7 4 45	

Continue this balance sheet on the next page.

Artistry, Inc.

Balance Sheet (continued)

December 31, 19--

Stockholders' Equity			
Capital Stock	300 0 0 0 00		
Retained Earnings	105 9 3 8 86		
Total Stockholders' Equity		405 9 3 8 86	
Total Liabilities & Stockholders' Equity		429 4 1 3 31	

GENERAL JOURNAL

PAGE 8

	DATE		ACCOUNT TITLE	POST. REF.	DEBIT	CREDIT	
1			*Adjusting Entries*				1
2	Dec.	31	Bad Debts Expense	6205	9 20 00		2
3			Allowance for Uncollectible Accounts	1120		9 20 00	3
4		31	Merchandise Inventory — Art Equipment	1125-1	11 3 05 05		4
5			Income Summary — Art Equipment	3115-1		11 3 05 05	5
6		31	Merchandise Inventory — Art Supplies	1125-2	4 5 99 55		6
7			Income Summary — Art Supplies	3115-2		4 5 99 55	7
8		31	Supplies Expense — Office	6240	1 5 80 20		8
9			Supplies — Office	1130		1 5 80 20	9
10		31	Supplies Expense — Store	6125	1 1 45 80		10
11			Supplies — Store	1135		1 1 45 80	11
12		31	Insurance Expense	6215	8 80 00		12
13			Prepaid Insurance	1140		8 80 00	13
14		31	Depreciation Expense — Office Equipment	6210	8 70 00		14
15			Accum. Depreciation — Office Equipment	1210		8 70 00	15
16		31	Depreciation Expense — Store Equipment	6115	9 40 00		16
17			Accum. Depreciation — Store Equipment	1220		9 40 00	17
18		31	Federal Income Tax	7105	3 22 40		18
19			Federal Income Tax Payable	2120		3 22 40	19
20							20
21							21
22							22
23							23
24							24
25							25
26							26
27							27
28							28
29							29
30							30
31							31
32							32
33							33

GENERAL JOURNAL

PAGE 9

	DATE		ACCOUNT TITLE	POST. REF.	DEBIT	CREDIT	
1			*Closing Entries*				1
2	19-- Dec.	31	**Income Summary — Art Equipment**	3115-1	11 3 0 5 05		2
3			**Income Summary — Art Supplies**	3115-2	4 5 9 9 55		3
4			**Sales — Art Equipment**	4105-1	243 8 5 5 90		4
5			**Sales — Art Supplies**	4105-2	244 1 5 0 40		5
6			**Purchases Returns & Allow. — Art Equipment**	5110-1	5 5 4 5 00		6
7			**Purchases Returns & Allow. — Art Supplies**	5110-2	4 3 8 5 70		7
8			**Purchases Discount — Art Equipment**	5115-1	3 4 1 6 36		8
9			**Purchases Discount — Art Supplies**	5115-2	3 4 3 1 61		9
10			Income Summary — General	3120		520 6 8 9 57	10
11		31	**Income Summary — General**	3120	492 2 7 6 41		11
12			Sales Returns & Allow. — Art Equipment	4110-1		1 9 3 5 00	12
13			Sales Returns & Allow. — Art Supplies	4110-2		3 8 8 0 20	13
14			Sales Discount — Art Equipment	4115-1		1 6 9 1 48	14
15			Sales Discount — Art Supplies	4115-2		1 9 4 8 70	15
16			Purchases — Art Equipment	5105-1		146 2 8 3 90	16
17			Purchases — Art Supplies	5105-2		143 6 5 5 70	17
18			Advertising Expense	6105		5 1 3 0 20	18
19			Credit Card Fee Expense	6110		5 2 4 4 80	19
20			Depreciation Expense — Store Equipment	6115		9 4 0 00	20
21			Salary Expense — Art Equipment	6120-1		54 0 2 2 20	21
22			Salary Expense — Art Supplies	6120-2		50 5 1 0 40	22
23			Supplies Expense — Store	6125		1 1 4 5 80	23
24			Bad Debts Expense	6205		9 2 0 00	24
25			Depreciation Expense — Office Equipment	6210		8 7 0 00	25
26			Insurance Expense	6215		8 8 0 00	26
27			Miscellaneous Expense	6220		5 3 3 0 20	27
28			Payroll Taxes Expense	6225		15 3 5 4 98	28
29			Rent Expense	6230		14 4 0 0 00	29
30			Salary Expense — Administrative	6235		31 2 3 0 25	30
31			Supplies Expense — Office	6240		1 5 8 0 20	31
32			Federal Income Tax	7105		5 3 2 2 40	32
33		31	**Income Summary — General**	3120	28 4 1 3 16		33
34			*Retained Earnings*	3110		28 4 1 3 16	34

Artistry, Inc.

Post-Closing Trial Balance

December 31, 19--

ACCOUNT TITLE	DEBIT	CREDIT
Cash	61 3 4 7 91	
Petty Cash	5 0 0 00	
Accounts Receivable	13 4 7 1 50	
Allowance for Uncollectible Accounts		1 2 6 0 20
Merchandise Inventory — Art Equipment	174 4 6 9 25	
Merchandise Inventory — Art Supplies	151 4 3 9 85	
Supplies — Office	4 6 3 5 00	
Supplies — Store	3 9 6 0 00	
Prepaid Insurance	4 4 0 0 00	
Office Equipment	19 2 1 0 00	
Accumulated Depreciation — Office Equipment		9 6 3 0 00
Store Equipment	21 4 3 0 00	
Accumulated Depreciation — Store Equipment		14 5 6 0 00
Accounts Payable		9 9 4 1 00
Employees Income Tax Payable — Federal		1 2 8 3 60
Employees Income Tax Payable — State		1 1 3 8 54
Federal Income Tax Payable		3 2 2 40
FICA Tax Payable		1 6 0 4 80
Sales Tax Payable		5 9 3 5 93
Unemployment Tax Payable — Federal		5 3 70
Unemployment Tax Payable — State		3 6 2 48
Hospital Insurance Premiums Payable		2 5 2 0 00
Life Insurance Premiums Payable		3 1 2 00
Capital Stock		300 0 0 0 00
Retained Earnings		105 9 3 8 86
	454 8 6 3 51	454 8 6 3 51

UNIT A—Identifying Accounting Terms

DIRECTIONS: Select the one term in Column I that best fits each definition in Column II. Print the letter identifying your choice in the Answers column.

	Column I	*Column II*	Answers	For Scoring
A.	automated accounting	**0.** Data put into a computer	K	**0.** ✔
B.	applications software	**1.** A set of instructions followed by a computer to process data	F	**1.**
C.	batch number			
D.	computer	**2.** A system using a computer to process data	E	**2.**
E.	computer information system	**3.** The number assigned to a group of journal entries	C	**3.**
F.	computer program	**4.** Information produced by a computer	Q	**4.**
G.	computer programmer	**5.** The date to be printed on reports prepared by a computer	T	**5.**
H.	diskette			
I.	file maintenance	**6.** Working with data according to precise instructions	S	**6.**
J.	hardware	**7.** Programs used to direct the operations of a computer	U	**7.**
K.	input			
L.	key-entering	**8.** Software prepared to tell the computer how to operate itself	W	**8.**
M.	mainframe computer	**9.** Computer units	J	**9.**
N.	manual accounting	**10.** Entering data on a computer keyboard	L	**10.**
O.	microcomputer			
P.	minicomputer	**11.** An accounting system in which data are recorded and reported mostly by hand	N	**11.**
Q.	output	**12.** A person who prepares a computer program	G	**12.**
R.	printout			
S.	processing	**13.** The procedure for arranging accounts in a ledger, selecting account numbers, and keeping records current	I	**13.**
T.	run date			
U.	software			
V.	storage			
W.	systems software			

	Answers	For Scoring
14. A flexible magnetic disk commonly used as secondary storage for microcomputers	H	**14.**
15. Computer output in printed, human-readable form	R	**15.**
16. Filing or holding data until needed	V	**16.**
17. An accounting system in which data are recorded and reported mostly by using automated machines	A	**17.**
18. A large-sized computer with the greatest computing speed, largest storage capacity, and the most powerful processing capability	M	**18.**
19. A machine that accepts data, applies procedures, and produces results according to stored instructions	D	**19.**
20. A small-sized computer with the slowest computing speed, smallest storage capacity, and the least processing capability	O	**20.**
21. Software prepared to direct the operations of a computer for specific applications	B	**21.**
22. A medium-sized computer with intermediate computing speed, storage capacity, and processing capability	P	**22.**

UNIT B—Analyzing Concepts and Procedures for an Automated Departmentalized Accounting System

DIRECTIONS: Place a check mark in the proper Answers column to show whether each of the following statements is true or false.

		Answers		For Scoring
		True	False	
0.	Accounting records must include details and facts that are current, accurate, and complete..	✔		0. ✔
23.	In automated accounting, accounting concepts are applied differently in each accounting cycle..		✔	23.
24.	Businesses that need to process large amounts of data at very fast processing speeds often choose a minicomputer................................		✔	24.
25.	Businesses with limited data to be processed and with a need for processing speed greater than can be achieved with manual methods often choose a microcomputer..	✔		25.
26.	Several computer programs are generally needed for a complete information system..	✔		26.
27.	Applications software is generally prepared by the computer manufacturer....		✔	27.
28.	Computer functions consist of input, processing, storage, and output..........	✔		28.
29.	A central processing unit has unlimited space for internal data storage.........		✔	29.
30.	A magnetic tape is the most widely used secondary storage......................		✔	30.
31.	Automated accounting is based on the same accounting concepts as manual accounting..	✔		31.
32.	Recording and reporting a business' financial information separately from the stockholders' personal financial information is an application of the Going Concern accounting concept..		✔	32.
33.	Automated accounting requires that general ledger accounts be numbered differently than accounts in a manual accounting system......................		✔	33.
34.	Each business numbers its general ledger accounts according to the size of the computer being used..		✔	34.
35.	Automated accounting uses the same subsidiary ledgers as manual accounting..	✔		35.
36.	Accounts in subsidiary ledgers are numbered in the same way for both manual and automated accounting..	✔		36.
37.	In a departmentalized accounting system, net income is figured for each department..		✔	37.
38.	In a departmentalized accounting system, all revenue, contra revenue, merchandise inventory, cost, and contra cost accounts are departmentalized..	✔		38.
39.	Using a memorandum as the source document to record an entry to divide an account balance is an application of the Adequate Disclosure accounting concept..		✔	39.

Performing file maintenance activities; adding and
deleting general ledger accounts

	GENERAL LEDGER	
RUN DATE 10 / 01 / -- MM DD YY	FILE MAINTENANCE Input Form	

	1	2	
	ACCOUNT NUMBER	**ACCOUNT TITLE**	
1	6111	*Credit Card Fee Expense*	1
2	6212	*Depreciation Expense—Computer Equipment*	2
3	6228	*Salary Expense—Administrative*	3
4	6110	*(Delete)*	4
5	6218	*(Delete)*	5
6	6235	*(Delete)*	6
7			7
8			8

Performing file maintenance activities; adding and
deleting subsidiary ledger accounts

PROBLEM 6-2, p. 136

	CUSTOMER	
RUN DATE 03 / 01 / -- MM DD YY	FILE MAINTENANCE Input Form	

	1	2	
	CUSTOMER NUMBER	**CUSTOMER NAME**	
1	115	*Thomas Arthur*	1
2	132	*Valerie Clevinger*	2
3	175	*Joseph Voison*	3
4	120	*(Delete)*	4
5	140	*(Delete)*	5
6	160	*(Delete)*	6
7			7
8			8

GENERAL LEDGER FILE MAINTENANCE
Input Form

RUN DATE _06_ / _01_ / _--_
MM   DD   YY

	1 ACCOUNT NUMBER	2 ACCOUNT TITLE	
1	1125-1	Merchandise Inventory — Hardware	1
2	1125-2	Merchandise Inventory — Plumbing	2
3	3120-1	Income Summary — Hardware	3
4	3120-2	Income Summary — Plumbing	4
5	4105-1	Sales — Hardware	5
6	4105-2	Sales — Plumbing	6
7	4110-1	Sales Returns and Allow. — Hardware	7
8	4110-2	Sales Returns and Allow. — Plumbing	8
9	4115-1	Sales Discount — Hardware	9
10	4115-2	Sales Discount — Plumbing	10
11	5105-1	Purchases — Hardware	11
12	5105-2	Purchases — Plumbing	12
13	5110-1	Purchases Returns and Allow. — Hardware	13
14	5110-2	Purchases Returns and Allow. — Plumbing	14
15	5115-1	Purchases Discount — Hardware	15
16	5115-2	Purchases Discount — Plumbing	16
17	6120-1	Salary Expense — Hardware	17
18	6120-2	Salary Expense — Plumbing	18
19			19
20			20
21			21
22			22
23			23
24			24
25			25

BATCH NO. __1__

RUN DATE __06 / 01 / --__
MM DD YY

JOURNAL ENTRIES
Input Form

PAGE __1__ OF __1__ PAGES

	1	2	3	4	5	6	
	DAY	DOC. NO.	VENDOR/ CUSTOMER NO.	GENERAL LEDGER ACCT. NO.	DEBIT	CREDIT	
1	01	M32		1125-1	172 640 00		1
2				1125-2	163 843 50		2
3				1125		336 483 50	3
25							25

PAGE TOTALS		
BATCH TOTALS	336 483 50	336 483 50

[3]

RUN DATE __06 / 01 / --__
MM DD YY

**GENERAL LEDGER
FILE MAINTENANCE**
Input Form

	1	2	
	ACCOUNT NUMBER	ACCOUNT TITLE	
1	1125	(Delete)	1
2	3120	(Delete)	2
3	4105	(Delete)	3
4	4110	(Delete)	4
5	4115	(Delete)	5
6	5105	(Delete)	6
7	5110	(Delete)	7
8	5115	(Delete)	8
9	6120	(Delete)	9
10			10

GENERAL LEDGER
FILE MAINTENANCE
Input Form

RUN DATE 07 / 01 / --
MM DD YY

	ACCOUNT NUMBER	ACCOUNT TITLE	
1	1108	Petty Cash	1
2	6108	Credit Card Fee Expense	2
3	6245	(Delete)	3
4	1120-1	Merchandise Inventory — Men's Shoes	4
5	1120-2	Merchandise Inventory — Women's Shoes	5
6	3120-1	Income Summary — Men's Shoes	6
7	3120-2	Income Summary — Women's Shoes	7
8	4105-1	Sales — Men's Shoes	8
9	4105-2	Sales — Women's Shoes	9
10	4110-1	Sales Returns & Allow. — Men's Shoes	10
11	4110-2	Sales Returns & Allow. — Women's Shoes	11
12	4115-1	Sales Discount — Men's Shoes	12
13	4115-2	Sales Discount — Women's Shoes	13
14	5105-1	Purchases — Men's Shoes	14
15	5105-2	Purchases — Women's Shoes	15
16	5110-1	Purch. Returns & Allow. — Men's Shoes	16
17	5110-2	Purch. Returns & Allow. — Women's Shoes	17
18	5115-1	Purchases Discount — Men's Shoes	18
19	5115-2	Purchases Discount — Women's Shoes	19
20	6115-1	Salary Expense — Men's Shoes	20
21	6115-2	Salary Expense — Women's Shoes	21
22			22
23			23
24			24
25			25

[2]

BATCH NO. ___1___

RUN DATE __07__ / __01__ / __--__
          MM DD YY

JOURNAL ENTRIES
Input Form

PAGE ___1___ OF ___1___ PAGES

	1	2	3	4	5	6	
	DAY	DOC. NO.	VENDOR/ CUSTOMER NO.	GENERAL LEDGER ACCT. NO.	DEBIT	CREDIT	
1	01	M43		1120-1	146 740 50		1
2				1120-2	180 100 00		2
3				1120		326 840 50	3
25							25

	PAGE TOTALS		
	BATCH TOTALS	326 840 50	326 840 50

[3]

RUN DATE __07__ / __01__ / __--__
        MM DD YY

GENERAL LEDGER
FILE MAINTENANCE
Input Form

	1	2	
	ACCOUNT NUMBER	ACCOUNT TITLE	
1	1120	(Delete)	1
2	3120	(Delete)	2
3	4105	(Delete)	3
4	4110	(Delete)	4
5	4115	(Delete)	5
6	5105	(Delete)	6
7	5110	(Delete)	7
8	5115	(Delete)	8
9	6115	(Delete)	9
10			10

CUSTOMER
FILE MAINTENANCE
Input Form

RUN DATE 07 / 01 / --
         MM DD YY

	CUSTOMER NUMBER	CUSTOMER NAME	
1	135	John Desai	1
2	155	Phyllis Mayan	2
3	125	(Delete)	3
4	170	(Delete)	4
5			5
6			6
7			7

Performing vendor file maintenance activities

CHALLENGE PROBLEM 6-C, p. 138

VENDOR
FILE MAINTENANCE
Input Form

RUN DATE 11 / 01 / --
         MM DD YY

	VENDOR NUMBER	VENDOR NAME	
1	220	(Delete)	1
2	225	(Delete)	2
3	248	(Delete)	3
4	278	(Delete)	4
5	220	Austin Store Supplies	5
6	235	Colburn Paint, Inc.	6
7	245	Garrett Wallcovering	7
8	272	Tabor Wallpaper Co.	8
9			9
10			10

Name _____

Deduct .... __   Date _____ Class _____

Your Score .... __   Checked by _____

UNIT A—Analyzing the Recording and Posting of Transactions in an Automated Accounting System

DIRECTIONS: Place a check mark in the proper Answers column to show whether each of the following statements is true or false.

	Answers True	Answers False	For Scoring
0. Transactions are analyzed into debit and credit parts in both manual and automated accounting systems	✔		0. ✔
1. In automated accounting, transaction data are key-entered into a computer and automatically posted to a general ledger stored on secondary storage	✔		1.
2. Using a one-month fiscal period is an application of the Consistent Reporting accounting concept...		✔	2.
3. The total number of pages is recorded on a journal entries input form after the entire batch has been recorded	✔		3.
4. In a departmental purchase on account transaction, the vendor account is increased by a debit		✔	4.
5. The run date recorded on a journal entries input form is the date on which data will be key-entered and processed	✔		5.
6. In a departmental purchases returns and allowances transaction, Accounts Payable is decreased by a credit..		✔	6.
7. Using a check stub as the source document for a cash payment is an application of the Objective Evidence accounting concept	✔		7.
8. In a departmental cash payment on account less discount transaction, the departmental purchases discount account is increased by a credit...............	✔		8.
9. In a departmental cash payment on account less discount transaction, the cash payment amount for a $8,650.00 purchase invoice less 1% discount is $8,562.50...		✔	9.
10. In a departmental cash payment to replenish petty cash transaction, Petty Cash is credited for the total amount of expenses paid out of the petty cash fund		✔	10.
11. Equality of debits and credits is proved for each page of journal entries.......	✔		11.
12. On a journal entries input form, some lines may be blank on individual pages of journal entries	✔		12.

UNIT B—Analyzing Departmentalized Transactions

DIRECTIONS: For each item below, select the choice that best completes the sentence. Print the letter identifying your choice in the Answers column.

	Answers	For Scoring

0. In a departmental purchases returns and allowances transaction, Purchases Returns and Allowances is   **(A)** increased by a debit   **(B)** increased by a credit   **(C)** decreased by a debit   **(D)** decreased by a credit...................................... — B — 0. ✔

13. In a departmental cash payment on account less discount transaction, the purchase discount amount for an $8,650.00 invoice less 1% discount is   **(A)** $0.87   **(B)** $8.65   **(C)** $86.50   **(D)** none of these.. — C — 13.

14. In a $500.00 departmental sale on account plus $25.00 sales tax transaction, the customer account is   **(A)** increased by a $500.00 debit   **(B)** increased by a $500.00 credit   **(C)** increased by a $525.00 debit   **(D)** increased by a $525.00 credit .... — C — 14.

15. In a $300.00 departmental sale on account plus $15.00 sales tax transaction, the revenue account is   **(A)** increased by a $300.00 debit   **(B)** increased by a $300.00 credit   **(C)** increased by a $315.00 debit   **(D)** increased by a $315.00 credit .... — B — 15.

16. In a departmental sales returns and allowances transaction, the customer account is   **(A)** increased by a debit   **(B)** decreased by a debit   **(C)** increased by a credit   **(D)** decreased by a credit................. — D — 16.

17. In a departmental cash received on account less 2% discount and less 5% sales tax transaction, the cash received for a sales invoice of $500.00 plus $25.00 sales tax is   **(A)** $489.50   **(B)** $513.97   **(C)** $514.50   **(D)** none of these.................. — C — 17.

18. In a departmental cash received on account less 2% discount and less 5% sales tax transaction, the sales tax payable decrease for a sales invoice of $1,200.00 plus $60.00 sales tax is   **(A)** $24.00   **(B)** $1.20   **(C)** $2.40   **(D)** none of these .... — B — 18.

19. In a cash received on account less 2% discount and less 5% sales tax transaction, the sales discount increase for a sales invoice of $2,000.00 plus $100.00 sales tax is   **(A)** $40.00   **(B)** $42.00   **(C)** $20.00   **(D)** none of these...................... — A — 19.

Recording departmental purchases on account and purchases returns and allowances

	BATCH NO.	1		JOURNAL ENTRIES		
	RUN DATE	08 / 06 / --		Input Form	PAGE 1 OF 1 PAGES	
		MM DD YY				

	1	2	3	4	5	6	
	DAY	DOC. NO.	VENDOR/ CUSTOMER NO.	GENERAL LEDGER ACCT. NO.	DEBIT	CREDIT	
1	01	P182	220	5105-2	1250 00		1
2				2105		1250 00	2
3	01	P183	240	5105-1	1635 00		3
4				2105		1635 00	4
5	02	P184	210	5105-1	860 00		5
6				2105		860 00	6
7	03	DM26	230	2105	427 00		7
8				5110-2		427 00	8
9	03	P185	215	5105-2	1480 00		9
10				2105		1480 00	10
11	04	DM27	210	2105	216 00		11
12				5110-1		216 00	12
13	05	DM28	220	2105	346 00		13
14				5110-2		346 00	14
15	05	P186	240	5105-1	735 00		15
16				2105		735 00	16
17	06	DM29	210	2105	135 00		17
18				5110-1		135 00	18
19							19
20							20
21							21
22							22
23							23
24							24
25							25
				PAGE TOTALS			
				BATCH TOTALS	7084 00	7084 00	

BATCH NO. 2

RUN DATE 10 / 15 / --

MM DD YY

JOURNAL ENTRIES
Input Form

PAGE 1 OF 2 PAGES

	DAY	DOC. NO.	VENDOR/ CUSTOMER NO.	GENERAL LEDGER ACCT. NO.	DEBIT	CREDIT	
1	10	C221		6105	138 00		1
2				1105		138 00	2
3	10	C222	230	2105	1250 00		3
4				1105		1225 00	4
5				5115-2		25 00	5
6	11	C223	210	2105	8360 00		6
7				1105		8192 80	7
8				5115-1		167 20	8
9	12	C224		1135	115 00		9
10				1105		115 00	10
11	12	C225	220	2105	650 00		11
12				1105		637 00	12
13				5115-2		13 00	13
14	13	C226	225	2105	9840 00		14
15				1105		9643 20	15
16				5115-1		196 80	16
17	14	C227		6225	88 00		17
18				1105		88 00	18
19	15	C228		1135	110 00		19
20				6105	93 00		20
21				6225	101 00		21
22				1105		304 00	22
23	15	C229	240	2105	13 140 00		23
24				1105		12 877 20	24
25				5115-1		262 80	25

PAGE TOTALS: 33 885 00 | 33 885 00

BATCH TOTALS:

BATCH NO. [2]

RUN DATE 10 / 15 / --
          MM DD YY

JOURNAL ENTRIES
Input Form

PAGE __2__ OF __2__ PAGES

	1	2	3	4	5	6	
	DAY	DOC. NO.	VENDOR/ CUSTOMER NO.	GENERAL LEDGER ACCT. NO.	DEBIT	CREDIT	
1	15	C230		6115-1	3820 00		1
2				6115-2	3580 00		2
3				6240	2040 00		3
4				2110		1260 30	4
5				2115		506 20	5
6				2125		660 80	6
7				2145		192 00	7
8				2150		136 00	8
9				1105		6684 70	9
10	15	C231		1135	93 00		10
11				1105		93 00	11
12							12
13							13
14							14
15							15
16							16
17							17
18							18
19							19
20							20
21							21
22							22
23							23
24							24
25							25
			PAGE TOTALS		9533 00	9533 00	
			BATCH TOTALS		43 418 00	43 418 00	

BATCH NO. **3**

RUN DATE $\underline{03}$ / $\underline{19}$ / $\underline{--}$
MM DD YY

JOURNAL ENTRIES
Input Form

PAGE $\underline{1}$ OF $\underline{1}$ PAGES

	1	2	3	4	5	6	
	DAY	DOC. NO.	VENDOR/ CUSTOMER NO.	GENERAL LEDGER ACCT. NO.	DEBIT	CREDIT	
1	14	S138	130	1115	399 00		1
2				2130		19 00	2
3				4105-1		380 00	3
4	14	S139	135	1115	1302 00		4
5				2130		62 00	5
6				4105-1		1240 00	6
7	15	CM27	110	2130	14 00		7
8				4110-2	280 00		8
9				1115		294 00	9
10	16	S140	120	1115	682 50		10
11				2130		32 50	11
12				4105-2		650 00	12
13	16	S141	140	1115	194 25		13
14				2130		9 25	14
15				4105-1		185 00	15
16	17	CM28	135	2130	11 25		16
17				4110-1	225 00		17
18				1115		236 25	18
19	18	CM29	130	2130	7 50		19
20				4110-1	150 00		20
21				1115		157 50	21
22	19	S142	110	1115	787 50		22
23				2130		37 50	23
24				4105-2		750 00	24
25							25

PAGE TOTALS		

BATCH TOTALS	4053 00	4053 00

Recording departmental cash receipts

BATCH NO. [1]

RUN DATE 02 / 06 / --
      MM DD YY

JOURNAL ENTRIES
Input Form

PAGE _1_ **OF** _1_ **PAGES**

	DAY	DOC. NO.	VENDOR/ CUSTOMER NO.	GENERAL LEDGER ACCT. NO.	DEBIT	CREDIT	
1	01	R45	130	1105	1646 40		1
2				2130	1 60		2
3				4115-1	32 00		3
4				1115		1680 00	4
5	01	R46	120	1105	2469 60		5
6				2130	2 40		6
7				4115-1	48 00		7
8				1115		2520 00	8
9	02	R47	110	1105	987 84		9
10				2130	96		10
11				4115-2	19 20		11
12				1115		1008 00	12
13	04	R48	115	1105	1378 86		13
14				2130	1 34		14
15				4115-2	26 80		15
16				1115		1407 00	16
17	05	R49	120	1105	3045 84		17
18				2130	2 96		18
19				4115-1	59 20		19
20				1115		3108 00	20
21	06	T6		1105	8379 00		21
22				2130		399 00	22
23				4105-1		4620 00	23
24				4105-2		3360 00	24
25							25

PAGE TOTALS

BATCH TOTALS   18 102 00   18 102 00

	BATCH NO. 1			JOURNAL ENTRIES Input Form		PAGE 1 OF 2 PAGES	

RUN DATE 11 / 05 / --
MM DD YY

	1	2	3	4	5	6	
	DAY	DOC. NO.	VENDOR/ CUSTOMER NO.	GENERAL LEDGER ACCT. NO.	DEBIT	CREDIT	
1	01	C310		6235	1200 00		1
2				1105		1200 00	2
3	01	C311		6115-1	3160 00		3
4				6115-2	3380 00		4
5				6240	2190 00		5
6				2110		760 20	6
7				2115		374 20	7
8				2125		611 10	8
9				2145		148 00	9
10				2150		102 00	10
11				1105		6734 50	11
12	01	P140	230	5105-1	3860 00		12
13				2105		3860 00	13
14	01	P141	250	5105-2	4620 00		14
15				2105		4620 00	15
16	02	DM22	240	2105	1275 00		16
17				5110-2		1275 00	17
18	02	S246	130	1115	892 50		18
19				2130		42 50	19
20				4105-1		850 00	20
21	02	C312	220	2105	1680 00		21
22				1105		1646 40	22
23				5115-2		33 60	23
24	02	C313		1135	86 00		24
25				1105		86 00	25

PAGE TOTALS	22 343 50	22 343 50
BATCH TOTALS		

BATCH NO. ___1___   **JOURNAL ENTRIES**

RUN DATE __11__ / __05__ / __--__   Input Form   PAGE __2__ OF __2__ PAGES

MM DD YY

	DAY	DOC. NO.	VENDOR/ CUSTOMER NO.	GENERAL LEDGER ACCT. NO.	DEBIT	CREDIT	
1	03	S247	140	1115	1176 00		1
2				2130		56 00	2
3				4105-2		1120 00	3
4	03	R209	110	1105	2932 65		4
5				2130	2 85		5
6				4115-1	57 00		6
7				1115		2992 50	7
8	04	CM19	130	2130	5 00		8
9				4110-1	100 00		9
10				1115		105 00	10
11	05	T5		1105	29 788 50		11
12				2130		1418 50	12
13				4105-1		16 520 00	13
14				4105-2		11 850 00	14
15							15
16							16
17							17
18							18
19							19
20							20
21							21
22							22
23							23
24							24
25							25

PAGE TOTALS   34 062 00   34 062 00

BATCH TOTALS   56 405 50   56 405 50

BATCH NO. 2
RUN DATE 11 / 12 / --
MM DD YY

JOURNAL ENTRIES
Input Form

PAGE 1 **OF** 1 **PAGES**

	DAY	DOC. NO.	VENDOR/ CUSTOMER NO.	GENERAL LEDGER ACCT. NO.	DEBIT	CREDIT	
1	07	P142	240	5105-2	14 920 00		1
2				2105		14 920 00	2
3	09	DM23	230	2105	1150 00		3
4				5110-1		1150 00	4
5	10	C314		1135	135 00		5
6				6105	93 00		6
7				6225	86 00		7
8				1105		314 00	8
9	11	C315	230	2105	2710 00		9
10				1105		2655 80	10
11				5115-1		54 20	11
12	11	C316	250	2105	4620 00		12
13				1105		4527 60	13
14				5115-2		92 40	14
15	12	R210	130	1105	771 75		15
16				2130	75		16
17				4115-1	15 00		17
18				1115		787 50	18
19	12	T12		1105	26 008 50		19
20				2130		1238 50	20
21				4105-1		14 920 00	21
22				4105-2		9850 00	22
23							23
24							24
25							25

PAGE TOTALS

BATCH TOTALS 50 510 00 | 50 510 00

Recording departmental business transactions

BATCH NO. **4**

RUN DATE **08** / **27** / **--**
MM DD YY

JOURNAL ENTRIES
Input Form

PAGE **1** OF **1** PAGES

	DAY	DOC. NO.	VENDOR/ CUSTOMER NO.	GENERAL LEDGER ACCT. NO.	DEBIT	CREDIT	
1	22	DM38	220	2105	776 00		1
2				5110-1		776 00	2
3	23	C273	210	2105	1235 00		3
4				1105		1210 30	4
5				5115-2		24 70	5
6	24	CM27	120	2130	2 50		6
7				4110-2	50 00		7
8				1115		52 50	8
9	25	R152	110	1105	740 88		9
10				2130	72		10
11				4115-1	14 40		11
12				1115		756 00	12
13	26	R153	130	1105	823 20		13
14				2130	80		14
15				4115-2	16 00		15
16				1115		840 00	16
17	27	C274	230	2105	1825 00		17
18				1105		1788 50	18
19				5115-1		36 50	19
20							20
21							21
22							22
23							23
24							24
25							25

PAGE TOTALS

BATCH TOTALS **5 484 50** **5 484 50**

JOURNAL ENTRIES
Input Form

BATCH NO. [   ]

RUN DATE ___ / ___ / ___
MM   DD   YY

PAGE ____ OF ____ PAGES

	1	2	3	4	5	6	
	DAY	DOC. NO.	VENDOR/ CUSTOMER NO.	GENERAL LEDGER ACCT. NO.	DEBIT	CREDIT	
1							1
2							2
3							3
4							4
5							5
6							6
7							7
8							8
9							9
10							10
11							11
12							12
13							13
14							14
15							15
16							16
17							17
18							18
19							19
20							20
21							21
22							22
23							23
24							24
25							25

PAGE TOTALS [|]

BATCH TOTALS [|]

Perfect Score. 26

Deduct .... __

Your Score .... __

Name _____

Date _____ Class _____

Checked by _____

STUDY
GUIDE
8

UNIT A—Analyzing End-of-Fiscal-Period Work in an Automated Accounting System

DIRECTIONS: Place a check mark in the proper Answers column to show whether each of the following statements is true or false.

	Answers		For
	True	False	Scoring
0. Financial statements must contain all pertinent information essential for a reader's understanding of a business' financial status	✔		0. ✔
1. In automated accounting, end-of-fiscal-period reports are prepared by a computer..	✔		1.
2. The run date used for all end-of-fiscal-period reports is the date on which the reports will be prepared		✔	2.
3. Computex prepares subsidiary ledger schedules to prove the accuracy of subsidiary ledger accounts and the controlling accounts in the general ledger..	✔		3.
4. Adjusting entries are made at the end of a fiscal period to bring subsidiary ledger account balances up to date..		✔	4.
5. Adjusting entries are recorded on a general ledger file maintenance input form		✔	5.
6. For a bad debts expense adjustment, Bad Debts Expense is increased by a debit	✔		6.
7. For a bad debts expense adjustment, Accounts Receivable is decreased by a credit		✔	7.
8. A departmental merchandise inventory adjustment for a $200,000.00 beginning and a $180,000.00 ending balance requires that the departmental income summary account be debited for $20,000.00...............................	✔		8.
9. A departmental merchandise inventory adjustment for a $150,000.00 beginning and a $160,000.00 ending balance requires that the departmental merchandise inventory account be credited for $10,000.00		✔	9.
10. For a supplies inventory adjustment, Supplies Expense is debited for the value of the ending supplies inventory		✔	10.
11. A supplies inventory adjustment for an $800.00 beginning and a $600.00 ending balance requires that the supplies account be credited for $200.00.....	✔		11.
12. For a prepaid insurance adjustment, Prepaid Insurance is adjusted to reflect the value of insurance used during the fiscal period..............................	✔		12.
13. For a federal income tax adjustment, the federal income tax account is increased by a credit...		✔	13.
14. An income statement for a departmentalized business reports departmental cost of merchandise sold and gross profit on operations for each department		✔	14.
15. An acceptable level of performance is indicated when the ratio of cost of merchandise sold is less than the acceptable performance standard..............	✔		15.
16. A statement of stockholders' equity is prepared to show details of changes in owner's equity during a fiscal period		✔	16.
17. A post-closing trial balance is prepared to prove equality of debits and credits after adjusting and closing entries have been posted	✔		17.

DIRECTIONS: For each item below, select the choice that best completes the sentence. Print the letter identifying your choice in the Answers column.

	Answers	For Scoring
0. For a bad debts expense adjustment, Allowance for Uncollectible Accounts is (**A**) increased by a debit (**B**) increased by a credit (**C**) decreased by a debit (**D**) decreased by a credit....................	B	0. ✔
18. A departmental merchandise inventory adjustment for a $120,000.00 beginning and a $90,000.00 ending balance requires that the departmental income summary account be (**A**) debited for $30,000.00 (**B**) credited for $30,000.00 (**C**) credited for $90,000.00 (**D**) none of these	A	18.
19. A departmental merchandise inventory adjustment for a $120,000.00 beginning and a $140,000.00 ending balance requires that the departmental merchandise inventory account be (**A**) increased by a $20,000.00 debit (**B**) increased by a $20,000.00 credit (**C**) decreased by a $20,000.00 debit (**D**) decreased by a $20,000.00 credit....................	A	19.
20. For a supplies inventory adjustment, the supplies account is (**A**) increased by a debit (**B**) increased by a credit (**C**) decreased by a debit (**D**) decreased by a credit....................	D	20.
21. A supplies inventory adjustment for a $1,000.00 beginning and an $800.00 ending balance requires that the supplies account be (**A**) increased by a $200.00 debit (**B**) increased by an $800.00 debit (**C**) decreased by a $200.00 credit (**D**) decreased by a $1,000.00 credit	C	21.
22. For a prepaid insurance adjustment, the prepaid insurance account is (**A**) increased by a debit (**B**) decreased by a debit (**C**) increased by a credit (**D**) decreased by a credit....................	D	22.
23. A prepaid insurance adjustment for a $700.00 beginning and a $550.00 ending prepaid insurance value requires that the insurance expense account be (**A**) debited for $150.00 (**B**) credited for $150.00 (**C**) debited for $550.00 (**D**) credited for $550.00....................	A	23.
24. For a depreciation expense adjustment, the accumulated depreciation account is (**A**) increased by a debit (**B**) decreased by a debit (**C**) increased by a credit (**D**) decreased by a credit....................	C	24.
25. A $600.00 depreciation expense adjustment requires that the depreciation expense account be (**A**) increased by a $600.00 debit (**B**) increased by a $600.00 credit (**C**) decreased by a $600.00 debit (**D**) decreased by a $600.00 credit	A	25.
26. For a federal income tax adjustment, the federal income tax account is (**A**) increased by a debit (**B**) decreased by a debit (**C**) increased by a credit (**D**) decreased by a credit....................	A	26.

Name _____ Date _____ Class _____

Recording adjusting entries on a journal entries input
form

BATCH NO.	5				

RUN DATE 10 / 31 / --
MM   DD   YY

JOURNAL ENTRIES
Input Form

PAGE __1__ OF __1__ PAGES

	1	2	3	4	5	6	
	DAY	DOC. NO.	VENDOR/ CUSTOMER NO.	GENERAL LEDGER ACCT. NO.	DEBIT	CREDIT	
1	31	ADJ. ENT.		6205	1250 20		1
2				1120		1250 20	2
3				1125-1	4079 90		3
4				3120-1		4079 90	4
5				3120-2	5126 50		5
6				1125-2		5126 50	6
7				6245	760 70		7
8				1130		760 70	8
9				6120	1508 70		9
10				1135		1508 70	10
11				6220	325 00		11
12				1140		325 00	12
13				6210	350 00		13
14				1210		350 00	14
15				6215	420 00		15
16				1220		420 00	16
17				6110	380 00		17
18				1230		380 00	18
19				9105	1280 00		19
20				2120		1280 00	20
21							21
22							22
23							23
24							24
25							25

	PAGE TOTALS		

	BATCH TOTALS	15 481 00	15 481 00

	BATCH NO. 5 RUN DATE 07 / 31 / -- MM DD YY		JOURNAL ENTRIES Input Form		PAGE 1 OF 1 PAGES	

	1	2	3	4	5	6	
	DAY	DOC. NO.	VENDOR/ CUSTOMER NO.	GENERAL LEDGER ACCT. NO.	DEBIT	CREDIT	
1	31	ADJ. ENT.		6205	436 75		1
2				1120		436 75	2
3				3120-1	1914 70		3
4				1125-1		1914 70	4
5				1125-2	2370 10		5
6				3120-2		2370 10	6
7				6245	609 60		7
8				1130		609 60	8
9				6120	650 20		9
10				1135		650 20	10
11				6220	350 00		11
12				1140		350 00	12
13				6210	410 00		13
14				1210		410 00	14
15				6215	360 00		15
16				1220		360 00	16
17				6110	340 00		17
18				1230		340 00	18
19				9105	1320 00		19
20				2120		1320 00	20
21							21
22							22
23							23
24							24
25							25
			PAGE TOTALS				
			BATCH TOTALS		8761 35	8761 35	

Recording adjusting entries on a journal entries input
form

BATCH NO.	5			JOURNAL ENTRIES			
RUN DATE	04 / 30 / --			Input Form		PAGE 1 OF 1 PAGES	
	MM DD YY						

	1	2	3	4	5	6	
	DAY	DOC. NO.	VENDOR/ CUSTOMER NO.	GENERAL LEDGER ACCT. NO.	DEBIT	CREDIT	
1	30	ADJ. ENT.		6205	387 20		1
2				1120		387 20	2
3				1125-1	2168 20		3
4				3120-1		2168 20	4
5				1125-2	2820 00		5
6				3120-2		2820 00	6
7				6245	729 70		7
8				1130		729 70	8
9				6120	380 50		9
10				1135		380 50	10
11				6220	250 00		11
12				1140		250 00	12
13				6210	380 00		13
14				1210		380 00	14
15				6215	420 00		15
16				1220		420 00	16
17				6110	340 00		17
18				1230		340 00	18
19				9105	1260 00		19
20				2120		1260 00	20
21							21
22							22
23							23
24							24
25							25
			PAGE TOTALS				
			BATCH TOTALS		9135 60	9135 60	

BATCH NO.

RUN DATE ___/___/___
MM DD YY

JOURNAL ENTRIES
Input Form

PAGE ____ **OF** ____ **PAGES**

	1	2	3	4	5	6	
	DAY	DOC. NO.	VENDOR/ CUSTOMER NO.	GENERAL LEDGER ACCT. NO.	DEBIT	CREDIT	
1							1
2							2
3							3
4							4
5							5
6							6
7							7
8							8
9							9
10							10
11							11
12							12
13							13
14							14
15							15
16							16
17							17
18							18
19							19
20							20
21							21
22							22
23							23
24							24
25							25

PAGE TOTALS

BATCH TOTALS

Perfect Score. 43

Deduct .... __

Your Score .... __

Name _____

Date _____ Class _____

Checked by _____

STUDY GUIDE 9

UNIT A — Identifying Accounting Terms

DIRECTIONS: Select the one term in Column I that best fits each definition in Column II. Print the letter identifying your choice in the Answers column.

Column I	Column II	Answers	For Scoring
A. accounts receivable turnover ratio	0. Accounts receivable that cannot be collected...............	F	0. ✔
B. aging accounts receivable	1. Canceling the balance of a customer account because the customer does not pay	G	1.
C. allowance method of recording losses from uncollectible accounts	2. Recording bad debts expense only when an amount is actually known to be uncollectible	E	2.
	3. Crediting the estimated value of uncollectible accounts to a contra account	C	3.
D. book value of accounts receivable	4. Analyzing accounts receivable according to when they are due........................	B	4.
E. direct write-off method of recording bad debts	5. The difference between the balance of Accounts Receivable and the estimated uncollectible accounts.......	D	5.
F. uncollectible accounts	6. The number of times the average amount of accounts receivable is collected annually	A	6.
G. writing off an account			

UNIT B — Analyzing Entries for Bad Debts Expense

DIRECTIONS: For each entry below, print in the proper Answers column the letters identifying which accounts are to be debited and credited.

Account Titles

A. Accounts Receivable
B. Allowance for Uncollectible Accounts
C. Bad Debts Collected
D. Bad Debts Expense
E. Cash

Transactions

(a) Direct write-off method:

		Answers		For Scoring	
		Debit	Credit	Debit	Credit
0–0.	Wrote off a customer's account as uncollectible	D	A	0. ✔	0. ✔
7–8.	Reopened an account previously written off....................................	A	C	7.	8.
9–10.	Received cash on account for balance owed by a customer previously written off as uncollectible	E	A	9.	10.

(b) Allowance method:

		Answers		For Scoring	
		Debit	Credit	Debit	Credit
11–12.	Recorded adjustment for bad debts expense............................	D	B	11.	12.
13–14.	Recorded adjustment for bad debts expense when using aging accounts receivable method to figure the amount	D	B	13.	14.
15–16.	Recorded adjustment for bad debts expense when using the percentage of accounts receivable account balance to figure the amount	D	B	15.	16.
17–18.	Wrote off a customer's account as uncollectible....................	B	A	17.	18.
19–20.	Reopened customer's account previously written off as uncollectible...	A	B	19.	20.
21–22.	Received cash for balance owed by customer described in question 19–20..	E	A	21.	22.

UNIT C—Analyzing Practices Involved in Recording Bad Debts Expense

DIRECTIONS: Place a check mark in the proper Answers column to show whether each of the following statements is true or false.

		Answers		For
		True	**False**	**Scoring**
0.	The Going Concern accounting concept is being applied when a business expects to continue in business indefinitely...	✔		0. ✔
23.	Uncollectible accounts are sometimes known as bad debts........................	✔		23.
24.	When a sale on account is made, the amount is recorded in Allowance for Uncollectible Accounts...		✔	24.
25.	Until a specific amount is actually known to be uncollectible, the amount remains recorded in Accounts Receivable...	✔		25.
26.	When a customer's account is known to be uncollectible, the account is no longer an asset..	✔		26.
27.	When a customer's account is known to be uncollectible, the amount becomes a business expense	✔		27.
28.	Because an uncollectible account may be collected in the future, the account should remain as part of the accounts receivable of a business..................		✔	28.
29.	Amounts owed by customers are recorded in a general ledger account titled Accounts Receivable	✔		29.
30.	When using the allowance method, an uncollectible account is closed by transferring the balance to a general ledger account titled Allowance for Uncollectible Accounts..	✔		30.
31.	A business with very few bad debts probably should use the allowance method of recording bad debts expense...		✔	31.
32.	One disadvantage of the direct write-off method of recording bad debts expense is that the expense may not be recorded in the same fiscal period as the revenue for the sale...	✔		32.
33.	Recording bad debts expense in the same fiscal period in which the original sale on account was made is an application of the accounting concept Matching Expenses with Revenue	✔		33.
34.	Because there is no way of knowing for sure which customers' accounts will become uncollectible, an estimate is made based on past history of bad debts expense	✔		34.
35.	The formula for figuring the amount of bad debts expense based on a percentage of net sales is: Net sales *times* percentage *equals* bad debts expense	✔		35.
36.	An adjusting entry is made at the end of a fiscal period to record the estimated bad debts expense	✔		36.
37.	Two accounts used for the bad debts expense adjustment are Bad Debts Expense and Accounts Receivable..		✔	37.
38.	Allowance for Uncollectible Accounts is a contra asset account	✔		38.
39.	Some businesses base their estimate of bad debts expense on a percentage of the total sales on account made during a fiscal period.........................	✔		39.
40.	The formula for figuring the estimated amount of bad debts expense when using a percentage of total sales on account is: Total sales on account *times* percentage *equals* bad debts expense..	✔		40.
41.	When using the allowance method of recording bad debts expense, regardless of the method used to figure the amount, the adjusting entry affects the same two accounts	✔		41.
42.	Most businesses today sell on credit to some customers...........................	✔		42.
43.	Regardless of the care taken in granting credit, some customers will not pay the amounts owed	✔		43.

Recording bad debts expense—direct write-off method

GENERAL JOURNAL
PAGE 12

	DATE	ACCOUNT TITLE	POST. REF.	DEBIT	CREDIT	
1	19-- Jan. 20	Bad Debts Expense		165 48		1
2		Accounts Receivable/Beth Quincy			165 48	2
3		M15				3
4	Feb. 15	Bad Debts Expense		52 00		4
5		Accounts Receivable/Edward Day			52 00	5
6		M21				6
7	Apr. 10	Accounts Receivable/Louise May		168 43		7
8		Bad Debts Collected			168 43	8
9		M34				9
10	June 14	Bad Debts Expense		89 97		10
11		Accounts Receivable/Charles Wagoner			89 97	11
12		M68				12
13	Oct. 5	Accounts Receivable/Beth Quincy		165 48		13
14		Bad Debts Collected			165 48	14
15		M104				15
16	Nov. 1	Accounts Receivable/Baker Olds		217 53		16
17		Bad Debts Collected			217 53	17
18		M127				18

CASH RECEIPTS JOURNAL
PAGE 10

	DATE	ACCOUNT TITLE	DOC. NO.	POST. REF.	GENERAL DEBIT	GENERAL CREDIT	ACCOUNTS RECEIVABLE CREDIT	SALES CREDIT	SALES TAX PAYABLE DEBIT	SALES TAX PAYABLE CREDIT	SALES DISCOUNT DEBIT	CASH DEBIT	
1	19-- Apr. 10	Louise May	R89				168 43					168 43	1
2	Oct. 5	Beth Quincy	R135				165 48					165 48	2
3	Nov. 1	Baker Olds	R139				217 53					217 53	3

Estimating amount of bad debts expense by using a percentage of net sales — allowance method

PROBLEM 9-2, p. 196
[1, 2]

GENERAL JOURNAL

PAGE 7

	DATE		ACCOUNT TITLE	POST. REF.	DEBIT	CREDIT	
1			*Adjusting Entries*				1
2	*Dec.* 19--	*31*	*Bad Debts Expense*		1 2 2 1 61		2
3			*Allowance for Uncollectible Accounts*			1 2 2 1 61	3
4							4
5							5
6							6
7							7
8							8
9							9
10							10
11							11
12							12

Estimating amount of bad debts expense by using a percentage of total sales on account — allowance method

PROBLEM 9-3, p. 197
[1, 2]

GENERAL JOURNAL

PAGE 5

	DATE		ACCOUNT TITLE	POST. REF.	DEBIT	CREDIT	
1			*Adjusting Entries*				1
2	*Dec.* 19--	*31*	*Bad Debts Expense*		1 6 8 7 17		2
3			*Allowance for Uncollectible Accounts*			1 6 8 7 17	3
4							4
5							5
6							6
7							7
8							8
9							9
10							10
11							11
12							12

Estimating the balance of Allowance for Uncollectible
Accounts by aging accounts receivable—allowance
method

Age Group	Amount	Percentage	Uncollectible
Not yet due	$ 9,619.18	.1 %	$ 9.62
1–30 days	1,254.83	.2 %	2.51
31–60 days	862.57	.3 %	2.59
61–90 days	1,574.57	.8 %	12.60
Over 90 days	350.90	50.0 %	175.45
Totals	$ 13,662.05		$ 202.77

[2]

GENERAL JOURNAL

PAGE 30

	DATE		ACCOUNT TITLE	POST. REF.	DEBIT	CREDIT	
1			*Adjusting Entries*				1
2	19-- Dec.	31	Bad Debts Expense		1 5 9 53		2
3			Allowance for Uncollectible Accounts			1 5 9 53	3
4							4
5							5

Estimating the balance of Allowance for Uncollectible
Accounts by using a percentage of the accounts
receivable account balance—allowance method

GENERAL JOURNAL

PAGE 17

	DATE		ACCOUNT TITLE	POST. REF.	DEBIT	CREDIT	
1			*Adjusting Entries*				1
2	19-- Dec.	31	Bad Debts Expense		2 3 0 00		2
3			Allowance for Uncollectible Accounts			2 3 0 00	3
4							4
5							5

GENERAL JOURNAL

PAGE 14

	DATE		ACCOUNT TITLE	POST. REF.	DEBIT	CREDIT	
1	Feb. 19--	11	Allowance for Uncollectible Accounts		5 7 00		1
2			Accounts Receivable/Wilbur Mason	/		5 7 00	2
3			M12				3
4	Apr.	15	Allowance for Uncollectible Accounts		1 2 9 58		4
5			Accounts Receivable/Mabel Bloom	/		1 2 9 58	5
6			M21				6
7	July	20	Allowance for Uncollectible Accounts		2 7 50		7
8			Accounts Receivable/Dan Hilyard	/		2 7 50	8
9			M39				9
10	Oct.	10	Allowance for Uncollectible Accounts		4 8 13		10
11			Accounts Receivable/LuAnn Boyd	/		4 8 13	11
12			M61				12
13							13
14							14
15							15
16							16
17							17
18							18
19							19
20							20
21							21
22							22
23							23
24							24
25							25
26							26
27							27
28							28
29							29
30							30
31							31
32							32
33							33

Recording the receipt of cash for written-off accounts—allowance method

GENERAL JOURNAL

PAGE 15

DATE		ACCOUNT TITLE	POST. REF.	DEBIT	CREDIT	
19-- Apr.	2	Accounts Receivable/Wilbur Mason	/	57 00		1
		Allowance for Uncollectible Accounts			57 00	2
		M17				3
May	14	Accounts Receivable/Mabel Bloom	/	129 58		4
		Allowance for Uncollectible Accounts			129 58	5
		M25				6
Dec.	5	Accounts Receivable/LuAnn Boyd	/	48 13		7
		Allowance for Uncollectible Accounts			48 13	8
		M81				9
						10
						11
						12

CASH RECEIPTS JOURNAL

PAGE 20

					1 GENERAL		2	3 ACCOUNTS RECEIVABLE CREDIT	4 SALES CREDIT	5 SALES TAX PAYABLE		6	7 SALES DISCOUNT DEBIT	8 CASH DEBIT	
DATE		ACCOUNT TITLE	DOC. NO.	POST. REF.	DEBIT	CREDIT				DEBIT	CREDIT				
19-- Apr.	2	Wilbur Mason	R43					57 00						57 00	1
May 14		Mabel Bloom	R47					129 58						129 58	2
Dec.	5	LuAnn Boyd	R103					48 13						48 13	3
															4
															5
															6

[1]

Business A $\dfrac{17{,}201.18 + 15{,}820.93}{2} = 16{,}511.06$ $\qquad$ $\dfrac{113{,}320.36}{16{,}511.06} = 6.9$

Business B $\dfrac{27{,}160.52 + 27{,}320.42}{2} = 27{,}240.47$ $\qquad$ $\dfrac{130{,}754.25}{27{,}240.47} = 4.8$

Business C $\dfrac{34{,}058.33 + 29{,}725.77}{2} = 31{,}892.05$ $\qquad$ $\dfrac{158{,}648.50}{31{,}892.05} = 5.0$

Business D $\dfrac{106{,}432.28 + 127{,}718.74}{2} = 117{,}075.51$ $\qquad$ $\dfrac{1{,}301{,}322.50}{117{,}075.51} = 11.1$

[2]

a. Best turnover ratio last year: **Business D**

Best turnover ratio this year: **Business D**

b. Worst turnover ratio last year: **Business C**

Worst turnover ratio this year: **Business B**

c. Greatest amount of improvement in turnover ratio from last year to this year: **Business D**

d. Least amount of improvement in turnover ratio from last year to this year: **Business B**

[1, 2]

Recording transactions for uncollectible accounts—
allowance method

GENERAL JOURNAL   PAGE 19

	DATE		ACCOUNT TITLE	POST. REF.	DEBIT	CREDIT	
1	19-- Jan.	9	Allowance for Uncollectible Accounts		534 65		1
2			Accounts Receivable/Joan Mueller			534 65	2
3			M20				3
4	Mar.	4	Allowance for Uncollectible Accounts		782 50		4
5			Accounts Receivable/James York			782 50	5
6			M29				6
7	Mar.	28	Accounts Receivable/Joan Mueller		534 65		7
8			Allowance for Uncollectible Accounts			534 65	8
9			M40				9
10	June	20	Allowance for Uncollectible Accounts		617 16		10
11			Accounts Receivable/Alice Armbruster			617 16	11
12			M58				12
13	Oct.	7	Allowance for Uncollectible Accounts		808 15		13
14			Accounts Receivable/Martha Hoggenboom			808 15	14
15			M74				15
16	Dec.	11	Accounts Receivable/James York		782 50		16
17			Allowance for Uncollectible Accounts			782 50	17
18			M82				18
19			Adjusting Entries				19
20		31	Bad Debts Expense		2 775 40		20
21			Allowance for Uncollectible Accounts			2 775 40	21
22							22
23							23
24							24

[2]

Sales		$280,065.10
Less Sales Returns and Allowances.................................	919.82	
Sales Discount...	1,605.70	2,525.52
Net Sales...		$277,539.58
Bad Debts Expense = Net Sales × 1% ($277,539.58 × 1%).............................		$ 2,775.40

CASH RECEIPTS JOURNAL

PAGE 30

	DATE	ACCOUNT TITLE	DOC. NO.	POST. REF.	GENERAL DEBIT	GENERAL CREDIT	ACCOUNTS RECEIVABLE CREDIT	SALES CREDIT	SALES TAX PAYABLE DEBIT	SALES TAX PAYABLE CREDIT	SALES DISCOUNT DEBIT	CASH DEBIT	
1	19-- Mar. 28	Joan Mueller	R24				534 65					534 65	1
2	Dec. 11	James York	R92				782 50					782 50	2
3													3
4													4
5													5
6													6
7													7
8													8
9													9
10													10
11													11
12													12

[1]

[3] Balance of Allowance for Uncollectible Accounts:

	Debits	Credits	Credit Balance
Beginning Balance			$1,463.89
	$534.65	$ 534.65	
	782.50	782.50	
	617.16	2,775.40	
	808.15		
Ending Balance			$2,813.98

Estimating and recording bad debts expense by aging
accounts receivable—allowance method

GENERAL JOURNAL

PAGE 26

	DATE		ACCOUNT TITLE	POST. REF.	DEBIT	CREDIT	
1	19-- Jan.	9	Allowance for Uncollectible Accounts		5 3 4 65		1
2			Accounts Receivable/Joan Mueller	/		5 3 4 65	2
3			M20				3
4	Mar.	4	Allowance for Uncollectible Accounts		7 8 2 50		4
5			Accounts Receivable/James York	/		7 8 2 50	5
6			M29				6
7	Mar.	28	Accounts Receivable/Joan Mueller	/	5 3 4 65		7
8			Allowance for Uncollectible Accounts			5 3 4 65	8
9			M40				9
10	June	20	Allowance for Uncollectible Accounts		6 1 7 16		10
11			Accounts Receivable/Alice Armbruster	/		6 1 7 16	11
12			M58				12
13	Oct.	7	Allowance for Uncollectible Accounts		8 0 8 15		13
14			Accounts Receivable/Martha Hoggenboom	/		8 0 8 15	14
15			M74				15
16	Dec.	11	Accounts Receivable/James York	/	7 8 2 50		16
17			Allowance for Uncollectible Accounts			7 8 2 50	17
18			M82				18
19			Adjusting Entries				19
20		31	Bad Debts Expense		7 7 7 36		20
21			Allowance for Uncollectible Accounts			7 7 7 36	21
22							22
23							23
24							24
25							25
26							26
27							27
28							28
29							29
30							30
31							31

[1]

CASH RECEIPTS JOURNAL

PAGE 35

	DATE	ACCOUNT TITLE	DOC. NO.	POST. REF.	GENERAL DEBIT	GENERAL CREDIT	ACCOUNTS RECEIVABLE CREDIT	SALES CREDIT	SALES TAX PAYABLE DEBIT	SALES TAX PAYABLE CREDIT	SALES DISCOUNT DEBIT	CASH DEBIT	
1	19-- Mar. 28	Joan Mueller	R24				534 65					534 65	1
2	Dec. 11	James York	R92				782 50					782 50	2
3													3
4													4
5													5
6													6
7													7
8													8
9													9
10													10
11													11
12													12

[2] Aging of Accounts Receivable:

$15,234.64 × .2% = $ 30.47
1,307.65 × .6% = 7.85
898.90 × 1.0% = 8.99
1,640.87 × 7.0% = 114.86
1,089.62 × 60.0% = 653.77

Total $815.94

Balance of Allowance for Uncollectible Accounts:

	Debits	Credits	Credit Balance
Beginning Balance			$1,463.89
	$534.65	$534.65	
	782.50	782.50	
	617.16		
	808.15		

Ending Balance (before adjusting entry) $ 38.58

Bad Debts Expense = $815.94 − 38.58 = $777.36

Perfect Score. 44

Deduct .... __

Your Score .... __

Name _____

Date _____ Class _____

Checked by _____

**STUDY
GUIDE
10**

UNIT A—Analyzing Depreciation and Disposing of Plant Assets Transactions

DIRECTIONS: Place a check mark in the proper Answers column to show whether each of the following statements is true or false.

	Answers		For
	True	False	Scoring
0. Plant assets are any asset that can be moved		✓	0. ✓
1. Recording the amount actually paid for a plant asset is an application of the accounting concept Historical Cost	✓		1.
2. At the time a plant asset is bought, the salvage value is only an estimated amount	✓		2.
3. Depreciation is a business operating expense	✓		3.
4. When a plant asset is discarded, no notation needs to be made on the plant asset record		✓	4.
5. The straight-line method of figuring depreciation expense is used most often because it best meets the IRS regulations		✓	5.
6. Because of land's permanent nature, no depreciation is recorded annually.....	✓		6.
7. Recording depreciation at the end of each fiscal period is an application of the accounting concept Matching Expenses with Revenue	✓		7.
8. The actual value and book value of a plant asset are usually the same amount		✓	8.
9. Depreciation expense for buildings is recorded the same as for other plant assets	✓		9.
10. A gain or loss on plant assets is not recorded when one plant asset is traded for a similar plant asset	✓		10.
11. Original cost, estimated useful life, and miles driven in a year are the three factors considered when figuring amount of annual depreciation		✓	11.
12. The actual cash paid is all that is ever considered as a plant asset's original cost		✓	12.
13. The formula for figuring a plant asset's annual amount of straight-line depreciation is: Original cost *minus* estimated salvage value *divided by* estimated useful life *equals* annual depreciation.....................	✓		13.
14. Three common ways of disposing of plant assets are discarding, selling, and trading-in	✓		14.
15. If a plant asset is disposed of during a fiscal year, depreciation expense for part of a year is recorded.....................	✓		15.
16. All plant assets depreciate an equal amount each year.....................		✓	16.

UNIT B—Identifying Accounting Terms

DIRECTIONS: Select the one term in Column I that best fits each definition in Column II. Print the letter identifying your choice in the Answers column.

	Column I		*Column II*	Answers	For Scoring
A.	assessed value	**0.**	Land and anything attached to the land	K	0. ✓
B.	book value of a plant asset	**17.**	An accounting form on which a business records information about each plant asset	I	17.
C.	declining-balance method of figuring depreciation	**18.**	The total costs paid to make a plant asset usable to a business	G	18.
D.	depletion	**19.**	The amount an owner expects to receive when a plant asset is removed from use	E	19.
E.	estimated salvage value	**20.**	The original cost of a plant asset minus accumulated depreciation	B	20.
F.	estimated useful life	**21.**	Charging an equal amount of depreciation expense for a plant asset each fiscal period	L	21.
G.	original cost	**22.**	Multiplying the book value at the end of each fiscal period by a constant depreciation rate	C	22.
H.	personal property				
I.	plant asset record	**23.**	Using fractions based on years of a plant asset's useful life	M	23.
J.	production-unit method of figuring depreciation	**24.**	Figuring estimated annual depreciation based on the amount of production expected from a plant asset	J	24.
K.	real property	**25.**	The decrease in a plant asset's value because of the removal of a natural resource	D	25.
L.	straight-line method of figuring depreciation	**26.**	All property not classified as real property	H	26.
		27.	An asset's value determined by tax authorities for the purpose of figuring taxes	A	27.
M.	sum-of-the-years-digits method of figuring depreciation	**28.**	The number of years a plant asset is expected to be productive for a business	F	28.

UNIT C—Analyzing Plant Asset Transactions

DIRECTIONS: For each transaction below, print in the proper Answers columns the identifying letter of the accounts to be debited and credited.

	Account Titles		*Transactions*	Answers Debit	Answers Credit	For Scoring Debit	For Scoring Credit
A.	Accumulated Depr.—Equipment	**0–0.**	Paid cash for new equipment	F	B	0. ✓	0. ✓
B.	Cash	**29–30.**	Recorded annual depreciation on equipment	C	A	29.	30.
C.	Depr. Expense—Equipment	**31–32.**	Discarded equipment with no book value	A	F	31.	32.
D.	Gain on Plant Assets	**33–34.**	Recorded depreciation for part of a year	C	A	33.	34.
E.	Loss on Plant Assets	**35–36.**	Discarded equipment with book value, all depreciation recorded	A, E	F	35.	36.
F.	Equipment	**37–38.**	Sold equipment for cash at less than book value, all depreciation recorded	A, B, E	F	37.	38.
G.	Property Tax Expense						
39–40.	Sold equipment for more than book value, all depreciation recorded			A, B	D, F	39.	40.
41–42.	Paid cash, $3,500.00, plus old equipment, cost $2,500.00; total accumulated depreciation recorded to date of trade, $500.00, for new office equipment			A, F	B, F	41.	42.
43–44.	Paid cash for property tax			G	B	43.	44.

Recording the buying of plant assets

The plant asset records used in Problem 10-1 are needed to complete Problems 10-2, 10-3, and 10-4.

[1]

GENERAL JOURNAL

PAGE 3

	DATE	ACCOUNT TITLE	POST. REF.	DEBIT	CREDIT	
1	1985 Jan. 3	Equipment—Office		3 5 0 00		1
2		Accounts Payable/Doarn, Inc.			3 5 0 00	2
3		M11				3
4	Mar. 31	Equipment—Warehouse		1 0 0 00		4
5		Accounts Payable/Bessler, Inc.			1 0 0 00	5
6		M24				6
7						7
8						8
9						9

[1]

CASH PAYMENTS JOURNAL

PAGE 5

	DATE	ACCOUNT TITLE	CHECK NO.	POST. REF.	GENERAL DEBIT	GENERAL CREDIT	ACCOUNTS PAYABLE DEBIT	PURCHASES DISCOUNT CREDIT	CASH CREDIT	
1	1985 Jan. 2	Equipment—Office	130		3 0 0 00				3 0 0 00	1
2	May 1	Equipment—Warehouse	210		8 5 0 00				8 5 0 00	2
3	July 1	Equipment—Store	250		5 0 0 00				5 0 0 00	3
4										4
5										5
6										6

Note: Students will complete section 1 of each plant asset record in Problem 10-1, section 2 in Problem 10-4, and Section 3 in Problem 10-3.

PLANT ASSET RECORD   Use _Office_

Description _File Cabinet_

| Date Bought | Jan. 2, 1985 | Serial Number | FC2467 | Original Cost | $300.00 |
| Estimated Useful Life | 5 years | Estimated Salvage Value | $50.00 | Annual Depreciation | $50.00 |

Disposed of: Discarded ✔   Sold ____   Traded ____
Date _Jan. 28, 1989_   Book Value _$95.83_

Year	Beginning Book Value	Annual Depreciation Expense	Accumulated Depreciation	Ending Book Value
1985	$300.00	$50.00	$ 50.00	$250.00
1986	250.00	50.00	100.00	200.00
1987	200.00	50.00	150.00	150.00
1988	150.00	50.00	200.00	100.00
1989	100.00	4.17	204.17	95.83

PLANT ASSET RECORD   Use _Office_

Description _Typewriter_

| Date Bought | Jan. 3, 1985 | Serial Number | X4672Y101 | Original Cost | $350.00 |
| Estimated Useful Life | 5 years | Estimated Salvage Value | None | Annual Depreciation | $70.00 |

Disposed of: Discarded ✔   Sold ____   Traded ____
Date _Jan. 21, 1989_   Book Value _$64.17_

Year	Beginning Book Value	Annual Depreciation Expense	Accumulated Depreciation	Ending Book Value
1985	$350.00	$70.00	$ 70.00	$280.00
1986	280.00	70.00	140.00	210.00
1987	210.00	70.00	210.00	140.00
1988	140.00	70.00	280.00	70.00
1989	70.00	5.83	285.83	64.17

PLANT ASSET RECORD   Use **Warehouse**

Description **Hand Truck**

| Date Bought **Mar. 31, 1985** | Serial Number **23D4689** | Original Cost **$100.00** |
| Estimated Useful Life **5 years** | Estimated Salvage Value **$25.00** | Annual Depreciation **$15.00** |

Disposed of: Discarded _____   Sold ✔   Traded _____
Date **Mar. 29, 1990**   Book Value **$25.00**

Year	Beginning Book Value	Annual Depreciation Expense	Accumulated Depreciation	Ending Book Value
1985	$100.00	$11.25	$11.25	$88.75
1986	88.75	15.00	26.25	73.75
1987	73.75	15.00	41.25	58.75
1988	58.75	15.00	56.25	43.75
1989	43.75	15.00	71.25	28.75
1990	28.75	3.75	75.00	25.00

PLANT ASSET RECORD   Use **Warehouse**

Description **Truck**

| Date Bought **May 1, 1985** | Serial Number **45J3257XF29** | Original Cost **$8,500.00** |
| Estimated Useful Life **5 years** | Estimated Salvage Value **$1,000.00** | Annual Depreciation **$1,500.00** |

Disposed of: Discarded _____   Sold _____   Traded ✔
Date **Dec. 31, 1990**   Book Value **$1,000.00**

Year	Beginning Book Value	Annual Depreciation Expense	Accumulated Depreciation	Ending Book Value
1985	$8,500.00	$1,000.00	$1,000.00	$7,500.00
1986	7,500.00	1,500.00	2,500.00	6,000.00
1987	6,000.00	1,500.00	4,000.00	4,500.00
1988	4,500.00	1,500.00	5,500.00	3,000.00
1989	3,000.00	1,500.00	7,000.00	1,500.00
1990	1,500.00	500.00	7,500.00	1,000.00

PLANT ASSET RECORD   Use _Store_____

Description _Shelving_____

Date Bought _____July 1, 1985_____   Serial Number _____None_____   Original Cost _____$500.00_____

Estimated Useful Life _____10 years_____   Estimated Salvage Value _____$25.00_____   Annual Depreciation _____$47.50_____

Disposed of: _____   Discarded _____   Sold _✔_   Traded _____

Date _____Dec. 31, 1990_____   Book Value _____ $238.75 _____

Year	Beginning Book Value	Annual Depreciation Expense	Accumulated Depreciation	Ending Book Value
1985	$500.00	$23.75	$ 23.75	$476.25
1986	476.25	47.50	71.25	428.75
1987	428.75	47.50	118.75	381.25
1988	381.25	47.50	166.25	333.75
1989	333.75	47.50	213.75	286.25
1990	286.25	47.50	261.25	238.75

Figuring depreciation using the straight-line method

PROBLEM 10-2, p. 222

The plant asset records used in Problem 10-1 are needed to complete Problem 10-2. The depreciation tables completed in Problem 10-2 are needed to complete Problem 10-3.

Plant asset: _____File Cabinet_____

Original cost: _____$300.00_____

Estimated salvage value: _____$50.00_____

Estimated useful life: _____5 years_____

Estimated annual depreciation: _____$50.00_____

Year	Beginning Book Value	Annual Depreciation	Accumulated Depreciation	Ending Book Value
1	$300.00	$50.00	$ 50.00	$250.00
2	250.00	50.00	100.00	200.00
3	200.00	50.00	150.00	150.00
4	150.00	50.00	200.00	100.00
5	100.00	50.00	250.00	50.00

Plant asset: _____Typewriter_____

Original cost: _____$350.00_____

Estimated salvage value: _____None_____

Estimated useful life: _____5 years_____

Estimated annual depreciation: _____$70.00_____

Year	Beginning Book Value	Annual Depreciation	Accumulated Depreciation	Ending Book Value
1	$350.00	$70.00	$ 70.00	$280.00
2	280.00	70.00	140.00	210.00
3	210.00	70.00	210.00	140.00
4	140.00	70.00	280.00	70.00
5	70.00	70.00	350.00	—

Plant asset: _____Truck_____

Original cost: _____$8,500.00_____

Estimated salvage value: _____$1,000.00_____

Estimated useful life: _____5 years_____

Estimated annual depreciation: _____$1,500.00_____

Year	Beginning Book Value	Annual Depreciation	Accumulated Depreciation	Ending Book Value
1	$8,500.00	$1,000.00	$1,000.00	$7,500.00
2	7,500.00	1,500.00	2,500.00	6,000.00
3	6,000.00	1,500.00	4,000.00	4,500.00
4	4,500.00	1,500.00	5,500.00	3,000.00
5	3,000.00	1,500.00	7,000.00	1,500.00
6	1,500.00	500.00	7,500.00	1,000.00

Plant asset: _____Hand Truck_____

Original cost: _____$100.00_____

Estimated salvage value: _____$25.00_____

Estimated useful life: _____5 years_____

Estimated annual depreciation: _____$15.00_____

Year	Beginning Book Value	Annual Depreciation	Accumulated Depreciation	Ending Book Value
1	$100.00	$11.25	$11.25	$88.75
2	88.75	15.00	26.25	73.75
3	73.75	15.00	41.25	58.75
4	58.75	15.00	56.25	43.75
5	43.75	15.00	71.25	28.75
6	28.75	3.75	75.00	25.00

Plant asset: _____**Shelving**_____

Original cost: _____**$500.00**_____

Estimated salvage value: _____**$25.00**_____

Estimated useful life: _____**10 years**_____

Estimated annual depreciation: _____**$47.50**_____

Year	Beginning Book Value	Annual Depreciation	Accumulated Depreciation	Ending Book Value
1	$500.00	$23.75	$ 23.75	$476.25
2	476.25	47.50	71.25	428.75
3	428.75	47.50	118.75	381.25
4	381.25	47.50	166.25	333.75
5	333.75	47.50	213.75	286.25
6	286.25	47.50	261.25	238.75
7	238.75	47.50	308.75	191.25
8	191.25	47.50	356.25	143.75
9	143.75	47.50	403.75	96.25
10	96.25	47.50	451.25	48.75
11	48.75	23.75	475.00	25.00

Recording estimated annual depreciation

PROBLEM 10-3, p. 222
[1, 3]

The plant asset records used in Problem 10-1 and the depreciation tables completed in Problem 10-2 are needed to complete Problem 10-3.

GENERAL JOURNAL

PAGE 12

	DATE		ACCOUNT TITLE	POST. REF.	DEBIT	CREDIT	
1			*Adjusting Entries*				1
2	1985 Dec.	31	Depreciation Expense—Office Equipment		1 2 0 00		2
3			Accum. Depr.—Office Equipment			1 2 0 00	3
4		31	Depreciation Expense—Warehouse Equip.		1 0 1 1 25		4
5			Accum. Depr.—Warehouse Equipment			1 0 1 1 25	5
6		31	Depreciation Expense—Store Equipment		2 3 75		6
7			Accum. Depr.—Store Equipment			2 3 75	7
8			*Adjusting Entries*				8
9	1986 Dec.	31	Depreciation Expense—Office Equipment		1 2 0 00		9
10			Accum. Depr.—Office Equipment			1 2 0 00	10
11		31	Depreciation Expense—Warehouse Equip.		1 5 1 5 00		11
12			Accum. Depr.—Warehouse Equipment			1 5 1 5 00	12
13		31	Depreciation Expense—Store Equipment		4 7 50		13
14			Accum. Depr.—Store Equipment			4 7 50	14

Recording transactions for disposing of plant assets

The plant asset records used in Problem 10-3 are needed to complete Problem 10-4.

GENERAL JOURNAL

PAGE 1

	DATE		ACCOUNT TITLE	POST. REF.	DEBIT	CREDIT	
1	1989 Jan.	21	Depreciation Expense — Office Equipment		5 83		1
2			Accum. Depr. — Office Equipment			5 83	2
3			M522				3
4		21	Accum. Depr. — Office Equipment		2 85 83		4
5			Loss on Plant Assets		64 17		5
6			Equipment — Office			3 50 00	6
7			M522				7
8		28	Depreciation Expense — Office Equipment		4 17		8
9			Accum. Depr. — Office Equipment			4 17	9
10			M523				10
11		28	Accum. Depr. — Office Equipment		2 04 17		11
12			Loss on Plant Assets		95 83		12
13			Equipment — Office			3 00 00	13
14			M523				14
15	1990 Mar.	29	Depreciation Expense — Warehouse Equipment		3 75		15
16			Accum. Depr. — Warehouse Equipment			3 75	16
17			M575				17
18	Dec.	31	Depreciation Expense — Store Equipment		47 50		18
19			Accum. Depr. — Store Equipment			47 50	19
20			M631				20
21		31	Depreciation Expense — Warehouse Equipment		5 00 00		21
22			Accum. Depr. — Warehouse Equipment			5 00 00	22
23			M632				23
24							24
25							25
26							26
27							27
28							28
29							29
30							30
31							31

CASH RECEIPTS JOURNAL

PAGE 4

				GENERAL		ACCOUNTS RECEIVABLE CREDIT	SALES CREDIT	SALES TAX PAYABLE		SALES DISCOUNT DEBIT	CASH DEBIT
DATE	ACCOUNT TITLE	DOC. NO.	POST. REF.	DEBIT	CREDIT			DEBIT	CREDIT		
				1	2	3	4	5	6	7	8
1990 Mar. 29	Accum. Depr. —										
	Warehouse Equip.	R645		75 00							10 00
	Loss on Plant Assets			15 00							
	Equipment — Warehouse				100 00						
Dec. 31	Accum. Depr. — Store Equip.	R733		2 61 25							250 00
	Gain on Plant Assets				11 25						
	Equipment — Store				500 00						

CASH PAYMENTS JOURNAL

PAGE 5

				GENERAL		ACCOUNTS PAYABLE DEBIT	PURCHASES DISCOUNT CREDIT	CASH CREDIT
DATE	ACCOUNT TITLE	CHECK NO.	POST. REF.	DEBIT	CREDIT			
				1	2	3	4	5
1990 Dec. 31	Equipment — Warehouse	815		900 00				800 00
	Accum. Depr. — Warehouse Equipment			750 00				
	Equipment — Warehouse				850 00			

Figuring depreciation using the straight-line, declining-balance, and sum-of-the-years-digits methods

Plant asset: _____Office Desk_____

Original cost: _____$3,200.00_____

Estimated salvage value: _____$200.00_____

Estimated useful life: _____4 years_____

Year	Straight-Line Method	Declining-Balance Method	Sum-of-the-Years-Digits Method
1	$ 750.00	$1,600.00	$1,200.00
2	750.00	800.00	900.00
3	750.00	400.00	600.00
4	750.00	200.00	300.00
Totals	$3,000.00	$3,000.00	$3,000.00
Ending Book Value	$ 200.00	$ 200.00	$ 200.00

Figuring depreciation using the production-unit method

Plant asset: _____Truck_____

Original cost: _____$9,000.00_____

Estimated salvage value: _____$1,000.00_____

Estimated total depreciation: _____$8,000.00_____

Depreciation rate: _____$0.14 per mile driven_____

Year	Beginning Book Value	Miles Driven	Annual Depreciation	Ending Book Value
1985	$9,000.00	10,500	$1,470.00	$7,530.00
1986	7,530.00	11,300	1,582.00	5,948.00
1987	5,948.00	9,900	1,386.00	4,562.00
1988	4,562.00	11,500	1,610.00	2,952.00
1989	2,952.00	12,200	1,708.00	1,244.00
Totals	—	55,400	$7,756.00	—

PROBLEM 10-7, p. 223

Figuring depletion

Plant asset: Mine
Original cost: $35,000.00
Estimated salvage value: $1,000.00
Estimated total depletion: $34,000.00
Depletion rate: $0.80 per ton mined

Year	Beginning Book Value	Tons Mined	Annual Depletion	Ending Book Value
1985	$35,000.00	8,000	$ 6,400.00	$28,600.00
1986	28,600.00	7,400	5,920.00	22,680.00
1987	22,680.00	9,000	7,200.00	15,480.00
1988	15,480.00	10,500	8,400.00	7,080.00
1989	7,080.00	7,200	5,760.00	1,320.00
Totals	—	42,100	$33,680.00	—

PROBLEM 10-8, p. 224

Figuring and recording property tax
[2]

CASH PAYMENTS JOURNAL

PAGE 5

				GENERAL		ACCOUNTS PAYABLE DEBIT	PURCHASES DISCOUNT CREDIT	CASH CREDIT
DATE	ACCOUNT TITLE	CHECK NO.	POST. REF.	DEBIT	CREDIT			
19-- Feb. 1	Property Tax Expense	124		6 7 5 0 00				6 7 5 0 00

[1]

Assessed Value times Rate equals Annual Tax
$300,000.00 × 4.5% = $13,500.00

Annual Tax divided by 2 equals Each Tax Payment
$13,500.00 ÷ 2 = $6,750.00

Recording transactions for plant assets

GENERAL JOURNAL

PAGE 22

	DATE		ACCOUNT TITLE	POST. REF.	DEBIT	CREDIT	
1	1988 Jan.	2	Accum. Depr. — Office Equipment		4 0 0 00		1
2			Loss on Plant Assets		1 2 0 00		2
3			Equipment — Office			5 2 0 00	3
4			M47				4
5	Mar.	29	Depreciation Expense — Office Equipment		1 5 00		5
6			Accum. Depr. — Office Equipment			1 5 00	6
7			M52				7
8		29	Accum. Depr. — Office Equipment		3 0 0 00		8
9			Loss on Plant Assets		5 0 00		9
10			Equipment — Office			3 5 0 00	10
11			M52				11
12		30	Depreciation Expense — Office Equipment		2 5 00		12
13			Accum. Depr. — Office Equipment			2 5 00	13
14			M54				14
15	June	29	Depreciation Expense — Office Equipment		1 2 50		15
16			Accum. Depr. — Office Equipment			1 2 50	16
17			M62				17
18	July	2	Depreciation Expense — Office Equipment		7 5 00		18
19			Accum. Depr. — Office Equipment			7 5 00	19
20			M70				20
21							21
22							22
23							23
24							24
25							25
26							26
27							27
28							28
29							29
30							30
31							31
32							32

CASH RECEIPTS JOURNAL

PAGE 44

					1 GENERAL	2 GENERAL	3 ACCOUNTS RECEIVABLE	4 SALES	5 SALES TAX PAYABLE	6 SALES TAX PAYABLE	7 SALES DISCOUNT	8 CASH	
DATE	ACCOUNT TITLE	DOC. NO.	POST. REF.		DEBIT	CREDIT	CREDIT	CREDIT	DEBIT	CREDIT	DEBIT	DEBIT	
1988 Mar. 30	Accum. Depr.—Office Equip.	R191			600 00							100 00	1
	Loss on Plant Assets				50 00								2
	Equipment—Office					750 00							3
June 29	Accum. Depr.—Office Equip.	R224			225 00							150 00	4
	Equipment—Office					300 00							5
	Gain on Plant Assets					75 00							6
													7
													8
													9

[1]

CASH PAYMENTS JOURNAL

PAGE 40

				1 GENERAL	2 GENERAL	3 ACCOUNTS PAYABLE	4 PURCHASES DISCOUNT	5 CASH	
DATE	ACCOUNT TITLE	CHECK NO.	POST. REF.	DEBIT	CREDIT	DEBIT	CREDIT	CREDIT	
1988 Jan. 2	Equipment—Office	122		1400 00				1400 00	1
July 2	Equipment—Office	239		550 00				50 00	2
	Accum. Depr.—Office Equipment				800 00				3
	Equipment—Office			750 00					4
									5
									6
									7
									8

[1]

PLANT ASSET RECORD   Use __Office__

Description __Filing Cabinet__

Date Bought __June 28, 1979__	Serial Number __FC125__	Original Cost __$300.00__
Estimated Useful Life __10 years__	Estimated Salvage Value __$50.00__	Annual Depreciation __$25.00__

Disposed of: Discarded _____   Sold __✔__   Traded _____
Date __June 29, 1988__   Book Value __$75.00__

Year	Beginning Book Value	Annual Depreciation Expense	Accumulated Depreciation	Ending Book Value
1979	$300.00	$12.50	$ 12.50	$287.50
1980	287.50	25.00	37.50	262.50
1981	262.50	25.00	62.50	237.50
1982	237.50	25.00	87.50	212.50
1983	212.50	25.00	112.50	187.50
1984	187.50	25.00	137.50	162.50
1985	162.50	25.00	162.50	137.50
1986	137.50	25.00	187.50	112.50
1987	112.50	25.00	212.50	87.50
1988	*87.50*	*12.50*	*225.00*	*75.00*

Continue record on back of card

PLANT ASSET RECORD   Use __Office__

Description __Typewriter__

Date Bought __Apr. 6, 1982__	Serial Number __TM48194H32__	Original Cost __$750.00__
Estimated Useful Life __6 years__	Estimated Salvage Value __$150.00__	Annual Depreciation __$100.00__

Disposed of: Discarded _____   Sold __✔__   Traded _____
Date __Mar. 30, 1988__   Book Value __$150.00__

Year	Beginning Book Value	Annual Depreciation Expense	Accumulated Depreciation	Ending Book Value
1982	$750.00	$ 75.00	$ 75.00	$675.00
1983	675.00	100.00	175.00	575.00
1984	575.00	100.00	275.00	475.00
1985	475.00	100.00	375.00	375.00
1986	375.00	100.00	475.00	275.00
1987	275.00	100.00	575.00	175.00
1988	*175.00*	*25.00*	*600.00*	*150.00*

PLANT ASSET RECORD   Use _Office_

Description _Desk_

Date Bought _Jan. 5, 1983_	Serial Number _D3481_	Original Cost _$520.00_	
Estimated Useful Life _5 years_	Estimated Salvage Value _$120.00_	Annual Depreciation _$80.00_	

Disposed of: Discarded ✔   Sold _____   Traded _____

Date _____ *Jan. 2, 1988* _____ Book Value _____ *$120.00* _____

Year	Beginning Book Value	Annual Depreciation Expense	Accumulated Depreciation	Ending Book Value
1983	$520.00	$80.00	$ 80.00	$440.00
1984	440.00	80.00	160.00	360.00
1985	360.00	80.00	240.00	280.00
1986	280.00	80.00	320.00	200.00
1987	200.00	80.00	400.00	120.00

PLANT ASSET RECORD   Use _Office_

Description _Table_

Date Bought _Mar. 29, 1983_	Serial Number _T3929_	Original Cost _$350.00_	
Estimated Useful Life _5 years_	Estimated Salvage Value _$50.00_	Annual Depreciation _$60.00_	

Disposed of: Discarded ✔   Sold _____   Traded _____

Date _____ *Mar. 29, 1988* _____ Book Value _____ *$50.00* _____

Year	Beginning Book Value	Annual Depreciation Expense	Accumulated Depreciation	Ending Book Value
1983	$350.00	$45.00	$ 45.00	$305.00
1984	305.00	60.00	105.00	245.00
1985	245.00	60.00	165.00	185.00
1986	185.00	60.00	225.00	125.00
1987	125.00	60.00	285.00	65.00
1988	*65.00*	*15.00*	*300.00*	*50.00*

PLANT ASSET RECORD   Use _Office_

Description _Copying Machine_

| Date Bought | July 1, 1983 | Serial Number | C56M203 | Original Cost | $800.00 |

| Estimated Useful Life | 5 years | Estimated Salvage Value | $50.00 | Annual Depreciation | $150.00 |

Disposed of: Discarded _____   Sold _____   Traded ✔

Date _____ *July 2, 1988* _____   Book Value _____ *$50.00*

Year	Beginning Book Value	Annual Depreciation Expense	Accumulated Depreciation	Ending Book Value
1983	$800.00	$ 75.00	$ 75.00	$725.00
1984	725.00	150.00	225.00	575.00
1985	575.00	150.00	375.00	425.00
1986	425.00	150.00	525.00	275.00
1987	275.00	150.00	675.00	125.00
1988	*125.00*	*75.00*	*750.00*	*50.00*

PLANT ASSET RECORD   Use *Office*

Description *Typewriter*

| Date Bought | *Jan. 2, 1988* | Serial Number | *SD345J267* | Original Cost | *$1,400.00* |

| Estimated Useful Life | *5 years* | Estimated Salvage Value | *$400.00* | Annual Depreciation | *$200.00* |

Disposed of: Discarded _____   Sold _____   Traded _____

Date _____   Book Value _____

Year	Beginning Book Value	Annual Depreciation Expense	Accumulated Depreciation	Ending Book Value

PLANT ASSET RECORD   Use _Office_

Description _Copying Machine_

| Date Bought | _July 2, 1988_ | Serial Number | _C35194_ | Original Cost | _$550.00_ |
| Estimated Useful Life | _5 years_ | Estimated Salvage Value | _$100.00_ | Annual Depreciation | _$90.00_ |

Disposed of: Discarded _____   Sold _____   Traded _____
Date _____ Book Value _____

Year	Beginning Book Value	Annual Depreciation Expense	Accumulated Depreciation	Ending Book Value

Continue record on back of card

Recording transactions for plant assets

GENERAL JOURNAL   PAGE 2

	DATE		ACCOUNT TITLE	POST. REF.	DEBIT	CREDIT	
1	1987 July	1	Depreciation Expense — Office Equipment		9 00		1
2			Accum. Depr. — Office Equipment			9 00	2
3			M66				3
4		1	Accum. Depr. — Office Equipment		3 6 00		4
5			Loss on Plant Assets		6 4 00		5
6			Equipment — Office			1 0 0 00	6
7			M66				7
8	Sept.	1	Depreciation Expense — Delivery Equipment		1 2 0 0 00		8
9			Accum. Depr. — Delivery Equipment			1 2 0 0 00	9
10			M70				10
11	Dec.	31	Depreciation Expense — Office Equipment		7 0 00		11
12			Accum. Depr. — Office Equipment			7 0 00	12
13			M81				13
14							14
15							15
16							16
17							17
18							18
19							19
20							20
21							21
22							22
23							23
24							24
25							25
26							26
27							27
28							28
29							29
30							30
31							31
32							32

CASH RECEIPTS JOURNAL

PAGE 3

	DATE	ACCOUNT TITLE	DOC. NO.	POST. REF.	GENERAL DEBIT	GENERAL CREDIT	ACCOUNTS RECEIVABLE CREDIT	SALES CREDIT	SALES TAX PAYABLE DEBIT	SALES TAX PAYABLE CREDIT	SALES DISCOUNT DEBIT	CASH DEBIT
1	1987 Dec. 31	Accum. Depr.—Office Equip.	R146		1 9 8 33							3 5 0 00
2		Gain on Plant Assets				4 8 33						
3		Equipment—Office				5 0 0 00						
4												
5												

CASH PAYMENTS JOURNAL

PAGE 4

	DATE	ACCOUNT TITLE	CHECK NO.	POST. REF.	GENERAL DEBIT	GENERAL CREDIT	ACCOUNTS PAYABLE DEBIT	PURCHASES DISCOUNT CREDIT	CASH CREDIT
1	1985 Jan. 3	Equipment—Office	130		5 0 0 00				5 0 0 00
2	Mar. 1	Equipment—Office	190		5 0 0 00				5 0 0 00
3	June 30	Equipment—Office	200		1 0 0 00				1 0 0 00
4	July 1	Equipment—Delivery	220		1 0 0 0 00				1 0 0 0 00
5	1987 Jan. 2	Equipment—Office	300		7 0 0 00				3 0 0 00
6		Accum. Depr.—Office Equipment			1 0 0 00	5 0 0 00			
7		Equipment—Office			1 1 1 0 00				5 0 0 00
8	Sept. 1	Equipment—Delivery	310		3 9 0 00				
9		Accum. Depr.—Delivery Equipment				1 0 0 0 0 00			
10		Equipment—Delivery							
11									
12									

Perfect Score. 51

Deduct .... __

Your Score .... __

Name _____

Date _____ Class _____

Checked by _____

STUDY
GUIDE
11

DIRECTIONS: Place a check mark in the proper Answers column to show whether each of the following statements is true or false.

| | Answers | | For |
	True	False	Scoring
0. Showing in accounting records all information needed to prepare a business' financial statements is an application of the accounting concept Adequate Disclosure	✔		**0.** ✔
1. When a note payable is issued for cash, Cash is debited and Notes Payable is credited	✔		**1.**
2. The length of time to maturity of a note may be expressed in months or in days	✔		**2.**
3. When a note's time is expressed in months, the time from a date in one month to the same date in the next month is counted as one month	✔		**3.**
4. When a note's time is expressed in days, the time from a date in one month to the same date in the next month is counted as 30 days......................		✔	**4.**
5. Reporting as expenses only that portion of prepaid expenses that has been used in the current fiscal period is an application of the accounting concept Historical Cost..		✔	**5.**
6. An adjusting entry is made at the end of a fiscal period to separate and record the asset and expense portions of prepaid supplies and insurance expenses	✔		**6.**
7. After adjusting entries are recorded and posted, the interest expense account balance includes all interest received or paid for the fiscal period..............		✔	**7.**
8. Recording accrued payroll is an application of the accounting concept Matching Expenses with Revenue	✔		**8.**
9. An adjusting entry for employer's payroll taxes is not made at the end of a fiscal period because the accrued payroll has not been paid yet.................		✔	**9.**
10. An adjusting entry for accrued employees' federal income taxes is made at the end of a fiscal period		✔	**10.**
11. If reversing entries are not made, some interest expense might be reported twice...	✔		**11.**
12. A reversing entry is usually just the opposite of the adjusting entry made to the same accounts...	✔		**12.**
13. When a note payable is discounted, interest is recorded on the note's maturity date		✔	**13.**

DIRECTIONS: Select the one term in Column I that best fits each definition in Column II. Print the letter identifying your choice in the Answers column.

Column I

A. accrued expenses
B. bank discount
C. date of a note
D. discounted note
E. interest
F. interest rate of a note
G. maturity date of a note
H. note payable
I. prepaid expenses
J. principal of a note
K. proceeds
L. promissory note
M. reversing entry

Column II

		Answers	For Scoring
0.	A written and signed promise to pay a sum of money ...	L	0. ✔
14.	A promissory note that a business issues to a creditor ...	H	14.
15.	The day a note is issued	C	15.
16.	The original amount of a note	J	16.
17.	The date a note is due	G	17.
18.	An amount paid for the use of money	E	18.
19.	The percentage of the principal that is paid for the use of the money	F	19.
20.	A note on which interest is paid in advance	D	20.
21.	Interest collected in advance on a note	B	21.
22.	The amount received for a note after the bank discount has been deducted	K	22.
23.	Expenses paid in one fiscal period but not reported as expenses until a later fiscal period	I	23.
24.	An entry made at the beginning of one fiscal period to reverse an adjusting entry made in the previous fiscal period	M	24.
25.	Expenses incurred in one fiscal period but not paid until a later fiscal period	A	25.

DIRECTIONS: For each transaction below, print in the proper Answers columns the identifying letter of the accounts to be debited and credited.

Account Titles

A. Cash
B. FICA Tax Payable
C. Insurance Expense
D. Interest Expense
E. Interest Payable
F. Notes Payable
G. Payroll Taxes Expense
H. Prepaid Insurance
I. Salary Expense
J. Salaries Payable
K. Supplies — Sales
L. Supplies Expense — Sales
M. Unemployment Tax Payable — Federal
N. Unemployment Tax Payable — State

Transactions

		Answers Debit	Answers Credit	For Scoring Debit	For Scoring Credit
0–0.	Issued a 3-month note to the bank for cash	A	F	0. ✔	0. ✔
26–27.	Issued a 60-day note to the bank for cash	A	F	26.	27.
28–29.	Paid bank for a note plus interest	D, F	A	28.	29.
30–31.	Discounted at the bank a 30-day note	A, D	F	30.	31.
32–33.	Adjusting entry for accrued payroll	I	J	32.	33.
34–35.	Adjusting entry for accrued payroll taxes	G	B, M, N	34.	35.
36–37.	Reversing entry for accrued payroll	J	I	36.	37.
38–39.	Reversing entry for accrued payroll taxes	B, M, N	G	38.	39.
Prepaid items recorded initially as expenses:					
40–41.	Adjusting entry for sales supplies	K	L	40.	41.
42–43.	Adjusting entry for prepaid insurance	H	C	42.	43.
44–45.	Adjusting entry for prepaid interest	E	D	44.	45.
46–47.	Reversing entry for sales supplies	L	K	46.	47.
48–49.	Reversing entry for prepaid insurance	C	H	48.	49.
50–51.	Reversing entry for prepaid interest	D	E	50.	51.

Recording the issuing, discounting, and paying of notes payable   [3]

CASH RECEIPTS JOURNAL

PAGE 8

| | | | | 1 | 2 | 3 | 4 | 5 | 6 | 7 | 8 |
| | | | | GENERAL | | ACCOUNTS RECEIVABLE CREDIT | SALES CREDIT | SALES TAX PAYABLE | | SALES DISCOUNT DEBIT | CASH DEBIT |
DATE	ACCOUNT TITLE	DOC. NO.	POST. REF.	DEBIT	CREDIT			DEBIT	CREDIT		
19-- Aug. 1	Notes Payable	NP1			1000 00						1000 00
Sept. 2	Interest Expense	NP2		16 44							983 56
	Notes Payable				1000 00						
Oct. 1	Notes Payable	NP3			500 00						500 00

[4]

CASH PAYMENTS JOURNAL

PAGE 10

| | | | | 1 | 2 | 3 | 4 | 5 |
| | | | | GENERAL | | ACCOUNTS PAYABLE DEBIT | PURCHASES DISCOUNT CREDIT | CASH CREDIT |
DATE	ACCOUNT TITLE	CHECK NO.	POST. REF.	DEBIT	CREDIT			
19-- Nov. 1	Notes Payable	45		1000 00				1025 00
	Interest Expense			25 00				
1	Notes Payable	52		1000 00				1000 00
30	Notes Payable	59		500 00				508 22
	Interest Expense			8 22				

[1]

Note	Maturity Date
1	November 1
2	November 1
3	November 30

[2]

Note	Interest at Maturity
1	$25.00
2	None—Paid in advance
3	$8.22

Recording adjusting entries and reversing entries for
prepaid expenses recorded initially as expenses

PROBLEM 11-2, p. 248
[1, 2]

GENERAL JOURNAL

PAGE 10

	DATE		ACCOUNT TITLE	POST. REF.	DEBIT	CREDIT	
1			*Adjusting Entries*				1
2	¹⁹⁻⁻ Dec.	31	Supplies—Sales		8 70 00		2
3			Supplies Expense—Sales			8 70 00	3
4		31	Supplies—Administrative		2 50 00		4
5			Supplies Expense—Administrative			2 50 00	5
6		31	Prepaid Insurance		7 20 00		6
7			Insurance Expense			7 20 00	7
8		31	Prepaid Interest		8 22		8
9			Interest Expense			8 22	9
10							10
11							11
12							12
13							13
14							14

[3]

GENERAL JOURNAL

PAGE 1

	DATE		ACCOUNT TITLE	POST. REF.	DEBIT	CREDIT	
1			*Reversing Entries*				1
2	¹⁹⁻⁻ Jan.	1	Supplies Expense—Sales		8 70 00		2
3			Supplies—Sales			8 70 00	3
4		1	Supplies Expense—Administrative		2 50 00		4
5			Supplies—Administrative			2 50 00	5
6		1	Insurance Expense		7 20 00		6
7			Prepaid Insurance			7 20 00	7
8		1	Interest Expense		8 22		8
9			Prepaid Interest			8 22	9
10							10
11							11
12							12
13							13
14							14

[1]

Recording adjusting and reversing entries for accrued expenses

GENERAL JOURNAL

PAGE 8

	DATE		ACCOUNT TITLE	POST. REF.	DEBIT	CREDIT	
1			*Adjusting Entries*				1
2	19-- Dec.	31	Interest Expense		4 15		2
3			Interest Payable			4 15	3
4		31	Salary Expense—Sales		4 0 0 00		4
5			Salary Expense—Administrative		5 0 0 00		5
6			Salaries Payable			9 0 0 00	6
7		31	Payroll Taxes Expense		1 1 8 80		7
8			FICA Tax Payable			6 3 00	8
9			Unemployment Tax Payable—Federal			7 20	9
10			Unemployment Tax Payable—State			4 8 60	10
11		31	Federal Income Tax		1 0 0 0 00		11
12			Federal Income Tax Payable			1 0 0 0 00	12
13							13

[2]

GENERAL JOURNAL

PAGE 1

	DATE		ACCOUNT TITLE	POST. REF.	DEBIT	CREDIT	
1			*Reversing Entries*				1
2	19-- Jan.	1	Interest Payable		4 15		2
3			Interest Expense			4 15	3
4		1	Salaries Payable		9 0 0 00		4
5			Salary Expense—Sales			4 0 0 00	5
6			Salary Expense—Administrative			5 0 0 00	6
7		1	FICA Tax Payable		6 3 00		7
8			Unemployment Tax Payable—Federal		7 20		8
9			Unemployment Tax Payable—State		4 8 60		9
10			Payroll Taxes Expense			1 1 8 80	10
11		1	Federal Income Tax Payable		1 0 0 0 00		11
12			Federal Income Tax			1 0 0 0 00	12
13							13

Recording adjusting and reversing entries for prepaid expenses recorded initially as expenses and for accrued expenses [2]

CASH RECEIPTS JOURNAL

PAGE 4

	DATE	ACCOUNT TITLE	DOC. NO.	POST. REF.	GENERAL DEBIT	GENERAL CREDIT	ACCOUNTS RECEIVABLE CREDIT	SALES CREDIT	SALES TAX PAYABLE DEBIT	SALES TAX PAYABLE CREDIT	SALES DISCOUNT DEBIT	CASH DEBIT	
1	19-- July 1	Notes Payable	NP1			5 0 0 00						5 0 0 00	1
2	Oct. 31	Notes Payable	NP2			1 0 0 0 00						1 0 0 0 00	2
3	Nov. 1	Notes Payable	NP3			1 5 0 0 00						1 5 0 0 00	3
4	Dec. 1	Interest Expense	NP4		1 3 15							7 8 6 85	4
5		Notes Payable				8 0 0 00							5
6													6
7													7

[2]

CASH PAYMENTS JOURNAL

PAGE 5

	DATE	ACCOUNT TITLE	CHECK NO.	POST. REF.	GENERAL DEBIT	GENERAL CREDIT	ACCOUNTS PAYABLE DEBIT	PURCHASES DISCOUNT CREDIT	CASH CREDIT	
1	19-- Sept. 1	Notes Payable	105		5 0 0 00				5 1 2 50	1
2		Interest Expense			1 2 50					2
3										3

[1]

Note	Maturity Date
2	January 31
3	January 30
4	January 30

GENERAL JOURNAL

PAGE 3

	DATE		ACCOUNT TITLE	POST. REF.	DEBIT	CREDIT	
1			*Adjusting Entries*				1
2	Dec. 19--	31	Supplies—Sales		2 00 00		2
3			Supplies Expense—Sales			2 00 00	3
4		31	Supplies—Administrative		1 00 00		4
5			Supplies Expense—Administrative			1 00 00	5
6		31	Prepaid Insurance		2 50 00		6
7			Insurance Expense			2 50 00	7
8		31	Prepaid Interest		6 58		8
9			Interest Expense			6 58	9
10		31	Interest Expense		4 1 33		10
11			Interest Payable			4 1 33	11
12		31	Salary Expense—Sales		3 15 00		12
13			Salary Expense—Administrative		2 50 00		13
14			Salaries Payable			5 65 00	14
15		31	Payroll Taxes Expense		7 9 12		15
16			FICA Tax Payable			3 9 55	16
17			Unemployment Tax Payable—Federal			2 83	17
18			Unemployment Tax Payable—State			3 6 74	18
19		31	Federal Income Tax		7 00 00		19
20			Federal Income Tax Payable			7 00 00	20
21							21
22							22
23							23
24							24
25							25
26							26
27							27
28							28
29							29
30							30
31							31
32							32
33							33

GENERAL JOURNAL

	DATE		ACCOUNT TITLE	POST. REF.	DEBIT	CREDIT	
1			*Reversing Entries*				1
2	19-- Jan.	1	Supplies Expense — Sales		2 0 0 00		2
3			Supplies — Sales			2 0 0 00	3
4		1	Supplies Expense — Administrative		1 0 0 00		4
5			Supplies — Administrative			1 0 0 00	5
6		1	Insurance Expense		2 5 0 00		6
7			Prepaid Insurance			2 5 0 00	7
8		1	Interest Expense		6 58		8
9			Prepaid Interest			6 58	9
10		1	Interest Payable		4 1 33		10
11			Interest Expense			4 1 33	11
12		1	Salaries Payable		5 6 5 00		12
13			Salary Expense — Sales			3 1 5 00	13
14			Salary Expense — Administrative			2 5 0 00	14
15		1	FICA Tax Payable		3 9 55		15
16			Unemployment Tax Payable — Federal		2 83		16
17			Unemployment Tax Payable — State		3 6 74		17
18			Payroll Taxes Expense			7 9 12	18
19		1	Federal Income Tax Payable		7 0 0 00		19
20			Federal Income Tax			7 0 0 00	20
21							21
22							22
23							23
24							24
25							25
26							26
27							27
28							28
29							29
30							30
31							31
32							32
33							33

Recording adjusting entries for prepaid expenses
recorded initially as assets and adjusting and
reversing entries for accrued expenses

[1]

Note	Maturity Date
4	*March 30*
5	*February 28*

[2]

CASH RECEIPTS JOURNAL

PAGE 12

	DATE	ACCOUNT TITLE	DOC. NO.	POST. REF.	GENERAL DEBIT	GENERAL CREDIT	ACCOUNTS RECEIVABLE CREDIT	SALES CREDIT	SALES TAX PAYABLE DEBIT	SALES TAX PAYABLE CREDIT	SALES DISCOUNT DEBIT	CASH DEBIT	
1	19-- Aug. 1	Notes Payable	NP3			1 0 0 0 00						1 0 0 0 00	1
2	Sept. 30	Notes Payable	NP4			1 5 0 0 00						1 5 0 0 00	2
3	Nov. 30	Prepaid Interest	NP5		9 86							3 9 0 14	3
4		Notes Payable				4 0 0 00							4

[3]

GENERAL JOURNAL

PAGE 7

	DATE	ACCOUNT TITLE	POST. REF.	DEBIT	CREDIT	
1		***Adjusting Entries***				1
2	19-- Dec. 31	Supplies Expense—Sales		3 5 0 00		2
3		Supplies—Sales			3 5 0 00	3
4	31	Supplies Expense—Administrative		3 0 0 00		4
5		Supplies—Administrative			3 0 0 00	5
6	31	Insurance Expense		3 5 0 00		6
7		Prepaid Insurance			3 5 0 00	7
8	31	Interest Expense		2 8 40		8
9		Prepaid Interest			2 8 40	9
10	31	Interest Expense		4 5 37		10
11		Interest Payable			4 5 37	11
12	31	Salary Expense—Sales		4 2 5 00		12
13		Salary Expense—Administrative		3 5 5 00		13
14		Salaries Payable			7 8 0 00	14
15	31	Payroll Taxes Expense		1 0 2 18		15
16		FICA Tax Payable			5 4 60	16
17		Unemployment Tax Payable—Federal			3 90	17
18		Unemployment Tax Payable—State			4 3 68	18
19	31	Federal Income Tax		9 0 0 00		19
20		Federal Income Tax Payable			9 0 0 00	20

[2]

CASH PAYMENTS JOURNAL

PAGE 11

	DATE		ACCOUNT TITLE	CHECK NO.	POST. REF.	GENERAL DEBIT	GENERAL CREDIT	ACCOUNTS PAYABLE DEBIT	PURCHASES DISCOUNT CREDIT	CASH CREDIT	
1	19-- Nov.	1	Notes Payable	95		1 0 0 0 00				1 0 2 5 00	1
2			Interest Expense			2 5 00					2
3											3
4											4
5											5
6											6
7											7
8											8
9											9
10											10
11											11

[4]

GENERAL JOURNAL

PAGE 1

	DATE		ACCOUNT TITLE	POST. REF.	DEBIT	CREDIT	
1			*Reversing Entries*				1
2	19-- Jan.	1	Interest Payable		4 5 37		2
3			Interest Expense			4 5 37	3
4		1	Salaries Payable		7 8 0 00		4
5			Salary Expense — Sales			4 2 5 00	5
6			Salary Expense — Administrative			3 5 5 00	6
7		1	FICA Tax Payable		5 4 60		7
8			Unemployment Tax Payable — Federal		3 90		8
9			Unemployment Tax Payable — State		4 3 68		9
10			Payroll Taxes Expense			1 0 2 18	10
11		1	Federal Income Tax Payable		9 0 0 00		11
12			Federal Income Tax			9 0 0 00	12
13							13
14							14
15							15
16							16
17							17
18							18
19							19
20							20

Name _____

Deduct .... __   Date _____   Class _____

Your Score .... __   Checked by _____

DIRECTIONS: Select the one term in Column I that best fits each definition in Column II. Print the letter identifying your choice in the Answers column.

Column I	Column II	Answers	For Scoring
A accrued revenue B. dishonored note C. notes receivable D. prepaid expenses E. unearned revenue	**0.** Expenses paid in one fiscal period but not reported as expenses until a later fiscal period	D	0. ✔
	1. Promissory notes that a business accepts from customers	C	1.
	2. A note that is not paid when due	B	2.
	3. Revenue received in one fiscal period but not earned until the next fiscal period	E	3.
	4. Revenue earned in one fiscal period but not received until a later fiscal period	A	4.

DIRECTIONS: For each transaction below, print in the proper Answers column the identifying letters of the accounts to be debited and credited.

Account Titles	Transactions	Answers Debit	Answers Credit	For Scoring Debit	For Scoring Credit
A. Accounts Receivable B. Cash C. FICA Tax Payable D. Interest Income E. Interest Receivable F. Notes Receivable G. Rent Income H. Unearned Rent	**0–0.** Accepted a 30-day, 10% note as extension of time to pay	F	A	0. ✔	0. ✔
	5–6. A note receivable is dishonored	A	D,F	5.	6.
	7–8. Received cash in payment of a note receivable	B	D,F	7.	8.
	9–10. Received cash for a previously dishonored note receivable	B	A,D	9.	10.
	Unearned revenue recorded initially as revenue:				
	11–12. Received cash for rent in advance	B	G	11.	12.
13–14. Adjusting entry for unearned rent income		G	H	13.	14.
15–16. Reversing entry for unearned rent income		H	G	15.	16.
Accrued revenue:					
17–18. Adjusting entry for accrued interest income..............................		E	D	17.	18.
19–20. Reversing entry for accrued interest income		D	E	19.	20.

DIRECTIONS: For each item below, select the choice that best completes the sentence. Print the letter identifying your choice in the Answers column.

	Answers	For Scoring

0. Rent received in advance is a liability until the rented space is actually (**A**) paid for   (**B**) used   (**C**) rented   (**D**) none of these.......................... — B — 0. ✔

21. At the end of a fiscal period, a business must show how much rent received in advance has become   (**A**) an expense   (**B**) a revenue   (**C**) an asset (**D**) none of these .... — B — 21.

22. When a business actually receives cash in advance for rent, the amount is recorded as   (**A**) a liability   (**B**) a revenue   (**C**) either a liability or a revenue (**D**) none of these .... — C — 22.

23. When a business actually receives cash in advance for rent, and records unearned income initially as revenue, the account credited is   (**A**) Cash   (**B**) Rent Income   (**C**) Notes Receivable   (**D**) none of these..................... — B — 23.

24. Recording an adjusting entry for accrued interest income is an application of the accounting concept   (**A**) Objective Evidence   (**B**) Historical Cost (**C**) Consistent Reporting   (**D**) Matching Expenses with Revenue..................... — D — 24.

25. When unearned revenue is recorded initially as a liability, the accounts affected by an entry for receipt of rent income in advance are   (**A**) Cash debit; Rent Income credit   (**B**) Cash debit; Unearned Rent credit   (**C**) Cash debit; Unearned Rent debit   (**D**) Rent Income debit; Unearned Rent credit..................... — B — 25.

26. The maturity date of a 60-day note receivable issued on December 27 is (**A**) February 27   (**B**) February 26   (**C**) February 25   (**D**) none of these.... — C — 26.

27. The interest on a 3-month, 10%, $1,000.00 note receivable is   (**A**) $25.00 (**B**) $100.00   (**C**) $24.66   (**D**) none of these.......................... — A — 27.

28. The interest on a 90-day, 10%, $2,000.00 note receivable is   (**A**) $50.00 (**B**) $200.00   (**C**) $49.32   (**D**) none of these.......................... — C — 28.

Recording entries for notes receivable

GENERAL JOURNAL PAGE 1

	DATE		ACCOUNT TITLE	POST. REF.	DEBIT	CREDIT	
1	19-- Aug.	1	Notes Receivable		100 00		1
2			Accounts Receivable/Moses Williams			100 00	2
3			NR1				3
4		1	Notes Receivable		200 00		4
5			Accounts Receivable/Gary Byrd			200 00	5
6			NR2				6
7	Sept.	30	Accounts Receivable/Moses Williams		101 64		7
8			Notes Receivable			100 00	8
9			Interest Income			1 64	9
10			M12				10
11	Oct.	1	Notes Receivable		500 00		11
12			Accounts Receivable/Melinda Cruz			500 00	12
13			NR3				13

CASH RECEIPTS JOURNAL PAGE 3

	DATE		ACCOUNT TITLE	DOC. NO.	POST. REF.	GENERAL DEBIT	GENERAL CREDIT	ACCOUNTS RECEIVABLE CREDIT	SALES CREDIT	SALES TAX PAYABLE DEBIT	SALES TAX PAYABLE CREDIT	SALES DISCOUNT DEBIT	CASH DEBIT	
						1	2	3	4	5	6	7	8	
1	19-- Oct.	1	Notes Receivable	R10			200 00						204 00	1
2			Interest Income				4 00							2
3	Dec.	1	Moses Williams	R32				101 64					103 37	3
4			Interest Income				1 73							4
5		1	Notes Receivable	R33			500 00						508 33	5
6			Interest Income				8 33							6

Recording adjusting and reversing entries for unearned revenue

PROBLEM 12-2, p. 262
[1, 2]

GENERAL JOURNAL   PAGE 4

	DATE		ACCOUNT TITLE	POST. REF.	DEBIT	CREDIT	
1			*Adjusting Entry*				1
2	19-- Dec.	31	Rent Income		2 000 00		2
3			Unearned Rent			2 000 00	3
4			*Reversing Entry*				4
5	19-- Jan.	1	Unearned Rent		2 000 00		5
6			Rent Income			2 000 00	6
7							7

Recording adjusting and reversing entries for accrued revenue

PROBLEM 12-3, p. 262
[2, 3]

GENERAL JOURNAL   PAGE 1

	DATE		ACCOUNT TITLE	POST. REF.	DEBIT	CREDIT	
1			*Adjusting Entry*				1
2	19-- Dec.	31	Interest Receivable		3 28		2
3			Interest Income			3 28	3
4			*Reversing Entry*				4
5	19-- Jan.	1	Interest Income		3 28		5
6			Interest Receivable			3 28	6
7							7

[1]

Note #	Accrued Interest Receivable
1	*$1.64*
2	*1.64*
Total	*$3.28*

Recording entries for notes receivable, unearned revenue, and accrued revenue

GENERAL JOURNAL

PAGE 3

	DATE		ACCOUNT TITLE	POST. REF.	DEBIT	CREDIT	
1	19-- July	1	*Notes Receivable*		2 0 0 00		1
2			*Accounts Receivable/Thomas Carlson*	╱		2 0 0 00	2
3			*NR12*				3
4		5	*Notes Receivable*		2 0 0 00		4
5			*Accounts Receivable/John Westmore*	╱		2 0 0 00	5
6			*NR13*				6
7	Sept.	29	*Accounts Receivable/Thomas Carlson*	╱	2 0 4 93		7
8			*Notes Receivable*			2 0 0 00	8
9			*Interest Income*			4 93	9
10			*M32*				10
11			*Adjusting Entries*				11
12	Dec.	31	*Interest Receivable*		1 0 24		12
13			*Interest Income*			1 0 24	13
14		31	*Rent Income*		4 0 0 00		14
15			*Unearned Rent*			4 0 0 00	15

[1]

CASH RECEIPTS JOURNAL

PAGE 4

	DATE	ACCOUNT TITLE	DOC. NO.	POST. REF.	GENERAL DEBIT	GENERAL CREDIT	ACCOUNTS RECEIVABLE CREDIT	SALES CREDIT	SALES TAX PAYABLE DEBIT	SALES TAX PAYABLE CREDIT	SALES DISCOUNT DEBIT	CASH DEBIT	
1	19-- Oct. 5	Notes Receivable	R65			2 0 0 00						2 0 6 00	1
2		Interest Income				6 00							2
3	Nov. 1	Rent Income	R70			1 2 0 0 00						1 2 0 0 00	3
4	Dec. 1	Thomas Carlson	R81				2 0 4 93					2 0 8 47	4
5		Interest Income				3 54							5

[3]

GENERAL JOURNAL

PAGE 4

	DATE		ACCOUNT TITLE	POST. REF.	DEBIT	CREDIT	
1			*Reversing Entries*				1
2	19-- Jan.	1	*Interest Income*		1 0 24		2
3			*Interest Receivable*			1 0 24	3
4		1	*Unearned Rent*		4 0 0 00		4
5			*Rent Income*			4 0 0 00	5

Recording entries for notes receivable, unearned revenue, and accrued revenue

CHALLENGE PROBLEM 12-C, p. 263
[1, 2]

GENERAL JOURNAL

PAGE 4

	DATE		ACCOUNT TITLE	POST. REF.	DEBIT	CREDIT	
1	19-- July	1	Notes Receivable		4 0 0 00		1
2			Accounts Receivable/Susan Bradley	/		4 0 0 00	2
3			NR26				3
4	Aug.	1	Notes Receivable		5 0 0 00		4
5			Accounts Receivable/Donald Murdock	/		5 0 0 00	5
6			NR27				6
7	Sept.	29	Accounts Receivable/Susan Bradley	/	4 1 3 81		7
8			Notes Receivable			4 0 0 00	8
9			Interest Income			1 3 81	9
10			M45				10
11	Dec.	1	Notes Receivable		3 0 0 00		11
12			Accounts Receivable/Janet Vincent	/		3 0 0 00	12
13			NR28				13
14			*Adjusting Entries*				14
15	Dec.	31	Interest Receivable		2 47		15
16			Interest Income			2 47	16
17		31	Rent Income		1 4 0 0 00		17
18			Unearned Rent			1 4 0 0 00	18
19							19
20							20
21							21
22							22
23							23
24							24
25							25
26							26
27							27
28							28
29							29
30							30
31							31
32							32
33							33

[1]

CASH RECEIPTS JOURNAL
PAGE 7

DATE	ACCOUNT TITLE	DOC. NO.	POST. REF.	GENERAL DEBIT	GENERAL CREDIT	ACCOUNTS RECEIVABLE CREDIT	SALES CREDIT	SALES TAX PAYABLE DEBIT	SALES TAX PAYABLE CREDIT	SALES DISCOUNT DEBIT	CASH DEBIT	
19-- Sept. 30	Notes Receivable	R70			5 0 0 00						5 0 9 86	1
	Interest Income				9 86							2
Nov. 15	Susan Bradley	R85				4 1 3 81					4 2 1 27	3
	Interest Income				7 46							4
Dec. 31	Rent Income	R97			2 1 0 0 00						2 1 0 0 00	5
												6
												7
												8
												9

[3]

GENERAL JOURNAL
PAGE 5

DATE	ACCOUNT TITLE	POST. REF.	DEBIT	CREDIT	
	Reversing Entries				1
19-- Jan. 1	Interest Income		2 47		2
	Interest Receivable			2 47	3
1	Unearned Rent		1400 00		4
	Rent Income			1400 00	5
					6
					7
					8
					9

Extra Form

GENERAL JOURNAL

PAGE

	DATE		ACCOUNT TITLE	POST. REF.	DEBIT	CREDIT	
1							1
2							2
3							3
4							4
5							5
6							6
7							7
8							8
9							9
10							10
11							11
12							12
13							13
14							14
15							15
16							16
17							17
18							18
19							19
20							20
21							21
22							22
23							23
24							24
25							25
26							26
27							27
28							28
29							29
30							30
31							31
32							32
33							33
34							34

Perfect Score. 36

Deduct .... __

Your Score .... __

Name _____

Date _____ Class _____

Checked by _____

STUDY GUIDE 13

UNIT A—Identifying Accounting Terms

DIRECTIONS: Select the one term in Column I that best fits each definition in Column II. Print the letter identifying your choice in the Answers column.

Column I	Column II	Answers	For Scoring
A. articles of incorporation	0. An owner of one or more shares of a corporation	R	0. ✔
B. board of directors	1. A group of persons elected by the stockholders to manage a corporation...	B	1.
C. charter	2. A written application requesting permission to form a corporation	A	2.
D. common stock	3. The approved articles of incorporation......................	C	3.
E. cumulative preferred stock	4. Stock that does not give stockholders any special preferences	D	4.
F. dividends	5. A value assigned to a share of stock and printed on the stock certificate..	L	5.
G. intangible assets	6. A share of stock that has an authorized value printed on the stock certificate...	N	6.
H. noncumulative preferred stock	7. A share of stock that has no authorized value printed on the stock certificate...	J	7.
I. nonparticipating preferred stock	8. No-par-value stock that is assigned a value by a corporation	P	8.
J. no-par-value stock	9. Earnings distributed to stockholders	F	9.
K. organization costs	10. Stock that gives stockholders preference in earnings and other rights...	O	10.
L. par value			
M. participating preferred stock	11. Preferred stock with a provision that unpaid dividends will accumulate from one year to another	E	11.
N. par-value stock			
O. preferred stock			
P. stated-value stock			
Q. stock certificate			
R. stockholder			
S. subscribing for capital stock			

12. Preferred stock for which unpaid dividends do not accumulate from one year to another .... | H | 12. |

13. Preferred stock with a right to share with common stock in dividends above a stated percentage or amount.. | M | 13. |

14. Preferred stock with no right to share with common stock in dividends above a stated percentage or amount.. | I | 14. |

15. Written evidence of the number of shares each stockholder owns in a corporation..... | Q | 15. |

16. Entering into an agreement with a corporation to buy capital stock and pay at a later date... | S | 16. |

17. Fees and other expenses of organizing a corporation.. | K | 17. |

18. Assets of a nonphysical nature that have value for a business............................. | G | 18. |

12.	H	12.
13.	M	13.
14.	I	14.
15.	Q	15.
16.	S	16.
17.	K	17.
18.	G	18.

UNIT B—Analyzing Transactions for Starting a Corporation

DIRECTIONS: For each transaction below, print in the proper Answers columns the identifying letters of the accounts to be debited and credited.

Account Titles

A. Capital Stock—Common
B. Capital Stock—Preferred
C. Cash
D. Interest Expense
E. Organization Costs
F. Organization Expense
G. Stock Subscribed—Common
H. Stock Subscribed—Preferred
I. Subscriptions Receivable

Transactions

0–0. Received subscription for preferred stock ....

19–20. Received cash from subscribers in part payment of preferred stock subscription ....

21–22. Paid cash for reimbursement of organization costs ....

23–24. Received cash from incorporators in full payment for common stock ....

25–26. Issued stock certificate to subscriber for common stock ....

Answers		For Scoring	
Debit	Credit	Debit	Credit
I	H	0. ✔	0. ✔
C	I	19.	20.
E	C	21.	22.
C	A	23.	24.
G	A	25.	26.

UNIT C—Analyzing Procedures and Concepts for Starting a Corporation

DIRECTIONS: Place a check mark in the proper Answers column to show whether each of the following statements is true or false.

		Answers		For Scoring
		True	False	
0.	A board of directors determines corporate policies	✔		0. ✔
27.	A board of directors handles day-to-day corporate management		✔	27.
28.	An application to start a new corporation is submitted to designated officials of the state in which the corporation is to be formed	✔		28.
29.	One preference usually given to preferred stock is the right to vote in stockholder meetings		✔	29.
30.	A corporation, by law, must issue only one kind of stock, either common or preferred..		✔	30.
31.	Stated value is similar to par value in that both must be printed on stock certificates..		✔	31.
32.	When starting a corporation, the initial capital is obtained from selling stock to incorporators..	✔		32.
33.	A corporation is restricted to selling a number of shares of stock up to the amount authorized in the corporation's charter	✔		33.
34.	A stock certificate is issued to a stock subscriber as soon as the stock subscription is received		✔	34.
35.	Usually one of the incorporators agrees to pay organization costs until the corporation's charter is granted..	✔		35.
36.	Recording organization costs initially as an intangible asset and then charging a portion each year as an expense is an application of the accounting concept Matching Expenses with Revenue	✔		36.

Figuring dividends of corporations

Corp.	Year	Dividends		
		Total	**Preferred**	**Common**
A	1987	$50,000.00	$50,000.00	–0–
	1988	70,000.00	60,000.00	$10,000.00
	1989	90,000.00	60,000.00	30,000.00
B	1987	$50,000.00	$50,000.00	–0–
	1988	70,000.00	70,000.00	–0–
	1989	90,000.00	60,000.00	$30,000.00
C	1987	$50,000.00	$50,000.00	–0–
	1988	70,000.00	60,000.00	$10,000.00
	1989	90,000.00	67,500.00	22,500.00
D	1987	$50,000.00	$50,000.00	–0–
	1988	70,000.00	70,000.00	–0–
	1989	90,000.00	67,500.00	$22,500.00

$10 × 20,000 × 10% = $20,000 common dividend before participation
$100 × 6,000 × 10% = $60,000 required preferred dividend
Total value of outstanding stock = ($10 × 20,000) + ($100 × 6,000) = $800,000

1987: Total $50,000 preferred

1988: A—$60,000 preferred, balance common
B—$60,000 + 10,000 unpaid in 1987 = $70,000 preferred
C—Same as A
D—Same as B

1989: A—$60,000 preferred, balance common
B—Same as A
C—$90,000 − 60,000 − 20,000 = $10,000 participating
$10,000 ÷ 800,000 = .0125 participating rate
.0125 × $10 × 20,000 = $2,500 common
.0125 × $100 × 6,000 = $7,500 preferred
Common: $20,000 + 2,500 = $22,500
Preferred: $60,000 + 7,500 = $67,500
D—Same as C

Recording transactions for starting a corporation [1]

CASH RECEIPTS JOURNAL

PAGE 1

	DATE	ACCOUNT TITLE	DOC. NO.	POST. REF.	GENERAL DEBIT 1	GENERAL CREDIT 2	ACCOUNTS RECEIVABLE CREDIT 3	SALES CREDIT 4	SALES TAX PAYABLE DEBIT 5	SALES TAX PAYABLE CREDIT 6	SALES DISCOUNT DEBIT 7	CASH DEBIT 8	
1	19-- Jan. 2	Capital Stock—Common	R1-3			337 5 0 0 00						337 5 0 0 00	1
2	10	Subscriptions Receivable	R4			7 5 0 0 00						7 5 0 0 00	2
3													3
4													4
5													5
6													6
7													7

GENERAL JOURNAL

PAGE 1

	DATE	ACCOUNT TITLE	POST. REF.	DEBIT 1	CREDIT 2	
1	19-- Jan. 5	Subscriptions Receivable		7 5 0 0 00		1
2		Stock Subscribed—Common			7 5 0 0 00	2
3		M2				3
4	10	Stock Subscribed—Common		7 5 0 0 00		4
5		Capital Stock—Common			7 5 0 0 00	5
6		M3				6
7						7
8						8
9						9

Name _____ Date _____ Class _____

Recording transactions for starting a corporation

CASH RECEIPTS JOURNAL

PAGE 1

	DATE	ACCOUNT TITLE	DOC. NO.	POST. REF.	GENERAL DEBIT	GENERAL CREDIT	ACCOUNTS RECEIVABLE CREDIT	SALES CREDIT	SALES TAX PAYABLE DEBIT	SALES TAX PAYABLE CREDIT	SALES DISCOUNT DEBIT	CASH DEBIT	
1	19-- Jan. 3	Capital Stock — Common	R1-3			240 0 0 0 00						240 0 0 0 00	1
2	Feb. 1	Subscriptions Receivable	R4			6 0 0 0 00						6 0 0 0 00	2
3	1	Subscriptions Receivable	R5			50 0 0 0 00						50 0 0 0 00	3
4	Mar. 1	Subscriptions Receivable	R6			50 0 0 0 00						50 0 0 0 00	4
5													5
6													6
7													7
8													8

CASH PAYMENTS JOURNAL

PAGE 1

	DATE	ACCOUNT TITLE	CHECK NO.	POST. REF.	GENERAL DEBIT	GENERAL CREDIT	ACCOUNTS PAYABLE DEBIT	PURCHASES DISCOUNT CREDIT	CASH CREDIT	
1	19-- Jan. 3	Organization Costs	1		1 0 0 0 00				1 0 0 0 00	1
2										2
3										3
4										4
5										5
6										6

GENERAL JOURNAL

PAGE 1

	DATE	ACCOUNT TITLE	POST. REF.	DEBIT	CREDIT	
1	19-- Jan. 5	Subscriptions Receivable		6 0 0 0 00		1
2		Stock Subscribed — Common			6 0 0 0 00	2
3		M1				3
4	10	Subscriptions Receivable		100 0 0 0 00		4
5		Stock Subscribed — Common			100 0 0 0 00	5
6		M2				6
7	Feb. 1	Stock Subscribed — Common		6 0 0 0 00		7
8		Capital Stock — Common			6 0 0 0 00	8
9		M3				9
10	15	Subscriptions Receivable		3 0 0 0 00		10
11		Stock Subscribed — Common			3 0 0 0 00	11
12		M4				12
13	Mar. 1	Stock Subscribed — Common		100 0 0 0 00		13
14		Capital Stock — Common			100 0 0 0 00	14
15		M5				15
16						16

Welbourne Corporation

Balance Sheet

March 1, 19--

Assets																
Current Assets:																
Cash	345	0	0	0	00											
Subscriptions Receivable	3	0	0	0	00											
Total Current Assets						348	0	0	0	00						
Intangible Asset:																
Organization Costs						1	0	0	0	00						
Total Assets											349	0	0	0	00	
Stockholders' Equity																
Paid-in Capital:																
Capital Stock—Common (34,600 shares,																
$10.00 stated value)	346	0	0	0	00											
Stock Subscribed—Common (300 shares)	3	0	0	0	00											
Total Paid-in Capital						349	0	0	0	00						
Total Stockholders' Equity											349	0	0	0	00	

Recording transactions for starting a corporation

CASH RECEIPTS JOURNAL   PAGE 1

	DATE	ACCOUNT TITLE	DOC. NO.	POST. REF.	GENERAL DEBIT	GENERAL CREDIT	ACCOUNTS RECEIVABLE CREDIT	SALES CREDIT	SALES TAX PAYABLE DEBIT	SALES TAX PAYABLE CREDIT	SALES DISCOUNT DEBIT	CASH DEBIT	
1	19-- Aug. 2	Capital Stock — Common	R1-3			750 0 0 0 00						750 0 0 0 00	1
2	Sept. 10	Subscriptions Receivable	R4			7 5 0 0 00						7 5 0 0 00	2
3	Oct. 1	Subscriptions Receivable	R5			7 5 0 0 00						7 5 0 0 00	3
4	Nov. 1	Subscriptions Receivable	R6			7 5 0 0 00						7 5 0 0 00	4
5													5
6													6
7													7
8													8

CASH PAYMENTS JOURNAL   PAGE 1

	DATE	ACCOUNT TITLE	CHECK NO.	POST. REF.	GENERAL DEBIT	GENERAL CREDIT	ACCOUNTS PAYABLE DEBIT	PURCHASES DISCOUNT CREDIT	CASH CREDIT	
1	19-- Aug. 2	Organization Costs	1		1 5 0 0 00				1 5 0 0 00	1
2										2
3										3
4										4
5										5

GENERAL JOURNAL   PAGE 1

	DATE	ACCOUNT TITLE	POST. REF.	DEBIT	CREDIT	
1	19-- Aug. 6	Subscriptions Receivable		7 5 0 0 00		1
2		Stock Subscribed — Common			7 5 0 0 00	2
3		M1				3
4	21	Subscriptions Receivable		15 0 0 0 00		4
5		Stock Subscribed — Common			15 0 0 0 00	5
6		M2				6
7	Sept. 10	Stock Subscribed — Common		7 5 0 0 00		7
8		Capital Stock — Common			7 5 0 0 00	8
9		M3				9
10	Oct. 15	Subscriptions Receivable		30 0 0 0 00		10
11		Stock Subscribed — Common			30 0 0 0 00	11
12		M4				12
13	Nov. 1	Stock Subscribed — Common		15 0 0 0 00		13
14		Capital Stock — Common			15 0 0 0 00	14
15		M5				15
16						16

Bauyo, Inc.

Balance Sheet

November 2, 19--

Assets																
Current Assets:																
Cash	771	0	0	0	00											
Subscriptions Receivable	30	0	0	0	00											
Total Current Assets						801	0	0	0	00						
Intangible Asset:																
Organization Costs						1	5	0	0	00						
Total Assets											802	5	0	0	00	
Stockholders' Equity																
Paid-in Capital:																
Capital Stock—Common (51,500 shares,																
$15.00 stated value)	772	5	0	0	00											
Stock Subscribed—Common (2,000 shares)	30	0	0	0	00											
Total Paid-in Capital						802	5	0	0	00						
Total Stockholders' Equity											802	5	0	0	00	

[3]

Total Dividend $25,000.00
Less Preferred Stock ($100,000.00 × 10% rate) 10,000.00
***Equals** Common Stock dividend $15,000.00

*Common Stock dividend is less than 53,500 × $15.00 × 10% rate;
therefore there are no participating dividends.

Figuring dividends for a corporation   [1]

Year	Dividends					Year's Total Dividend
	Preferred			Common		
	Initial	Cumulative	Participating	Initial	Participating	
1984	$18,000.00	–0–	–0–	–0–	–0–	$18,000.00
1985	15,000.00	–0–	–0–	–0–	–0–	15,000.00
1986	18,000.00	$3,000.00	$2,000.00	$9,000.00	$1,000.00	33,000.00
1987	12,000.00	–0–	–0–	–0–	–0–	12,000.00
1988	17,000.00	–0–	–0–	–0–	–0–	17,000.00
1989	18,000.00	7,000.00	2,000.00	9,000.00	1,000.00	37,000.00

[2]

Year	Preferred				Common			
	Total Dividend	÷	Total Par Value	= %	Total Dividend	÷	Total Stated Value	= %
1984	$18,000.00		$200,000.00	9.0%	–0–		$100,000.00	0.0%
1985	15,000.00		200,000.00	7.5%	–0–		100,000.00	0.0%
1986	23,000.00		200,000.00	11.5%	$10,000.00		100,000.00	10.0%
1987	12,000.00		200,000.00	6.0%	–0–		100,000.00	0.0%
1988	17,000.00		200,000.00	8.5%	–0–		100,000.00	0.0%
1989	27,000.00		200,000.00	13.5%	10,000.00		100,000.00	10.0%

Perfect Score. 44

Deduct .... __

Your Score .... __

Name _____

Date _____ Class _____

Checked by _____

STUDY GUIDE 14

UNIT A—Analyzing Transactions for Capital Stock and Bonds

DIRECTIONS: For each transaction below, print in the proper Answers columns the identifying letters of the accounts to be debited and credited.

Account Titles

A. Bond Sinking Fund
B. Bonds Payable
C. Capital Stock—Common
D. Capital Stock—Preferred
E. Cash
F. Discount on Sale of Capital Stock
G. Interest Expense
H. Interest Income
I. Office Equipment
J. Organization Costs
K. Paid-in Capital in Excess of Par/Stated Value
L. Paid-in Capital from Sale of Treasury Stock
M. Treasury Stock

_____

Transactions

	Transactions	Debit (Answers)	Credit (Answers)	Debit (For Scoring)	Credit (For Scoring)
0–0.	Received cash for common stock at stated value	E	C	0. ✔	0. ✔
1–2.	Received cash for preferred stock at par value	E	D	1.	2.
3–4.	Received cash for common stock at an amount greater than stated value	E	C,K	3.	4.
5–6.	Received cash for preferred stock at an amount less than par value	E,F	D	5.	6.
7–8.	Received office equipment for common stock at stated value	I	C	7.	8.
9–10.	Paid cash for shares of the corporation's own common stock	M	E	9.	10.
11–12.	Received cash from sale of treasury stock at the original cost	E	M	11.	12.
13–14.	Received cash from sale of treasury stock at less than the original cost	E,L	M	13.	14.
15–16.	Received cash from sale of treasury stock at more than the original cost	E	M,L	15.	16.
17–18.	Received cash for a bond issue	E	B	17.	18.
19–20.	Paid semiannual interest on bonds	G	E	19.	20.
21–22.	Paid cash to bond trustee for first annual deposit to the bond sinking fund	A	E	21.	22.
23–24.	Paid cash to bond trustee for second annual deposit to the bond sinking fund and recorded interest earned on the fund	A	E,H	23.	24.
25–26.	Received notice that the bond trustee used the bond sinking fund to retire the bond issue	B	A	25.	26.

UNIT B—Identifying Accounting Terms

DIRECTIONS: Select the one term in Column I that best fits each definition in Column II. Print the letter identifying your choice in the Answers column.

Column I	
A.	amortization
B.	bond
C.	bond issue
D.	bond sinking fund
E.	discount on capital stock
F.	retiring a bond issue
G.	serial bonds
H.	term bonds
I.	treasury stock
J.	trustee

Column II	Answers	For Scoring
0. An amount less than par or stated value at which capital stock is sold	E	0. ✔
27. A corporation's own stock that has been issued and reacquired	I	27.
28. A printed, long-term promise to pay a specified amount on a specified date, and to pay interest at stated intervals	B	28.
29. Bonds that all mature on the same date	H	29.
30. All the bonds representing the total amount of a loan	C	30.
31. A person or institution, usually a bank, who is given legal authorization to administer property for the benefit of property owners	J	31.
32. An amount set aside to pay a bond issue when due	D	32.
33. Recognizing a portion of an expense or amount owed in each of several years	A	33.
34. Paying the amounts owed to bondholders for a bond issue	F	34.
35. Portions of a bond issue that mature on different dates	G	35.

UNIT C—Analyzing Accounting Practices Related to Capital Stock and Bonds

DIRECTIONS: Place a check mark in the proper Answers column to show whether each of the following statements is true or false.

	Answers True	Answers False	For Scoring
0. The treasury stock account is classified as a contra-capital account	✔		0. ✔
36. Par-value of stock is equal to the market value of the stock		✔	36.
37. When stated-value common stock is sold for cash, the accounts affected are Treasury Stock and Capital Stock—Common		✔	37.
38. When a corporation buys its own common stock, the account debited is Treasury Stock	✔		38.
39. The account Bond Sinking Fund is classified as a liability		✔	39.
40. When preferred stock is sold for more than par-value, the accounts affected are Capital Stock—Preferred, Cash, and Paid-in Capital in Excess of Par/Stated Value	✔		40.
41. Treasury stock is an asset of the corporation		✔	41.
42. Voting rights for treasury stock rest with the corporation		✔	42.
43. An advantage of selling stock instead of issuing bonds is that the capital brought into the corporation is relatively permanent	✔		43.
44. Recording treasury stock at the price paid per share regardless of the stock's par or stated value is an application of the accounting concept Objective Evidence		✔	44.

Recording capital stock transactions

CASH RECEIPTS JOURNAL

PAGE 15

DATE		ACCOUNT TITLE	DOC. NO.	POST. REF.	GENERAL DEBIT	GENERAL CREDIT	ACCOUNTS RECEIVABLE CREDIT	SALES CREDIT	SALES TAX PAYABLE DEBIT	SALES TAX PAYABLE CREDIT	SALES DISCOUNT DEBIT	CASH DEBIT	
19-- Jan.	6	Capital Stock—Common	R400			5 000 00 0						5 000 00 0	1
Mar.	13	Discount on Sale of											2
		Capital Stock	R482		1 500 0							1 350 00 0	3
		Capital Stock—Common				1 500 00							4
Apr.	15	Capital Stock—Preferred	R518			40 000 00 0						40 000 00 0	5
June	5	Discount on Sale of				5 000 00							6
		Capital Stock	R601		5 000 00							45 000 00 0	7
		Capital Stock—Preferred				50 000 00							8
													9
													10
													11
													12

GENERAL JOURNAL

PAGE 3

DATE		ACCOUNT TITLE	POST. REF.	DEBIT	CREDIT	
19-- July	1	Office Equipment		12 500 00		1
		Capital Stock—Preferred			12 500 00	2
		M48				3
						4
						5

Recording treasury stock transactions

CASH RECEIPTS JOURNAL

PAGE 6

	DATE	ACCOUNT TITLE	DOC. NO.	POST. REF.	GENERAL DEBIT	GENERAL CREDIT	ACCOUNTS RECEIVABLE CREDIT	SALES CREDIT	SALES TAX PAYABLE DEBIT	SALES TAX PAYABLE CREDIT	SALES DISCOUNT DEBIT	CASH DEBIT	
1	Jan. 31	Treasury Stock	R115			2 25 0 00						2 25 0 00	1
2	Apr. 15	Treasury Stock	R151			1 00 0 00						1 20 0 00	2
3		Paid-in Capital from Sale of											3
4		Treasury Stock				2 0 0 00							4
5	July 30	Paid-in Capital from Sale of			3 0 0 00								5
6		Treasury Stock	R203			3 30 0 00						3 00 0 00	6
7		Treasury Stock											7
8													8
9													9
10													10

CASH PAYMENTS JOURNAL

PAGE 9

	DATE	ACCOUNT TITLE	CHECK NO.	POST. REF.	GENERAL DEBIT	GENERAL CREDIT	ACCOUNTS PAYABLE DEBIT	PURCHASES DISCOUNT CREDIT	CASH CREDIT	
1	Jan. 21	Treasury Stock	100		3 25 0 00				3 25 0 00	1
2	Mar. 22	Treasury Stock	138		8 25 0 00				8 25 0 00	2
3										3
4										4
5										5
6										6

Recording bonds payable transactions

CASH RECEIPTS JOURNAL

PAGE 3

	DATE	ACCOUNT TITLE	DOC. NO.	POST. REF.	GENERAL DEBIT	GENERAL CREDIT	ACCOUNTS RECEIVABLE CREDIT	SALES CREDIT	SALES TAX PAYABLE DEBIT	SALES TAX PAYABLE CREDIT	SALES DISCOUNT DEBIT	CASH DEBIT	
1	1989 Jan. 1	Bonds Payable	R104			100 0 0 0 00						100 0 0 0 00	1
2													2
3													3
4													4
5													5
6													6

CASH PAYMENTS JOURNAL

PAGE 2

	DATE	ACCOUNT TITLE	CHECK NO.	POST. REF.	GENERAL DEBIT	GENERAL CREDIT	ACCOUNTS PAYABLE DEBIT	PURCHASES DISCOUNT CREDIT	CASH CREDIT	
1	1989 June 30	Interest Expense	300		4 5 0 0 00				4 5 0 0 00	1
2	30	Bond Sinking Fund	301		5 0 0 0 00				5 0 0 0 00	2
3	Dec. 31	Interest Expense	504		4 5 0 0 00				4 5 0 0 00	3
4	31	Bond Sinking Fund	505		5 0 0 0 00				4 6 0 0 00	4
5		Interest Income				4 0 0 00				5
6										6

GENERAL JOURNAL

PAGE 1

	DATE		ACCOUNT TITLE	POST. REF.	DEBIT	CREDIT	
1	1999 Jan.	31	Bonds Payable		100 0 0 0 00		1
2			Bond Sinking Fund			100 0 0 0 00	2
3			M159				3
4							4
5							5
6							6
7							7
8							8
9							9
10							10
11							11
12							12
13							13
14							14
15							15
16							16
17							17
18							18
19							19
20							20
21							21
22							22
23							23
24							24
25							25
26							26
27							27
28							28
29							29
30							30
31							31
32							32
33							33

Recording transactions for stocks and bonds

CASH RECEIPTS JOURNAL

PAGE 3

	DATE		ACCOUNT TITLE	DOC. NO.	POST. REF.	GENERAL DEBIT	GENERAL CREDIT	ACCOUNTS RECEIVABLE CREDIT	SALES CREDIT	SALES TAX PAYABLE DEBIT	SALES TAX PAYABLE CREDIT	SALES DISCOUNT DEBIT	CASH DEBIT	
1	1989 Jan.	1	Bonds Payable	R204			100 0 0 0 00						100 0 0 0 00	1
2		6	Capital Stock—Common	R210			100 0 0 0 00						100 0 0 0 00	2
3		31	Treasury Stock	R215			4 5 0 0 00						4 5 0 0 00	3
4	Mar.	13	Capital Stock—Common	R220			3 0 0 0 00						3 3 0 0 00	4
5			Paid-in Capital in											5
6			Excess of Par/											6
7			Stated Value				3 0 0 00							7
8	Apr.	15	Treasury Stock	R231			2 0 0 0 00						2 2 0 0 00	8
9			Paid-in Capital from											9
10			Sale of Treasury Stock				2 0 0 00							10
11		15	Discount on Sale of Capital Stock	R232		2 0 0 0 00							78 0 0 0 00	11
12			Capital Stock—Preferred				80 0 0 0 00							12
13	June	5	Capital Stock—Preferred	R307			100 0 0 0 00						100 0 0 0 00	13
14	July	30	Paid-in Capital from											14
15			Sale of Treasury Stock	R353		2 0 0 00							6 0 0 0 00	15
16			Treasury Stock				6 2 0 0 00							16
17														17
18														18
19														19
20														20
21														21
22														22

CASH PAYMENTS JOURNAL

PAGE 2

	DATE	ACCOUNT TITLE	CHECK NO.	POST. REF.	GENERAL DEBIT	GENERAL CREDIT	ACCOUNTS PAYABLE DEBIT	PURCHASES DISCOUNT CREDIT	CASH CREDIT	
1	1989 Jan. 21	Treasury Stock	100		8 5 0 0 00				8 5 0 0 00	1
2	Mar. 22	Treasury Stock	138		15 7 5 00				15 7 5 00	2
3	June 30	Interest Expense	200		4 5 0 0 00				4 5 0 0 00	3
4	30	Bond Sinking Fund	201		5 0 0 0 00				5 0 0 0 00	4
5	Dec. 31	Interest Expense	504		4 5 0 0 00				4 5 0 0 00	5
6	31	Bond Sinking Fund	505		5 0 0 0 00				4 6 0 0 00	6
7		Interest Income				4 0 0 00				7
8										8
9										9

GENERAL JOURNAL

PAGE 1

	DATE	ACCOUNT TITLE	POST. REF.	DEBIT	CREDIT	
1	1989 July 1	Office Equipment		25 0 0 0 00		1
2		Capital Stock—Preferred			25 0 0 0 00	2
3		M98				3
4	1999 Jan. 1	Bonds Payable		100 0 0 0 00		4
5		Bond Sinking Fund			100 0 0 0 00	5
6		M381				6
7						7
8						8

Recording transactions for stocks and bonds

CASH RECEIPTS JOURNAL

	DATE	ACCOUNT TITLE	DOC. NO.	POST. REF.	GENERAL DEBIT	GENERAL CREDIT	ACCOUNTS RECEIVABLE CREDIT	SALES CREDIT	SALES TAX PAYABLE DEBIT	SALES TAX PAYABLE CREDIT	SALES DISCOUNT DEBIT	CASH DEBIT	
1	1989 Jan. 2	Bonds Payable	R251			300 0 0 0 00						300 0 0 0 00	1
2	24	Capital Stock—Common	R264			150 0 0 0 00						180 0 0 0 00	2
3		Paid-in Capital in Excess of Par/											3
4		Stated Value				30 0 0 0 00							4
5	Feb. 20	Capital Stock—Preferred	R305			500 0 0 0 00						500 0 0 0 00	5
6	May 26	Treasury Stock	R410			24 0 0 0 00						24 0 0 0 00	6
7	July 10	Discount on Sale of Capital Stock	R487		3 0 0 0 00							297 0 0 0 00	7
8		Capital Stock—Preferred				300 0 0 0 00							8
9	Sept. 18	Treasury Stock	R561			30 0 0 0 00						37 5 0 0 00	9
10		Paid-in Capital from Sale of											10
11		Treasury Stock				7 5 0 0 00							11
12	Oct. 14	Discount on Sale of Capital Stock	R600		1 5 0 0 00							148 5 0 0 00	12
13		Capital Stock—Preferred				150 0 0 0 00							13
14													14
15													15
16													16
17													17
18													18
19													19
20													20
21													21
22													22

CASH PAYMENTS JOURNAL

PAGE 2

	DATE	ACCOUNT TITLE	CHECK NO.	POST. REF.	GENERAL DEBIT	GENERAL CREDIT	ACCOUNTS PAYABLE DEBIT	PURCHASES DISCOUNT CREDIT	CASH CREDIT	
1	1989 Feb. 5	Treasury Stock	233		12 000 00				12 000 00	1
2	June 30	Interest Expense	389		12 000 00				12 000 00	2
3	30	Bond Sinking Fund	390		15 000 00				15 000 00	3
4	Dec. 31	Interest Expense	634		12 000 00				12 000 00	4
5	31	Bond Sinking Fund	635		15 000 00				12 800 00	5
6		Interest Income				2 200 00				6
7										7
8										8
9										9

GENERAL JOURNAL

PAGE 1

	DATE	ACCOUNT TITLE	POST. REF.	DEBIT	CREDIT	
1	1989 Mar. 14	Office Equipment		7 000 00		1
2		Capital Stock—Common			7 000 00	2
3		M195				3
4	1999 Jan. 2	Bonds Payable		300 000 00		4
5		Bond Sinking Fund			300 000 00	5
6		M428				6
7						7
8						8

UNIT A—Identifying Accounting Terms

DIRECTIONS: Select the one term in Column I that best fits each definition in Column II. Print the letter identifying your choice in the Answers column.

Column I	Column II	Answers	For Scoring
A. date of declaration B. date of payment C. date of record D. declaring a dividend E. earnings per share F. equity per share G. market value H. price-earnings ratio I. rate earned on average stockholders' equity J. rate earned on average total assets	0. The amount of total stockholders' equity belonging to a single share of stock...............	F	0. ✔
	1. The amount of net income belonging to a single share of stock................................	E	1.
	2. The price at which a share of stock may be sold on the stock market	G	2.
	3. The relationship between a stock's market value per share and earnings per share	H	3.
	4. Action of a board of directors to distribute a portion of corporate earnings to stockholders on a specific date	D	4.
	5. The relationship between net income and the average stockholders' equity	I	5.
	6. The date on which a board of directors votes to distribute a dividend..............................	A	6.
	7. The relationship between net income and average total assets...........................	J	7.
	8. The date that determines which stockholders are to receive dividends....................	C	8.
	9. The date on which dividends are actually to be paid to stockholders	B	9.

UNIT B—Analyzing Corporate Accounting Principles, Concepts, and Procedures

DIRECTIONS: Place a check mark in the proper Answers column to show whether each of the following statements is true or false.

	Answers True	False	For Scoring
0. The date on which a corporate board of directors votes for a dividend payment is called the date of declaration	✔		0. ✔
10. The sequence of dividend dates is (a) date of record, (b) date of declaration, and (c) date of payment...		✔	10.
11. When a corporate board of directors declares a dividend, a corporate liability is incurred...	✔		11.
12. If a corporation pays estimated federal income tax quarterly, an annual income tax report does not have to be submitted to the IRS....................		✔	12.
13. All information on a statement of stockholders' equity should also be shown on the balance sheet		✔	13.
14. A stock's market value should be recorded on the company's records..........		✔	14.
15. Federal income tax is a corporate expense	✔		15.
16. The amount of total stockholders' equity belonging to a single share of stock is called equity per share	✔		16.

UNIT C—Analyzing a Corporation's End-of-Fiscal-Period and Dividend Transactions

DIRECTIONS: For each transaction below, print in the Debit and Credit Answers columns the letter identifying the accounts to be debited and credited.

Account Titles

A. Accumulated Depreciation—Office Equipment
B. Allowance for Uncollectible Accounts
C. Bad Debts Expense
D. Cash
E. Depreciation Expense—Office Equipment
F. Dividends Payable
G. Dividends—Common
H. Dividends—Preferred
I. Federal Income Tax
J. Federal Income Tax Payable
K. Income Summary
L. Organization Costs
M. Organization Expense
N. Paid-in Capital in Excess of Par/Stated Value
O. Paid-in Capital from Sale of Treasury Stock
P. Retained Earnings
Q. Supplies—Office
R. Supplies Expense—Office
S. Treasury Stock

Transactions

Transactions		Accounts to be		For Scoring	
		Debited	Credited	Debit	Credit
0–0.	Adjust office supplies account	R	Q	0. ✔	0. ✔
17–18.	Record estimated bad debts expense	C	B	17.	18.
19–20.	Record estimated depreciation of office equipment	E	A	19.	20.
21–22.	Write off part of the organization costs	M	L	21.	22.
23–24.	Record adjustment for accrued federal income tax	I	J	23.	24.
25–26.	Record declaration of a dividend including both common and preferred stock	G,H	F	25.	26.
27–28.	Record payment of dividend previously declared	F	D	27.	28.
29–30.	Entry to close Income Summary and record net income	K	P	29.	30.
31–32.	Entry to close Dividends—Common and Dividends—Preferred	P	G,H	31.	32.

Recording entries for corporate dividends

GENERAL JOURNAL

PAGE 10

	DATE	ACCOUNT TITLE	POST. REF.	DEBIT	CREDIT	
1	1989 Nov. 25	Dividends—Preferred Stock		10 000 00		1
2		Dividends—Common Stock		23 000 00		2
3		Dividends Payable			33 000 00	3
4		M65				4
5						5
6						6
7						7
8						8
9						9

CASH PAYMENTS JOURNAL

PAGE 13

					1 GENERAL		2	3 ACCOUNTS PAYABLE DEBIT	4 PURCHASES DISCOUNT CREDIT	5 CASH CREDIT	
	DATE	ACCOUNT TITLE	CHECK NO.	POST. REF.	DEBIT	CREDIT					
1	1990 Feb. 1	Dividends Payable	139		33 000 00					33 000 00	1
2											2
3											3
4											4
5											5
6											6
7											7
8											8

Preparing a work sheet for a corporation

The work sheet prepared in Problem 15-2 is needed to complete Problems 15-3, 15-4, 15-5, and 15-6.

PROBLEM 15-2, p. 324

Tolton, Inc.

Work Sheet

For Year Ended December 31, 19--

#	ACCOUNT TITLE	TRIAL BALANCE DEBIT	TRIAL BALANCE CREDIT	ADJUSTMENTS DEBIT	ADJUSTMENTS CREDIT	INCOME STATEMENT DEBIT	INCOME STATEMENT CREDIT	BALANCE SHEET DEBIT	BALANCE SHEET CREDIT
1	Cash	37 08 4 97						37 08 4 97	
2	Petty Cash	3 00 00						3 00 00	
3	Notes Receivable	9 24 91						9 24 91	
4	Interest Receivable			(a) 10 17				10 17	
5	Accounts Receivable	30 83 0 48						30 83 0 48	
6	Allowance for Uncollectible Accounts		9 2 49		(b)1 26 4 05				1 35 6 54
7	Merchandise Inventory	51 61 0 22			(c) 15 9 99			51 45 0 23	
8	Supplies—Sales	2 89 8 07			(d)1 69 5 37			1 20 2 70	
9	Supplies—Delivery	3 66 8 83			(e)2 61 5 88			1 05 2 95	
10	Supplies—Administrative	5 02 5 37			(f)4 06 5 52			9 5 985	
11	Prepaid Insurance	4 06 9 62			(g)2 63 3 04			1 43 6 58	
12	Prepaid Interest			(h) 1 85				1 85	
13	Bond Sinking Fund	4 00 0 00						4 00 0 00	
14	Store Equipment	13 62 7 07						13 62 7 07	
15	Accum. Depr.—Store Equip.		1 30 8 20		(i)1 29 4 57				2 60 2 77
16	Delivery Equipment	27 53 1 62						27 53 1 62	
17	Accum. Depr.—Delivery Equip.		1 67 9 43		(j)2 75 3 16				4 43 2 59
18	Office Equipment	30 49 1 34						30 49 1 34	
19	Accum. Depr.—Office Equip.		3 07 9 63		(k)3 01 8 64				6 09 8 27
20	Building	29 00 0 00						29 00 0 00	
21	Accum. Depr.—Building		3 21 9 00		(l)1 45 0 00				4 66 9 00
22	Land	21 48 8 84						21 48 8 84	
23	Organization Costs	2 00 00			(m) 5 00			1 5 000	
24	Notes Payable		3 08 30						3 08 30
25	Interest Payable				(n)4 00 2 57				4 00 2 57
26	Accounts Payable		2 77 47						2 77 47
27	Employees Inc. Tax Payable		2 46 64						2 46 64

Chapter 15 • 216

	ACCOUNT TITLE	TRIAL BALANCE DEBIT	TRIAL BALANCE CREDIT	ADJUSTMENTS DEBIT	ADJUSTMENTS CREDIT	INCOME STATEMENT DEBIT	INCOME STATEMENT CREDIT	BALANCE SHEET DEBIT	BALANCE SHEET CREDIT
28	Federal Income Tax Payable				(q) 4152				4152
29	FICA Tax Payable		14880		(p) 5712				20592
30	Salaries Payable				(o) 81597				81597
31	Sales Tax Payable		43163						43163
32	Unemploy. Tax Pay. — Federal		4921		(p) 653				5574
33	Unemploy. Tax Pay. — State		33278		(p) 4406				37684
34	Hospital Ins. Prem. Payable		9249						9249
35	Dividends Payable		880563						880563
36	Bonds Payable		4000000						4000000
37	Capital Stock — Common		10900000						10900000
38	Capital Stock — Preferred		4200000						4200000
39	Pd.-in Cap. in Ex. Par/Stated Val.		110000						110000
40	Disc. on Sale of Cap. Stock	200000						200000	
41	Treasury Stock	70000						70000	
42	Pd.-in Cap. from Sale of Tr. Stock		14000						14000
43	Retained Earnings		1341126						1341126
44	Dividends — Common Stock	460563						460563	
45	Dividends — Preferred Stock	420000						420000	
46	Income Summary			(c) 15999		15999			
47	Sales		19440119				19440119		
48	Sales Ret. & Allowances	58320				58320			
49	Sales Discount	38880				38880			
50	Purchases	9230646				9230646			
51	Purchases Ret. & Allow.		55384				55384		
52	Purchases Discount		156921				156921		
53	Advertising Expense	234312				234312			
54	Credit Card Fee Expense	265142				265142			
55	Depr. Exp. — Store Equip.			(i) 129457		129457			
56	Misc. Expense — Sales	114073				114073			
57	Salary Expense — Sales	1399704		(o) 15397		1415101			

#	ACCOUNT TITLE	TRIAL BALANCE DEBIT	TRIAL BALANCE CREDIT	ADJUSTMENTS DEBIT	ADJUSTMENTS CREDIT	INCOME STATEMENT DEBIT	INCOME STATEMENT CREDIT	BALANCE SHEET DEBIT	BALANCE SHEET CREDIT
58	Supplies Expense—Sales			(d)1 6 9 5 37		1 6 9 5 37			
59	Depr. Exp.—Deliv. Equip.			(j)2 7 5 3 16		2 7 5 3 16			
60	Misc. Expense—Delivery	2 9 9 0 56				2 9 9 0 56			
61	Salary Expense—Delivery	6 2 2 7 76		(o) 6 8 51		6 2 9 6 27			
62	Supplies Expense—Delivery			(e)2 6 1 5 88		2 6 1 5 88			
63	Bad Debts Expense			(b)1 2 6 4 05		1 2 6 4 05			
64	Depr. Exp.—Office Equip.			(k)3 0 1 8 64		3 0 1 8 64			
65	Depr. Expense—Building			(l)1 4 5 0 00		1 4 5 0 00			
66	Insurance Expense			(g)2 6 3 3 04		2 6 3 3 04			
67	Misc. Expense—Admin.	3 2 6 8 03				3 2 6 8 03			
68	Payroll Taxes Expense	3 3 8 1 86		(p) 1 0 7 71		3 4 8 9 57			
69	Property Tax Expense	1 3 0 0 00				1 3 0 0 00			
70	Salary Expense—Admin.	5 3 9 5 33		(o) 5 9 3 49		5 9 8 8 82			
71	Supplies Expense—Admin.			(f)4 0 6 5 52		4 0 6 5 52			
72	Utilities Expense	5 5 1 8 66				5 5 1 8 66			
73	Interest Income		1 2 33		(a) 1 0 17		1 3 3 50		
74	Interest Expense	2 6 2 0 59		(n)4 0 0 2 57	(h) 1 85	6 6 2 1 31			
75	Organization Expense			(m) 5 0 00		5 0 00			
76	Federal Income Tax	4 0 0 0 00		(q) 4 1 52		4 0 4 1 52			
77		4 2 2 3 7 0 53	4 2 2 3 7 0 53	2 5 9 8 0 01	2 5 9 8 0 01	1 7 4 0 7 9 70	1 9 6 6 5 7 74	2 6 3 0 4 9 19	2 4 0 4 7 1 15
78	*Net Income after Federal Income Tax*					2 2 5 7 8 04			2 2 5 7 8 04
79						1 9 6 6 5 7 74	1 9 6 6 5 7 74	2 6 3 0 4 9 19	2 6 3 0 4 9 19
80									
81									
82									
83									
84									
85									
86									
87									

Preparing a corporate income statement

The work sheet prepared in Problem 15-2 is needed to complete Problem 15-3.

Tolton, Inc.

Income Statement

For Year Ended December 31, 19--

				% OF NET SALES
Operating Revenue:				
Sales			194 40 1 19	
Less: Sales Ret. & Allow.		5 83 20		
Sales Discount		3 88 80	9 72 00	
Net Sales				193 4 29 19	100.0
Cost of Merchandise Sold:				
Mdse. Inventory, January 1, 19--			51 6 10 22	
Purchases		92 3 06 46		
Less: Pur. Ret. & Allow.	5 53 84			
Purchases Discount	1 5 69 21	2 1 23 05		
Net Purchases			90 1 83 41	
Total Cost of Mdse. Avail. for Sale			141 7 93 63	
Less Mdse. Inv., Dec. 31, 19--			51 4 50 23	
Cost of Merchandise Sold				90 3 43 40	46.7
Gross Profit from Operations				103 0 85 79	53.3
Operating Expenses:				
Selling Expenses:				
Advertising Expense		2 3 43 12		
Credit Card Fee Expense		2 6 51 42		
Depr. Exp.—Store Equip.		1 2 94 57		
Misc. Expense—Sales		1 1 40 73		
Salary Expense—Sales		14 1 51 01		
Supplies Expense—Sales		1 6 95 37		
Total Selling Expenses			23 2 76 22	
Delivery Expenses:				
Depr. Exp.—Deliv. Equip.		2 7 53 16		
Misc. Expense—Delivery		2 9 90 56		
Salary Expense—Delivery		6 2 96 27		
Supplies Expense—Delivery		2 6 15 88		
Total Delivery Expenses			14 6 55 87	

Continue this income statement on the next page.

Tolton, Inc.

Income Statement (continued)

For Year Ended December 31, 19--

			% OF NET SALES
Administrative Expenses:			
Bad Debts Expense	1 2 6 4 05		
Depr. Exp. — Office Equip.	3 0 1 8 64		
Depr. Expense — Building	1 4 5 0 00		
Insurance Expense	2 6 3 3 04		
Misc. Expense — Admin.	3 2 6 8 03		
Payroll Taxes Expense	3 4 8 9 57		
Property Tax Expense	1 3 0 0 00		
Salary Expense — Admin.	5 9 8 8 82		
Supplies Expense — Admin.	4 0 6 5 52		
Utilities Expense	5 5 1 8 66		
Total Admin. Expenses		31 9 9 6 33	
Total Operating Expenses			69 9 2 8 42	36.2
Income from Operations			33 1 5 7 37	
Other Revenue:			
Interest Income		1 3 3 50	
Other Expenses:			
Interest Expense	6 6 2 1 31		
Organization Expense	5 0 00		
Total Other Expenses		6 6 7 1 31	
Net Deduction			6 5 3 7 81	
Net Income before Fed. Income Tax			26 6 1 9 56	13.8
Less Federal Income Tax			4 0 4 1 52	2.1
Net Income after Fed. Income Tax			22 5 7 8 04	11.7

Earnings per share:

Stock	Share of Net Income	÷	Shares Outstanding	=	Earnings per share
Preferred	$ 4,200.00	÷	420	=	$10.00
Common	18,378.04	÷	10,830	=	$ 1.70

Preparing a corporate statement of stockholders' equity

The work sheet prepared in Problem 15-2 is needed to complete Problem 15-4. The statement of stockholders' equity prepared in Problem 15-4 is needed to complete Problem 15-5.

Tolton, Inc.

Statement of Stockholders' Equity

For Year Ended December 31, 19--

Paid-in Capital:			
Common Stock, $10.00 Per Share			
Jan. 1, 19--, 10,000 Shares Issued	100 000 00		
Issued during 19--, 900 Shares	9 000 00		
Balance, Dec. 31, 19--, 10,900 Shares Issued		109 000 00	
Preferred Stock, $100.00 Per Share			
Jan. 1, 19--, 320 Shares Issued	32 000 00		
Issued during 19--, 100 Shares	10 000 00		
Balance, Dec. 31, 19--, 420 Shares Issued		42 000 00	
Total Value of Capital Stock Issued			151 000 00
Additional Paid-in Capital:			
Pd.-in Cap. in Ex. of Par/Stated Val.	1 100 00		
Pd.-in Cap. from Sale of Treas. Stock	1 40 00	1 240 00	
Less Disc. on Sale of Cap. Stock		2 000 00	
Total Additional Paid-in Capital			(7 60 00)
Total Paid-in Capital			150 240 00
Retained Earnings:			
January 1, 19--		13 411 26	
Net Income after Federal Income Tax for 19--	22 578 04		
Less Dividends Declared	8 805 63		
Net Increase during 19--		13 772 41	
Balance, December 31, 19--			27 183 67
Total Pd.-in Capital & Retained Earnings			177 423 67
Less Treasury Stock, 70 Shares of			
Common Stock, December 31, 19--			7 00 00
Total Stockholders' Equity, Dec. 31, 19--			176 723 67

a. Equity per share:

Stock	Equity	÷	Shares Outstanding	=	Equity per share
Preferred	$ 42,000.00	÷	420	=	$100.00
Common	134,723.67	÷	10,830	=	$12.44

b. Price-earnings ratio:

Stock	Market Price	÷	Earnings per share	=	Price-earnings ratio
Common	$11.00	÷	$1.70	=	6.47 times

Preparing a corporate balance sheet

PROBLEM 15-5, p. 326
[1]

The work sheet prepared in Problem 15-2 and the statement of stockholders' equity prepared in Problem 15-4 are needed to complete Problem 15-5.

Tolton, Inc.

Balance Sheet

December 31, 19--

Assets			
Current Assets:			
Cash		37 0 8 4 97	
Petty Cash		3 0 0 00	
Notes Receivable		9 2 4 91	
Interest Receivable		1 0 17	
Accounts Receivable	30 8 3 0 48		
Less Allow. for Uncoll. Accounts	1 3 5 6 54	29 4 7 3 94	
Merchandise Inventory		51 4 5 0 23	
Supplies—Sales		1 2 0 2 70	
Supplies—Delivery		1 0 5 2 95	
Supplies—Administrative		9 5 9 85	
Prepaid Insurance		1 4 3 6 58	
Prepaid Interest		1 85	
Total Current Assets			123 8 9 8 15
Long-Term Investment:			
Bond Sinking Fund			4 0 0 0 00
Plant Assets:			
Store Equipment	13 6 2 7 07		
Less Accum. Depr.—Store Equip.	2 6 0 2 77	11 0 2 4 30	

Continue this balance sheet on the next page.

Tolton, Inc.

Balance Sheet (continued)

December 31, 19--

Delivery Equipment	27 5 3 1 62		
Less Accum. Depr.—Deliv. Equip.	4 4 3 2 59	23 0 9 9 03	
Office Equipment	30 4 9 1 34		
Less Accum. Depr.—Office Equip.	6 0 9 8 27	24 3 9 3 07	
Building	29 0 0 0 00		
Less Accum. Depr.—Building	4 6 6 9 00	24 3 3 1 00	
Land		21 4 8 8 84	
Total Plant Assets			104 3 3 6 24
Intangible Asset:			
Organization Costs			1 5 0 00
Total Assets			232 3 8 4 39
Liabilities			
Current Liabilities:			
Notes Payable		3 0 8 30	
Interest Payable		4 0 0 2 57	
Accounts Payable		2 7 7 47	
Employees Income Tax Payable		2 4 6 64	
Federal Income Tax Payable		4 1 52	
FICA Tax Payable		2 0 5 92	
Salaries Payable		8 1 5 97	
Sales Tax Payable		4 3 1 63	
Unemploy. Tax Payable—Federal		5 5 74	
Unemploy. Tax Payable—State		3 7 6 84	
Hospital Insurance Premiums Payable		9 2 49	
Dividends Payable		8 8 0 5 63	
Total Current Liabilities			15 6 6 0 72
Long-Term Liability:			
Bonds Payable			40 0 0 0 00
Total Liabilities			55 6 6 0 72
Stockholders' Equity			
Total Stockholders' Equity			176 7 2 3 67
Total Liabilities & Stockholders' Equity			232 3 8 4 39

a. Rate earned on average stockholders' equity:

January 1 Equity	December 31 Equity	Average
$143,951.26	$176,723.67	$160,337.47

Net Income	÷	Average Equity	=	Rate
$22,578.04	÷	$160,337.47	=	14.1%

b. Rate earned on average total assets:

January 1 Assets	December 31 Assets	Average
$233,699.75	$232,384.39	$233,042.07

Net Income	÷	Average Assets	=	Rate
$22,578.04	÷	$233,042.07	=	9.7%

Completing other end-of-fiscal period work

PROBLEM 15-6, p. 326
[1]

The work sheet prepared in Problem 15-2 is needed to complete Problem 15-6.

GENERAL JOURNAL

PAGE 12

	DATE		ACCOUNT TITLE	POST. REF.	DEBIT	CREDIT	
1			*Adjusting Entries*				1
2	19-- Dec.	31	Interest Receivable		1 0 17		2
3			Interest Income			1 0 17	3
4		31	Bad Debts Expense		1 2 6 4 05		4
5			Allowance for Uncollectible Accounts			1 2 6 4 05	5
6		31	Income Summary		1 5 9 99		6
7			Merchandise Inventory			1 5 9 99	7
8		31	Supplies Expense — Sales		1 6 9 5 37		8
9			Supplies — Sales			1 6 9 5 37	9
10		31	Supplies Expense — Delivery		2 6 1 5 88		10
11			Supplies — Delivery			2 6 1 5 88	11
12		31	Supplies Expense — Administrative		4 0 6 5 52		12
13			Supplies — Administrative			4 0 6 5 52	13
14		31	Insurance Expense		2 6 3 3 04		14
15			Prepaid Insurance			2 6 3 3 04	15
16		31	Prepaid Interest		1 85		16
17			Interest Expense			1 85	17

GENERAL JOURNAL   PAGE 13

	DATE		ACCOUNT TITLE	POST. REF.	DEBIT	CREDIT	
1	19-- Dec.	31	Depreciation Expense—Store Equipment		1 2 9 4 57		1
2			Accum. Depr.—Store Equipment			1 2 9 4 57	2
3		31	Depreciation Expense—Delivery Equipment		2 7 5 3 16		3
4			Accum. Depr.—Delivery Equipment			2 7 5 3 16	4
5		31	Depreciation Expense—Office Equipment		3 0 1 8 64		5
6			Accum. Depr.—Office Equipment			3 0 1 8 64	6
7		31	Depreciation Expense—Building		1 4 5 0 00		7
8			Accum. Depr.—Building			1 4 5 0 00	8
9		31	Organization Expense		5 0 00		9
10			Organization Costs			5 0 00	10
11		31	Interest Expense		4 0 0 2 57		11
12			Interest Payable			4 0 0 2 57	12
13		31	Salary Expense—Sales		1 5 3 97		13
14			Salary Expense—Delivery		6 8 51		14
15			Salary Expense—Administrative		5 9 3 49		15
16			Salaries Payable			8 1 5 97	16
17		31	Payroll Taxes Expense		1 0 7 71		17
18			FICA Tax Payable			5 7 12	18
19			Unemployment Tax Payable—Federal			6 53	19
20			Unemployment Tax Payable—State			4 4 06	20
21		31	Federal Income Tax		4 1 52		21
22			Federal Income Tax Payable			4 1 52	22
23							23
24							24
25							25
26							26
27							27
28							28
29							29
30							30
31							31
32							32
33							33

| Form **1120**
Department of the Treasury
Internal Revenue Service | **U.S. Corporation Income Tax Return**
For calendar 19-- or tax year beginning _____, 19--, ending _____, 19 ____
► For Paperwork Reduction Act Notice, see page 1 of the instructions. | OMB No. 1545-0123 |

Check if a—	Use IRS label. Otherwise please print or type.	Name Tolton, Inc.	**D** Employer identification number 65-0243548
A Consolidated return ☐			
B Personal Holding Co. ☐		Number and street 952 South Liberty Road	**E** Date incorporated 1/2/--
C Business Code No. (See the list in the Instructions) 5995		City or town, state, and ZIP code Salem, OR 97302-6438	**F** Total assets (see Specific Instructions)

G Check box if there has been a change in address from the previous year . . . . ► ☐ $ 232,384 39

			Dollars	Cents
Income	1 **a** Gross receipts or sales 194,012.39 **b** Less returns and allowances 583.20 Balance ►	1c	193,429	19
	2 Cost of goods sold and/or operations (Schedule A) .	2	90,343	40
	3 Gross profit (line 1c less line 2)	3	103,085	79
	4 Dividends (Schedule C)	4	–0–	
	5 Interest	5	133	50
	6 Gross rents	6	–0–	
	7 Gross royalties	7	–0–	
	8 Capital gain net income (attach separate Schedule D) .	8	–0–	
	9 Net gain or (loss) from Form 4797, line 17, Part II (attach Form 4797)	9	–0–	
	10 Other income (see instructions—attach schedule).	10	–0–	
	11 TOTAL. income—Add lines 3 through 10 and enter here . . . . ►	11	103,219	29
Deductions	12 Compensation of officers (Schedule E) . . .	12	6,609	02
	13 **a** Salaries and wages 19,827.08 **b** Less jobs credit –0– Balance ►	13c	19,827	08
	14 Repairs	14	–0–	
	15 Bad debts (Schedule F if reserve method is used)	15	1,264	05
	16 Rents	16	–0–	
	17 Taxes	17	4,789	57
	18 Interest	18	6,621	31
	19 Contributions (**see Instructions for 10% limitation**)	19	–0–	
	20 Depreciation (attach Form 4562) . . 20 8,516 37			
	21 Less depreciation claimed in Schedule A and elsewhere on return . 21a –0–	21b	8,516	37
	22 Depletion	22	–0–	
	23 Advertising	23	2,343	12
	24 Pension, profit-sharing, etc. plans	24	–0–	
	25 Employee benefit programs	25	–0–	
	26 Other deductions (attach schedule)	26	26,629	21
	27 TOTAL deductions—Add lines 12 through 26 and enter here . . . ►	27	76,599	73
	28 Taxable income before net operating loss deduction and special deductions (line 11 less line 27) .	28	26,619	56
	29 **Less: a** Net operating loss deduction (see instructions) . . . . 29a –0–			
	b Special deductions (Schedule C) . . . . 29b –0–	29c	–0–	
Tax and Payments	30 Taxable income (line 28 less line 29c)	30	26,619	56
	31 TOTAL TAX (Schedule J).	31	4,041	52
	32 **Payments:**			
	a 19-- overpayment allowed as a credit . . . –0–			
	b 19-- estimated tax payments 4,000 00			
	c Less 19-- refund applied for on Form 4466 . . (–0–) 4,000 00			
	d Tax deposited with Form 7004 . . . . –0–			
	e Credit from regulated investment companies (attach Form 2439) . . –0–			
	f Credit for Federal tax on gasoline and special fuels (attach Form 4136) –0–	32	4,000	00
	33 Enter any **PENALTY** for underpayment of estimated tax—check ► ☐ if Form 2220 is attached .	33	–0–	
	34 **TAX DUE**—If the total of lines 31 and 33 is larger than line 32, enter AMOUNT OWED	34	41	52
	35 **OVERPAYMENT**—If line 32 is larger than the total of lines 31 and 33, enter AMOUNT OVERPAID	35		
	36 Enter amount of line 35 you want: **Credited to 19--** estimated tax ► Refunded ►	36		

Please Sign Here

Under penalties of perjury, I declare that I have examined this return, including accompanying schedules and statements, and to the best of my knowledge and belief, it is true, correct, and complete. Declaration of preparer (other than taxpayer) is based on all information of which preparer has any knowledge.

► _____ Signature of officer   Date   ► _____ Title

Paid Preparer's Use Only	Preparer's signature ►	Date	Check if self-employed ► ☐	Preparer's social security number
	Firm's name (or yours, if self-employed) and address ►		E.I. No. ►	
			ZIP code ►	

GENERAL JOURNAL

PAGE 14

	DATE		ACCOUNT TITLE	POST. REF.	DEBIT	CREDIT	
1			*Closing Entries*				1
2	19-- Dec.	31	Sales		194 401 19		2
3			Purchases Returns and Allowances		5 53 84		3
4			Purchases Discount		1 5 69 21		4
5			Interest Income		1 33 50		5
6			Income Summary			196 657 74	6
7		31	Income Summary		173 919 71		7
8			Sales Returns and Allowances			5 83 20	8
9			Sales Discount			3 88 80	9
10			Purchases			92 306 46	10
11			Advertising Expense			2 343 12	11
12			Credit Card Fee Expense			2 651 42	12
13			Depreciation Expense—Store Equip.			1 294 57	13
14			Miscellaneous Expense—Sales			1 140 73	14
15			Salary Expense—Sales			14 151 01	15
16			Supplies Expense—Sales			1 695 37	16
17			Depreciation Expense—Delivery Equip.			2 753 16	17
18			Miscellaneous Expense—Delivery			2 990 56	18
19			Salary Expense—Delivery			6 296 27	19
20			Supplies Expense—Delivery			2 615 88	20
21			Bad Debts Expense			1 264 05	21
22			Depreciation Expense—Office Equip.			3 018 64	22
23			Depreciation Expense—Building			1 450 00	23
24			Insurance Expense			2 633 04	24
25			Miscellaneous Expense—Admin.			3 268 03	25
26			Payroll Taxes Expense			3 489 57	26
27			Property Tax Expense			1 300 00	27
28			Salary Expense—Administrative			5 988 82	28
29			Supplies Expense—Administrative			4 065 52	29
30			Utilities Expense			5 518 66	30
31			Interest Expense			6 621 31	31
32			Organization Expense			50 00	32
33			Federal Income Tax			4 041 52	33

GENERAL JOURNAL

PAGE 15

	DATE		ACCOUNT TITLE	POST. REF.	DEBIT	CREDIT	
1	19-- Dec.	31	Income Summary		22 5 7 8 04		1
2			Retained Earnings			22 5 7 8 04	2
3		31	Retained Earnings		8 8 0 5 63		3
4			Dividends — Common Stock			4 6 0 5 63	4
5			Dividends — Preferred Stock			4 2 0 0 00	5
6			Reversing Entries				6
7	19-- Jan.	1	Interest Income		1 0 17		7
8			Interest Receivable			1 0 17	8
9		1	Interest Expense		1 85		9
10			Prepaid Interest			1 85	10
11		1	Interest Payable		4 0 0 2 57		11
12			Interest Expense			4 0 0 2 57	12
13		1	Salaries Payable		8 1 5 97		13
14			Salary Expense — Sales			1 5 3 97	14
15			Salary Expense — Delivery			6 8 51	15
16			Salary Expense — Administrative			5 9 3 49	16
17		1	FICA Tax Payable		5 7 12		17
18			Unemployment Tax Payable — Federal		6 53		18
19			Unemployment Tax Payable — State		4 4 06		19
20			Payroll Taxes Expense			1 0 7 71	20
21		1	Federal Income Tax Payable		4 1 52		21
22			Federal Income Tax			4 1 52	22
23							23
24							24
25							25
26							26
27							27
28							28
29							29
30							30
31							31
32							32
33							33

End-of-fiscal-period work for a corporation   [1]

Wescox, Inc.

Work Sheet

For Year Ended December 31, 1989

	TRIAL BALANCE		ADJUSTMENTS		INCOME STATEMENT		BALANCE SHEET	
ACCOUNT TITLE	DEBIT	CREDIT	DEBIT	CREDIT	DEBIT	CREDIT	DEBIT	CREDIT
1 Cash	50 5 6 0 24						50 5 6 0 24	
2 Petty Cash	5 0 0 0 00						5 0 0 0 00	
3 Notes Receivable	1 5 6 1 77						1 5 6 1 77	
4 Interest Receivable			(a) 17 18				17 18	
5 Accounts Receivable	52 0 5 8 86						52 0 5 8 86	
6 Allowance for Uncollectible Accounts		1 5 6 18		(b) 2 1 3 4 41				2 2 9 0 59
7 Merchandise Inventory	87 1 4 6 53			(c) 2 7 0 15			86 8 7 6 38	
8 Supplies—Sales	4 8 9 3 53			(d) 2 8 6 2 71			2 0 3 0 82	
9 Supplies—Delivery	6 1 9 5 01			(e) 4 4 1 7 04			1 7 7 7 97	
10 Supplies—Administrative	8 4 8 5 59			(f) 6 8 6 4 84			1 6 2 0 75	
11 Prepaid Insurance	6 8 7 1 77			(g) 4 4 4 6 04			2 4 2 5 73	
12 Prepaid Interest			(h) 3 12				3 12	
13 Bond Sinking Fund	7 0 0 0 00						7 0 0 0 00	
14 Store Equipment	51 4 8 6 21						51 4 8 6 21	
15 Accum. Depr.—Store Equip.		5 2 0 0 11		(i) 5 0 9 7 14				10 2 9 7 25
16 Delivery Equipment	46 4 8 8 56						46 4 8 8 56	
17 Accum. Depr.—Delivery Equip.		2 8 3 5 80		(j) 4 6 4 8 86				7 4 8 4 66
18 Office Equipment	23 0 1 0 02						23 0 1 0 02	
19 Accum. Depr.—Office Equip.		2 2 0 8 96		(k) 2 1 8 5 95				4 3 9 4 91
20 Building	48 0 0 0 00						48 0 0 0 00	
21 Accum. Depr.—Building		5 3 2 8 00		(l) 2 4 0 0 00				7 7 2 8 00
22 Land	36 2 8 5 03						36 2 8 5 03	
23 Organization Costs	3 0 0 0 00			(m) 75 00			2 2 5 00	
24 Notes Payable		5 2 0 59						5 2 0 59
25 Interest Payable				(n) 7 0 0 4 34				7 0 0 4 34
26 Accounts Payable		10 4 6 8 53						10 4 6 8 53
27 Employees Inc. Tax Payable		4 1 6 47						4 1 6 47

[1]

	Account Title	Trial Balance Debit (1)	Trial Balance Credit (2)	Adjustments Debit (3)	Adjustments Credit (4)	Income Statement Debit (5)	Income Statement Credit (6)	Balance Sheet Debit (7)	Balance Sheet Credit (8)	
28	Federal Income Tax Payable				(q) 2437				2437	28
29	FICA Tax Payable		25126		(p) 9645				34771	29
30	Salaries Payable				(o) 137778				137778	30
31	Sales Tax Payable		72882						72882	31
32	Unemploy. Tax Pay. — Federal		8309		(p) 1102				9411	32
33	Unemploy. Tax Pay. — State		56192		(p) 7440				63632	33
34	Hospital Ins. Prem. Payable		15618						15618	34
35	Dividends Payable		1492280						1492280	35
36	Bonds Payable		7000000						7000000	36
37	Capital Stock — Common		18400000						18400000	37
38	Capital Stock — Preferred		7200000						7200000	38
39	Pd. in Cap. in Ex. Par/Stated Val.		1800000						1800000	39
40	Disc. on Sale of Cap. Stock	300000						300000		40
41	Treasury Stock	120000						120000		41
42	Pd.-in Cap. from Sale of Tr. Stock		24000						24000	42
43	Retained Earnings		2264560						2264560	43
44	Dividends — Common Stock	772280						772280		44
45	Dividends — Preferred Stock	720000						720000		45
46	Income Summary			(c) 27015		27015				46
47	Sales		29673550				29673550			47
48	Sales Ret. & Allowances	89021				89021				48
49	Sales Discount	59347				59347				49
50	Purchases	15565599				15565599				50
51	Purchases Ret. & Allow.		93394				93394			51
52	Purchases Discount		264615				264615			52
53	Advertising Expense	395647				395647				53
54	Credit Card Fee Expense	447706				447706				54
55	Depr. Exp. — Store Equip.			(i) 509714		509714				55
56	Misc. Expense — Sales	192618				192618				56
57	Salary Expense — Sales	2363472		(o) 25998		2389470				57

[1]

	TRIAL BALANCE		ADJUSTMENTS		INCOME STATEMENT		BALANCE SHEET		
ACCOUNT TITLE	DEBIT	CREDIT	DEBIT	CREDIT	DEBIT	CREDIT	DEBIT	CREDIT	
Supplies Expense—Sales			(d) 2 8 6 2 71		2 8 6 2 71				58
Depr. Exp.—Deliv. Equip.			(j) 4 6 4 8 86		4 6 4 8 86				59
Misc. Expense—Delivery	5 0 4 9 71				5 0 4 9 71				60
Salary Expense—Delivery	10 5 1 5 89		(o) 1 1 5 67		10 6 3 1 56				61
Supplies Expense—Delivery			(e) 4 4 1 7 04		4 4 1 7 04				62
Bad Debts Expense			(b) 2 1 3 4 41		2 1 3 4 41				63
Depr. Exp.—Office Equip.			(k) 2 1 8 5 95		2 1 8 5 95				64
Depr. Expense—Building			(l) 2 4 0 0 00		2 4 0 0 00				65
Insurance Expense			(g) 4 4 4 6 04		4 4 4 6 04				66
Misc. Expense—Admin.	5 5 1 8 24				5 5 1 8 24				67
Payroll Taxes Expense	5 7 1 0 44		(p) 1 8 1 87		5 8 9 2 31				68
Property Tax Expense	2 3 0 0 00				2 3 0 0 00				69
Salary Expense—Admin.	9 1 1 0 30		(o) 1 0 0 2 13		10 1 1 2 43				70
Supplies Expense—Admin.			(f) 6 8 6 4 84		6 8 6 4 84				71
Utilities Expense	9 3 1 8 54				9 3 1 8 54				72
Interest Income		2 0 8 24	(a)	1 7 18		2 2 5 42			73
Interest Expense	4 4 2 5 00		(n) 7 0 0 4 34	(h) 3 12	11 4 2 6 22				74
Organization Expense			(m) 7 5 00		7 5 00				75
Federal Income Tax	2 0 0 0 00		(q) 2 4 37		2 0 2 4 37				76
	695 0 4 8 14	695 0 4 8 14	44 0 1 0 80	44 0 1 0 80	289 0 9 6 60	300 5 4 1 01	431 0 5 0 44	419 5 7 9 03	77
Net Income after Federal Income Tax					11 4 7 1 41			11 4 7 1 41	78
					300 5 4 1 01	300 5 4 1 01	431 0 5 0 44	431 0 5 0 44	79
									80
									81
									82
									83
									84
									85
									86
									87

Wescox, Inc.

Income Statement

For Year Ended December 31, 1989

					% OF NET SALES
Operating Revenue:					
Sales			296 7 3 5 50		
Less: Sales Ret. & Allow.		8 9 0 21			
Sales Discount		5 9 3 47	1 4 8 3 68		
Net Sales				295 2 5 1 82	100.0
Cost of Merchandise Sold:					
Mdse. Inventory, January 1, 1989			87 1 4 6 53		
Purchases		155 6 5 5 99			
Less: Pur. Ret. & Allow.	9 3 3 94				
Purchases Discount	2 6 4 6 15	3 5 8 0 09			
Net Purchases			152 0 7 5 90		
Total Cost of Mdse. Avail. for Sale			239 2 2 2 43		
Less Mdse. Inv., Dec. 31, 1989			86 8 7 6 38		
Cost of Merchandise Sold				152 3 4 6 05	51.6
Gross Profit from Operations				142 9 0 5 77	48.4
Operating Expenses:					
Selling Expenses:					
Advertising Expense		3 9 5 6 47			
Credit Card Fee Expense		4 4 7 7 06			
Depr. Exp.—Store Equip.		5 0 9 7 14			
Misc. Expense—Sales		1 9 2 6 18			
Salary Expense—Sales		23 8 9 4 70			
Supplies Expense—Sales		2 8 6 2 71			
Total Selling Expenses			42 2 1 4 26		
Delivery Expenses:					
Depr. Exp.—Deliv. Equip.		4 6 4 8 86			
Misc. Expense—Delivery		5 0 4 9 71			
Salary Expense—Delivery		10 6 3 1 56			
Supplies Expense—Delivery		4 4 1 7 04			
Total Delivery Expenses			24 7 4 7 17		
Administrative Expenses:					
Bad Debts Expense		2 1 3 4 41			

Continue this income statement on the next page.

Wescox, Inc.

Income Statement (continued)

For Year Ended December 31, 1989

			% OF NET SALES
Depr. Exp. — Office Equip.	2 1 8 5 95		
Depr. Expense — Building	2 4 0 0 00		
Insurance Expense	4 4 4 6 04		
Misc. Expense — Admin.	5 5 1 8 24		
Payroll Taxes Expense	5 8 9 2 31		
Property Tax Expense	2 3 0 0 00		
Salary Expense — Admin.	10 1 1 2 43		
Supplies Expense — Admin.	6 8 6 4 84		
Utilities Expense	9 3 1 8 54		
Total Admin. Expenses		51 1 7 2 76	
Total Operating Expenses			118 1 3 4 19	40.0
Income from Operations			24 7 7 1 58	
Other Revenue:				
Interest Income		2 2 5 42	
Other Expenses:				
Interest Expense	11 4 2 6 22		
Organization Expense	7 5 00		
Total Other Expenses		11 5 0 1 22	
Net Deduction			11 2 7 5 80	
Net Income before Fed. Income Tax			13 4 9 5 78	4.6
Less Federal Income Tax			2 0 2 4 37	0.7
Net Income after Fed. Income Tax			11 4 7 1 41	3.9

Earnings per share:

Stock	Share of Net Income	÷	Shares Outstanding	=	Earnings per share
Preferred	$7,200.00	÷	720	=	$10.00
Common	4,271.41	÷	18,280	=	$ .23

Wescox, Inc.

Statement of Stockholders' Equity

For Year Ended December 31, 1989

Paid-in Capital:			
Common Stock, $10.00 Per Share			
Jan. 1, 1989, 18,000 Shares Issued	180 000 00		
Issued during 1989, 400 Shares	4 000 00		
Balance, Dec. 31, 1989, 18,400 Shares Issued		184 000 00	
Preferred Stock, $100.00 Per Share			
Jan. 1, 1989, 600 Shares Issued	60 000 00		
Issued during 1989, 120 Shares	12 000 00		
Balance, Dec. 31, 1989, 720 Shares Issued		72 000 00	
Total Value of Capital Stock Issued			256 000 00
Additional Paid-in Capital:			
Pd.-in Cap. in Ex. of Par/Stated Val.	1 800 00		
Pd.-in Cap. from Sale of Treas. Stock	2 40 00	2 040 00	
Less Disc. on Sale of Cap. Stock		3 000 00	
Total Additional Paid-in Capital			(9 60 00)
Total Paid-in Capital			255 040 00
Retained Earnings:			
January 1, 1989		22 645 60	
Net Income after Federal Income Tax for 1989	11 471 41		
Less Dividends Declared	14 922 80		
Net Decrease during 1989		3 451 39	
Balance, December 31, 1989			19 194 21
Total Pd.-in Capital & Retained Earnings			274 234 21
Less Treasury Stock, 120 Shares of			
Common Stock, December 31, 1989			1 200 00
Total Stockholders' Equity, Dec. 31, 1989			273 034 21

a. Equity per share:

Stock	Equity	÷	Shares Outstanding	=	Equity per share
Preferred	$ 72,000.00	÷	720	=	$100.00
Common	201,034.21	÷	18,280	=	$ 11.00

b. Price-earnings ratio:

Stock	Market Price	÷	Earnings per share	=	Price-earnings ratio
Common	$10.00	÷	$.23	=	43.5 times

[5]

Wescox, Inc.

Balance Sheet

December 31, 1989

Assets			
Current Assets:			
Cash		50 5 6 0 24	
Petty Cash		5 0 0 00	
Notes Receivable		1 5 6 1 77	
Interest Receivable		1 7 18	
Accounts Receivable	52 0 5 8 86		
Less Allow. for Uncoll. Accounts	2 2 9 0 59	49 7 6 8 27	
Merchandise Inventory		86 8 7 6 38	
Supplies — Sales		2 0 3 0 82	
Supplies — Delivery		1 7 7 7 97	
Supplies — Administrative		1 6 2 0 75	
Prepaid Insurance		2 4 2 5 73	
Prepaid Interest		3 12	
Total Current Assets			197 1 4 2 23
Long-Term Investment:			
Bond Sinking Fund			7 0 0 0 00
Plant Assets:			
Store Equipment	51 4 8 6 21		
Less Accum. Depr. — Store Equip.	10 2 9 7 25	41 1 8 8 96	
Delivery Equipment	46 4 8 8 56		
Less Accum. Depr. — Deliv. Equip.	7 4 8 4 66	39 0 0 3 90	
Office Equipment	23 0 1 0 02		
Less Accum. Depr. — Office Equip.	4 3 9 4 91	18 6 1 5 11	

Continue this balance sheet on the next page.

Wescox, Inc.

Balance Sheet (continued)

December 31, 1989

Building	48	0	0	0	00													
Less Accum. Depr.—Building	7	7	2	8	00	40	2	7	2	00								
Land						36	2	8	5	03								
Total Plant Assets											175	3	6	5	00			
Intangible Asset:																		
Organization Costs												2	2	5	00			
Total Assets											379	7	3	2	23			
Liabilities																		
Current Liabilities:																		
Notes Payable						5	2	0	59									
Interest Payable						7	0	0	4	34								
Accounts Payable						10	4	6	8	53								
Employees Income Tax Payable						4	1	6	47									
Federal Income Tax Payable						2	4	37										
FICA Tax Payable						3	4	7	71									
Salaries Payable						1	3	7	7	78								
Sales Tax Payable						7	2	8	82									
Unemploy. Tax Payable—Federal						9	4	11										
Unemploy. Tax Payable—State						6	3	6	32									
Hospital Insurance Premiums Payable						1	5	6	18									
Dividends Payable						14	9	2	2	80								
Total Current Liabilities											36	6	9	8	02			
Long-Term Liability:																		
Bonds Payable											70	0	0	0	00			
Total Liabilities											106	6	9	8	02			
Stockholders' Equity																		
Total Stockholders' Equity											273	0	3	4	21			
Total Liabilities & Stockholders' Equity											379	7	3	2	23			

[6]

a. Rate earned on average stockholders' equity:

January 1 Equity	*December 31 Equity*	*Average*
$260,485.60	$273,034.21	$266,759.91

Net Income	÷	*Average Equity*	=	*Rate*
$11,471.41	÷	$266,759.91	=	4.3%

b. Rate earned on average total assets:

January 1 Assets	*December 31 Assets*	*Average*
$347,548.29	$379,732.23	$363,640.26

Net Income	÷	*Average Assets*	=	*Rate*
$11,471.41	÷	$363,640.26	=	3.2%

[7]

GENERAL JOURNAL

PAGE 12

	DATE		ACCOUNT TITLE	POST. REF.	DEBIT	CREDIT	
1			**Adjusting Entries**				1
2	1989 Dec.	31	Interest Receivable		1 7 18		2
3			Interest Income			1 7 18	3
4		31	Bad Debts Expense		2 1 3 4 41		4
5			Allowance for Uncollectible Accounts			2 1 3 4 41	5
6		31	Income Summary		2 7 0 15		6
7			Merchandise Inventory			2 7 0 15	7
8		31	Supplies Expense—Sales		2 8 6 2 71		8
9			Supplies—Sales			2 8 6 2 71	9
10		31	Supplies Expense—Delivery		4 4 1 7 04		10
11			Supplies—Delivery			4 4 1 7 04	11
12		31	Supplies Expense—Administrative		6 8 6 4 84		12
13			Supplies—Administrative			6 8 6 4 84	13
14		31	Insurance Expense		4 4 4 6 04		14
15			Prepaid Insurance			4 4 4 6 04	15
16		31	Prepaid Interest		3 12		16
17			Interest Expense			3 12	17
18		31	Depreciation Expense—Store Equipment		5 0 9 7 14		18
19			Accum. Depr.—Store Equipment			5 0 9 7 14	19
20		31	Depreciation Expense—Delivery Equipment		4 6 4 8 86		20
21			Accum. Depr.—Delivery Equipment			4 6 4 8 86	21

GENERAL JOURNAL

PAGE 13

	DATE		ACCOUNT TITLE	POST. REF.	DEBIT	CREDIT	
1	1989 Dec.	31	Depreciation Expense — Office Equipment		2 1 8 5 95		1
2			Accum. Depr. — Office Equipment			2 1 8 5 95	2
3		31	Depreciation Expense — Building		2 4 0 0 00		3
4			Accum. Depr. — Building			2 4 0 0 00	4
5		31	Organization Expense		7 5 00		5
6			Organization Costs			7 5 00	6
7		31	Interest Expense		7 0 0 4 34		7
8			Interest Payable			7 0 0 4 34	8
9		31	Salary Expense — Sales		2 5 9 98		9
10			Salary Expense — Delivery		1 1 5 67		10
11			Salary Expense — Administrative		1 0 0 2 13		11
12			Salaries Payable			1 3 7 7 78	12
13		31	Payroll Taxes Expense		1 8 1 87		13
14			FICA Tax Payable			9 6 45	14
15			Unemployment Tax Payable — Federal			1 1 02	15
16			Unemployment Tax Payable — State			7 4 40	16
17		31	Federal Income Tax		2 4 37		17
18			Federal Income Tax Payable			2 4 37	18
19							19
20							20
21							21
22							22
23							23
24							24
25							25
26							26
27							27
28							28
29							29
30							30
31							31
32							32
33							33

GENERAL JOURNAL   PAGE 14

	DATE		ACCOUNT TITLE	POST. REF.	DEBIT	CREDIT	
1			*Closing Entries*				1
2	1989 Dec.	31	Sales		296 735 50		2
3			Purchases Returns and Allowances		9 33 94		3
4			Purchases Discount		2 646 15		4
5			Interest Income		2 25 42		5
6			Income Summary			300 541 01	6
7		31	Income Summary		288 799 45		7
8			Sales Returns and Allowances			8 90 21	8
9			Sales Discount			5 93 47	9
10			Purchases			155 655 99	10
11			Advertising Expense			3 956 47	11
12			Credit Card Fee Expense			4 477 06	12
13			Depreciation Expense—Store Equip.			5 097 14	13
14			Miscellaneous Expense—Sales			1 926 18	14
15			Salary Expense—Sales			23 894 70	15
16			Supplies Expense—Sales			2 862 71	16
17			Depreciation Expense—Delivery Equip.			4 648 86	17
18			Miscellaneous Expense—Delivery			5 049 71	18
19			Salary Expense—Delivery			10 631 56	19
20			Supplies Expense—Delivery			4 417 04	20
21			Bad Debts Expense			2 134 41	21
22			Depreciation Expense—Office Equip.			2 185 95	22
23			Depreciation Expense—Building			2 400 00	23
24			Insurance Expense			4 446 04	24
25			Miscellaneous Expense—Admin.			5 518 24	25
26			Payroll Taxes Expense			5 892 31	26
27			Property Tax Expense			2 300 00	27
28			Salary Expense—Administrative			10 112 43	28
29			Supplies Expense—Administrative			6 864 84	29
30			Utilities Expense			9 318 54	30
31			Interest Expense			11 426 22	31
32			Organization Expense			75 00	32
33			Federal Income Tax			2 024 37	33

GENERAL JOURNAL

PAGE 15

	DATE		ACCOUNT TITLE	POST. REF.	DEBIT	CREDIT	
1	1989 Dec.	31	Income Summary		11 4 7 1 41		1
2			Retained Earnings			11 4 7 1 41	2
3		31	Retained Earnings		14 9 2 2 80		3
4			Dividends—Common Stock			7 7 2 2 80	4
5			Dividends—Preferred Stock			7 2 0 0 00	5
6			Reversing Entries				6
7	1990 Jan.	1	Interest Income		1 7 18		7
8			Interest Receivable			1 7 18	8
9		1	Interest Expense		3 12		9
10			Prepaid Interest			3 12	10
11		1	Interest Payable		7 0 0 4 34		11
12			Interest Expense			7 0 0 4 34	12
13		1	Salaries Payable		1 3 7 7 78		13
14			Salary Expense—Sales			2 5 9 98	14
15			Salary Expense—Delivery			1 1 5 67	15
16			Salary Expense—Administrative			1 0 0 2 13	16
17		1	FICA Tax Payable		9 6 45		17
18			Unemployment Tax Payable—Federal		1 1 02		18
19			Unemployment Tax Payable—State		7 4 40		19
20			Payroll Taxes Expense			1 8 1 87	20
21		1	Federal Income Tax Payable		2 4 37		21
22			Federal Income Tax			2 4 37	22

[10]

GENERAL JOURNAL

PAGE 17

DATE		ACCOUNT TITLE	POST. REF.	DEBIT	CREDIT	
1990 Nov.	24	Dividends—Common Stock		24 4 3 7 50		1
		Dividends—Preferred Stock		7 2 0 0 00		2
		Dividends Payable			31 6 3 7 50	3
		M72				4
						5
						6
						7
						8
						9

CASH PAYMENTS JOURNAL

PAGE 21

DATE		ACCOUNT TITLE	CHECK NO.	POST. REF.	GENERAL DEBIT	GENERAL CREDIT	ACCOUNTS PAYABLE DEBIT	PURCHASES DISCOUNT CREDIT	CASH CREDIT	
1991 Feb.	1	Dividends Payable	164		31 6 3 7 50				31 6 3 7 50	1
										2
										3
										4
										5
										6
										7
										8

End-of-fiscal-period work for a corporation   [1]

Knoll, Inc.

Work Sheet

For Year Ended December 31, 19--

	ACCOUNT TITLE	TRIAL BALANCE		ADJUSTMENTS		INCOME STATEMENT		BALANCE SHEET	
		DEBIT	CREDIT	DEBIT	CREDIT	DEBIT	CREDIT	DEBIT	CREDIT
1	Cash	84240 52						84240 52	
2	Petty Cash	400 00						400 00	
3	Notes Receivable	937 06						937 06	
4	Interest Receivable			(a) 10 31				10 31	
5	Accounts Receivable	31073 23						31073 23	
6	Allowance for Uncollectible Accounts		93 71		(b) 1280 65				1374 36
7	Merchandise Inventory	67450 01			(c) 162 09			67287 92	
8	Supplies—Sales	2936 12			(d) 1717 63			1218 49	
9	Supplies—Delivery	3717 00			(e) 2650 22			1066 78	
10	Supplies—Administrative	5091 36			(f) 4118 91			972 45	
11	Prepaid Insurance	4123 06			(g) 2667 62			1455 44	
12	Prepaid Interest			(h) 1 87				1 87	
13	Bond Sinking Fund	4000 00						4000 00	
14	Store Equipment	13806 01						13806 01	
15	Accum. Depr.—Store Equip.		1325 38		(i) 1311 57				2636 95
16	Delivery Equipment	27893 14						27893 14	
17	Accum. Depr.—Delivery Equip.		1701 48		(j) 2789 31				4490 79
18	Office Equipment	30891 73						30891 73	
19	Accum. Depr.—Office Equip.		3120 06		(k) 3058 28				6178 34
20	Building	29000 00						29000 00	
21	Accum. Depr.—Building		3219 00		(l) 1450 00				4669 00
22	Land	21771 02						21771 02	
23	Organization Costs	200 00			(m) 50 00			150 00	
24	Notes Payable		3123 5						3123 5
25	Interest Payable				(n) 4002 64				4002 64
26	Accounts Payable		20281 12						20281 12
27	Employees Inc. Tax Payable		249 88						249 88

[1]

#	ACCOUNT TITLE	TRIAL BALANCE Debit	TRIAL BALANCE Credit	ADJUSTMENTS Debit	ADJUSTMENTS Credit	INCOME STATEMENT Debit	INCOME STATEMENT Credit	BALANCE SHEET Debit	BALANCE SHEET Credit
28	Federal Income Tax Payable				(q) 2689 45				2689 45
29	FICA Tax Payable		150 76		(p) 57 87				208 63
30	Salaries Payable				(o) 826 67				826 67
31	Sales Tax Payable		437 29						437 29
32	Unemploy. Tax Pay.—Federal		49 85		(p) 6 61				56 46
33	Unemploy. Tax Pay.—State		337 15		(p) 44 64				381 79
34	Hospital Ins. Prem. Payable		93 71						93 71
35	Dividends Payable		20720 00						20720 00
36	Bonds Payable		40000 00						40000 00
37	Capital Stock—Common		110000 00						110000 00
38	Capital Stock—Preferred		43000 00						43000 00
39	Pd.-in Cap. in Ex. Par/Stated Val.		1100 00						1100 00
40	Disc. on Sale of Cap. Stock	2000 00						2000 00	
41	Treasury Stock	700 00						700 00	
42	Pd.-in Cap. from Sale of Tr. Stock		140 00						140 00
43	Retained Earnings		13587 36						13587 36
44	Dividends—Common Stock	16420 00						16420 00	
45	Dividends—Preferred Stock	4300 00						4300 00	
46	Income Summary			(c) 162 09		162 09			
47	Sales		299585 24				299585 24		
48	Sales Ret. & Allowances	508 76				508 76			
49	Sales Discount	339 17				339 17			
50	Purchases	143393 61				143393 61			
51	Purchases Ret. & Allow.		560 36				560 36		
52	Purchases Discount		1587 69				1587 69		
53	Advertising Expense	2373 88				2373 88			
54	Credit Card Fee Expense	2686 24				2686 24			
55	Depr. Exp.—Store Equip.			(i) 1311 57		1311 57			
56	Misc. Expense—Sales	1155 71				1155 71			
57	Salary Expense—Sales	14180 84		(o) 155 99		14336 83			

[1]

		TRIAL BALANCE		ADJUSTMENTS		INCOME STATEMENT		BALANCE SHEET	
	ACCOUNT TITLE	DEBIT	CREDIT	DEBIT	CREDIT	DEBIT	CREDIT	DEBIT	CREDIT
58	Supplies Expense—Sales			(d) 1717 63		1717 63			
59	Depr. Exp.—Deliv. Equip.			(j) 2789 31		2789 31			
60	Misc. Expense—Delivery	3029 83				3029 83			
61	Salary Expense—Delivery	6309 53		(o) 69 40		6378 93			
62	Supplies Expense—Delivery			(e) 2650 22		2650 22			
63	Bad Debts Expense			(b) 1280 65		1280 65			
64	Depr. Exp.—Office Equip.			(k) 3058 28		3058 28			
65	Depr. Expense—Building			(l) 1450 00		1450 00			
66	Insurance Expense			(g) 2667 62		2667 62			
67	Misc. Expense—Admin.	3310 94				3310 94			
68	Payroll Taxes Expense	3426 26		(p) 109 12		3535 38			
69	Property Tax Expense	1400 00				1400 00			
70	Salary Expense—Admin.	5466 18		(o) 601 28		6067 46			
71	Supplies Expense—Admin.			(f) 4118 91		4118 91			
72	Utilities Expense	5591 12				5591 12			
73	Interest Income		124 94		(a) 10 31		135 25		
74	Interest Expense	2655 00		(n) 4002 64	(h) 1 87	6655 77			
75	Organization Expense			(m) 50 00		50 00			
76	Federal Income Tax	15000 00		(q) 2689 45		17689 45			
77		561777 33	561777 33	28896 34	28896 34	239709 36	301868 54	339595 97	277436 79
78	Net Income after Federal Income Tax					62159 18			62159 18
79						301868 54	301868 54	339595 97	339595 97

$79,848.63 Net Income before Federal Tax:

Portion	Rate	Tax Amount
$25,000.00	15%	$ 3,750.00
25,000.00	18%	4,500.00
25,000.00	30%	7,500.00
4,848.63	40%	1,939.45
		$17,689.45

Total Tax $17,689.45
Account Balance   15,000.00
Tax Adjustment $ 2,689.45

Knoll, Inc.

Income Statement

For Year Ended December 31, 19--

					% OF NET SALES
Operating Revenue:					
Sales			299 5 8 5 24		
Less: Sales Ret. & Allow.		5 0 8 76			
Sales Discount		3 3 9 17	8 4 7 93		
Net Sales				298 7 3 7 31	100.0
Cost of Merchandise Sold:					
Mdse. Inv., Jan. 1, 19--			67 4 5 0 01		
Purchases		143 3 9 3 61			
Less: Pur. Ret. & Allow.	5 6 0 36				
Purchases Discount	1 5 8 7 69	2 1 4 8 05			
Net Purchases			141 2 4 5 56		
Total Cost of Mdse. Avail. for Sale			208 6 9 5 57		
Less Mdse. Inv., Dec. 31, 19--			67 2 8 7 92		
Cost of Merchandise Sold				141 4 0 7 65	47.3
Gross Profit from Operations				157 3 2 9 66	52.7
Operating Expenses:					
Selling Expenses:					
Advertising Expense		2 3 7 3 88			
Credit Card Fee Expense		2 6 8 6 24			
Depr. Exp. — Store Equip.		1 3 1 1 57			
Misc. Expense — Sales		1 1 5 5 71			
Salary Expense — Sales		14 3 3 6 83			
Supplies Expense — Sales		1 7 1 7 63			
Total Selling Expenses			23 5 8 1 86		
Delivery Expenses:					
Depr. Exp. — Deliv. Equip.		2 7 8 9 31			
Misc. Expense — Delivery		3 0 2 9 83			
Salary Expense — Delivery		6 3 7 8 93			
Supplies Expense — Delivery		2 6 5 0 22			
Total Delivery Expenses			14 8 4 8 29		
Administrative Expenses:					
Bad Debts Expense		1 2 8 0 65			

Continue this income statement on the next page.

Knoll, Inc.

Income Statement (continued)

For Year Ended December 31, 19--

			% OF NET SALES
Depr. Exp. — Office Equip.	3 0 5 8 28		
Depr. Expense — Building	1 4 5 0 00		
Insurance Expense	2 6 6 7 62		
Misc. Expense — Admin.	3 3 1 0 94		
Payroll Taxes Expense	3 5 3 5 38		
Property Tax Expense	1 4 0 0 00		
Salary Expense — Admin.	6 0 6 7 46		
Supplies Expense — Admin.	4 1 1 8 91		
Utilities Expense — Admin.	5 5 9 1 12		
Total Admin. Expenses		32 4 8 0 36	
Total Operating Expenses			70 9 1 0 51	23.7
Income from Operations			86 4 1 9 15	
Other Revenue:				
Interest Income		1 3 5 25	
Other Expenses:				
Interest Expense	6 6 5 5 77		
Organization Expense	5 0 00		
Total Other Expenses		6 7 0 5 77	
Net Deduction			6 5 7 0 52	
Net Income before Fed. Income Tax			79 8 4 8 63	26.7
Less Federal Income Tax			17 6 8 9 45	5.9
Net Income after Fed. Income Tax			62 1 5 9 18	20.8

Earnings per share:

Stock	Share of Net Income	÷	Shares Outstanding	=	Earnings per share
Preferred	$ 4,300.00	÷	430	=	$10.00
Common	57,859.18	÷	10,930	=	$ 5.29

15

Knoll, Inc.

Statement of Stockholders' Equity

For Year Ended December 31, 19--

Paid-in Capital:			
Common Stock, $10.00 Per Share			
Jan. 1, 19--, 10,000 Shares Issued	100 0 0 0 00		
Issued during 19--, 1,000 Shares	10 0 0 0 00		
Balance, Dec. 31, 19--, 11,000 Shares Issued		110 0 0 0 00	
Preferred Stock, $100.00 Per Share			
Jan. 1, 19--, 300 Shares Issued	30 0 0 0 00		
Issued during 19--, 130 Shares	13 0 0 0 00		
Balance, Dec. 31, 19--, 430 Shares Issued		43 0 0 0 00	
Total Value of Capital Stock Issued			153 0 0 0 00
Additional Paid-in Capital:			
Pd.-in Cap. in Ex. of Par/Stated Val.	1 1 0 0 00		
Pd.-in Cap. from Sale of Treas. Stock	1 4 0 00	1 2 4 0 00	
Less Disc. on Sale of Cap. Stock		2 0 0 0 00	
Total Additional Paid-in Capital			(7 6 0 00)
Total Paid-in Capital			152 2 4 0 00
Retained Earnings:			
January 1, 19--		13 5 8 7 36	
Net Income after Federal Income Tax for 19--	62 1 5 9 18		
Less Dividends Declared	20 7 2 0 00		
Net Increase during 19--		41 4 3 9 18	
Balance, December 31, 19--			55 0 2 6 54
Total Paid-in Capital & Retained Earnings			207 2 6 6 54
Less Treasury Stock, 70 Shares of			
Common Stock, December 31, 19--			7 0 0 00
Total Stockholders' Equity, Dec. 31, 19--			206 5 6 6 54

a. Equity per share:

Stock	Equity	÷	Shares Outstanding	=	Equity per share
Preferred	$ 43,000.00	÷	430	=	$100.00
Common	163,566.54	÷	10,930	=	$ 14.96

b. Price-earnings ratio:

Stock	Market Price	÷	Earnings per share	=	Price-earnings ratio
Common	$9.75	÷	$5.29	=	1.84 times

[5]

Knoll, Inc.

Balance Sheet

December 31, 19--

Assets			
Current Assets:			
Cash		84 240 52	
Petty Cash		400 00	
Notes Receivable		937 06	
Interest Receivable		10 31	
Accounts Receivable	31 073 23		
Less Allow. for Uncoll. Accounts	1 374 36	29 698 87	
Merchandise Inventory		67 287 92	
Supplies — Sales		1 218 49	
Supplies — Delivery		1 066 78	
Supplies — Administrative		972 45	
Prepaid Insurance		1 455 44	
Prepaid Interest		1 87	
Total Current Assets			187 289 71
Long-Term Investment:			
Bond Sinking Fund			4 000 00
Plant Assets:			
Store Equipment	13 806 01		
Less Accum. Depr. — Store Equip.	2 636 95	11 169 06	
Delivery Equipment	27 893 14		
Less Accum. Depr. — Deliv. Equip.	4 490 79	23 402 35	
Office Equipment	30 891 73		
Less Accum. Depr. — Office Equip.	6 178 34	24 713 39	

Continue this balance sheet on the next page.

Knoll, Inc.

Balance Sheet (continued)

December 31, 19--

Building	29 0 0 0 00		
Less Accum. Depr.—Building	4 6 6 9 00	24 3 3 1 00	
Land		21 7 7 1 02	
Total Plant Assets			105 3 8 6 82
Intangible Asset:			
Organization Costs			1 5 0 00
Total Assets			296 8 2 6 53
Liabilities			
Current Liabilities:			
Notes Payable		3 1 2 35	
Interest Payable		4 0 0 2 64	
Accounts Payable		20 2 8 1 12	
Employees Income Tax Payable		2 4 9 88	
Federal Income Tax Payable		2 6 8 9 45	
FICA Tax Payable		2 0 8 63	
Salaries Payable		8 2 6 67	
Sales Tax Payable		4 3 7 29	
Unemploy. Tax Payable—Federal		5 6 46	
Unemploy. Tax Payable—State		3 8 1 79	
Hospital Insurance Premiums Payable		9 3 71	
Dividends Payable		20 7 2 0 00	
Total Current Liabilities			50 2 5 9 99
Long-Term Liability:			
Bonds Payable			40 0 0 0 00
Total Liabilities			90 2 5 9 99
Stockholders' Equity			
Total Stockholders' Equity			206 5 6 6 54
Total Liabilities & Stockholders' Equity			296 8 2 6 53

[6]

a. Rate earned on average stockholders' equity:

January 1 Equity		December 31 Equity		Average
$142,127.36		$206,566.54		$174,346.95

Net Income	÷	Average Equity	=	Rate
$62,159.18	÷	$174,346.95	=	35.7%

b. Rate earned on average total assets:

January 1 Assets		December 31 Assets		Average
$199,116.94		$296,826.53		$247,971.74

Net Income	÷	Average Assets	=	Rate
$62,159.18	÷	$247,971.74	=	25.1%

[7]

GENERAL JOURNAL

PAGE 12

	DATE		ACCOUNT TITLE	POST. REF.	DEBIT	CREDIT	
1			*Adjusting Entries*				1
2	19-- Dec.	31	Interest Receivable		1 0 31		2
3			Interest Income			1 0 31	3
4		31	Bad Debts Expense		1 2 8 0 65		4
5			Allowance for Uncollectible Accounts			1 2 8 0 65	5
6		31	Income Summary		1 6 2 09		6
7			Merchandise Inventory			1 6 2 09	7
8		31	Supplies Expense—Sales		1 7 1 7 63		8
9			Supplies—Sales			1 7 1 7 63	9
10		31	Supplies Expense—Delivery		2 6 5 0 22		10
11			Supplies—Delivery			2 6 5 0 22	11
12		31	Supplies Expense—Administrative		4 1 1 8 91		12
13			Supplies—Administrative			4 1 1 8 91	13
14		31	Insurance Expense		2 6 6 7 62		14
15			Prepaid Insurance			2 6 6 7 62	15
16		31	Prepaid Interest		1 87		16
17			Interest Expense			1 87	17
18		31	Depreciation Expense—Store Equipment		1 3 1 1 57		18
19			Accum. Depr.—Store Equipment			1 3 1 1 57	19
20		31	Depreciation Expense—Delivery Equipment		2 7 8 9 31		20
21			Accum. Depr.—Delivery Equipment			2 7 8 9 31	21

GENERAL JOURNAL

PAGE 13

	DATE		ACCOUNT TITLE	POST. REF.	DEBIT	CREDIT	
1	19-- Dec.	31	Depreciation Expense—Office Equipment		3 0 5 8 28		1
2			Accum. Depr.—Office Equipment			3 0 5 8 28	2
3		31	Depreciation Expense—Building		1 4 5 0 00		3
4			Accum. Depr.—Building			1 4 5 0 00	4
5		31	Organization Expense		5 0 00		5
6			Organization Costs			5 0 00	6
7		31	Interest Expense		4 0 0 2 64		7
8			Interest Payable			4 0 0 2 64	8
9		31	Salary Expense—Sales		1 5 5 99		9
10			Salary Expense—Delivery		6 9 40		10
11			Salary Expense—Administrative		6 0 1 28		11
12			Salaries Payable			8 2 6 67	12
13		31	Payroll Taxes Expense		1 0 9 12		13
14			FICA Tax Payable			5 7 87	14
15			Unemployment Tax Payable—Federal			6 61	15
16			Unemployment Tax Payable—State			4 4 64	16
17		31	Federal Income Tax		2 6 8 9 45		17
18			Federal Income Tax Payable			2 6 8 9 45	18
19							19
20							20
21							21
22							22
23							23
24							24
25							25
26							26
27							27
28							28
29							29
30							30
31							31
32							32
33							33

GENERAL JOURNAL

PAGE 14

	DATE		ACCOUNT TITLE	POST. REF.	DEBIT	CREDIT	
1			*Closing Entries*				1
2	Dec.¹⁹⁻⁻	31	Sales		299 585 24		2
3			Purchases Returns and Allowances		5 60 36		3
4			Purchases Discount		1 587 69		4
5			Interest Income		1 35 25		5
6			Income Summary			301 868 54	6
7		31	Income Summary		239 547 27		7
8			Sales Returns and Allowances			5 08 76	8
9			Sales Discount			3 39 17	9
10			Purchases			143 393 61	10
11			Advertising Expense			2 373 88	11
12			Credit Card Fee Expense			2 686 24	12
13			Depreciation Expense—Store Equip.			1 311 57	13
14			Miscellaneous Expense—Sales			1 155 71	14
15			Salary Expense—Sales			14 336 83	15
16			Supplies Expense—Sales			1 717 63	16
17			Depreciation Expense—Delivery Equip.			2 789 31	17
18			Miscellaneous Expense—Delivery			3 029 83	18
19			Salary Expense—Delivery			6 378 93	19
20			Supplies Expense—Delivery			2 650 22	20
21			Bad Debts Expense			1 280 65	21
22			Depreciation Expense—Office Equip.			3 058 28	22
23			Depreciation Expense—Building			1 450 00	23
24			Insurance Expense			2 667 62	24
25			Misc. Expense—Administrative			3 310 94	25
26			Payroll Taxes Expense			3 535 38	26
27			Property Tax Expense			1 400 00	27
28			Salary Expense—Administrative			6 067 46	28
29			Supplies Expense—Administrative			4 118 91	29
30			Utilities Expense			5 591 12	30
31			Interest Expense			6 655 77	31
32			Organization Expense			50 00	32
33			Federal Income Tax			17 689 45	33

GENERAL JOURNAL

PAGE 15

	DATE		ACCOUNT TITLE	POST. REF.	DEBIT	CREDIT	
1	19-- Dec.	31	Income Summary		62 1 5 9 18		1
2			Retained Earnings			62 1 5 9 18	2
3		31	Retained Earnings		20 7 2 0 00		3
4			Dividends — Common Stock			16 4 2 0 00	4
5			Dividends — Preferred Stock			4 3 0 0 00	5
6			Reversing Entries				6
7	19-- Jan.	1	Interest Income		1 0 31		7
8			Interest Receivable			1 0 31	8
9		1	Interest Expense		1 87		9
10			Prepaid Interest			1 87	10
11		1	Interest Payable		4 0 0 2 64		11
12			Interest Expense			4 0 0 2 64	12
13		1	Salaries Payable		8 2 6 67		13
14			Salary Expense — Sales			1 5 5 99	14
15			Salary Expense — Delivery			6 9 40	15
16			Salary Expense — Administrative			6 0 1 28	16
17		1	FICA Tax Payable		5 7 87		17
18			Unemployment Tax Payable — Federal		6 61		18
19			Unemployment Tax Payable — State		4 4 64		19
20			Payroll Taxes Expense			1 0 9 12	20
21		1	Federal Income Tax Payable		2 6 8 9 45		21
22			Federal Income Tax			2 6 8 9 45	22
23							23
24							24
25							25
26							26
27							27
28							28
29							29
30							30
31							31
32							32
33							33

GENERAL JOURNAL

PAGE

	DATE		ACCOUNT TITLE	POST. REF.	DEBIT	CREDIT	
1							1
2							2
3							3
4							4
5							5
6							6
7							7
8							8
9							9
10							10
11							11
12							12
13							13
14							14
15							15
16							16
17							17
18							18
19							19
20							20
21							21
22							22
23							23
24							24
25							25
26							26
27							27
28							28
29							29
30							30
31							31
32							32
33							33

Recording Selected Accounting Transactions and Completing End-of-Fiscal-Period Work for a Corporation   [1,2]

CASH RECEIPTS JOURNAL

PAGE 15

	DATE	ACCOUNT TITLE	DOC. NO.	POST. REF.	GENERAL DEBIT	GENERAL CREDIT	ACCOUNTS RECEIVABLE CREDIT	SALES CREDIT	SALES TAX PAYABLE DEBIT	SALES TAX PAYABLE CREDIT	SALES DISCOUNT DEBIT	CASH DEBIT
1	19-- Dec. 1	Unearned Rent	R126			1800 00						1800 00
2	5	Notes Payable	NP6			2000 00						2000 00
3	6	Capital Stock—Common	R134			7000 00						7700 00
4		Paid-in Capital										
5		in Excess of										
6		Par/Stated Value				700 00						
7	7	Notes Receivable	R136			150 00						152 47
8		Interest Income				2 47						
9	11	Accum. Depr.—Office Equip.	R138		600 00							70 00
10		Loss on Plant Assets			30 00							
11		Office Equipment				700 00						
12	13	Capital Stock—Common	R140			2000 00						2000 00
13	14	Notes Receivable	R141			247 50						251 57
14		Interest Income				4 07						
15	20	Jane Gerard	R143				166 50					166 50
16	27	Interest Expense	NP7		98 63							4901 37
17		Notes Payable				5000 00						
18	28	Treasury Stock	R146			90 00						130 00
19		Paid-in Capital										
20		from Sale of										
21		Treasury Stock				40 00						
22	29	Accum. Depr.—Store Equip.	R147		1040 00							800 00
23		Store Equipment				1600 00						
24		Gain on Plant Assets				240 00						

Continue this journal on the next page.

[1, 2]

CASH RECEIPTS JOURNAL

	DATE	ACCOUNT TITLE	DOC. NO.	POST. REF.	GENERAL DEBIT (1)	GENERAL CREDIT (2)	ACCOUNTS RECEIVABLE CREDIT (3)	SALES CREDIT (4)	SALES TAX PAYABLE DEBIT (5)	SALES TAX PAYABLE CREDIT (6)	SALES DISCOUNT DEBIT (7)	CASH DEBIT (8)	
25	Dec. 29	Rick Plunkett	R148				153 70					154 75	25
26		Interest Income				1 05							26
27	29	Subscriptions Receivable	R149			3 000 00						3 000 00	27
28	31	Totals			17 686 63	24 575 09	320 20					23 126 66	28
29													29
30													30
31													31

PAGE 14

CASH PAYMENTS JOURNAL

	DATE	ACCOUNT TITLE	CHECK NO.	POST. REF.	GENERAL DEBIT (1)	GENERAL CREDIT (2)	ACCOUNTS PAYABLE DEBIT (3)	PURCHASES DISCOUNT CREDIT (4)	CASH CREDIT (5)	
1	Dec. 2	Office Equipment	296		755 00				755 00	1
2	5	Interest Expense	297		24 000 00				24 000 00	2
3	5	Bond Sinking Fund	298		20 000 00				18 400 00	3
4		Interest Income				16 000 00				4
5	11	Treasury Stock	302		540 00				540 00	5
6	12	Notes Payable	303		300 00				306 00	6
7		Interest Expense			6 00					7
8	16	Notes Payable	309		1 000 00				1016 44	8
9		Interest Expense			16 44					9
10	21	Office Equipment	315		990 00				800 00	10
11		Accum. Depr.— Office Equipment			810 00					11
12		Office Equipment				10 000 00				12
13	30	Dividends Payable	319		7 910 00				7 910 00	13
14	31	Totals			56 327 44	26 000 00			53 727 44	14
15										15

GENERAL JOURNAL

PAGE 11

	DATE		ACCOUNT TITLE	POST. REF.	DEBIT	CREDIT	
1	19-- Dec.	1	*Dividends—Common Stock*		5 8 9 0 00		1
2			*Dividends—Preferred Stock*		2 0 2 0 00		2
3			*Dividends Payable*			7 9 1 0 00	3
4			*M21*				4
5		1	*Allowance for Uncollectible Accounts*		1 6 6 50		5
6			*Accounts Receivable/Jane Gerard*	/		1 6 6 50	6
7			*M22*				7
8		1	*Depreciation Expense—Store Equipment*		3 6 67		8
9			*Accum. Depr.—Store Equipment*			3 6 67	9
10			*M23*				10
11		1	*Accum. Depr.—Store Equipment*		2 0 0 00		11
12			*Store Equipment*			2 0 0 00	12
13			*M23*				13
14		1	*Subscriptions Receivable*		3 0 0 0 00		14
15			*Stock Subscribed—Preferred*			3 0 0 0 00	15
16			*M24*				16
17		4	*Accounts Receivable/Rick Plunkett*	/	1 5 3 70		17
18			*Notes Receivable*			1 5 0 00	18
19			*Interest Income*			3 70	19
20			*M25*				20
21		4	*Depreciation Expense—Office Equipment*		5 0 00		21
22			*Accum. Depr.—Office Equipment*			5 0 00	22
23			*M26*				23
24		4	*Accum. Depr.—Office Equipment*		2 0 0 00		24
25			*Loss on Plant Assets*		5 0 00		25
26			*Office Equipment*			2 5 0 00	26
27			*M26*				27
28		4	*Notes Receivable*		5 0 0 00		28
29			*Accounts Receivable/Alice Wendson*	/		5 0 0 00	29
30			*NR5*				30
31		11	*Depreciation Expense—Office Equipment*		1 0 0 00		31
32			*Accum. Depr.—Office Equipment*			1 0 0 00	32
33			*M28*				33

GENERAL JOURNAL

PAGE 12

	DATE		ACCOUNT TITLE	POST. REF.	DEBIT	CREDIT	
1	19-- Dec.	19	Office Equipment		1 0 0 0 00		1
2			Capital Stock — Preferred			1 0 0 0 00	2
3			M30				3
4		20	Accounts Receivable/Jane Gerard		1 6 6 50		4
5			Allowance for Uncollectible Accounts			1 6 6 50	5
6			M31				6
7		21	Depreciation Expense — Office Equipment		9 0 00		7
8			Accum. Depr. — Office Equipment			9 0 00	8
9			M32				9
10		29	Depreciation Expense — Store Equipment		1 4 4 00		10
11			Accum. Depr. — Store Equipment			1 4 4 00	11
12			M36				12
13		29	Stock Subscribed — Preferred		3 0 0 0 00		13
14			Capital Stock — Preferred			3 0 0 0 00	14
15			M37				15
16							16
17							17
18							18
19							19
20							20
21							21
22							22
23							23
24							24
25							25
26							26
27							27
28							28
29							29
30							30
31							31
32							32
33							33

Eastland, Inc.

Work Sheet

For Year Ended December 31, 19--

	ACCOUNT TITLE	TRIAL BALANCE DEBIT	TRIAL BALANCE CREDIT	ADJUSTMENTS DEBIT	ADJUSTMENTS CREDIT	INCOME STATEMENT DEBIT	INCOME STATEMENT CREDIT	BALANCE SHEET DEBIT	BALANCE SHEET CREDIT
1	Cash	33 7 3 4 92						33 7 3 4 92	
2	Petty Cash	3 0 0 00						3 0 0 00	
3	Notes Receivable	5 0 0 00						5 0 0 00	
4	Interest Receivable			(a) 3 70				3 70	
5	Accounts Receivable	32 7 5 7 65						32 7 5 7 65	
6	Allowance for Uncollectible Accounts		4 1 9 28		(b) 2 2 3 47				6 4 2 75
7	Subscriptions Receivable								
8	Merchandise Inventory	153 5 4 6 33			(c) 12 2 2 7 70			141 3 1 8 63	
9	Supplies — Sales	3 4 0 6 78			(d) 1 9 8 8 93			1 4 1 7 85	
10	Supplies — Administrative	1 9 4 7 28			(e) 1 2 1 7 28			7 3 0 00	
11	Prepaid Insurance	1 7 6 4 00			(f) 7 9 4 00			9 7 0 00	
12	Prepaid Interest			(g) 9 2 06				9 2 06	
13	Bond Sinking Fund	60 0 0 0 00						60 0 0 0 00	
14	Store Equipment	93 4 0 0 00						93 4 0 0 00	
15	Accum. Depr. — Store Equip.		28 0 2 0 00		(h) 8 3 0 0 00				36 3 2 0 00
16	Office Equipment	31 5 6 8 00						31 5 6 8 00	
17	Accum. Depr. — Office Equip.		9 4 7 0 40		(i) 1 1 5 0 00				10 6 2 0 40
18	Building	80 0 0 0 00						80 0 0 0 00	
19	Accum. Depr. — Building		4 5 0 0 00		(j) 1 5 0 0 00				6 0 0 0 00
20	Land	20 0 0 0 00						20 0 0 0 00	
21	Organization Costs	6 0 0 00			(k) 3 0 0 00			3 0 0 00	
22	Notes Payable		7 0 0 0 00						7 0 0 0 00
23	Interest Payable				(l) 2 0 2 5 00				2 0 2 5 00
24	Accounts Payable		22 8 2 0 00						22 8 2 0 00
25	Employees Inc. Tax Payable		1 6 3 4 40						1 6 3 4 40
26	Federal Income Tax Payable				(p) 8 9 6 87				8 9 6 87
27	FICA Tax Payable		1 8 7 72		(n) 2 7 6 40				4 6 4 12

[3]

	ACCOUNT TITLE	TRIAL BALANCE DEBIT	TRIAL BALANCE CREDIT	ADJUSTMENTS DEBIT	ADJUSTMENTS CREDIT	INCOME STATEMENT DEBIT	INCOME STATEMENT CREDIT	BALANCE SHEET DEBIT	BALANCE SHEET CREDIT	
28	Salaries Payable				(m) 3 9 4 8 54				3 9 4 8 54	28
29	Sales Tax Payable		9 5 1 42						9 5 1 42	29
30	Unearned Rent		8 4 0 0 00	(o) 7 2 0 0 00					1 2 0 0 00	30
31	Unemploy. Tax Pay.—Federal		1 0 72		(n) 1 5 79				2 6 51	31
32	Unemploy. Tax Pay.—State		7 2 36		(n) 1 0 6 58				1 7 8 94	32
33	Hospital Ins. Prem. Payable		2 1 5 40						2 1 5 40	33
34	Dividends Payable									34
35	Bonds Payable		200 0 0 0 00						200 0 0 0 00	35
36	Capital Stock—Common		126 8 0 0 00						126 8 0 0 00	36
37	Stock Subscribed—Common									37
38	Capital Stock—Preferred		44 0 0 0 00						44 0 0 0 00	38
39	Stock Subscribed—Preferred									39
40	Pd.-in Cap. in Ex. Par/Stated Val.		1 5 0 0 00						1 5 0 0 00	40
41	Treasury Stock	4 5 0 0 00						4 5 0 0 00		41
42	Pd.-in Cap. from Sale of Tr. Stock		4 0 00						4 0 00	42
43	Retained Earnings		23 7 5 9 39						23 7 5 9 39	43
44	Dividends—Common Stock	11 7 8 0 00						11 7 8 0 00		44
45	Dividends—Preferred Stock	4 0 4 0 00						4 0 4 0 00		45
46	Income Summary			(c) 12 2 2 7 70		12 2 2 7 70				46
47	Sales		545 6 1 5 96				545 6 1 5 96			47
48	Sales Ret. & Allowances	4 4 1 5 16				4 4 1 5 16				48
49	Sales Discount	4 2 7 57				4 2 7 57				49
50	Purchases	346 1 2 6 27				346 1 2 6 27				50
51	Purchases Ret. & Allow.		2 1 1 2 17				2 1 1 2 17			51
52	Purchases Discount		1 7 4 2 32				1 7 4 2 32			52
53	Advertising Expense	3 1 9 44				3 1 9 44				53
54	Credit Card Fee Expense	6 7 2 1 83				6 7 2 1 83				54
55	Depr. Exp.—Store Equip.	1 8 0 67		(h) 8 3 0 0 00		8 4 8 0 67				55
56	Misc. Expense—Sales	4 7 6 30				4 7 6 30				56
57	Salary Expense—Sales	84 0 3 3 00		(m) 3 2 3 2 04		87 2 6 5 04				57

	ACCOUNT TITLE	TRIAL BALANCE DEBIT	TRIAL BALANCE CREDIT	ADJUSTMENTS DEBIT	ADJUSTMENTS CREDIT	INCOME STATEMENT DEBIT	INCOME STATEMENT CREDIT	BALANCE SHEET DEBIT	BALANCE SHEET CREDIT
58	Supplies Expense—Sales			(d)1 9 8 8 93		1 9 8 8 93			
59	Bad Debts Expense			(b)2 2 3 47		2 2 3 47			
60	Depr. Exp.—Office Equip.	2 4 0 00		(i)1 1 5 0 00		1 3 9 0 00			
61	Depr. Expense—Building			(j)1 5 0 0 00		1 5 0 0 00			
62	Insurance Expense			(f)7 9 4 00		7 9 4 00			
63	Misc. Expense—Admin.	3 9 0 00				3 9 0 00			
64	Payroll Taxes Expense	9 6 6 0 15		(n)3 9 8 77		1 0 0 5 8 92			
65	Property Tax Expense	4 0 0 0 00				4 0 0 0 00			
66	Salary Expense—Admin.	13 5 5 1 38		(m)7 1 6 50		1 4 2 6 7 88			
67	Supplies Expense—Admin.			(e)1 2 1 7 28		1 2 1 7 28			
68	Utilities Expense	3 4 1 1 87				3 4 1 1 87			
69	Gain on Plant Assets		2 4 0 00				2 4 0 00		
70	Interest Income		1 6 1 1 29		(a) 3 70		1 6 1 4 99		
71	Rent Income				(o)7 2 0 0 00		7 2 0 0 00		
72	Interest Expense	24 1 3 4 23		(l)2 0 2 5 00	(g) 9 2 06	2 6 0 6 7 17			
73	Loss on Plant Assets	6 4 0 00				6 4 0 00			
74	Organization Expense			(k) 3 0 0 00		3 0 0 00			
75	Federal Income Tax	3 0 0 0 00		(p)8 9 6 87		3 8 9 6 87			
76		1031 5 2 2 83	1031 5 2 2 83	42 6 6 32	42 6 6 32	536 6 0 6 37	558 5 2 5 44	513 3 6 2 81	491 4 4 3 74
77	Net Income after Federal Income Tax					21 9 1 9 07			21 9 1 9 07
78						558 5 2 5 44	558 5 2 5 44	513 3 6 2 81	513 3 6 2 81

Eastland, Inc.

Income Statement

For Year Ended December 31, 19--

						% OF NET SALES
Operating Revenue:						
Sales				545 6 1 5 96		
Less: Sales Ret. & Allow.		4 4 1 5 16				
Sales Discount		4 2 7 57	4 8 4 2 73			
Net Sales					540 7 7 3 23	100.0
Cost of Merchandise Sold:						
Mdse. Inventory, January 1, 19--				153 5 4 6 33		
Purchases		346 1 2 6 27				
Less: Pur. Ret. & Allow.	2 1 1 2 17					
Purchases Discount	1 7 4 2 32	3 8 5 4 49				
Net Purchases				342 2 7 1 78		
Total Cost of Mdse. Avail. for Sale				495 8 1 8 11		
Less Mdse. Inv., Dec. 31, 19--				141 3 1 8 63		
Cost of Merchandise Sold					354 4 9 9 48	65.6
Gross Profit from Operations					186 2 7 3 75	34.4
Operating Expenses:						
Selling Expenses:						
Advertising Expense		3 1 9 44				
Credit Card Fee Expense		6 7 2 1 83				
Depr. Exp.—Store Equip.		8 4 8 0 67				
Misc. Expense—Sales		4 7 6 30				
Salary Expense—Sales		87 2 6 5 04				
Supplies Expense—Sales		1 9 8 8 93				
Total Selling Expenses				105 2 5 2 21		
Administrative Expenses:						
Bad Debts Expense		2 2 3 47				
Depr. Exp.—Office Equip.		1 3 9 0 00				
Depr. Expense—Building		1 5 0 0 00				
Insurance Expense		7 9 4 00				
Misc. Expense—Admin.		3 9 0 00				
Payroll Taxes Expense		10 0 5 8 92				
Property Tax Expense		4 0 0 0 00				

Continue this income statement on the next page.

Eastland, Inc.

Income Statement (continued)

For Year Ended December 31, 19--

									% OF NET SALES
Salary Expense—Admin.			14 2 6 7 88						
Supplies Expense—Admin.			1 2 1 7 28						
Utilities Expense			3 4 1 1 87						
Total Admin. Expenses				37 2 5 3 42					
Total Operating Expenses						142 5 0 5 63			26.4
Income from Operations						43 7 6 8 12			
Other Revenue:									
Gain on Plant Assets			2 4 0 00						
Interest Income			1 6 1 4 99						
Rent Income			7 2 0 0 00						
Total Other Revenue				9 0 5 4 99					
Other Expenses:									
Interest Expense			26 0 6 7 17						
Loss on Plant Assets			6 4 0 00						
Organization Expense			3 0 0 00						
Total Other Expenses				27 0 0 7 17					
Net Deduction						17 9 5 2 18			
Net Income before Fed. Income Tax						25 8 1 5 94			4.8
Less Federal Income Tax						3 8 9 6 87			0.7
Net Income after Fed. Income Tax						21 9 1 9 07			4.1

Earnings per share:

Stock	Share of Net Income	÷	Shares Outstanding	=	Earnings per share
Preferred	$ 4,440.00	÷	444	=	$10.00
Common	17,479.07	÷	12,630	=	$ 1.38

Eastland, Inc.

Statement of Stockholders' Equity

For Year Ended December 31, 19--

Paid-in Capital:				
Common Stock, $10.00 Per Share				
Jan. 1, 19--, 11,780 Shares Issued	117 800 00			
Issued during 19--, 900 Shares	9 000 00			
Balance, Dec. 31, 19--, 12,680 Shares Issued		126 800 00		
Preferred Stock, $100.00 Per Share				
Jan. 1, 19--, 404 Shares Issued	40 400 00			
Issued during 19--, 40 Shares	4 000 00			
Balance, Dec. 31, 19--, 444 Shares Issued		44 400 00		
Total Value of Capital Stock Issued			171 200 00	
Additional Paid-in Capital:				
Pd.-in Cap. in Ex. of Par/Stated Val.		1 500 00		
Pd.-in Cap. from Sale of Treas. Stock		40 00		
Total Additional Paid-in Capital			1 540 00	
Total Paid-in Capital			172 740 00	
Retained Earnings:				
January 1, 19--		23 759 39		
Net Income after Federal Income Tax for 19--	21 919 07			
Less Dividends Declared	15 820 00			
Net Increase during 19--		6 099 07		
Balance, December 31, 19--			29 858 46	
Total Pd.-in Capital & Retained Earnings			202 598 46	
Less Treasury Stock, 50 Shares of				
Common Stock, December 31, 19--			4 50 00	
Total Stockholders' Equity, Dec. 31, 19--			202 148 46	

a. Equity per share:

Stock	Equity	÷	Shares Outstanding	=	Equity per share
Preferred	$ 44,400.00	÷	444	=	$100.00
Common	157,748.46	÷	12,630	=	$ 12.49

b. Price-earnings ratio:

Stock	Market Price	÷	Earnings per share	=	Price-earnings ratio
Common	$10.00	÷	$1.38	=	7.2 times

[7]

Eastland, Inc.

Balance Sheet

December 31, 19--

Assets					
Current Assets:					
Cash			33 7 3 4 92		
Petty Cash			3 0 0 00		
Notes Receivable			5 0 0 00		
Interest Receivable			3 70		
Accounts Receivable	32 7 5 7 65				
Less Allow. for Uncoll. Accounts	6 4 2 75		32 1 1 4 90		
Merchandise Inventory			141 3 1 8 63		
Supplies—Sales			1 4 1 7 85		
Supplies—Administrative			7 3 0 00		
Prepaid Insurance			9 7 0 00		
Prepaid Interest			9 2 06		
Total Current Assets				211 1 8 2 06	
Long-Term Investment:					
Bond Sinking Fund				60 0 0 0 00	
Plant Assets:					
Store Equipment	93 4 0 0 00				
Less Accum. Depr.—Store Equip.	36 3 2 0 00		57 0 8 0 00		
Office Equipment	31 5 6 8 00				
Less Accum. Depr.—Office Equip.	10 6 2 0 40		20 9 4 7 60		
Building	80 0 0 0 00				
Less Accum. Depr.—Building	6 0 0 0 00		74 0 0 0 00		

Continue this balance sheet on the next page.

Eastland, Inc.

Balance Sheet (continued)

December 31, 19--

Land	20 0 0 0 00	
Total Plant Assets		172 0 2 7 60
Intangible Asset:		
Organization Costs		3 0 0 00
Total Assets		443 5 0 9 66
Liabilities		
Current Liabilities:		
Notes Payable	7 0 0 0 00	
Interest Payable	2 0 2 5 00	
Accounts Payable	22 8 2 0 00	
Employees Income Tax Payable	1 6 3 4 40	
Federal Income Tax Payable	8 9 6 87	
FICA Tax Payable	4 6 4 12	
Salaries Payable	3 9 4 8 54	
Sales Tax Payable	9 5 1 42	
Unearned Rent	1 2 0 0 00	
Unemploy. Tax Payable—Federal	2 6 51	
Unemploy. Tax Payable—State	1 7 8 94	
Hospital Insurance Premiums Payable	2 1 5 40	
Total Current Liabilities		41 3 6 1 20
Long-Term Liability:		
Bonds Payable		200 0 0 0 00
Total Liabilities		241 3 6 1 20
Stockholders' Equity		
Total Stockholders' Equity		202 1 4 8 46
Total Liabilities & Stockholders' Equity		443 5 0 9 66

a. Rate earned on average stockholders' equity:

January 1 Equity		*December 31 Equity*		*Average*
$182,759.39		*$202,148.46*		*$192,453.93*

Net Income	÷	*Average Equity*	=	*Rate*
$21,919.07	÷	*$192,453.93*	=	*11.4%*

b. Rate earned on average total assets:

January 1 Assets		*December 31 Assets*		*Average*
$399,822.40		*$443,509.66*		*$421,666.03*

Net Income	÷	*Average Assets*	=	*Rate*
$21,919.07	÷	*$421,666.03*	=	*5.2%*

c. Accounts receivable turnover ratio:

Beginning Book Value of Accounts Receivable	+	*Ending Book Value of Accounts Receivable*	÷	*2*	=	*Avg. Book Value of Accounts Receivable*
$27,178.59	+	*$32,114.90*	÷	*2*	=	*$29,646.75*

		Avg. Book Value of Accounts Receivable		=		*Accounts Receivable Turnover Ratio*
Net Sales on Account	÷			=		
$234,436.51	÷	*$29,646.75*		=		*7.9 times*

d. Average number of days for payment:

Days in a Year	÷	*Turnover Ratio*	=	*Avg. Number of days for Payment*
365	÷	*7.9 times*	=	*46.2 days*

GENERAL JOURNAL

PAGE 13

	DATE		ACCOUNT TITLE	POST. REF.	DEBIT	CREDIT	
1			*Adjusting Entries*				1
2	19-- Dec.	31	Interest Receivable		3 70		2
3			Interest Income			3 70	3
4		31	Bad Debts Expense		2 23 47		4
5			Allowance for Uncollectible Accounts			2 23 47	5
6		31	Income Summary		12 2 27 70		6
7			Merchandise Inventory			12 2 27 70	7
8		31	Supplies Expense — Sales		1 9 88 93		8
9			Supplies — Sales			1 9 88 93	9
10		31	Supplies Expense — Administrative		1 2 17 28		10
11			Supplies — Administrative			1 2 17 28	11
12		31	Insurance Expense		7 94 00		12
13			Prepaid Insurance			7 94 00	13
14		31	Prepaid Interest		9 2 06		14
15			Interest Expense			9 2 06	15
16		31	Depreciation Expense — Store Equipment		8 3 00 00		16
17			Accum. Depr. — Store Equipment			8 3 00 00	17
18		31	Depreciation Expense — Office Equipment		1 1 50 00		18
19			Accum. Depr. — Office Equipment			1 1 50 00	19
20		31	Depreciation Expense — Building		1 5 00 00		20
21			Accum. Depr. — Building			1 5 00 00	21
22		31	Organization Expense		3 00 00		22
23			Organization Costs			3 00 00	23
24		31	Interest Expense		2 0 25 00		24
25			Interest Payable			2 0 25 00	25
26		31	Salary Expense — Sales		3 2 32 04		26
27			Salary Expense — Administrative		7 16 50		27
28			Salaries Payable			3 9 48 54	28
29		31	Payroll Taxes Expense		3 98 77		29
30			FICA Tax Payable			2 76 40	30
31			Unemployment Tax Payable — Federal			15 79	31
32			Unemployment Tax Payable — State			1 06 58	32

GENERAL JOURNAL

PAGE 14

	DATE		ACCOUNT TITLE	POST. REF.	DEBIT	CREDIT	
1	19-- Dec.	31	Unearned Rent		7 2 0 0 00		1
2			Rent Income			7 2 0 0 00	2
3		31	Federal Income Tax		8 9 6 87		3
4			Federal Income Tax Payable			8 9 6 87	4
5			Closing Entries				5
6	19-- Dec.	31	Sales		545 6 1 5 96		6
7			Purchases Returns and Allowances		2 1 1 2 17		7
8			Purchases Discount		1 7 4 2 32		8
9			Gain on Plant Assets		2 4 0 00		9
10			Interest Income		1 6 1 4 99		10
11			Rent Income		7 2 0 0 00		11
12			Income Summary			558 5 2 5 44	12
13		31	Income Summary		524 3 7 8 67		13
14			Sales Returns and Allowances			4 4 1 5 16	14
15			Sales Discount			4 2 7 57	15
16			Purchases			346 1 2 6 27	16
17			Advertising Expense			3 1 9 44	17
18			Credit Card Fee Expense			6 7 2 1 83	18
19			Depreciation Expense—Store Equip.			8 4 8 0 67	19
20			Miscellaneous Expense—Sales			4 7 6 30	20
21			Salary Expense—Sales			87 2 6 5 04	21
22			Supplies Expense—Sales			1 9 8 8 93	22
23			Bad Debts Expense			2 2 3 47	23
24			Depreciation Expense—Office Equip.			1 3 9 0 00	24
25			Depreciation Expense—Building			1 5 0 0 00	25
26			Insurance Expense			7 9 4 00	26
27			Miscellaneous Expense—Admin.			3 9 0 00	27
28			Payroll Taxes Expense			10 0 5 8 92	28
29			Property Tax Expense			4 0 0 0 00	29
30			Salary Expense—Administrative			14 2 6 7 88	30
31			Supplies Expense—Administrative			1 2 1 7 28	31

GENERAL JOURNAL

PAGE 15

	DATE		ACCOUNT TITLE	POST. REF.	DEBIT	CREDIT	
1	19-- Dec.	31	Utilities Expense			3 4 1 1 87	1
2			Interest Expense			26 0 6 7 17	2
3			Loss on Plant Assets			6 4 0 00	3
4			Organization Expense			3 0 0 00	4
5			Federal Income Tax			3 8 9 6 87	5
6		31	Income Summary		21 9 1 9 07		6
7			Retained Earnings			21 9 1 9 07	7
8		31	Retained Earnings		15 8 2 0 00		8
9			Dividends — Common			11 7 8 0 00	9
10			Dividends — Preferred			4 0 4 0 00	10
11			*Reversing Entries*				11
12	19-- Jan.	1	Interest Income		3 70		12
13			Interest Receivable			3 70	13
14		1	Interest Expense		9 2 06		14
15			Prepaid Interest			9 2 06	15
16		1	Interest Payable		2 0 2 5 00		16
17			Interest Expense			2 0 2 5 00	17
18		1	Salaries Payable		3 9 4 8 54		18
19			Salary Expense — Sales			3 2 3 2 04	19
20			Salary Expense — Administrative			7 1 6 50	20
21		1	FICA Tax Payable		2 7 6 40		21
22			Unemployment Tax Payable — Federal		1 5 79		22
23			Unemployment Tax Payable — State		1 0 6 58		23
24			Payroll Taxes Expense			3 9 8 77	24
25		1	Federal Income Tax Payable		8 9 6 87		25
26			Federal Income Tax			8 9 6 87	26
27							27
28							28
29							29
30							30
31							31

Automated Accounting Cycle for a Corporation: Completing End-of-Fiscal-Period Work

BATCH NO. 54

RUN DATE 12 / 31 / 89
       MM DD YY

JOURNAL ENTRIES
Input Form

PAGE 1 **OF** 2 **PAGES**

	DAY	DOC. NO.	VENDOR/ CUSTOMER NO.	GENERAL LEDGER ACCT. NO.	DEBIT	CREDIT	
1	31	ADJ.ENT.		1120	17 18		1
2				7105		17 18	2
3				6305	2134 41		3
4				1130		2134 41	4
5				3150	270 15		5
6				1135		270 15	6
7				6130	2862 71		7
8				1140		2862 71	8
9				6220	4417 04		9
10				1145		4417 04	10
11				6345	6864 84		11
12				1150		6864 84	12
13				6320	4446 04		13
14				1155		4446 04	14
15				1160	3 12		15
16				8105		3 12	16
17				6115	5097 14		17
18				1310		5097 14	18
19				6205	4648 86		19
20				1320		4648 86	20
21				6310	2185 95		21
22				1330		2185 95	22
23				6315	2400 00		23
24				1340		2400 00	24
25							25

PAGE TOTALS   35347 44   35347 44

BATCH TOTALS

BATCH NO. __54__

RUN DATE __12__ / __31__ / __89__
MM   DD   YY

JOURNAL ENTRIES
Input Form

PAGE __2__ OF __2__ PAGES

	1	2	3	4	5	6	
	DAY	DOC. NO.	VENDOR/ CUSTOMER NO.	GENERAL LEDGER ACCT. NO.	DEBIT	CREDIT	
1	31	ADJ.ENT.		8110	75 00		1
2				1405		75 00	2
3				8105	7004 34		3
4				2110		7004 34	4
5				6125	259 98		5
6				6215	115 67		6
7				6340	1002 13		7
8				2135		1377 78	8
9				6330	181 87		9
10				2130		96 45	10
11				2145		11 02	11
12				2150		74 40	12
13				9105	24 37		13
14				2125		24 37	14
15							15
16							16
17							17
18							18
19							19
20							20
21							21
22							22
23							23
24							24
25							25

PAGE TOTALS   8663 36   8663 36

BATCH TOTALS   44010 80   44010 80

BATCH NO. 1

RUN DATE 01 / 01 / 90
             MM DD YY

JOURNAL ENTRIES
Input Form

PAGE 1 OF 1 PAGES

	1	2	3	4	5	6	
	DAY	DOC. NO.	VENDOR/ CUSTOMER NO.	GENERAL LEDGER ACCT. NO.	DEBIT	CREDIT	
1	01	REV.ENT.		7105	17 18		1
2				1120		17 18	2
3				8105	3 12		3
4				1160		3 12	4
5				2110	7004 34		5
6				8105		7004 34	6
7				2135	1377 78		7
8				6125		259 98	8
9				6215		115 67	9
10				6340		1002 13	10
11				2130	96 45		11
12				2145	11 02		12
13				2150	74 40		13
14				6330		181 87	14
15				2125	24 37		15
16				9105		24 37	16
17							17
18							18
19							19
20							20
21							21
22							22
23							23
24							24
25							25

	DEBIT	CREDIT
PAGE TOTALS		
BATCH TOTALS	8608 66	8608 66

BATCH NO. **49**

RUN DATE 11 / 24 / 90
         MM DD YY

JOURNAL ENTRIES
Input Form

PAGE __1__ OF __1__ PAGES

	1	2	3	4	5	6	
	DAY	DOC. NO.	VENDOR/ CUSTOMER NO.	GENERAL LEDGER ACCT. NO.	DEBIT	CREDIT	
1	24	M72		3140	24437 50		1
2				3145	7200 00		2
3				2160		31637 50	3
25							25
			PAGE TOTALS				
			BATCH TOTALS		31637 50	31637 50	

[15]

BATCH NO. **6**

RUN DATE 02 / 02 / 91
         MM DD YY

JOURNAL ENTRIES
Input Form

PAGE __1__ OF __1__ PAGES

	1	2	3	4	5	6	
	DAY	DOC. NO.	VENDOR/ CUSTOMER NO.	GENERAL LEDGER ACCT. NO.	DEBIT	CREDIT	
1	01	C164		2160	31637 50		1
2				1105		31637 50	2
3							3
25							25
			PAGE TOTALS				
			BATCH TOTALS		31637 50	31637 50	

Perfect Score. 32

Deduct .... —

Your Score .... —

Name _____

Date _____ Class _____

Checked by _____

STUDY GUIDE 16

UNIT A—Identifying Accounting Terms

DIRECTIONS: Select the one term in Column I that best fits each definition in Column II. Print the letter identifying your choice in the Answers column.

Column I	Column II	Answers	For Scoring
A. average number of days' sales in merchandise inventory	**0.** Goods which are given to a business to sell, but for which the title remains with the vendor...................	C	0. ✔
B. consignee	**1.** The person or business who receives goods on consignment..	B	1.
C. consignment			
D. consignor	**2.** The person or business who gives goods on consignment..	D	2.
E. first-in, first-out inventory costing method	**3.** The period of time needed to sell an average amount of merchandise inventory......................................	A	3.
F. last-in, first-out inventory costing method	**4.** A form used to show kind of merchandise, quantity received, quantity sold, and balance on hand..............	K	4.
G. lower of cost or market inventory costing method	**5.** A file of stock records for all merchandise.................	J	5.
	6. Charging the cost of merchandise purchased first to the cost of merchandise sold first................................	E	6.
H. merchandise inventory turnover ratio	**7.** Charging the cost of merchandise purchased last to the cost of merchandise sold first................................	F	7.
I. retail method of estimating inventory	**8.** Charging the average cost of beginning inventory plus merchandise purchased during a fiscal period to the cost of merchandise sold	L	8.
J. stock ledger			
K. stock record	**9.** Charging the lower of cost or market price to ending merchandise inventory	G	9.
L. weighted-average inventory costing method	**10.** Estimating inventory value by using a percentage based on both cost and retail prices	I	10.
	11. The number of times the average amount of merchandise inventory is sold during a specific period of time	H	11.

DIRECTIONS: Place a check mark in the proper Answers column to show whether each of the following statements is true or false.

	Answers		For Scoring
	True	False	
0. The value of merchandise available for sale consists of the value of the beginning inventory and the purchases added to inventory during the fiscal period...............	✔		**0.** ✔
12. At the end of each fiscal period, the cost of merchandise available for sale is divided into the ending inventory and net purchases............		✔	**12.**
13. If the value of the ending merchandise inventory is overstated, the net income will be understated...............		✔	**13.**
14. If the value of ending merchandise inventory is understated, the cost of merchandise sold will be understated...............		✔	**14.**
15. If the value of ending merchandise inventory is understated, the total stockholders' equity will be understated............	✔		**15.**
16. Typically, a business counts as part of its inventory all goods for sale legally owned by the business...............	✔		**16.**
17. When the terms of sale for goods in transit are FOB shipping point, the title to the goods passes to the buyer when the goods are received by the buyer...		✔	**17.**
18. When the terms of sale for goods in transit are FOB destination, the title to the goods passes to the buyer when the goods are received by the buyer......	✔		**18.**
19. When goods are sent to a business on consignment, title to the goods passes to the business accepting the consignment when the consignor delivers the goods to a transportation business...............		✔	**19.**
20. A perpetual inventory provides an easy way for management to determine when to reorder merchandise items...............	✔		**20.**
21. Because of the expense, many businesses take a periodic inventory only once a year...............	✔		**21.**
22. Businesses using a perpetual inventory method never need to take a periodic inventory...............		✔	**22.**
23. The weighted-average inventory costing method is based on the assumption that each item in the ending inventory has a value equal to the average price paid for similar items...............	✔		**23.**
24. In the lower of cost or market inventory costing method, if the cost price is higher than the current market price, the inventory value is marked down to the market price...............	✔		**24.**
25. During a period of increasing prices, the weighted-average inventory costing method usually will give the lowest total inventory value............		✔	**25.**
26. During a period of decreasing prices, the weighted-average inventory costing method usually will give the lowest total inventory value............		✔	**26.**
27. Taking a periodic inventory once a month for interim monthly financial statements is usually too expensive to be worthwhile............	✔		**27.**
28. Businesses that need an ending inventory value for monthly interim financial statements usually take a monthly periodic inventory............		✔	**28.**
29. A business keeping a perpetual inventory and also preparing monthly interim financial statements will need to estimate monthly ending inventory............		✔	**29.**
30. Using the retail method of estimating ending inventory is more expensive than the gross profit method because more records must be kept............	✔		**30.**
31. A merchandise inventory turnover ratio expresses a relationship between an average inventory and the cost of goods sold............	✔		**31.**
32. Figuring an accurate merchandise inventory value in order to adequately report a business' progress is an application of the accounting concept Adequate Disclosure............	✔		**32.**

Keeping perpetual inventory records

STOCK RECORD

Description	Lamp shades, beige				Stock No.	S51
Reorder	20		Minimum	5	Location	Bin 12
1	2	3	4	5	6	7
INCREASES			DECREASES			BALANCE
Date	Purchase Invoice No.	Quantity	Date	Sales Invoice No.	Quantity	Quantity
May 1 [19--]						11
			May 4	21	4	7
			13	24	2	5
15	16	20				25
			17	25	10	15
			21	27	10	5
			25	29	5	—0—
30	18	20				20

STOCK RECORD

Description	Electric cords, brown				Stock No.	C10
Reorder	25		Minimum	5	Location	Bin 40
1	2	3	4	5	6	7
INCREASES			DECREASES			BALANCE
Date	Purchase Invoice No.	Quantity	Date	Sales Invoice No.	Quantity	Quantity
May 1 [19--]						15
			May 6	22	5	10
			12	23	6	4
18	17	25				29
			20	26	10	19
			21	28	15	4
			26	30	3	1
31	19	25				26

Valuing inventory using fifo, lifo, and weighted-average methods

PROBLEM 16-2, p. 357
[1, 2]

| Stock No. | Dec. 31 Inventory | Inventory Costing Method | | | | | |
| | | Fifo | | Lifo | | Weighted-Average | |
		Unit Cost	Value	Unit Cost	Value	Unit Cost	Value
A15	30	10 @ 6.00 10 @ 8.00 10 @ 7.00	210.00	10 @ 5.00 10 @ 6.00 10 @ 7.00	180.00	30 @ 6.40	192.00
B10	20	5 @ 4.00 10 @ 5.00 5 @ 6.00	100.00	12 @ 4.00 5 @ 4.00 3 @ 6.00	86.00	20 @ 4.54	90.80
C8	35	10 @ 6.00 10 @ 7.00 10 @ 8.00 5 @ 9.00	255.00	6 @ 9.00 10 @ 9.00 10 @ 8.00 9 @ 7.00	287.00	35 @ 7.70	269.50
D23	15	5 @ 5.00 5 @ 5.00 5 @ 6.00	80.00	5 @ 6.00 5 @ 6.00 5 @ 6.00	90.00	15 @ 5.60	84.00
E30	45	10 @ 2.00 10 @ 3.00 10 @ 5.00 10 @ 4.00 5 @ 3.00	155.00	15 @ 3.00 10 @ 4.00 10 @ 5.00 10 @ 3.00	165.00	45 @ 3.36	151.20
Total Values			800.00		808.00		787.50

[3]

Highest method: _____lifo_____

Lowest method: _____weighted-average_____

Valuing inventory using lower of cost or market method

PROBLEM 16-3, p. 358
[1, 2]

| Stock No. | Inventory | Price to Use | | Total Value |
		Cost	Market	
N50	20	$ 3.25		$ 65.00
P23	35		$ 1.75	61.25
R10	5	19.00		95.00
T55	11	8.00		88.00
V2	8		15.00	120.00
W16	3	25.00		75.00
X58	15		10.00	150.00
Total				$654.25

Name _____ Date _____ Class _____

Estimating ending merchandise inventory

ESTIMATED MERCHANDISE INVENTORY SHEET
Gross Profit Method

Company __Miley, Inc.__   Date __August 31, 19--__

1	Beginning inventory, January 1	$ _16,200.00_
2	Net purchases to date..	_65,100.00_
3	Merchandise available for sale...	$ _81,300.00_
4	Net sales to date .... $ _81,900.00_	
5	Less estimated gross profit .... _24,570.00_	
	(Net sales × Estimated gross profit _30_ %)	
6	Estimated cost of merchandise sold...	_57,330.00_
7	Estimated ending inventory..	$ _23,970.00_

ESTIMATED MERCHANDISE INVENTORY SHEET
Gross Profit Method

Company __Dowsage, Inc.__   Date __August 31, 19--__

1	Beginning inventory, January 1	$ _37,200.00_
2	Net purchases to date..	_108,600.00_
3	Merchandise available for sale...	$ _145,800.00_
4	Net sales to date .... $ _141,000.00_	
5	Less estimated gross profit .... _56,400.00_	
	(Net sales × Estimated gross profit _40_ %)	
6	Estimated cost of merchandise sold...	_84,600.00_
7	Estimated ending inventory..	$ _61,200.00_

ESTIMATED MERCHANDISE INVENTORY SHEET
Retail Method

Company **Miley, Inc.**   Date **August 31, 19--**

		Cost	Retail
1	Beginning inventory, January 1	$ 16,200.00	$ 34,885.00
2	Net purchases to date..	65,100.00	99,265.00
3	Merchandise available for sale...............................	$ 81,300.00	$ 134,150.00
4	Less net sales to date...		94,550.00
5	Estimated ending inventory at retail........................		$ 39,600.00
6	Estimated ending inventory at cost (Inventory at Retail × percentage **60.6%**)..............	$ 23,997.60	

ESTIMATED MERCHANDISE INVENTORY SHEET
Retail Method

Company **Dowsage, Inc.**   Date **August 31, 19--**

		Cost	Retail
1	Beginning inventory, January 1	$ 37,200.00	$ 80,106.00
2	Net purchases to date..	108,600.00	165,594.00
3	Merchandise available for sale...............................	$ 145,800.00	$ 245,700.00
4	Less net sales to date...		142,833.00
5	Estimated ending inventory at retail........................		$ 102,867.00
6	Estimated ending inventory at cost (Inventory at Retail × percentage **59.3%**)..............	$ 61,000.13	

Figuring merchandise inventory turnover ratio and average number
of days' sales in merchandise inventory

Corporation A:

Beginning Merchandise Inventory	+	**Ending Merchandise Inventory**	÷ 2 =	**Average Merchandise Inventory**
$49,200.00	+	$53,000.00	÷ 2 =	$51,100.00

Cost of Merchandise Sold	÷	**Average Merchandise Inventory**	=	**Merchandise Inventory Turnover Ratio**
$480,700.00	÷	$51,100.00	=	9.4 times

Corporation B:

Beginning Merchandise Inventory	+	**Ending Merchandise Inventory**	÷ 2 =	**Average Merchandise Inventory**
$50,000.00	+	$49,300.00	÷ 2 =	$49,650.00

Cost of Merchandise Sold	÷	**Average Merchandise Inventory**	=	**Merchandise Inventory Turnover Ratio**
$422,100.00	÷	$49,650.00	=	8.5 times

Corporation C:

Beginning Merchandise Inventory	+	**Ending Merchandise Inventory**	÷ 2 =	**Average Merchandise Inventory**
$52,100.00	+	$47,500.00	÷ 2 =	$49,800.00

Cost of Merchandise Sold	÷	**Average Merchandise Inventory**	=	**Merchandise Inventory Turnover Ratio**
$525,600.00	÷	$49,800.00	=	10.6 times

[2]

Corporation A:

Days in a Year	÷	**Turnover Ratio**	=	**Average Number of Days' Sales in Merchandise Inventory**
365	÷	9.4 times	=	38.8 days

Corporation B:

Days in a Year	÷	**Turnover Ratio**	=	**Average Number of Days' Sales in Merchandise Inventory**
365	÷	8.5 times	=	42.9 days

Corporation C:

Days in a Year	÷	**Turnover Ratio**	=	**Average Number of Days' Sales in Merchandise Inventory**
365	÷	10.6 times	=	34.4 days

[3]

Best Turnover Ratio: *Corporation C.*

Valuing merchandise inventory; figuring merchandise inventory turnover ratio and average number of days' sales in merchandise inventory

MASTERY PROBLEM 16-M, p. 359
[1, 2]

Stock No.	Dec. 31 Inventory	Inventory Costing Method					
		Fifo		Lifo		Weighted-Average	
		Unit Cost	Value	Unit Cost	Value	Unit Cost	Value
G25	25	15 @ 9.00 10 @ 8.00	215.00	14 @ 7.00 11 @ 8.00	186.00	8.02	200.50
J15	30	10 @ 8.00 10 @ 5.00 10 @ 5.00	180.00	16 @ 5.00 10 @ 5.00 4 @ 8.00	162.00	5.83	174.90
K10	25	15 @ 11.00 10 @ 11.00	275.00	8 @ 12.00 15 @ 11.00 2 @ 11.00	283.00	11.21	280.25
M35	10	7 @ 8.00 3 @ 8.00	80.00	7 @ 8.00 3 @ 8.00	80.00	8.00	80.00
N52	5	5 @ 7.00	35.00	5 @ 4.00	20.00	6.00	30.00
Total Values			785.00		731.00		765.65

[3]

Stock No.	Inventory	Price to Use		Total Value
		Cost	Market	
G25	25	$8.02		$200.50
J15	30	5.83		174.90
K10	25		$10.00	250.00
M35	10	8.00		80.00
N52	5	6.00		30.00
Total				$735.40

[6]

Beginning Merchandise Inventory	+	Ending Merchandise Inventory	÷ 2 =	Average Merchandise Inventory
$19,400.00	+	$29,080.00	÷ 2 =	$24,240.00

Cost of Merchandise Sold	÷	Average Merchandise Inventory	=	Merchandise Inventory Turnover Ratio
$58,320.00	÷	$24,240.00	=	2.4 times

[7]

Days in a Year	÷	Turnover Ratio	=	Average Number of Days' Sales in Merchandise Inventory
365	÷	2.4 times	=	152.1 days

Chapter 16 • 282

[4]

ESTIMATED MERCHANDISE INVENTORY SHEET
Gross Profit Method

Company __*Bandee, Inc.*_____ Date *December 31, 19--*

1	Beginning inventory, January 1..	$	19,400.00
2	Net purchases to date...		68,000.00
3	Merchandise available for sale...	$	87,400.00
4	Net sales to date .... $	97,200.00	
5	Less estimated gross profit	38,880.00	
	(Net sales × Estimated gross profit __40__ %)		
6	Estimated cost of merchandise sold...............................		58,320.00
7	Estimated ending inventory..	$	29,080.00

[5]

ESTIMATED MERCHANDISE INVENTORY SHEET
Retail Method

Company __*Bandee, Inc.*_____ Date *December 31, 19--*

		Cost	Retail
1	Beginning inventory, January 1.........................	$ 19,400.00	$ 48,740.00
2	Net purchases to date......................................	68,000.00	142,800.00
3	Merchandise available for sale..........................	$ 87,400.00	$ 191,540.00
4	Less net sales to date......................................		129,300.00
5	Estimated ending inventory at retail.....................		$ 62,240.00
6	Estimated ending inventory at cost		
	(Inventory at Retail × percentage __45.6%__).............	$ 28,381.44	

Valuing merchandise inventory; figuring merchandise inventory turnover ratio and average number of days' sales in merchandise inventory

CHALLENGE PROBLEM 16-C, p. 360
[1, 2]

Stock No.	Jan. 31 Inventory	Inventory Costing Method					
		Fifo		Lifo		Weighted-Average	
		Unit Cost	Value	Unit Cost	Value	Unit Cost	Value
H15	2,500	1,500 @ 9.00 1,000 @ 8.00	21,500.00	2,400 @ 7.00 100 @ 8.00	17,600.00	7.83	19,575.00
J35	2,500	1,000 @ 8.00 1,000 @ 5.00 500 @ 5.00	15,500.00	1,600 @ 5.00 900 @ 5.00	12,500.00	5.83	14,575.00
M40	250	150 @ 11.00 100 @ 11.00	2,750.00	250 @ 12.00	3,000.00	11.73	2,932.50
Q75	650	300 @ 8.00 300 @ 8.00 50 @ 8.00	5,200.00	650 @ 8.00	5,200.00	8.00	5,200.00
V22	400	100 @ 7.00 100 @ 6.00 200 @ 4.00	2,100.00	400 @ 4.00	1,600.00	4.71	1,884.00
Total Values			47,050.00		39,900.00		44,166.50

[3]

Stock No.	Inventory	Price to Use		Total Value
		Cost	Market	
H15	2,000	$9.00		$18,000.00
J35	1,500	5.00		7,500.00
M40	200		$9.00	1,800.00
Q75	300	8.00		2,400.00
V22	300	4.00		1,200.00
Total				$30,900.00

[6]

Beginning Merchandise Inventory	+	Ending Merchandise Inventory	÷ 2 =	Average Merchandise Inventory
$42,000.00	+	$74,675.00	÷ 2 =	$58,337.50

Cost of Merchandise Sold	÷	Average Merchandise Inventory	=	Merchandise Inventory Turnover Ratio
$117,645.00	÷	$58,337.50	=	2.0 times

[7]

Days in a Year	÷	Turnover Ratio	=	Average Number of Days' Sales in Merchandise Inventory
365	÷	2.0 times	=	182.5 days

ESTIMATED MERCHANDISE INVENTORY SHEET
Gross Profit Method

Company __Minder, Inc._____ Date __December 31, 19--__

1	Beginning inventory, January 1..	$	42,000.00
2	Net purchases to date..		150,320.00
3	Merchandise available for sale..	$	192,320.00
4	Net sales to date	$ 213,900.00	
5	Less estimated gross profit .... (Net sales × Estimated gross profit __45__ %)	96,255.00	
6	Estimated cost of merchandise sold..		117,645.00
7	Estimated ending inventory..	$	74,675.00

[5]

ESTIMATED MERCHANDISE INVENTORY SHEET
Retail Method

Company __Minder, Inc._____ Date __December 31, 19--__

		Cost	Retail
1	Beginning inventory, January 1..............................	$ 42,000.00	$ 135,420.00
2	Net purchases to date...	150,320.00	377,300.00
3	Merchandise available for sale..............................	$ 192,320.00	$ 512,720.00
4	Less net sales to date...		319,200.00
5	Estimated ending inventory at retail......................		$ 193,520.00
6	Estimated ending inventory at cost (Inventory at Retail × percentage __37.5%__)..............	$ 72,570.00	

ESTIMATED MERCHANDISE INVENTORY SHEET
Gross Profit Method

Company _____ Date _____

1   Beginning inventory, January 1 .... $_____
2   Net purchases to date... _____
3   Merchandise available for sale.. $_____
4   Net sales to date .... $_____
5   Less estimated gross profit .... _____
    (Net sales × Estimated gross profit _____%)
6   Estimated cost of merchandise sold................................. _____
7   Estimated ending inventory.. $_____

ESTIMATED MERCHANDISE INVENTORY SHEET
Retail Method

Company _____ Date _____

		Cost	Retail
1	Beginning inventory, January 1	$_____	$_____
2	Net purchases to date...	_____	_____
3	Merchandise available for sale................................	$_____	$_____
4	Less net sales to date...		_____
5	Estimated ending inventory at retail........................		$_____
6	Estimated ending inventory at cost (Inventory at Retail × percentage _____)...............	$_____	

STUDY GUIDE 17

UNIT A—Identifying Accounting Terms

DIRECTIONS: Select the one term in Column I that best fits each definition in Column II. Print the letter identifying your choice in the Answers column.

	Column I	Column II	Answers	For Scoring
A.	budget	**0.** A comparison between two numbers showing how many times one number exceeds the other	F	0. ✔
B.	budget period	**1.** A report showing a comparison of budgeted and actual amounts for a specific period of time........................	E	1.
C.	budgeting	**2.** The length of time covered by a budget.....................	B	2.
D.	comparative income statement	**3.** An income statement containing revenue, cost, and expense information for two or more years..................	D	3.
E.	performance report	**4.** A written financial plan of a business for a specific period of time, expressed in dollars...........................	A	4.
F.	ratio	**5.** Planning the financial operations of a business	C	5.

UNIT B—Analyzing Procedures for Budgetary Planning and Control

DIRECTIONS: For each item below, select the choice that best completes the sentence. Print the letter identifying your choice in the Answers column.

	Answers	For Scoring
0. Budget preparation begins with **(A)** estimating selling expenses **(B)** preparing an income statement for the current year **(C)** determining company goals **(D)** preparing a cash budget....................................	C	0. ✔
6. Preparing the sales budget of a business is usually the responsibility of the **(A)** treasurer **(B)** accountant **(C)** administrative manager **(D)** sales manager..	D	6.
7. In preparing a purchases budget schedule, cost of purchases is estimated as **(A)** beginning inventory in units plus estimated sales in units minus estimated inventory in units times estimated unit cost **(B)** estimated unit cost times estimated purchases less ending inventory plus estimated beginning inventory **(C)** estimated ending inventory in units plus estimated sales in units minus beginning inventory in units times estimated unit cost **(D)** estimated sales in units times estimated unit cost	C	7.
8. One of the two annual budgets frequently prepared by businesses is **(A)** trial balance **(B)** cash budget **(C)** statement of retained earnings **(D)** none of these..	B	8.
9. The first budget schedule that is usually prepared is the **(A)** purchases budget schedule **(B)** sales budget schedule **(C)** selling expense budget schedule **(D)** cash payments schedule..................................	B	9.
10. Expressing financial information in dollars on a budget is an application of the accounting concept **(A)** Materiality **(B)** Adequate Disclosure **(C)** Consistency **(D)** Unit of Measurement	D	10.
11. Of the following, the only item included in a cash payments budget schedule is **(A)** buying equipment **(B)** sales **(C)** depreciation expense on delivery equipment **(D)** issuance of note payable	A	11.
12. A report which shows a comparison between actual and budgeted amounts for a specific period of time is **(A)** a comparative income statement **(B)** a performance report **(C)** a cash budget **(D)** a post-closing trial balance	B	12.

UNIT C—Analyzing Accounting Principles for Budgetary Planning and Control

DIRECTIONS: Place a check mark in the proper Answers column to show whether each of the following statements is true or false.

		Answers		For Scoring
		True	False	
0.	Budgets are estimates of what will happen in the future expressed in financial terms...	✔		0. ✔
13.	A budgeted income statement is an estimate of a business' expected revenue, expenses, and cash receipts for a fiscal period......................		✔	13.
14.	In planning a budgeted income statement, price trends usually are considered..	✔		14.
15.	Since some information will be in conflict with other information, budget decisions are based finally on company records...........................		✔	15.
16.	Financial planning is an important part of a business' overall planning process...	✔		16.
17.	By comparing actual expenses with expected or budgeted expenses, a business can identify where action is needed to control expenses...............	✔		17.
18.	Usually a company budget is for a fiscal period of one year....................	✔		18.
19.	If a cash budget has been correctly prepared, net income for the fiscal period will be shown..		✔	19.
20.	Explanations should be required only for significant differences between budgeted and actual amounts......................................	✔		20.
21.	Sales and the trend in sales for a period of two or more years are considered in preparing a sales budget schedule...........................	✔		21.
22.	A comparative income statement shows trends that may be taking place in certain revenue or expense items..	✔		22.
23.	In preparing a purchases budget schedule, the estimated amount of merchandise inventory at the end of the budget year must be taken into consideration..	✔		23.
24.	Unit cost is not needed to prepare a purchases budget schedule..............		✔	24.
25.	The selling expense budget schedule is prepared before amounts are budgeted for each selling expense item..		✔	25.
26.	The purchases budget schedule is prepared before the sales budget has been approved..		✔	26.
27.	The estimated amount of future sales determines to some extent the amount that a business can spend for future salaries..................................	✔		27.
28.	The amount of estimated depreciation expense is listed on the cash payments schedule...		✔	28.
29.	The amount of estimated bad debts expense is listed on the administrative expenses budget schedule..	✔		29.
30.	The amount of payroll taxes expense paid is listed on the cash payments schedule...	✔		30.
31.	The sources of all cash receipts listed on a cash budget are cash sales or collections on account from customers..		✔	31.
32.	In planning a cash payments schedule, consideration is given to expected receipts from customers on account...		✔	32.
33.	In planning a cash receipts schedule, consideration is given to the effect of anticipated cash sales..	✔		33.
34.	In planning a cash receipts schedule, consideration is given to anticipated purchases of equipment and other assets..		✔	34.

Preparing a sales budget schedule and a purchases budget schedule   [1]

Harrison Corporation
Sales Budget Schedule
For Year Ended December 31, 1989

Schedule 1

	1988 Actual		1989 Budget	
	Units	Actual Amount @ $5.70/Unit	Units	Estimated Amount @ $6.00/Unit
1st Quarter	92,900	$ 529,530	97,500	$ 585,000
2d Quarter	95,200	542,640	100,000	600,000
3d Quarter	90,600	516,420	95,100	570,600
4th Quarter	99,500	567,150	104,500	627,000
	378,200	$2,155,740	397,100	$2,382,600

[2]

Harrison Corporation
Purchases Budget Schedule
For Year Ended December 31, 1989

Schedule 2

	Ending Inventory	+	Sales	=	Total Needed	−	Beginning Inventory	=	Purchases	×	Unit Cost	=	Cost of Purchases
1st Quarter	62,600		97,500		160,100		52,700		107,400		$3.60		$ 386,640
2d Quarter	60,000		100,000		160,000		62,600		97,400		3.60		350,640
3d Quarter	65,400		95,100		160,500		60,000		100,500		3.60		361,800
4th Quarter	65,400		104,500		169,900		65,400		104,500		3.60		376,200
Year	65,400		397,100		462,500		52,700		409,800		$3.60		$1,475,280

Samson Company
Selling Expenses Budget Schedule
For Year Ended December 31, 1989   Schedule 3

	1989 Budget	1989 — By Quarters			
		1st	2d	3d	4th
Advertising Expense........................	$ 19,200	$ 3,840	$ 4,800	$ 5,760	$ 4,800
Delivery Expense............................	7,200	1,440	1,800	2,160	1,800
Depr. Exp. — Delivery Equipment.......	2,880	720	720	720	720
Depr. Exp. — Store Equipment	4,560	1,140	1,140	1,140	1,140
Miscellaneous Exp. — Sales...............	4,320	1,080	1,080	1,080	1,080
Salary Exp. — Sales	60,000	12,000	15,000	18,000	15,000
Supplies Exp. — Sales......................	12,000	2,400	3,000	3,600	3,000
Total Selling Expenses......................	$110,160	$22,620	$27,540	$32,460	$27,540

[1]

Samson Company
Administrative Expenses Budget Schedule
For Year Ended December 31, 1989   Schedule 4

	1989 Budget	1989 — By Quarters			
		1st	2d	3d	4th
Bad Debts Expense..........................	$ 6,000	$ 1,200	$ 1,500	$ 1,800	$ 1,500
Depr. Exp. — Office Equipment..........	3,280	820	820	820	820
Insurance Expense...........................	7,280	1,820	1,820	1,820	1,820
Miscellaneous Exp. — Admin.	5,520	1,380	1,380	1,380	1,380
Payroll Taxes Expense......................	9,450	2,090	2,360	2,630	2,360
Rent Expense	15,840	3,960	3,960	3,960	3,960
Salary Exp. — Admin.	45,000	11,250	11,250	11,250	11,250
Supplies Exp. — Office......................	6,640	1,660	1,660	1,660	1,660
Utilities Expense.............................	19,680	4,920	4,920	4,920	4,920
Total Admin. Expenses	$118,690	$29,100	$29,670	$30,240	$29,670

Samson Company
Budgeted Income Statement
For Year Ended December 31, 1989

	Total for year	1989 — By Quarters			
		1st	2d	3d	4th
Operating Revenue: Sales (Schedule 1)........................	$1,200,000	$240,000	$300,000	$360,000	$300,000
Cost of Merchandise Sold: Beginning Inventory (Schedule 2)..	$ 88,250	$ 88,250	$111,500	$132,500	$110,500
Purchases (Schedule 2)..............	749,750	162,000	208,500	203,000	176,250
Total Merchandise Available........	$ 838,000	$250,250	$320,000	$335,500	$286,750
Less Ending Inv. (Schedule 2)...	$ 99,250	$111,500	$132,500	$110,500	$ 99,250
Cost of Merchandise Sold...........	$ 738,750	$138,750	$187,500	$225,000	$187,500
Gross Profit on Operations	$ 461,250	$101,250	$112,500	$135,000	$112,500
Operating Expenses: Selling Expenses (Schedule 3)........	$ 110,160	$ 22,620	$ 27,540	$ 32,460	$ 27,540
Admin. Expenses (Schedule 4)	118,690	29,100	29,670	30,240	29,670
Total Operating Expenses..................	$ 228,850	$ 51,720	$ 57,210	$ 62,700	$ 57,210
Net Income before Fed. Income Tax...	$ 232,400	$ 49,530	$ 55,290	$ 72,300	$ 55,290
Federal Income Tax	58,100	12,380	13,820	18,080	13,820
Net Income after Fed. Income Tax	$ 174,300	$ 37,150	$ 41,470	$ 54,220	$ 41,470

[1]

Giant Mart
Cash Receipts Schedule
For Year Ended December 31, 1989   Schedule A

Quarter	1st	2d	3d	4th
From Sales:				
Cash Sales...	$ 55,760	$ 57,490	$ 56,180	$ 58,160
A/R Collections (this quarter sales)......................	278,800	287,450	280,900	290,800
A/R Collections (last quarter sales)......................	209,270	220,250	227,090	221,910
Total Receipts from Sales	$543,830	$565,190	$564,170	$570,870
From Other Sources:				
Note Payable to Bank		24,000		
Total Cash Receipts	$543,830	$589,190	$564,170	$570,870

[2]

Giant Mart
Cash Payments Schedule
For Year Ended December 31, 1989   Schedule B

Quarter	1st	2d	3d	4th
For Merchandise:				
Cash Purchases...	$ 46,910	$ 47,160	$ 46,120	$ 48,230
A/P Payments (this quarter purchases).................	187,640	188,640	184,480	192,920
A/P Payments (last quarter purchases).................	219,120	234,550	235,800	230,600
Total Cash Payments for Purchases	$453,670	$470,350	$466,400	$471,750
Total Cash Expenses	$ 64,100	$ 70,200	$ 82,400	$ 76,800
For Other Cash Payments:				
Federal Income Tax	$ 4,800	$ 6,720	$ 3,600	$ 4,560
Equipment..		21,600		
Cash Dividend...			28,800	
Note Payable and Interest				26,880
Total Other Cash Payments	$ 4,800	$ 28,320	$ 32,400	$ 31,440
Total Cash Payments......................................	$522,570	$568,870	$581,200	$579,990

[3]

Giant Mart
Cash Budget
For Year Ended December 31, 1989

Quarter	1st	2d	3d	4th
Cash Balance — Beginning	$ 45,720	$ 66,980	$ 87,300	$ 70,270
Cash Receipts (Schedule A)...............................	543,830	589,190	564,170	570,870
Cash Available..	$589,550	$656,170	$651,470	$641,140
Less Cash Payments (Schedule B)	522,570	568,870	581,200	579,990
Cash Balance — Ending	$ 66,980	$ 87,300	$ 70,270	$ 61,150

Preparing a budgeted income statement and a cash budget with supporting schedules   [1]

Zack's Sporting Goods
Sales Budget Schedule
For Year Ended December 31, 1989

Schedule 1

	1988 Actual		1989 Budget	
	Units	Actual Amount @ $5.60/Unit	Units	Estimated Amount @ $6.30/Unit
1st Quarter	22,000	$123,200	22,400	$141,120
2d Quarter	26,600	148,960	27,100	170,730
3d Quarter	28,000	156,800	28,600	180,180
4th Quarter	30,500	170,800	31,100	195,930
	107,100	$599,760	109,200	$687,960

[2]

Zack's Sporting Goods
Purchases Budget Schedule
For Year Ended December 31, 1989

Schedule 2

	Ending Inventory	+	Sales	=	Total Needed	−	Beginning Inventory	=	Purchases	×	Unit Cost	=	Cost of Purchases
1st Quarter	13,700		22,400		36,100		12,500		23,600		$4.50		$106,200
2d Quarter	14,000		27,100		41,100		13,700		27,400		4.50		123,300
3d Quarter	15,600		28,600		44,200		14,000		30,200		4.50		135,900
4th Quarter	13,300		31,100		44,400		15,600		28,800		4.50		129,600
Year	13,300		109,200		122,500		12,500		110,000		$4.50		$495,000

Zack's Sporting Goods
Selling Expenses Budget Schedule
For Year Ended December 31, 1989   Schedule 3

	1989 Budget	1989 — By Quarters			
		1st	2d	3d	4th
Advertising Expense..........................	$ 6,880	$ 1,410	$ 1,710	$ 1,800	$ 1,960
Delivery Expense............................	4,130	850	1,020	1,080	1,180
Depr. Exp. — Delivery Equipment.......	1,760	440	440	440	440
Depr. Exp. — Store Equipment	5,360	1,340	1,340	1,340	1,340
Miscellaneous Exp. — Sales...............	2,750	560	680	720	780
Salary Exp. — Sales	34,400	7,060	8,540	9,010	9,800
Supplies Exp. — Sales......................	5,500	1,130	1,370	1,440	1,570
Total Selling Expenses......................	$60,780	$12,790	$15,100	$15,830	$17,070

[4]

Zack's Sporting Goods
Administrative Expenses Budget Schedule
For Year Ended December 31, 1989   Schedule 4

	1989 Budget	1989 — By Quarters			
		1st	2d	3d	4th
Bad Debts Expense..........................	$ 4,130	$ 850	$ 1,020	$ 1,080	$ 1,180
Depr. Exp. — Office Equipment..........	1,800	450	450	450	450
Insurance Expense...........................	2,680	670	670	670	670
Miscellaneous Exp. — Admin.	3,000	750	750	750	750
Payroll Taxes Expense......................	5,360	1,200	1,340	1,380	1,450
Rent Expense.................................	9,600	2,400	2,400	2,400	2,400
Salary Exp. — Admin.	25,200	6,300	6,300	6,300	6,300
Supplies Exp. — Office.....................	2,800	700	700	700	700
Utilities Expense.............................	12,380	2,540	3,070	3,240	3,530
Total Admin. Expenses	$66,950	$15,860	$16,700	$16,970	$17,430

[5]

	Zack's Sporting Goods Other Revenue and Expenses Budget Schedule For Year Ended December 31, 1989				Schedule 5
	1989 Budget	**1989 — By Quarters**			
		1st	**2d**	**3d**	**4th**
Other Expenses: Interest Expense.........................	*$3,000*	*$750*	*$750*	*$750*	*$750*

[6]

	Zack's Sporting Goods Budgeted Income Statement For Year Ended December 31, 1989				
	Total for year	**1989 — By Quarters**			
		1st	**2d**	**3d**	**4th**
Operating Revenue: Sales (Schedule 1).......................	*$687,960*	*$141,120*	*$170,730*	*$180,180*	*$195,930*
Cost of Merchandise Sold: Beginning Inventory (Schedule 2)..	*$ 50,000*	*$ 50,000*	*$ 61,650*	*$ 63,000*	*$ 70,200*
Purchases (Schedule 2)..............	*495,000*	*106,200*	*123,300*	*135,900*	*129,600*
Total Merchandise Available........	*$545,000*	*$156,200*	*$184,950*	*$198,900*	*$199,800*
Less Ending Inv. (Schedule 2)...	*59,850*	*61,650*	*63,000*	*70,200*	*59,850*
Cost of Merchandise Sold...........	*$485,150*	*$ 94,550*	*$121,950*	*$128,700*	*$139,950*
Gross Profit on Operations	*$202,810*	*$ 46,570*	*$ 48,780*	*$ 51,480*	*$ 55,980*
Operating Expenses: Selling Expenses (Schedule 3)........	*$ 60,780*	*$ 12,790*	*$ 15,100*	*$ 15,830*	*$ 17,070*
Admin. Expenses (Schedule 4).......	*66,950*	*15,860*	*16,700*	*16,970*	*17,430*
Total Operating Expenses.................	*$127,730*	*$ 28,650*	*$ 31,800*	*$ 32,800*	*$ 34,500*
Income from Operations	*$ 75,080*	*$ 17,920*	*$ 16,980*	*$ 18,680*	*$ 21,480*
Other Expense Deduction (Schedule 5).	*$ (3,000)*	*$ (750)*	*$ (750)*	*$ (750)*	*$ (750)*
Net Income before Fed. Income Tax...	*$ 72,080*	*$ 17,170*	*$ 16,230*	*$ 17,930*	*$ 20,730*
Federal Income Tax	*18,020*	*4,290*	*4,060*	*4,480*	*5,180*
Net Income after Fed. Income Tax	*$ 54,060*	*$ 12,880*	*$ 12,170*	*$ 13,450*	*$ 15,550*

Inventory January 1 cost $4.00 per unit. All other inventories cost $4.50 per unit.

Zack's Sporting Goods
Cash Payments Schedule
For Year Ended December 31, 1989

Schedule B

Quarter	1st	2d	3d	4th
For Merchandise:				
Cash Purchases...............................	$ 10,620	$ 12,330	$ 13,590	$ 12,960
A/P Payments (this quarter purchases).................	58,410	67,820	74,750	71,280
A/P Payments (last quarter purchases).................	36,960	37,170	43,160	47,570
Total Cash Payments for Purchases	$105,990	$117,320	$131,500	$131,810
For Operating Expenses:				
Cash Selling Expenses:				
Advertising Expense......................	$ 1,410	$ 1,710	$ 1,800	$ 1,960
Delivery Expense..........................	850	1,020	1,080	1,180
Miscellaneous Expense — Sales........................	560	680	720	780
Salary Expense — Sales	7,060	8,540	9,010	9,800
Supplies Expense — Sales.............................	1,130	1,370	1,440	1,570
Total Cash Selling Expenses............................	$ 11,010	$ 13,320	$ 14,050	$ 15,290
Cash Administrative Expenses:				
Insurance Expense.........................	$ 670	$ 670	$ 670	$ 670
Miscellaneous Expense — Admin.	750	750	750	750
Payroll Taxes Expense...........................	1,200	1,340	1,380	1,450
Rent Expense...............................	2,400	2,400	2,400	2,400
Salary Expense — Administrative....................	6,300	6,300	6,300	6,300
Supplies Expense — Office..........................	700	700	700	700
Utilities Expense..............................	2,540	3,070	3,240	3,530
Total Cash Admin. Expenses.........................	$ 14,560	$ 15,230	$ 15,440	$ 15,800
For Other Cash Payments:				
Federal Income Tax	$ 4,290	$ 4,060	$ 4,480	$ 5,180
Equipment...................................	30,000			
Cash Dividend..............................	10,000	10,000	10,000	10,000
Note Payable and Interest				23,000
Total Other Cash Payments	$ 44,290	$ 14,060	$ 14,480	$ 38,180
Total Cash Payments.......................................	$175,850	$159,930	$175,470	$201,080

[7]

Zack's Sporting Goods
Cash Receipts Schedule
For Year Ended December 31, 1989   Schedule A

Quarter	1st	2d	3d	4th
From Sales:				
Cash Sales..............................	$ 14,110	$ 17,070	$ 18,020	$ 19,590
A/R Collections (this quarter sales).....................	56,450	68,290	72,070	78,370
A/R Collections (last quarter sales).....................	84,380	69,710	84,340	89,010
Total Receipts from Sales	$154,940	$155,070	$174,430	$186,970
From Other Sources:				
Note Payable to Bank	20,000			
Total Cash Receipts	$174,940	$155,070	$174,430	$186,970

[9]

Zack's Sporting Goods
Cash Budget
For Year Ended December 31, 1989

Quarter	1st	2d	3d	4th
Cash Balance — Beginning	$ 32,300	$ 31,390	$ 26,530	$ 25,490
Cash Receipts (Schedule A).............................	174,940	155,070	174,430	186,970
Cash Available..	$207,240	$186,460	$200,960	$212,460
Less Cash Payments (Schedule B)	175,850	159,930	175,470	201,080
Cash Balance — Ending	$ 31,390	$ 26,530	$ 25,490	$ 11,380

Preparing a budgeted income statement and a cash budget with supporting schedules   [1]

Brownwood Industries
Sales Budget Schedule
For Year Ended December 31, 1989

Schedule 1

| | 1988 Actual | | 1989 Budget | |
	Units	Actual Amount @ $4.50/Unit	Units	Estimated Amount @ $4.50/Unit
1st Quarter	112,200	$ 504,900	110,000	$ 495,000
2d Quarter	115,300	518,850	113,000	508,500
3d Quarter	110,200	495,900	108,000	486,000
4th Quarter	120,400	541,800	118,000	531,000
	458,100	$2,061,450	449,000	$2,020,500

[2]

Brownwood Industries
Purchases Budget Schedule
For Year Ended December 31, 1989

Schedule 2

	Ending Inventory	+	Sales	=	Total Needed	−	Beginning Inventory	=	Purchases	×	Unit Cost	=	Cost of Purchases
1st Quarter	71,600		110,000		181,600		63,400		118,200		$2.80		$ 330,960
2d Quarter	68,400		113,000		181,400		71,600		109,800		2.80		307,440
3d Quarter	74,800		108,000		182,800		68,400		114,400		2.80		320,320
4th Quarter	71,200		118,000		189,200		74,800		114,400		2.80		320,320
Year	71,200		449,000		520,200		63,400		456,800		$2.80		$1,279,040

[3]

Brownwood Industries
Selling Expenses Budget Schedule
For Year Ended December 31, 1989

Schedule 3

	1989 Budget	1989 — By Quarters			
		1st	2d	3d	4th
Advertising Expense.........................	$ 36,370	$ 8,910	$ 9,150	$ 8,750	$ 9,560
Delivery Expense.............................	28,290	6,930	7,120	6,800	7,430
Depr. Exp. — Delivery Equipment.......	4,320	1,080	1,080	1,080	1,080
Depr. Exp. — Store Equipment	5,560	1,390	1,390	1,390	1,390
Miscellaneous Exp. — Sales...............	20,210	4,950	5,090	4,860	5,310
Salary Exp. — Sales	161,640	39,600	40,680	38,880	42,480
Supplies Exp. — Sales......................	28,290	6,930	7,120	6,800	7,430
Total Selling Expenses	$284,680	$69,790	$71,630	$68,560	$74,680

[4]

Brownwood Industries
Administrative Expenses Budget Schedule
For Year Ended December 31, 1989

Schedule 4

	1989 Budget	1989 — By Quarters			
		1st	2d	3d	4th
Bad Debts Expense..........................	$ 12,120	$ 2,970	$ 3,050	$ 2,920	$ 3,190
Depr. Exp. — Office Equipment..........	4,680	1,170	1,170	1,170	1,170
Insurance Expense...........................	13,800	3,450	3,450	3,450	3,450
Miscellaneous Exp. — Admin.	16,120	4,030	4,030	4,030	4,030
Payroll Taxes Expense......................	26,460	6,540	6,640	6,480	6,800
Rent Expense.................................	27,600	6,900	6,900	6,900	6,900
Salary Exp. — Admin.	132,400	33,100	33,100	33,100	33,100
Supplies Exp. — Office......................	11,280	2,820	2,820	2,820	2,820
Utilities Expense.............................	44,300	11,080	11,080	11,080	11,080
Total Admin. Expenses	$288,760	$72,060	$72,240	$71,950	$72,540

	Total for year	1989 — By Quarters			
		1st	2d	3d	4th
Brownwood Industries					
Budgeted Income Statement					
For Year Ended December 31, 1989					
Operating Revenue:					
Sales (Schedule 1).....................	$2,020,500	$495,000	$508,500	$486,000	$531,000
Cost of Merchandise Sold:					
Beginning Inventory (Schedule 2)..	$ 164,840 *	*$164,840	*$200,480	*$191,520	*$209,440
Purchases (Schedule 2)..............	1,279,040	330,960	307,440	320,320	320,320
Total Merchandise Available........	$1,443,880	$495,800	$507,920	$511,840	$529,760
Less Ending Inv. (Schedule 2)...	199,360	200,480	191,520	209,440	199,360
Cost of Merchandise Sold...........	$1,244,520	$295,320	$316,400	$302,400	$330,400
Gross Profit on Operations	$ 775,980	$199,680	$192,100	$183,600	$200,600
Operating Expenses:					
Selling Expenses (Schedule 3)........	$ 284,680	$ 69,790	$ 71,630	$ 68,560	$ 74,680
Admin. Expenses (Schedule 4).......	288,760	72,060	72,240	71,950	72,540
Total Operating Expenses.................	$ 573,440	$141,850	$143,870	$140,510	$147,220
Income from Operations	$ 202,540	$ 57,830	$ 48,230	$ 43,090	$ 53,380
Other Expense Deduction (Schedule 5) .	$ (4,500)	—	$ (1,500)	$ (1,500)	$ (1,500)
Net Income before Fed. Income Tax...	$ 198,040	$ 57,830	$ 46,730	$ 41,590	$ 51,880
Federal Income Tax	70,850 **	**20,690	**16,720	**14,880	**18,560
Net Income after Fed. Income Tax	$ 127,190	$ 37,140	$ 30,010	$ 26,710	$ 33,320

Inventory January 1 cost $2.60 per unit. All other inventories cost $2.80 per unit.

Federal Income Tax Computation:

$25,000 × 15% = $ 3,750
25,000 × 18% = 4,500
25,000 × 30% = 7,500
25,000 × 40% = 10,000
98,040 × 46% = 45,100
$70,850

$57,830 ÷ $198,040 = 29.2% × $70,850 = $20,690
$46,730 ÷ $198,040 = 23.6% × $70,850 = $16,720
$41,590 ÷ $198,040 = 21.0% × $70,850 = $14,880
$51,880 ÷ $198,040 = 26.2% × $70,850 = $18,560

[5]

<table>
<tr><td colspan="6">Brownwood Industries
Other Revenue and Expenses Budget Schedule
For Year Ended December 31, 1989
 Schedule 5 </td></tr>
<tr><td rowspan="2"></td><td rowspan="2">1989
Budget</td><td colspan="4">1989 — By Quarters</td></tr>
<tr><td>1st</td><td>2d</td><td>3d</td><td>4th</td></tr>
<tr><td>Other Expenses:
  Interest Expense...........................</td><td>$4500</td><td></td><td>$1,500</td><td>$1,500</td><td>$1,500</td></tr>
</table>

[7]

<table>
<tr><td colspan="5">Brownwood Industries
Cash Receipts Schedule
For Year Ended December 31, 1989
 Schedule A </td></tr>
<tr><td>Quarter</td><td>1st</td><td>2d</td><td>3d</td><td>4th</td></tr>
<tr><td>From Sales:
  Cash Sales..</td><td>$ 49,500</td><td>$ 50,850</td><td>$ 48,600</td><td>$ 53,100</td></tr>
<tr><td> A/R Collections (this quarter sales).....................</td><td>247,500</td><td>254,250</td><td>243,000</td><td>265,500</td></tr>
<tr><td> A/R Collections (last quarter sales).....................</td><td>213,470</td><td>195,030</td><td>200,350</td><td>191,480</td></tr>
<tr><td> Total Receipts from Sales ....</td><td>$510,470</td><td>$500,130</td><td>$491,950</td><td>$510,080</td></tr>
<tr><td>From Other Sources:
  Note Payable to Bank ....</td><td></td><td>40,000</td><td></td><td></td></tr>
<tr><td>Total Cash Receipts ....</td><td>$510,470</td><td>$540,130</td><td>$491,950</td><td>$510,080</td></tr>
</table>

[8]

Brownwood Industries
Cash Payments Schedule
For Year Ended December 31, 1989 — Schedule B

Quarter	1st	2d	3d	4th
For Merchandise:				
Cash Purchases	$ 33,100	$ 30,740	$ 32,030	$ 32,030
A/P Payments (this quarter purchases)	132,380	122,980	128,130	128,130
A/P Payments (last quarter purchases)	157,100	165,480	153,720	160,160
Total Cash Payments for Purchases	$322,580	$319,200	$313,880	$320,320
For Operating Expenses:				
Cash Selling Expenses:				
Advertising Expense	$ 8,910	$ 9,150	$ 8,750	$ 9,560
Delivery Expense	6,930	7,120	6,800	7,430
Miscellaneous Expense — Sales	4,950	5,090	4,860	5,310
Salary Expense — Sales	39,600	40,680	38,880	42,480
Supplies Expense — Sales	6,930	7,120	6,800	7,430
Total Cash Selling Expenses	$ 67,320	$ 69,160	$ 66,090	$ 72,210
Cash Administrative Expenses:				
Insurance Expense	$ 3,450	$ 3,450	$ 3,450	$ 3,450
Miscellaneous Expense — Admin.	4,030	4,030	4,030	4,030
Payroll Taxes Expense	6,540	6,640	6,480	6,800
Rent Expense	6,900	6,900	6,900	6,900
Salary Expense — Administrative	33,100	33,100	33,100	33,100
Supplies Expense — Office	2,820	2,820	2,820	2,820
Utilities Expense	11,080	11,080	11,080	11,080
Total Cash Admin. Expenses	$ 67,920	$ 68,020	$ 67,860	$ 68,180
For Other Cash Payments:				
Federal Income Tax	$ 20,690	$ 16,720	$ 14,880	$ 18,560
Equipment		40,000		
Cash Dividend	35,000		35,000	
Note Payable and Interest				44,500
Total Other Cash Payments	$ 55,690	$ 56,720	$ 49,880	$ 63,060
Total Cash Payments	$513,510	$513,100	$497,710	$523,770

[9]

Brownwood Industries
Cash Budget
For Year Ended December 31, 1989

Quarter	1st	2d	3d	4th
Cash Balance — Beginning	$ 49,820	$ 46,780	$ 73,810	$ 68,050
Cash Receipts (Schedule A)	510,470	540,130	491,950	510,080
Cash Available	$560,290	$586,910	$565,760	$578,130
Less Cash Payments (Schedule B)	513,510	513,100	497,710	523,770
Cash Balance — Ending	$ 46,780	$ 73,810	$ 68,050	$ 54,360

Perfect Score. 37   Name _____

Deduct .... —   Date _____ Class _____

Your Score .... —   Checked by _____

STUDY GUIDE 18

UNIT A—Identifying Accounting Terms

DIRECTIONS: Select the one term in Column I that best fits each definition in Column II. Print the letter identifying your choice in the Answers column.

Column I	Column II	Answers	For Scoring
	0. An amount spent for one of a specific product or service .	F	0. ✔
A. breakeven point	**1.** The amount of sales at which sales revenue is exactly the same as total costs..............................	A	1.
B. contribution margin			
C. fixed costs	**2.** Costs that remain constant regardless of change in business activity	C	2.
D. sales mix		D	3.
E. total costs	**3.** Relative distribution of sales among various products		
F. unit cost	**4.** Income determined by subtracting all variable costs from sales revenue	B	4.
G. variable costs		E	5.
	5. All costs for a specific period of time.........................	G	6.
	6. Costs which change in direct proportion to the change in number of units...............		

UNIT B—Analyzing Accounting Principles for Management Decision Information

DIRECTIONS: Place a check mark in the proper Answers column to show whether each of the following statements is true or false.

	Answers True	Answers False	For Scoring
0. An income statement is one source of information on which a manager can base decisions..	✔		0. ✔
7. Selling expenses are another part of cost of merchandise sold		✔	7.
8. Sales less fixed costs equals contribution margin		✔	8.
9. If one unit of a product costs $10.00 and ten units of that product cost $100.00, the cost is a variable cost........................	✔		9.
10. Variable costs plotted on a graph become a straight line parallel with the base of the graph...		✔	10.
11. Fixed costs plotted on a graph become a straight line parallel with the base of the graph	✔		11.
12. Sales less selling and administrative expenses equals marginal income.........		✔	12.
13. Variable costs change in direct proportion to changes in sales activity	✔		13.
14. Figuring the sales dollar breakeven point determines the selling price for one unit of product...		✔	14.
15. The sales line plotted on a graph represents unit sales price times number of units sold	✔		15.
16. The point at which no net income is earned and no loss is incurred is called the gross profit point		✔	16.
17. The breakeven point equals fixed costs divided by total revenue		✔	17.
18. The contribution margin is determined by subtracting total variable costs from total revenue	✔		18.
19. Total fixed costs increase as sales increase.............................		✔	19.
20. Total variable costs increase as sales increase	✔		20.
21. When net income is declining, providing a manager with greater detail about unit costs, variable costs, and fixed costs than the typical financial reports contain is an application of the Realization of Revenue concept................		✔	21.
22. Contribution margin must be more than fixed costs before any net income can be earned	✔		22.

UNIT C—Examining Procedures for Preparing Management Decision Information

DIRECTIONS: For each item below, select the choice that best completes the sentence. Print the letter identifying your choice in the Answers column.

	Answers	For Scoring
0. Units should be expressed in meaningful terms such as **(A)** total costs **(B)** gallons **(C)** net income **(D)** variable costs..................................	B	0. ✔
23. A major business objective is **(A)** spending money **(B)** providing employment for as many people as possible **(C)** increasing selling prices of products **(D)** earning a favorable net income..............................	D	23.
24. Unit costs are figured by **(A)** dividing total costs by number of units **(B)** multiplying total costs by number of units **(C)** dividing unit costs by variable costs **(D)** multiplying unit costs by variable costs......................	A	24.
25. Costs can be separated into the two parts of variable and **(A)** selling **(B)** administrative **(C)** fixed **(D)** cost of merchandise sold.......................	C	25.
26. When sales increase, the cost that always increases in the same direct proportion is **(A)** fixed costs **(B)** variable costs **(C)** selling expenses **(D)** administrative expenses..................................	B	26.
27. Gross profit is determined by **(A)** subtracting cost of merchandise sold from sales **(B)** subtracting variable costs from sales **(C)** adding net income to administrative expenses **(D)** subtracting net income from sales......................	A	27.
28. Contribution margin is determined by **(A)** subtracting cost of merchandise sold from sales **(B)** subtracting variable costs from sales **(C)** adding net income to administrative expenses **(D)** subtracting net income from sales	B	28.
29. The relationship of sales to other items is shown in the equation **(A)** sales equals variable costs less gross profit plus net income **(B)** sales equals variable costs plus fixed costs plus gross profit **(C)** sales equals variable costs plus fixed costs plus net income **(D)** sales equals gross profit plus variable costs plus fixed costs plus net income.................	C	29.
30. On a graph showing the relationship of sales and costs **(A)** the total cost line is always above the sales line **(B)** the sales line is always above the total cost line **(C)** the sales line crosses the total cost line at the point variable costs are all paid **(D)** the sales line crosses the total cost line at the breakeven point.......................	D	30.
31. The $4.00 paid by a commercial photographer for each roll of camera film is a **(A)** variable cost **(B)** total cost **(C)** fixed cost **(D)** breakeven cost........	A	31.
32. The $800.00 per month rent paid by an office supply company is a **(A)** total cost **(B)** fixed cost **(C)** breakeven cost **(D)** variable cost..............................	B	32.
33. The items of information needed to compute the breakeven point are total revenue, **(A)** total fixed costs, and total unit costs **(B)** total fixed costs, and total variable costs **(C)** total unit costs, and total variable costs **(D)** total costs, and total variable costs	B	33.
34. The first step in figuring the breakeven point is to figure the **(A)** unit cost **(B)** contribution margin rate **(C)** contribution margin **(D)** breakeven cost.....	C	34.
35. To make a sales mix more profitable, a company should strive to increase the sales of products that have **(A)** high variable costs **(B)** high contribution margin **(C)** high fixed costs **(D)** low fixed costs and high variable costs..................	B	35.
36. To earn a net income of $1,000.00, a business with variable costs of $12,000.00 and fixed costs of $4,000.00 will need sales of **(A)** $12,000.00 **(B)** $16,000.00 **(C)** $17,000.00 **(D)** $24,000.00	C	36.
37. If a business with sales of $10,000.00, variable costs of $6,000.00, and fixed costs of $2,000.00, reduces its unit selling prices 10% and the number of units sold remains the same, net income will be reduced **(A)** 10% **(B)** 20% **(C)** 40% **(D)** 50%	D	37.

Preparing an income statement reporting contribution margin

Pebble Creek Glass Company

Income Statement

For Month Ended November 30, 19--

Operating Revenue:			
Sales (14,400 units @ $16.20)		233 280 00	
Less Variable Costs:			
Cost of Units (14,400 @ $7.20)	103 680 00		
Sales Commission (14,400 @ $1.30)	18 720 00		
Installation Costs (14,400 @ $1.80)	25 920 00		
Other Variable Selling Costs (14,400 @ $.62)	8 928 00		
Variable Administrative Costs (14,400 @ $.42)	6 048 00		
Total Variable Costs		163 296 00	
Contribution Margin		69 984 00	
Less Fixed Costs:			
Fixed Selling Costs	11 970 00		
Rent	2 700 00		
Insurance	180 00		
Other Fixed Administrative Costs	17 955 00		
Total Fixed Costs		32 805 00	
Net Income		37 179 00	

(1) Figure the contribution margin:

$$Total\ Revenue - Total\ Variable\ Costs = Contribution\ Margin$$
$$\$1,350,000.00 - \$1,080,000.00 = \$270,000.00$$

◀ CONTRIBUTION
   MARGIN

[2] Figure the contribution margin rate:

$$Contribution\ Margin \div Total\ Revenue = Contribution\ Margin\ Rate$$
$$\frac{\$270,000.00}{\$1,350,000.00} = .20 = 20\%$$

◀ CONTRIBUTION
   MARGIN
   RATE

[3] Figure the breakeven point in
     (a) sales dollars:

$$Total\ Fixed\ Costs \div Contribution\ Margin\ Rate = Breakeven\ Point\ in\ Sales\ Dollars$$
$$\frac{\$190,200.00}{.20} = \$951,000.00$$

BREAKEVEN
POINT IN ◀
SALES
DOLLARS

(b) units:

$$\begin{array}{ccc} Sales\ Price & Variable\ Costs & Contribution\ Margin \\ per\ Unit & - \quad per\ Unit & = \quad per\ Unit \\ \$1,500.00 & - \quad \$1,200.00 & = \quad \$300.00 \end{array}$$

$$Total\ Fixed\ Costs \div Contribution\ Margin\ Per\ Unit = Breakeven\ Point\ in\ Units$$
$$\frac{\$190,200.00}{\$300.00} = 634\ trees$$

BREAKEVEN
POINT IN ◀
UNITS

Figuring plans for net income

[1] Figure the breakeven point for the year

(a) in total sales dollars:

$$\frac{Contribution\ Margin}{Total\ Revenue} = \frac{\$3.00}{\$12.00} = .25 = 25\%\ Contribution\ Margin\ Rate$$

$$\frac{Total\ Fixed\ Costs}{Contribution\ Margin\ Rate} = \frac{\$99,000.00}{.25} = \$396,000.00\ Breakeven\ Point\ in\ Sales\ Dollars$$

(b) in gallons of paint:

$$Sales\ Price\ Per\ Unit\ -\ Variable\ Costs\ Per\ Unit\ =\ Contribution\ Margin\ Per\ Unit$$
$$\$12.00 \quad - \quad \$9.00 \quad = \quad \$3.00$$

$$\frac{Total\ Fixed\ Costs}{Contribution\ Margin\ Per\ Unit} = \frac{\$99,000.00}{\$3.00} = 33,000\ gallons\ of\ paint\ (Breakeven\ Point\ in\ Units)$$

[2] If a $27,000 annual net income is desired, figure the required

(a) sales dollars:

$$\frac{Total\ Fixed\ Costs\ +\ Net\ Income}{Contribution\ Margin\ Rate} = \frac{\$99,000.00\ +\ \$27,000.00}{.25} = \begin{array}{c}\$504,000.00\ Sales\ Dollars\\ to\ Cover\ Fixed\ Costs\ and\\ Net\ Income\end{array}$$

(b) number of gallons of paint to be sold:

$$\$504,000 \div \$12.00 = 42,000\ gallons\ of\ paint\ \underline{or}$$

$$\frac{\$27,000}{\$3.00} = 9,000\ gallons\ +\ 33,000\ gallons\ (Breakeven\ point\ in\ Units)\ =\ 42,000\ gallons\ \underline{or}$$

$$\frac{\$99,000\ +\ \$27,000}{\$3.00} = 42,000\ gallons\ of\ paint$$

[3] Figure the breakeven point, if it is decided that an additional $36,000 in salaries will be paid in place of the $.60 per gallon sales commission

(a) in sales dollars:

$$\frac{Contribution\ Margin}{Total\ Revenue} = \frac{\$12.00\ -\ \$8.40}{\$12.00} = \frac{\$3.60}{\$12.00} = .30 = 30\%\ Contribution\ Margin\ Rate$$

$$\frac{Total\ Fixed\ Costs}{Contribution\ Margin\ Rate} = \frac{\$99,000\ +\ \$36,000}{.30} = \$450,000.00\ Sales\ Dollars$$

(b) in gallons of paint:

$$\$450,000.00 \div \$12.00\ per\ gallon = 37,500\ gallons\ of\ paint\ \underline{or}$$

$$\frac{Total\ Fixed\ Costs}{Contribution\ Margin} = \frac{\$99,000\ +\ \$36,000}{\$3.60} = 37,500\ gallons\ of\ paint$$

Figuring the effects on net income of changes in
selling price, variable costs, fixed costs, and volume

PROBLEM 18-4, p. 410

Jenkins Frame Shop

Income Statement

For Year Ended December 31, 19--

(a) Unit selling price increases 20%:

Sales (80,000 frames @ $48.00)	3,840 0 0 0 00
Less Variable Costs (80,000 frames @ $25.00)	2,000 0 0 0 00
Contribution Margin	1,840 0 0 0 00
Less Fixed Costs	800 0 0 0 00
Net Income	1,040 0 0 0 00

(b) Unit variable costs increase 20%:

Sales (80,000 frames @ $40.00)	3,200 0 0 0 00
Less Variable Costs (80,000 frames @ $30.00)	2,400 0 0 0 00
Contribution Margin	800 0 0 0 00
Less Fixed Costs	800 0 0 0 00
Net Income	–0–

(c) Total fixed costs increase 20%:

Sales (80,000 frames @ $40.00)	3,200 0 0 0 00
Less Variable Costs (80,000 frames @ $25.00)	2,000 0 0 0 00
Contribution Margin	1,200 0 0 0 00
Less Fixed Costs	960 0 0 0 00
Net Income	240 0 0 0 00

(d) Unit selling price decreases 10% and units sold increase 20%:

Sales (96,000 frames @ $36.00)	3,456 0 0 0 00
Less Variable Costs (96,000 frames @ $25.00)	2,400 0 0 0 00
Contribution Margin	1,056 0 0 0 00
Less Fixed Costs	800 0 0 0 00
Net Income	256 0 0 0 00

Figuring effects of sales mix changes

Bostwick Incorporated
Income Statement
For Month Ended January 31, 19--

Sales:				
Desk Lamps (9,300 @ $20.00)	186 0 0 0 00			
Desks (465 @ $400.00)	186 0 0 0 00			
Total Sales		372 0 0 0 00		
Variable Costs:				
Desk Lamps (9,300 @ $16.00)	148 8 0 0 00			
Desks (465 @ $200.00)	93 0 0 0 00			
Total Variable Costs		241 8 0 0 00		
Contribution Margin		130 2 0 0 00		
Less Fixed Costs		80 0 0 0 00		
Net Income		50 2 0 0 00		

Figuring effects of sales mix changes

MASTERY PROBLEM 18-M, p. 411

Colonial Music
Income Statement
For Month Ended January 31, 19--

Sales:				
Guitars (320 @ $300.00)	96 0 0 0 00			
Pianos (40 @ $2,400.00)	96 0 0 0 00			
Total Sales		192 0 0 0 00		
Variable Costs:				
Guitars (320 @ $225.00)	72 0 0 0 00			
Pianos (40 @ $1,200.00)	48 0 0 0 00			
Total Variable Costs		120 0 0 0 00		
Contribution Margin		72 0 0 0 00		
Less Fixed Costs		70 0 0 0 00		
Net Income		2 0 0 0 00		

Figuring the effects on net income of changes in
selling price, variable costs, fixed costs, and volume

(a) Figure the required sales dollars to increase net income by $60,000.00:

$$\frac{Contribution\ Margin}{Total\ Revenue} = \frac{\$\ 480,000.00}{\$1,600,000.00} = .30\ or\ 30\%\ Contribution\ Margin\ Rate$$

$$\frac{Total\ Fixed\ Costs\ +\ Net\ Income\ +\ Increase\ in\ Net\ Income}{Contribution\ Margin\ Rate} =$$

$$\frac{\$425,000.00\ +\ \$55,000.00\ +\ \$60,000.00}{.30} = \begin{array}{l} \$1,800,000.00\ Sales\ Dollars \\ to\ increase\ Net\ Income\ \$60,000.00. \end{array}$$

(b) Figure the required number of machines to increase net income by $60,000.00:

$$\frac{Total\ Fixed\ Costs\ +\ Net\ Income\ +\ Increase\ in\ Net\ Income}{Contribution\ Margin\ Per\ Unit} =$$

$$\frac{\$425,000.00\ +\ \$55,000.00\ +\ \$60,000.00}{\$60.00} = 9,000\ sewing\ machines$$

Sew-Right

Income Statement

For Year Ended December 31, 19--

(a) Unit selling price increases 10%:

Sales (8,000 machines @ $220.00)	1,760	0 0 0	00	
Less Variable Costs (8,000 machines @ $140.00)	1,120	0 0 0	00	
Contribution Margin	640	0 0 0	00	
Less Fixed Costs	425	0 0 0	00	
Net Income	215	0 0 0	00	

(b) Unit selling price decreases 10%:

Sales (8,000 machines @ $180.00)	1,440	0 0 0	00	
Less Variable Costs (8,000 machines @ $140.00)	1,120	0 0 0	00	
Contribution Margin	320	0 0 0	00	
Less Fixed Costs	425	0 0 0	00	
Net Loss	105	0 0 0	00	

(c) Unit variable costs increase 10%:

Sales (8,000 machines @ $200.00)	1,600	0 0 0	00	
Less Variable Costs (8,000 machines @ $154.00)	1,232	0 0 0	00	
Contribution Margin	368	0 0 0	00	
Less Fixed Costs	425	0 0 0	00	
Net Loss	57	0 0 0	00	

(d) Unit variable costs decrease 10%:

Sales (8,000 machines @ $200.00)	1,600	0 0 0	00	
Less Variable Costs (8,000 machines @ $126.00)	1,008	0 0 0	00	
Contribution Margin	592	0 0 0	00	
Less Fixed Costs	425	0 0 0	00	
Net Income	167	0 0 0	00	

(e) Total fixed costs increase 10%:

Sew-Right

Income Statement

For Year Ended December 31, 19--

Sales (8,000 machines @ $200.00)	1,600	0 0 0	00	
Less Variable Costs (8,000 machines @ $140.00)	1,120	0 0 0	00	
Contribution Margin	480	0 0 0	00	
Less Fixed Costs	467	5 0 0	00	
Net Income	12	5 0 0	00	

(f) Total fixed costs decrease 10%:

Sales (8,000 machines @ $200.00)	1,600	0 0 0	00	
Less Variable Costs (8,000 machines @ $140.00)	1,120	0 0 0	00	
Contribution Margin	480	0 0 0	00	
Less Fixed Costs	382	5 0 0	00	
Net Income	97	5 0 0	00	

(g) Unit selling price decreases 10% and units sold increase 20%:

Sales (9,600 machines @ $180.00)	1,728	0 0 0	00	
Less Variable Costs (9,600 machines @ $140.00)	1,344	0 0 0	00	
Contribution Margin	384	0 0 0	00	
Less Fixed Costs	425	0 0 0	00	
Net Loss	41	0 0 0	00	

(h) All changes of Parts (a), (c), and (e) occur:

Sales (8,000 machines @ $220.00)	1,760	0 0 0	00	
Less Variable Costs (8,000 machines @ $154.00)	1,232	0 0 0	00	
Contribution Margin	528	0 0 0	00	
Less Fixed Costs	467	5 0 0	00	
Net Income	60	5 0 0	00	

Perfect Score. 34

Deduct .... __

Your Score .... __

Name _____

Date _____ Class _____

Checked by _____

STUDY
GUIDE
19

UNIT A—Identifying Accounting Terms

DIRECTIONS: Select the one term in Column I that best fits each definition in Column II. Print the letter identifying your choice in the Answers column.

Column I	*Column II*	Answers	For Scoring
A. acid-test ratio	**0.** Financial statements providing information for each of two or more years	B	**0.** ✔
B. comparative financial statements	**1.** Those current assets that are cash or that can be quickly turned into cash	F	**1.**
C. current ratio	**2.** The ratio found by dividing total liabilities by total assets..	D	**2.**
D. debt ratio	**3.** A ratio that shows the numeric relationship of current assets to current liabilities.......................................	C	**3.**
E. equity ratio	**4.** A comparison of the relationship between one item on a financial statement and the same item on a previous year's financial statement		
F. quick assets			
G. trend analysis		G	**4.**
5. A ratio that shows the numeric relationship of quick assets to current liabilities		A	**5.**
6. The ratio found by dividing stockholders' equity by total assets		E	**6.**

UNIT B—Analyzing Financial Analysis Practices

DIRECTIONS: Place a check mark in the proper Answers column to show whether each of the following statements is true or false.

	Answers True	Answers False	For Scoring
0. A guide many businesses use to determine acceptable levels of performance is the business' previous performance...	✔		**0.** ✔
7. Financial statements for two or more years are needed to prepare component percentage analyses...		✔	**7.**
8. Figuring that cost of merchandise sold increased 9% this year over last year is an example of a component percentage..		✔	**8.**
9. Rate earned on average total assets measures profitability	✔		**9.**
10. A rate earned on average total assets of 12 percent means that for each $1.00 in assets the business earned 12 cents	✔		**10.**
11. Usually, only a small portion of a business' assets are in accounts receivable and merchandise inventory		✔	**11.**
12. An accounts receivable turnover ratio of 7.5 indicates that the average amount of accounts receivable is being collected 7.5 times a year	✔		**12.**
13. A decrease in accounts receivable turnover ratio from 8.5 times to 7.0 times is considered a favorable trend		✔	**13.**
14. Merchandise inventory turnover ratio is figured by dividing net sales by average merchandise inventory		✔	**14.**
15. A current ratio of 2.4 means that the business owns $1.00 in current assets for each $2.40 needed to pay current liabilities		✔	**15.**
16. Merchandise inventory normally is considered to be a quick asset		✔	**16.**
17. Long-term financial strength requires a balance between stockholders' capital and borrowed capital	✔		**17.**
18. Equity per share is an effective measure of a business' short-term financial strength		✔	**18.**
19. Consistent preparation and reporting of financial information is an application of the Consistent Reporting concept..	✔		**19.**

UNIT C—Preparing Financial Analysis

DIRECTIONS: For each item below, select the choice that best completes the sentence. Print the letter identifying your choice in the Answers column.

	Answers	For Scoring
0. If net sales are $100,000.00 in 1989 and $125,000.00 in 1990, the change in net sales is **(A)** 20% increase **(B)** 25% increase **(C)** 400% increase **(D)** none of these	B	0. ✔
20. If net sales are $100,000.00 and cost of merchandise sold is $50,000.00, the component percentage for cost of merchandise sold is **(A)** 50% **(B)** 100% **(C)** 200% **(D)** none of these...	A	20.
21. If December 31, 1989, total assets are $100,000.00 and December 31, 1988, total assets are $120,000.00, the average total assets for 1989 are **(A)** $50,000.00 **(B)** $220,000.00 **(C)** $110,000.00 **(D)** none of these	C	21.
22. If 1989 average total assets are $100,000.00 and 1989 net income after income tax is $20,000.00, the 1989 rate earned on average total assets is **(A)** 20% **(B)** 50% **(C)** 5% **(D)** none of these..................................	A	22.
23. If 1989 average stockholders' equity is $100,000.00 and 1989 net income after income tax is $40,000.00, the 1989 rate earned on average stockholders' equity is **(A)** 4% **(B)** 60% **(C)** 25% **(D)** none of these	D	23.
24. If 1989 net income after income tax is $5,000.00 and 1989 net sales are $100,000.00, the 1989 rate earned on sales is **(A)** 95% **(B)** 20% **(C)** 5% **(D)** none of these	C	24.
25. If 1989 net income after income tax is $100,000.00 and shares of stock outstanding on December 31, 1989, are 20,000, the 1989 earnings per share is **(A)** $5.00 **(B)** 20 cents **(C)** $20.00 **(D)** none of these	A	25.
26. If 1989 earnings per share is $5.00 and market price of stock on December 31, 1989 is $50.00 per share, the 1989 price-earnings ratio is **(A)** 5 times **(B)** 10 times **(C)** 20 times **(D)** none of these	B	26.
27. If 1989 average accounts receivable are $40,000.00 and 1989 net sales on account are $100,000.00, the 1989 accounts receivable turnover ratio is **(A)** 0.4 times **(B)** 0.6 times **(C)** 2.5 times **(D)** none of these	C	27.
28. If 1989 average merchandise inventory is $40,000.00, 1989 net sales are $100,000.00, and 1989 cost of merchandise sold is $80,000.00, the 1989 merchandise inventory turnover ratio is **(A)** 0.5 times **(B)** 0.8 times **(C)** 2.5 times **(D)** none of these	D	28.
29. If for 1989, quick assets are $50,000.00, current assets are $100,000.00, and current liabilities are $25,000.00, the 1989 current ratio is **(A)** 1.0 times **(B)** 2.0 times **(C)** 4 times **(D)** none of these..........................	C	29.
30. If for 1989, quick assets are $100,000.00, current assets are $200,000.00, and current liabilities are $100,000.00, the 1989 acid-test ratio is **(A)** 0.5 times **(B)** 1.0 times **(C)** 2 times **(D)** none of these..........................	B	30.
31. If for 1989, cash is $20,000.00, accounts receivable is $20,000.00, merchandise inventory is $40,000.00, and current liabilities are $20,000.00, the 1989 current ratio is **(A)** 1.0 times **(B)** 2.0 times **(C)** 4.0 times **(D)** none of these	C	31.
32. If on December 31, 1989, total assets are $100,000.00, total stockholders' equity is $60,000.00, and total liabilities are $40,000.00, the 1989 debt ratio is **(A)** 40% **(B)** 60% **(C)** 250% **(D)** none of these..	A	32.
33. If on December 31, 1989, total assets are $100,000.00, total stockholders' equity is $60,000.00, and total liabilities are $40,000.00, the 1989 equity ratio is **(A)** 40% **(B)** 60% **(C)** 250% **(D)** none of these..	B	33.
34. If on December 31, 1989, total assets are $100,000.00, total stockholders' equity is $60,000.00, total liabilities are $40,000.00, and 10,000 shares of stock are outstanding, the equity per share is **(A)** $10.00 **(B)** $6.00 **(C)** $4.00 **(D)** none of these	B	34.

Name _____ Date _____ Class _____

Preparing comparative financial statements with trend analysis

The comparative financial statements prepared in Problem 19-1 are needed to complete Problems 19-3, 19-4, 19-5, and 19-6.

Metrocom

Comparative Income Statement

For Years Ended December 31, 1989 and 1988

	1989	1988	INCREASE/DECREASE AMOUNT	%
Operating Revenue:				
Net Sales	919 9 80 00	828 8 00 00	91 1 80 00	11.0
Cost of Merchandise Sold:				
Merchandise Inv., January 1	203 8 40 00	102 4 10 00	101 4 30 00	99.0
Net Purchases	777 5 60 00	747 8 90 00	29 6 70 00	4.0
Cost of Merchandise Available	981 4 00 00	850 3 00 00	131 1 00 00	15.4
Less Merchandise Inv., December 31	309 8 20 00	203 8 40 00	105 9 80 00	52.0
Cost of Merchandise Sold	671 5 80 00	646 4 60 00	25 1 20 00	3.9
Gross Profit on Operations	248 4 00 00	182 3 40 00	66 0 60 00	36.2
Operating Expenses:				
Selling Expenses:				
Advertising Expense	7 3 60 00	5 8 00 00	1 5 60 00	26.9
Delivery Expense	13 8 00 00	12 4 30 00	1 3 70 00	11.0
Salary Expense — Sales	59 8 00 00	49 7 30 00	10 0 70 00	20.2
Supplies Expense	2 7 60 00	2 4 90 00	2 70 00	10.8
Other Selling Expenses	3 6 80 00	3 3 10 00	3 70 00	11.2
Total Selling Expenses	87 4 00 00	73 7 60 00	13 6 40 00	18.5
Administrative Expenses:				
Bad Debts Expense	9 2 00 00	4 1 40 00	5 0 60 00	122.2
Salary Expense — Administrative	22 0 80 00	20 7 20 00	1 3 60 00	6.6
Other Administrative Expenses	11 0 40 00	9 9 50 00	1 0 90 00	11.0
Total Administrative Expenses	42 3 20 00	34 8 10 00	7 5 10 00	21.6
Total Operating Expenses	129 7 20 00	108 5 70 00	21 1 50 00	19.5
Income from Operations	118 6 80 00	73 7 70 00	44 9 10 00	60.9
Other Expenses:				
Interest Expense	18 4 00 00	15 7 50 00	2 6 50 00	16.8
Net Income before Federal Income Tax	100 2 80 00	58 0 20 00	42 2 60 00	72.8
Federal Income Tax	25 8 80 00	10 6 60 00	15 2 20 00	142.8
Net Income after Federal Income Tax	74 4 00 00	47 3 60 00	27 0 40 00	57.1

Metrocom

Comparative Statement of Stockholders' Equity

For Years Ended December 31, 1989 and 1988

	1989	1988	INCREASE/DECREASE AMOUNT	%
Capital Stock, January 1	200 0 0 0 00	200 0 0 0 00	-0-	0.0
Additional Capital Stock Issued	50 0 0 0 00	-0-	50 0 0 0 00	—
Capital Stock, December 31	250 0 0 0 00	200 0 0 0 00	50 0 0 0 00	25.0
Retained Earnings, January 1	122 2 0 0 00	114 8 4 0 00	7 3 6 0 00	6.4
Net Income after Federal Income Tax	74 4 0 0 00	47 3 6 0 00	27 0 4 0 00	57.1
Total	196 6 0 0 00	162 2 0 0 00	34 4 0 0 00	21.2
Less Dividends Declared	60 0 0 0 00	40 0 0 0 00	20 0 0 0 00	50.0
Retained Earnings, December 31	136 6 0 0 00	122 2 0 0 00	14 4 0 0 00	11.8
Total Stockholders' Equity, December 31	386 6 0 0 00	322 2 0 0 00	64 4 0 0 00	20.0

Metrocom

Comparative Balance Sheet

December 31, 1989 and 1988

	1989	1988	INCREASE/DECREASE AMOUNT	%
Assets				
Current Assets:				
Cash	149 740 00	153 030 00	−3 290 00	−2.1
Accounts Receivable (book value)	82 760 00	81 220 00	1 540 00	1.9
Merchandise Inventory	309 820 00	203 840 00	105 980 00	52.0
Other Current Assets	10 800 00	10 570 00	230 00	2.2
Total Current Assets	553 120 00	448 660 00	104 460 00	23.3
Plant Assets (book value)	211 980 00	216 940 00	−4 960 00	−2.3
Total Assets	765 100 00	665 600 00	99 500 00	14.9
Liabilities				
Current Liabilities:				
Notes Payable	86 250 00	57 530 00	28 720 00	49.9
Interest Payable	5 460 00	4 720 00	740 00	15.7
Accounts Payable	164 660 00	161 080 00	3 580 00	2.2
Income Tax Payable — Federal	5 220 00	2 130 00	3 090 00	145.1
Other Current Liabilities	21 080 00	16 270 00	4 810 00	29.6
Total Current Liabilities	282 670 00	241 730 00	40 940 00	16.9
Long-Term Liability:				
Mortgage Payable	95 830 00	101 670 00	−5 840 00	−5.7
Total Liabilities	378 500 00	343 400 00	35 100 00	10.2
Stockholders' Equity				
Capital Stock	250 000 00	200 000 00	50 000 00	25.0
Retained Earnings	136 600 00	122 200 00	14 400 00	11.8
Total Stockholders' Equity	386 600 00	322 200 00	64 400 00	20.0
Total Liabilities & Stockholders' Equity	765 100 00	665 600 00	99 500 00	14.9
Capital Stock Shares Outstanding	5 000	4 000	1 000	25.0

(a)	Net sales: +11.0%	Trend: *Favorable*
		
		Reason: *Possible causes are:*
		
		  1) *The increase in advertising expense increased demand.*
		
		  2) *The increase in salary expense for sales personnel provided more or better sales.*

(b)	Net income: +57.1%	Trend: *Favorable* Reason: *The percentage increase in net sales is much larger than the percentage increase in cost of merchandise sold.*
(c)	Total stockholders' equity: +20.0%	Trend: *Favorable* Reason: *Retained earnings and net income have increased. Also, additional capital stock was issued.*
(d)	Total assets: +14.9%	Trend: *Favorable* Reason: *Although current liabilities increased significantly, total stockholders' equity increased more than total liabilities. However, most of the increase in assets is due to the significant increase in merchandise inventory, which may account for the increase in sales, but could be unfavorable.*

Preparing comparative financial statements with component percentage analysis

Metrocom

Comparative Income Statement

For Years Ended December 31, 1989 and 1988

	1989		1988	
	AMOUNT	% OF NET SALES	AMOUNT	% OF NET SALES
Operating Revenue:				
Net Sales	919 9 8 0 00	100.0	828 8 0 0 00	100.0
Cost of Merchandise Sold:				
Merchandise Inv., January 1	203 8 4 0 00	22.2	102 4 1 0 00	12.4
Net Purchases	777 5 6 0 00	84.5	747 8 9 0 00	90.2
Cost of Merchandise Available	981 4 0 0 00	106.7	850 3 0 0 00	102.6
Less Merchandise Inv., December 31	309 8 2 0 00	33.7	203 8 4 0 00	24.6
Cost of Merchandise Sold	671 5 8 0 00	73.0	646 4 6 0 00	78.0
Gross Profit on Operations	248 4 0 0 00	27.0	182 3 4 0 00	22.0
Operating Expenses:				
Selling Expenses:				
Advertising Expense	7 3 6 0 00	0.8	5 8 0 0 00	0.7
Delivery Expense	13 8 0 0 00	1.5	12 4 3 0 00	1.5
Salary Expense — Sales	59 8 0 0 00	6.5	49 7 3 0 00	6.0
Supplies Expense	2 7 6 0 00	0.3	2 4 9 0 00	0.3
Other Selling Expenses	3 6 8 0 00	0.4	3 3 1 0 00	0.4
Total Selling Expenses	87 4 0 0 00	9.5	73 7 6 0 00	8.9
Administrative Expenses:				
Bad Debts Expense	9 2 0 0 00	1.0	4 1 4 0 00	0.5
Salary Expense — Administrative	22 0 8 0 00	2.4	20 7 2 0 00	2.5
Other Administrative Expenses	11 0 4 0 00	1.2	9 9 5 0 00	1.2
Total Administrative Expenses	42 3 2 0 00	4.6	34 8 1 0 00	4.2
Total Operating Expenses	129 7 2 0 00	14.1	108 5 7 0 00	13.1
Income from Operations	118 6 8 0 00	12.9	73 7 7 0 00	8.9
Other Expenses:				
Interest Expense	18 4 0 0 00	2.0	15 7 5 0 00	1.9
Net Income before Federal Income Tax	100 2 8 0 00	10.9	58 0 2 0 00	7.0
Federal Income Tax	25 8 8 0 00	2.8	10 6 6 0 00	1.3
Net Income after Federal Income Tax	74 4 0 0 00	8.1	47 3 6 0 00	5.7

Metrocom

Comparative Statement of Stockholders' Equity

For Years Ended December 31, 1989 and 1988

	1989		1988	
	AMOUNT	PERCENT	AMOUNT	PERCENT
Capital Stock, January 1	200 0 0 0 00	51.7	200 0 0 0 00	62.1
Additional Capital Stock Issued	50 0 0 0 00	12.9	-0-	0.0
Capital Stock, December 31	250 0 0 0 00	64.7	200 0 0 0 00	62.1
Retained Earnings, January 1	122 2 0 0 00	31.6	114 8 4 0 00	35.6
Net Income after Federal Income Tax	74 4 0 0 00	19.2	47 3 6 0 00	14.7
Total	196 6 0 0 00	50.9	162 2 0 0 00	50.3
Less Dividends Declared	60 0 0 0 00	15.5	40 0 0 0 00	12.4
Retained Earnings, December 31	136 6 0 0 00	35.3	122 2 0 0 00	37.9
Total Stockholders' Equity, December 31	386 6 0 0 00	100.0	322 2 0 0 00	100.0

Metrocom

Comparative Balance Sheet

December 31, 1989 and 1988

	1989		1988	
	AMOUNT	PERCENT	AMOUNT	PERCENT
Assets				
Current Assets:				
Cash	149 740 00	19.6	153 030 00	23.0
Accounts Receivable (book value)	82 760 00	10.8	81 220 00	12.2
Merchandise Inventory	309 820 00	40.5	203 840 00	30.6
Other Current Assets	10 800 00	1.4	10 570 00	1.6
Total Current Assets	553 120 00	72.3	448 660 00	67.4
Plant Assets (book value)	211 980 00	27.7	216 940 00	32.6
Total Assets	765 100 00	100.0	665 600 00	100.0
Liabilities				
Current Liabilities:				
Notes Payable	86 250 00	11.3	57 530 00	8.6
Interest Payable	5 460 00	0.7	4 720 00	0.7
Accounts Payable	164 660 00	21.5	161 080 00	24.2
Income Tax Payable — Federal	5 220 00	0.7	2 130 00	0.3
Other Current Liabilities	21 080 00	2.8	16 270 00	2.4
Total Current Liabilities	282 670 00	36.9	241 730 00	36.3
Long-Term Liability:				
Mortgage Payable	95 830 00	12.5	101 670 00	15.3
Total Liabilities	378 500 00	49.5	343 400 00	51.6
Stockholders' Equity				
Capital Stock	250 000 00	32.7	200 000 00	30.0
Retained Earnings	136 600 00	17.9	122 200 00	18.4
Total Stockholders' Equity	386 600 00	50.5	322 200 00	48.4
Total Liabilities and Stockholders' Equity	765 100 00	100.0	665 600 00	100.0
Capital Stock Shares Outstanding	5 000		4 000	

(a)	As a Percentage of Net Sales:	
(1)	Cost of merchandise sold: 1988: **78.0%** 1989: **73.0%**	Trend: *Favorable* Reason: *Cost of merchandise sold as a percentage of net sales has decreased. A decreasing percentage of the revenue from sales is being used to pay for merchandise sold.*
(2)	Gross profit on operations: 1988: **22.0%** 1989: **27.0%**	Trend: *Favorable* Reason: *The decreased percentage of cost of merchandise sold has resulted in a higher gross profit percentage.*
(3)	Total operating expenses: 1988: **13.1%** 1989: **14.1%**	Trend: *Unfavorable* Reason: *The percentage of operating expenses to net sales has increased. The cost of operating the business has increased so the business is operating less economically.*
(4)	Net income after federal income tax: 1988: **5.7%** 1989: **8.1%**	Trend: *Favorable* Reason: *Cost of merchandise sold decreased more than the percentage increase in total operating expenses. Thus a larger percentage of sales revenue is retained as net income.*

(b) As a Percentage of Total Stockholders' Equity:

(1) Retained earnings:

1988: **37.9%**

1989: **35.3%**

Trend: *Unfavorable*

Reason: *Metrocom paid 50% more dividends in 1989 than 1988. While this high dividend payout reflects favorably on the market price of its stock, Metrocom is left with lower retained earnings.*

(2) Capital stock:

1988: **62.1%**

1989: **64.7%**

Trend: *Favorable*

Reason: *If additional stock is issued to expand the business, this is a favorable trend. However, this trend also indicates a relative reduction in retained earnings which could be unfavorable if caused by decreasing net income.*

(c) As a Percentage of Total Assets:

(1) Current assets:

1988: **67.4%**

1989: **72.3%**

Trend: *Favorable*

Reason: *Current assets provide the company's working capital—the capital used to operate the business. A higher portion of current assets means more assets are available for the daily profit making activities of the business.*

(2) Current liabilities:

1988: **36.3%**

1989: **36.9%**

Trend: *Unfavorable*

Reason: *Increased liabilities place restrictions on funding and weaken Metrocom's cash position.*

Analyzing earnings performance from comparative financial statements

The comparative statements prepared in Problem 19-1 are needed to complete Problem 19-3.

(a)	Rate earned on average total assets: 1988: $\$47{,}360 \div \dfrac{544{,}200 + 665{,}600}{2} = 7.8\%$ 1989: $\$74{,}400 \div \dfrac{665{,}600 + 765{,}100}{2} = 10.4\%$	Trend: *Favorable* Reason: *For each dollar in company assets, the net income has increased from 7.8¢ to 10.4¢.*
(b)	Rate earned on average stock-holders' equity: 1988: $\$47{,}360 \div \dfrac{314{,}840 + 322{,}200}{2} = 14.9\%$ 1989: $\$74{,}400 \div \dfrac{322{,}200 + 386{,}600}{2} = 21.0\%$	Trend: *Favorable* Reason: *For each dollar of stockholders' equity, the net income increased from 14.9¢ to 21.0¢.*
(c)	Rate earned on net sales: 1988: $\$47{,}360 \div 828{,}800 = 5.7\%$ 1989: $\$74{,}400 \div 919{,}980 = 8.1\%$	Trend: *Favorable* Reason: *For each dollar of sales, the net income increased from 5.7¢ to 8.1¢.*
(d)	Earnings per share: 1988: $\$47{,}360 \div 4{,}000 = \$11.84$ 1989: $\$74{,}400 \div 5{,}000 = \$14.88$	Trend: *Favorable* Reason: *The net income earned for each share of capital stock increased from $11.84 to $14.88.*
(e)	Price-earnings ratio: 1988: $\$150.00 \div 11.84 = 12.7$ times 1989: $\$220.00 \div 14.88 = 14.8$ times	Trend: *Favorable* Reason: *The increase shows that stock market investors have increased confidence in the profitability of Metrocom.*

Name _____ Date _____ Class _____

Analyzing efficiency from comparative financial statements

The comparative statements prepared in Problem 19-1 are needed to complete Problem 19-4.

(a)	Accounts receivable turnover ratio: 1988: $$\$828{,}800 \div \frac{77{,}160 + 81{,}220}{2} = 10.5 \text{ times}$$ 1989: $$\$919{,}980 \div \frac{81{,}220 + 82{,}760}{2} = 11.2 \text{ times}$$	Trend: *Favorable* Reason: *There is increasing collection efficiency of accounts receivable by reduction of the average collection period.*
(b)	Average number of days for payment: 1988: *365 ÷ 10.5 = 34.8 days* 1989: *365 ÷ 11.2 = 32.6 days*	Trend: *Favorable* Reason: *There is increasing efficiency of collection of accounts receivable. Accounts are collected, on average, in 2.2 fewer days.*
(c)	Merchandise inventory turnover ratio: 1988: $$\$646{,}460 \div \frac{102{,}410 + 203{,}840}{2} = 4.2 \text{ times}$$ 1989: $$\$671{,}580 \div \frac{203{,}840 + 309{,}820}{2} = 2.6 \text{ times}$$	Trend: *Unfavorable* Reason: *The number of times the average amount of inventory is sold each year has decreased from 4.2 to 2.6. The amount of sales relative to inventory on hand has decreased—an indication of inefficiency.*
(d)	Number of days' sales in merchandise inventory: 1988: *365 ÷ 4.2 = 86.9 days* 1989: *365 ÷ 2.6 = 140.4 days*	Trend: *Unfavorable* Reason: *It is taking longer to sell merchandise items—an increase from 86.9 days to 140.4 days to sell the average level of inventory.*

Analyzing short-term financial strength from a
comparative balance sheet

PROBLEM 19-5, p. 436
[1, 2]

The comparative balance sheet prepared in Problem 19-1 is needed to complete
Problem 19-5.

(a)

Current ratio:

1988: **$448,660 ÷ 241,730 = 1.9 times**

1989: **$553,120 ÷ 282,670 = 2.0 times**

Trend: **Favorable**

Reason: **The amount of current assets in relation to current liabilities is increasing to a satisfactory level.**

(b)

Acid-test ratio:

1988: **$234,250 ÷ 241,730 = 1.0 times**

1989: **$232,500 ÷ 282,670 = .8 times**

Trend: **Unfavorable**

Reason: **Quick assets have decreased and current liabilities have increased. All current liabilities could not be paid immediately if necessary.**

Analyzing long-term financial strength from a comparative balance sheet

The comparative balance sheet prepared in Problem 19-1 is needed to complete Problem 19-6.

(a)	Debt ratio: 1988: **$343,400 ÷ 665,600 = 51.6%** 1989: **$378,500 ÷ 765,100 = 49.5%**	Trend: **Favorable** Reason: **The per dollar assets owned that are financed with borrowed capital decreased from 51.6¢ to 49.5¢.**
(b)	Equity ratio: 1988: **$322,200 ÷ 665,600 = 48.4%** 1989: **$386,600 ÷ 765,100 = 50.5%**	Trend: **Favorable** Reason: **The per dollar assets owned that are provided by stockholders' equity has increased from 48.4¢ to 50.5¢.**
(c)	Equity per share: 1988: **$322,200 ÷ 4,000 = $80.55** 1989: **$386,600 ÷ 5,000 = $77.32**	Trend: **Unfavorable** Reason: **The ownership of the total equity per share of stock has decreased from $80.55 to $77.32.**

Customaire

Comparative Income Statement

For Years Ended December 31, 1989 and 1988

	1989	1988	INCREASE/DECREASE	
			AMOUNT	%
Operating Revenue:				
Net Sales	1,907 0 0 0 00	1,453 0 0 0 00	454 0 0 0 00	31.2
Cost of Merchandise Sold:				
Merchandise Inv., January 1	169 5 0 0 00	53 7 6 0 00	115 7 4 0 00	215.3
Net Purchases	1,201 6 0 0 00	1,047 1 1 0 00	154 4 9 0 00	14.8
Cost of Merchandise Available	1,371 1 0 0 00	1,100 8 7 0 00	270 2 3 0 00	24.5
Less Merchandise Inv., December 31	179 2 0 0 00	169 5 0 0 00	9 7 0 0 00	5.7
Cost of Merchandise Sold	1,191 9 0 0 00	931 3 7 0 00	260 5 3 0 00	28.0
Gross Profit on Operations	715 1 0 0 00	521 6 3 0 00	193 4 7 0 00	37.1
Operating Expenses:				
Selling Expenses:				
Advertising Expense	15 2 6 0 00	10 1 7 0 00	5 0 9 0 00	50.0
Delivery Expense	22 8 8 0 00	17 4 4 0 00	5 4 4 0 00	31.2
Salary Expense — Sales	286 0 5 0 00	216 5 0 0 00	69 5 5 0 00	32.1
Supplies Expense	13 3 5 0 00	10 1 7 0 00	3 1 8 0 00	31.3
Other Selling Expenses	38 1 4 0 00	30 5 1 0 00	7 6 3 0 00	25.0
Total Selling Expenses	375 6 8 0 00	284 7 9 0 00	90 8 9 0 00	31.9
Administrative Expenses:				
Bad Debts Expense	11 4 4 0 00	7 2 7 0 00	4 1 7 0 00	57.4
Salary Expense — Administrative	80 0 9 0 00	63 9 3 0 00	16 1 6 0 00	25.3
Other Administrative Expenses	57 2 1 0 00	47 9 5 0 00	9 2 6 0 00	19.3
Total Administrative Expenses	148 7 4 0 00	119 1 5 0 00	29 5 9 0 00	24.8
Total Operating Expenses	524 4 2 0 00	403 9 4 0 00	120 4 8 0 00	29.8
Income from Operations	190 6 8 0 00	117 6 9 0 00	72 9 9 0 00	62.0
Other Expenses:				
Interest Expense	25 5 6 0 00	22 5 0 0 00	3 0 6 0 00	13.6
Net Income before Federal Income Tax	165 1 2 0 00	95 1 9 0 00	69 9 3 0 00	73.5
Federal Income Tax	55 7 0 0 00	23 5 4 0 00	32 1 6 0 00	136.6
Net Income after Federal Income Tax	109 4 2 0 00	71 6 5 0 00	37 7 7 0 00	52.7

Customaire

Comparative Statement of Stockholders' Equity

For Years Ended December 31, 1989 and 1988

	1989	1988	INCREASE/DECREASE	
			AMOUNT	%
Capital Stock, January 1	200 0 0 0 00	200 0 0 0 00	-0-	0.0
Additional Capital Stock Issued	40 0 0 0 00	-0-	40 0 0 0 00	—
Capital Stock, December 31	240 0 0 0 00	200 0 0 0 00	40 0 0 0 00	20.0
Retained Earnings, January 1	163 5 0 0 00	131 8 5 0 00	31 6 5 0 00	24.0
Net Income after Federal Income Tax	109 4 2 0 00	71 6 5 0 00	37 7 7 0 00	52.7
Total	272 9 2 0 00	203 5 0 0 00	69 4 2 0 00	34.1
Less Dividends Declared	60 0 0 0 00	40 0 0 0 00	20 0 0 0 00	50.0
Retained Earnings, December 31	212 9 2 0 00	163 5 0 0 00	49 4 2 0 00	30.2
Total Stockholders' Equity, December 31	452 9 2 0 00	363 5 0 0 00	89 4 2 0 00	24.6

Customaire

Comparative Balance Sheet

December 31, 1989 and 1988

	1989	1988	INCREASE/DECREASE AMOUNT	%
Assets				
Current Assets:				
Cash	86 8 8 0 00	45 4 8 0 00	41 4 0 0 00	91.0
Accounts Receivable (book value)	198 3 0 0 00	231 6 6 0 00	−33 3 6 0 00	−14.4
Merchandise Inventory	179 2 0 0 00	169 5 0 0 00	9 7 0 0 00	5.7
Other Current Assets	10 9 2 0 00	8 5 2 0 00	2 4 0 0 00	28.2
Total Current Assets	475 3 0 0 00	455 1 6 0 00	20 1 4 0 00	4.4
Plant Assets (book value)	372 0 0 0 00	264 0 0 0 00	108 0 0 0 00	40.9
Total Assets	847 3 0 0 00	719 1 6 0 00	128 1 4 0 00	17.8
Liabilities				
Current Liabilities:				
Notes Payable	64 8 6 0 00	93 3 7 0 00	−28 5 1 0 00	−30.5
Interest Payable	5 1 6 0 00	8 0 4 0 00	−2 8 8 0 00	−35.8
Accounts Payable	136 7 0 0 00	160 4 7 0 00	−23 7 7 0 00	−14.8
Income Tax Payable — Federal	5 5 0 0 00	1 2 8 0 00	4 2 2 0 00	329.7
Other Current Liabilities	2 1 6 0 00	2 5 0 0 00	− 3 4 0 00	−13.6
Total Current Liabilities	214 3 8 0 00	265 6 6 0 00	−51 2 8 0 00	−19.3
Long-Term Liability:				
Mortgage Payable	180 0 0 0 00	90 0 0 0 00	90 0 0 0 00	100.0
Total Liabilities	394 3 8 0 00	355 6 6 0 00	38 7 2 0 00	10.9
Stockholders' Equity				
Capital Stock	240 0 0 0 00	200 0 0 0 00	40 0 0 0 00	20.0
Retained Earnings	212 9 2 0 00	163 5 0 0 00	49 4 2 0 00	30.2
Total Stockholders' Equity	452 9 2 0 00	363 5 0 0 00	89 4 2 0 00	24.6
Total Liabilities & Stockholders' Equity	847 3 0 0 00	719 1 6 0 00	128 1 4 0 00	17.8
Capital Stock Shares Outstanding	4 8 0 0	4 0 0 0	8 0 0	20.0

(a) Net sales: **+31.2%**

Trend: *Favorable*

Reason: *Possible reasons are:*
  1) Increased advertising efforts.
  2) Increased sales efforts as shown by increased spending for advertising and sales salaries.

(b) Net income: **+52.7%**

Trend: *Favorable*

Reason: *The percentage increase in net sales is larger than the percentage increase in cost of merchandise sold.*

(c) Total stockholders' equity: **+24.6%**

Trend: *Favorable*

Reason: *Retained earnings and net income have increased. Additional capital stock was issued.*

(d) Total assets: **+17.8%**

Trend: *Favorable*

Reason: *Significant increases in cash and plant assets resulting from an increase in long-term liabilities and stockholders' equity.*

Customaire

Comparative Income Statement

For Years Ended December 31, 1989 and 1988

	1989		1988	
	AMOUNT	% OF NET SALES	AMOUNT	% OF NET SALES
Operating Revenue:				
Net Sales	1,907 0 0 0 00	100.0	1,453 0 0 0 00	100.0
Cost of Merchandise Sold:				
Merchandise Inv., January 1	169 5 0 0 00	8.9	53 7 6 0 00	3.7
Net Purchases	1,201 6 0 0 00	63.0	1,047 1 1 0 00	72.1
Cost of Merchandise Available	1,371 1 0 0 00	71.9	1,100 8 7 0 00	75.8
Less Merchandise Inv., December 31	179 2 0 0 00	9.4	169 5 0 0 00	11.7
Cost of Merchandise Sold	1,191 9 0 0 00	62.5	931 3 7 0 00	64.1
Gross Profit on Operations	715 1 0 0 00	37.5	521 6 3 0 00	35.9
Operating Expenses:				
Selling Expenses:				
Advertising Expense	15 2 6 0 00	0.8	10 1 7 0 00	0.7
Delivery Expense	22 8 8 0 00	1.2	17 4 4 0 00	1.2
Salary Expense — Sales	286 0 5 0 00	15.0	216 5 0 0 00	14.9
Supplies Expense	13 3 5 0 00	0.7	10 1 7 0 00	0.7
Other Selling Expenses	38 1 4 0 00	2.0	30 5 1 0 00	2.1
Total Selling Expenses	375 6 8 0 00	19.7	284 7 9 0 00	19.6
Administrative Expenses:				
Bad Debts Expense	11 4 4 0 00	0.6	7 2 7 0 00	0.5
Salary Expense — Administrative	80 0 9 0 00	4.2	63 9 3 0 00	4.4
Other Administrative Expenses	57 2 1 0 00	3.0	47 9 5 0 00	3.3
Total Administrative Expenses	148 7 4 0 00	7.8	119 1 5 0 00	8.2
Total Operating Expenses	524 4 2 0 00	27.5	403 9 4 0 00	27.8
Income from Operations	190 6 8 0 00	10.0	117 6 9 0 00	8.1
Other Expenses:				
Interest Expense	25 5 6 0 00	1.3	22 5 0 0 00	1.5
Net Income before Federal Income Tax	165 1 2 0 00	8.7	95 1 9 0 00	6.6
Federal Income Tax	55 7 0 0 00	2.9	23 5 4 0 00	1.6
Net Income after Federal Income Tax	109 4 2 0 00	5.7	71 6 5 0 00	4.9

(a)   As a Percentage of Net Sales:

(1)   Cost of merchandise sold:

     1988:   **64.1%**

     1989:   **62.5%**

Trend: *Favorable*

Reason: **A decreasing percentage of the revenue from sales is being used to pay for merchandise sold.**

(2)   Gross profit on operations:

     1988:   **35.9%**

     1989:   **37.5%**

Trend: *Favorable*

Reason: **The decreased percentage of cost of merchandise sold has resulted in a higher gross profit percentage.**

(3)   Total operating expenses:

     1988:   **27.8%**

     1989:   **27.5%**

Trend: *Favorable*

Reason: **The cost of operating the business has decreased so the business is operating more economically.**

(4)   Net income after federal income tax:

     1988:   **4.9%**

     1989:   **5.7%**

Trend: *Favorable*

Reason: **Cost of merchandise sold and operating expenses decreased.**

(b) As a Percentage of Total Stockholders' Equity:	
(1) Retained earnings:	Trend: *Favorable*
1988: *$163,500 ÷ 363,500 = 45.0%*	Reason: *Net income increased and more was retained in the business.*
1989: *$212,920 ÷ 452,920 = 47.0%*	
(2) Capital stock:	Trend: *Favorable*
1988: *$200,000 ÷ 363,500 = 55.0%*	Reason: *A larger portion of the business is being financed through increased earnings and less from invested capital.*
1989: *$240,000 ÷ 452,920 = 53.0%*	
(c) As a Percentage of Total Assets:	
(1) Current assets:	Trend: *Unfavorable*
1988: *$455,160 ÷ 719,160 = 63.3%*	Reason: *Plant assets increased over 40%. Although current assets increased, the increase was only 4.4%, compared to the 40% plant asset increase.*
1989: *$475,300 ÷ 847,300 = 56.1%*	
(2) Current liabilities:	Trend: *Favorable*
1988: *$265,660 ÷ 719,160 = 36.9%*	Reason: *Current liabilities declined 19.3% while long-term liabilities increased 100% and total liabilities increased 10.9%. The additional long-term liabilities probably were used to reduce current liabilities.*
1989: *$214,380 ÷ 847,300 = 25.3%*	

(a) Rate earned on average total assets:

1988:
$$\$71,650 \div \frac{693,200 + 719,160}{2} = 10.1\%$$

1989:
$$\$109,420 \div \frac{719,160 + 847,300}{2} = 14.0\%$$

Trend: *Favorable*

Reason: *For each dollar in company assets, the net income has increased from 10.1¢ to 14.0¢.*

(b) Rate earned on average stockholders' equity:

1988:
$$\$71,650 \div \frac{331,850 + 363,500}{2} = 20.6\%$$

1989:
$$\$109,420 \div \frac{363,500 + 452,900}{2} = 26.8\%$$

Trend: *Favorable*

Reason: *For each dollar of stockholders' equity, the net income increased from 20.6¢ to 26.8¢.*

(c) Rate earned on net sales:

1988: $\$71,650 \div 1,453,000 = 4.9\%$

1989: $\$109,420 \div 1,907,000 = 5.7\%$

Trend: *Favorable*

Reason: *For each dollar of sales the net income increased from 4.9¢ to 5.7¢.*

(d) Earnings per share:

1988: $\$71,650 \div 4,000 = \$17.91$

1989: $\$109,420 \div 4,800 = \$22.80$

Trend: *Favorable*

Reason: *The net income earned for each share of capital stock increased from \$17.91 to \$22.80.*

(e) Price-earnings ratio:

1988: $\$300.00 \div 17.91 = 16.8$ times

1989: $\$367.00 \div 22.80 = 16.1$ times

Trend: *Unfavorable*

Reason: *The market price of the company's stock has not increased as much relatively as the earnings.*

[10, 11]
(a)

Accounts receivable turnover ratio:

1988:
$$\$1,453,000 \div \frac{222,400 + 231,660}{2} =$$
6.4 times

1989:
$$\$1,907,000 \div \frac{231,660 + 198,300}{2} =$$
8.9 times

Trend: *Favorable*

Reason: *The number of times the average accounts receivable balance has been collected increased from 6.4 to 8.9. Thus accounts receivable are being collected more quickly than in the previous year.*

(b)

Merchandise inventory turnover ratio:

1988:
$$\$931,370 \div \frac{53,760 + 169,500}{2} = 8.3 \text{ times}$$

1989:
$$\$1,191,900 \div \frac{169,500 + 179,200}{2} = 6.8 \text{ times}$$

Trend: *Unfavorable*

Reason: *The number of times the average amount of inventory is sold each year decreased from 8.3 to 6.8 times.*

[12, 13]
(a)

Current ratio:

1988: $\$455,160 \div 265,660 = 1.7 \text{ times}$

1989: $\$475,300 \div 214,380 = 2.2 \text{ times}$

Trend: *Favorable*

Reason: *The amount of current assets in relation to current liabilities is increasing.*

(b)

Acid-test ratio:

1988: $\$277,140 \div 265,660 = 1.0 \text{ times}$
($45,480 + 231,660 = 277,140$)

1989: $\$285,180 \div 214,380 = 1.3 \text{ times}$
($86,880 + 198,300 = 285,180$)

Trend: *Favorable*

Reason: *The amount of the most liquid current assets in relation to current liabilities is increasing.*

(a) Debt ratio: 1988: *$355,660 ÷ 719,160 = 49.5%* 1989: *$394,380 ÷ 847,300 = 46.5%*	Trend: *Favorable* Reason: *The per dollar assets owned that are financed with borrowed capital decreased from 49.5¢ to 46.5¢.*
(b) Equity ratio: 1988: *$363,500 ÷ 719,160 = 50.5%* 1989: *$452,920 ÷ 847,300 = 53.5%*	Trend: *Favorable* Reason: *The per dollar assets owned that are provided by stockholders' equity has increased from 50.5¢ to 53.5¢.*
(c) Equity per share: 1988: *$363,500 ÷ 4,000 = $90.88* 1989: *$452,920 ÷ 4,800 = $94.36*	Trend: *Favorable* Reason: *The ownership of the total equity per share of stock has increased from $90.88 to $94.36.*

[1]

ExCell

Comparative Income Statement

For Years Ended December 31, 1989 and 1988

	1989	1988	INCREASE/DECREASE AMOUNT	%
Operating Revenue:				
Net Sales	1,070 0 0 0 00	1,320 0 0 0 00	−250 0 0 0 00	−18.9
Cost of Merchandise Sold:				
Merchandise Inv., January 1	352 4 2 0 00	253 5 0 0 00	98 9 2 0 00	39.0
Net Purchases	705 7 3 0 00	918 6 4 0 00	−212 9 1 0 00	−23.2
Cost of Merchandise Available	1,058 1 5 0 00	1,172 1 4 0 00	−113 9 9 0 00	−9.7
Less Merchandise Inv., December 31	361 5 8 0 00	352 4 2 0 00	9 1 6 0 00	2.6
Cost of Merchandise Sold	696 5 7 0 00	819 7 2 0 00	−123 1 5 0 00	−15.0
Gross Profit on Operations	373 4 3 0 00	500 2 8 0 00	−126 8 5 0 00	−25.4
Operating Expenses:				
Selling Expenses:				
Advertising Expense	20 3 3 0 00	26 4 0 0 00	−6 0 7 0 00	−23.0
Delivery Expense	33 1 7 0 00	40 9 2 0 00	−7 7 5 0 00	−18.9
Salary Expense — Sales	86 6 7 0 00	116 1 6 0 00	−29 4 9 0 00	−25.4
Supplies Expense	8 5 6 0 00	10 5 6 0 00	−2 0 0 0 00	−18.9
Other Selling Expenses	37 4 5 0 00	46 2 0 0 00	−8 7 5 0 00	−18.9
Total Selling Expenses	186 1 8 0 00	240 2 4 0 00	−54 0 6 0 00	−22.5
Administrative Expenses:				
Bad Debts Expense	4 2 8 0 00	9 2 4 0 00	−4 9 6 0 00	−53.7
Salary Expense — Administrative	64 2 0 0 00	77 8 8 0 00	−13 6 8 0 00	−17.6
Other Administrative Expenses	55 6 4 0 00	66 0 0 0 00	−10 3 6 0 00	−15.7
Total Administrative Expenses	124 1 2 0 00	153 1 2 0 00	−29 0 0 0 00	−18.9
Total Operating Expenses	310 3 0 0 00	393 3 6 0 00	−83 0 6 0 00	−21.1
Income from Operations	63 1 3 0 00	106 9 2 0 00	−43 7 9 0 00	−41.0
Other Expenses:				
Interest Expense	31 0 3 0 00	26 4 0 0 00	4 6 3 0 00	17.5
Net Income before Federal Income Tax	32 1 0 0 00	80 5 2 0 00	−48 4 2 0 00	−60.1
Federal Income Tax	5 0 3 0 00	17 9 6 0 00	−12 9 3 0 00	−72.0
Net Income after Federal Income Tax	27 0 7 0 00	62 5 6 0 00	−35 4 9 0 00	−56.7

ExCell

Comparative Statement of Stockholders' Equity

For Years Ended December 31, 1989 and 1988

	1989	1988	INCREASE/DECREASE AMOUNT	%
Capital Stock, January 1	500 000 00	500 000 00	-0-	0.0
Additional Capital Stock Issued	-0-	-0-	-0-	—
Capital Stock, December 31	500 000 00	500 000 00	-0-	0.0
Retained Earnings, January 1	75 900 00	53 340 00	22 560 00	42.3
Net Income after Federal Income Tax	27 070 00	62 560 00	−35 490 00	−56.7
Total	102 970 00	115 900 00	−12 930 00	−11.2
Less Dividends Declared	20 000 00	40 000 00	−20 000 00	−50.0
Retained Earnings, December 31	82 970 00	75 900 00	7 070 00	9.3
Total Stockholders' Equity, December 31	582 970 00	575 900 00	7 070 00	1.2

ExCell

Comparative Balance Sheet

December 31, 1989 and 1988

	1989	1988	INCREASE/DECREASE AMOUNT	%
Assets				
Current Assets:				
Cash	157 7 6 0 00	173 8 5 0 00	−16 0 9 0 00	−9.3
Accounts Receivable (book value)	77 2 0 0 00	118 8 0 0 00	−41 6 0 0 00	−35.0
Merchandise Inventory	361 5 8 0 00	352 4 2 0 00	9 1 6 0 00	2.6
Other Current Assets	145 8 3 0 00	125 1 3 0 00	20 7 0 0 00	16.5
Total Current Assets	742 3 7 0 00	770 2 0 0 00	−27 8 3 0 00	−3.6
Plant Assets (book value)	270 9 3 0 00	278 6 0 0 00	−7 6 7 0 00	−2.8
Total Assets	1,013 3 0 0 00	1,048 8 0 0 00	−35 5 0 0 00	−3.4
Liabilities				
Current Liabilities:				
Notes Payable	142 0 0 0 00	112 2 0 0 00	29 8 0 0 00	26.6
Interest Payable	3 1 0 0 00	2 6 0 0 00	5 0 0 00	19.2
Accounts Payable	130 4 0 0 00	198 2 2 0 00	−67 8 2 0 00	−34.2
Income Tax Payable — Federal	5 0 0 00	3 0 0 0 00	−2 5 0 0 00	−83.3
Other Current Liabilities	34 3 3 0 00	24 8 8 0 00	9 4 5 0 00	38.0
Total Current Liabilities	310 3 3 0 00	340 9 0 0 00	−30 5 7 0 00	−9.0
Long-Term Liability:				
Mortgage Payable	120 0 0 0 00	132 0 0 0 00	−12 0 0 0 00	−9.1
Total Liabilities	430 3 3 0 00	472 9 0 0 00	−42 5 7 0 00	−9.0
Stockholders' Equity				
Capital Stock	500 0 0 0 00	500 0 0 0 00	-0-	0.0
Retained Earnings	82 9 7 0 00	75 9 0 0 00	7 0 7 0 00	9.3
Total Stockholders' Equity	582 9 7 0 00	575 9 0 0 00	7 0 7 0 00	1.2
Total Liabilities & Stockholders' Equity	1,013 3 0 0 00	1,048 8 0 0 00	−35 5 0 0 00	−3.4
Capital Stock Shares Outstanding	20 0 0 0	20 0 0 0	-0-	0.0

(a) Net sales: **−18.9%**	Trend: *Unfavorable* Reason: *Sales are down 18.9% and most costs and expenses are down 15% to 20%. However, bad debts expense is down 53.7% and sales salary expenses are down 25.4%. In an attempt to cut costs, the company may have decreased its sales efforts and become too restrictive on credit, thus decreasing sales.*
(b) Net income: **−56.7%**	Trend *Unfavorable* Reason: *Sales decreased 18.9%. However, gross profit and operating expenses decreased at an even higher rate, 25.4% and 21.1% respectively.*
(c) Total stockholders' equity: **+1.2%**	Trend: *Favorable* Reason: *Although the company experienced a significant reduction in net income, it managed to maintain approximately the same relative stockholders' equity — a 1.2% increase. This was achieved by reducing the cash dividends by 50%.*
(d) Total assets: **−3.4%**	Trend: *Unfavorable* Reason: *A significant portion of the decrease was caused by a 35.0% decrease in accounts receivable. This result could be positive if it is an indication of more efficient collection efforts. However, this effect could be caused by reduced sales efforts and stricter credit practices (as noted in (a) above).*

ExCell

Comparative Income Statement

For Years Ended December 31, 1989 and 1988

	1989 AMOUNT	1989 % OF NET SALES	1988 AMOUNT	1988 % OF NET SALES
Operating Revenue:				
Net Sales	1,070 0 0 0 00	100.0	1,320 0 0 0 00	100.0
Cost of Merchandise Sold:				
Merchandise Inv., January 1	352 4 2 0 00	32.9	253 5 0 0 00	19.2
Net Purchases	705 7 3 0 00	66.0	918 6 4 0 00	69.6
Cost of Merchandise Available	1,058 1 5 0 00	98.9	1,172 1 4 0 00	88.8
Less Merchandise Inv., December 31	361 5 8 0 00	33.8	352 4 2 0 00	26.7
Cost of Merchandise Sold	696 5 7 0 00	65.1	819 7 2 0 00	62.1
Gross Profit on Operations	373 4 3 0 00	34.9	500 2 8 0 00	37.9
Operating Expenses:				
Selling Expenses:				
Advertising Expense	20 3 3 0 00	1.9	26 4 0 0 00	2.0
Delivery Expense	33 1 7 0 00	3.1	40 9 2 0 00	3.1
Salary Expense — Sales	86 6 7 0 00	8.1	116 1 6 0 00	8.8
Supplies Expense	8 5 6 0 00	0.8	10 5 6 0 00	0.8
Other Selling Expenses	37 4 5 0 00	3.5	46 2 0 0 00	3.5
Total Selling Expenses	186 1 8 0 00	17.4	240 2 4 0 00	18.2
Administrative Expenses:				
Bad Debts Expense	4 2 8 0 00	0.4	9 2 4 0 00	0.7
Salary Expense — Administrative	64 2 0 0 00	6.0	77 8 8 0 00	5.9
Other Administrative Expenses	55 6 4 0 00	5.2	66 0 0 0 00	5.0
Total Administrative Expenses	124 1 2 0 00	11.6	153 1 2 0 00	11.6
Total Operating Expenses	310 3 0 0 00	29.0	393 3 6 0 00	29.8
Income from Operations	63 1 3 0 00	5.9	106 9 2 0 00	8.1
Other Expenses:				
Interest Expense	31 0 3 0 00	2.9	26 4 0 0 00	2.0
Net Income before Federal Income Tax	32 1 0 0 00	3.0	80 5 2 0 00	6.1
Federal Income Tax	5 0 3 0 00	0.5	17 9 6 0 00	1.4
Net Income after Federal Income Tax	27 0 7 0 00	2.5	62 5 6 0 00	4.7

(a) As a Percentage of Net Sales:	
(1) Cost of merchandise sold: 1988: ***62.1%*** 1989: ***65.1%***	Trend: *Unfavorable* Reason: *The cost of merchandise sold has increased from 62.1¢ to 65.1¢ per dollar of net sales. Therefore, in 1989 there is 3.0¢ less per sales dollar that is available for net income.*
(2) Gross profit on operations: 1988: ***37.9%*** 1989: ***34.9%***	Trend *Unfavorable* Reason: *Cost of merchandise sold increased 3.0¢ per sales dollar. Therefore, the company has 3.0¢ less per sales dollar available for net income and operating expenses.*
(3) Total operating expenses: 1988: ***29.8%*** 1989: ***29.0%***	Trend: *Favorable* Reason: *Increased efficiency decreased the operating expenses from 29.8¢ per sales dollar to 29.0¢, a 0.8¢ decrease.*
(4) Net income after federal income tax: 1988: ***4.7%*** 1989: ***2.5%***	Trend: *Unfavorable* Reason: *Net income decreased from 4.7¢ per sales dollar to 2.5¢, a 2.2¢ reduction. This decrease per sales dollar was caused by the following changes in costs:* *Cost of merchandise ....3.0¢ increase* *Operating expenses........................0.8¢ decrease* *Net increase in costs and decrease* *in net income..............................2.2¢.*

(b) As a Percentage of Total Stockholders' Equity:	
(1) Retained earnings:	Trend: *Favorable*
1988: *$75,900 ÷ 575,900 = 13.2%*	Reason: *Although earnings were down, cash dividends were decreased enough to retain a slightly larger portion of earnings.*
1989: *$82,970 ÷ 582,970 = 14.2%*	
(2) Capital stock:	Trend: *Favorable*
1988: *$500,000 ÷ 575,900 = 86.8%*	Reason: *The company has increased its proportion of retained earnings and, as a result, the proportion of capital stock has decreased.*
1989: *$500,000 ÷ 582,970 = 85.8%*	
(c) As a Percentage of Total Assets:	
(1) Current assets:	Trend: *Unfavorable*
1988: *$770,200 ÷ 1,048,800 = 73.4%*	Reason: *Accounts receivable decreased by $41,600. See also response to 19 [4] (d).*
1989: *$742,370 ÷ 1,013,300 = 73.3%*	
(2) Current liabilities:	Trend: *Favorable*
1988: *$340,900 ÷ 1,048,800 = 32.5%*	Reason: *Accounts payable decreased by $67,820. Decreased liabilities strengthen the cash position.*
1989: *$310,330 ÷ 1,013,300 = 30.6%*	

[8, 9]

(a) Rate earned on average total assets:

1988:
$62,560 ÷ $\dfrac{1,052,400 + 1,048,800}{2}$ = 6.0%

1989:
$27,070 ÷ $\dfrac{1,048,800 + 1,013,300}{2}$ = 2.6%

Trend: *Unfavorable*

Reason: *The net income for each dollar in company assets has decreased from 6.0¢ to 2.6¢.*

(b) Rate earned on average stockholders' equity:

1988:
$62,560 ÷ $\dfrac{553,340 + 575,900}{2}$ = 11.1%

1989:
$27,070 ÷ $\dfrac{575,900 + 582,970}{2}$ = 4.7%

Trend: *Unfavorable*

Reason: *The net income for each dollar of stockholders' equity decreased from 11.1¢ to 4.7¢.*

(c) Rate earned on net sales:

1988: $62,560 ÷ 1,320,000 = 4.7%

1989: $27,070 ÷ 1,070,000 = 2.5%

Trend: *Unfavorable*

Reason: *The amount earned per sales dollar decreased from 4.7¢ to 2.5¢.*

(d) Earnings per share:

1988: $62,560 ÷ 20,000 = $3.13

1989: $27,070 ÷ 20,000 = $1.35

Trend: *Unfavorable*

Reason: *Annual net income per share decreased from $3.13 to $1.35.*

(e) Price-earnings ratio:

1988: $32.00 ÷ 3.13 = 10.2 times

1989: $6.50 ÷ 1.35 = 4.8 times

Trend: *Unfavorable*

Reason: *Investors considered the stock less valuable and were not willing to pay as much for the stock per dollar earned by the corporation in 1989 as in 1988.*

[10, 11]

(a) Accounts receivable turnover ratio:

1988:
$1,320,000 ÷ $\dfrac{126,400 + 118,800}{2}$ = 10.8 times

1989:
$1,070,000 ÷ $\dfrac{118,800 + 77,200}{2}$ = 10.9 times

Trend: *Favorable*

Reason: *Collection efficiency was increased by reducing the collection period slightly.*

[10, 11] (b)	Merchandise inventory turnover ratio: 1988: $$\$819{,}720 \div \frac{253{,}500 + 352{,}420}{2} =$$ **2.7 times** 1989: $$\$696{,}570 \div \frac{352{,}420 + 361{,}580}{2} =$$ **2.0 times**	Trend: *Unfavorable* Reason: *The number of times the average amount of inventory is sold in a year has decreased from 2.7 to 2.0.*
[12, 13] (a)	Current ratio: 1988: *$770,200 ÷ 340,900 = 2.3 times* 1989: *$742,370 ÷ 310,330 = 2.4 times*	Trend: *Favorable* Reason: *The amount of current assets in relation to current liabilities is increasing.*
(b)	Acid-test ratio: 1988: *$292,650 ÷ 340,900 = 0.9 times* *($173,850 + 118,800 = 292,650)* 1989: *$234,960 ÷ 310,330 = 0.8 times* *($157,760 + 77,200 = 234,960)*	Trend: *Unfavorable* Reason: *Many businesses consider an acid-test ratio of 1.0 times as satisfactory. The company's ratio is declining below this. It is probably having difficulty paying current liabilities without borrowing.*
[14, 15] (a)	Debt ratio: 1988: *$472,900 ÷ 1,048,800 = 45.1%* 1989: *$430,330 ÷ 1,013,300 = 42.5%*	Trend: *Favorable* Reason: *The per dollar assets owned that are financed with borrowed capital decreased from 45.1¢ to 42.5¢.*
(b)	Equity ratio: 1988: *$575,900 ÷ 1,048,800 = 54.9%* 1989: *$582,970 ÷ 1,013,300 = 57.5%*	Trend: *Favorable* Reason: *The per dollar assets owned that are provided by stockholders' equity has increased from 54.9¢ to 57.5¢.*
(c)	Equity per share: 1988: *$575,900 ÷ 20,000 = $28.80* 1989: *$582,970 ÷ 20,000 = $29.15*	Trend: *Favorable* Reason: *The ownership of the total equity per share of stock has increased from $28.80 to $29.15.*

UNIT A—Analyzing Cost Accounting for a Departmentalized Merchandising Business

DIRECTIONS: For each item below, select the choice that best completes the sentence. Print the letter identifying your choice in the Answers column.

	Answers	For Scoring
0. Manufacturing businesses **(A)** make products **(B)** store products **(C)** display products **(D)** use products...	A	0. ✔
1. A departmentalized merchandising business' general ledger normally contains separate departmental accounts for **(A)** capital stock **(B)** accounts receivable **(C)** cash **(D)** purchases..	D	1.
2. On a departmentalized merchandising business' work sheet, purchases should be extended to **(A)** the appropriate Departmental Margin Statement column **(B)** an Adjustments column **(C)** a Balance Sheet column **(D)** an Income Statement column	A	2.
3. The accounting concept applied when both direct and indirect expenses are reported in the same way each fiscal period is **(A)** Historical Cost **(B)** Materiality **(C)** Consistent Reporting **(D)** Adequate Disclosure	C	3.
4. One difference in adjusting and closing entries for a merchandising business preparing departmental margin statements and merchandising businesses that are not departmentalized is **(A)** the fiscal period used **(B)** the method used to figure federal income tax **(C)** the journal used **(D)** the number of income summary accounts used	D	4.
5. On a departmentalized merchandising business' work sheet, indirect expenses should be extended to **(A)** an Adjustments column **(B)** a Balance Sheet column **(C)** the appropriate Departmental Margin Statement column **(D)** an Income Statement column	D	5.
6. Tracing revenues and costs to the individual managers responsible for decisions about those revenues and costs is known as **(A)** revenue accounting **(B)** financial accounting **(C)** responsibility accounting **(D)** cost accounting. .	C	6.
7. Costs shown on a merchandising business' departmental margin statements consist of **(A)** direct and indirect expenses **(B)** cost of merchandise and direct expenses **(C)** salaries and depreciation **(D)** cost of merchandise and indirect expenses	B	7.
8. To figure what percent the cost of merchandise sold is of net sales **(A)** divide net sales by gross sales **(B)** multiply cost of merchandise sold by net sales **(C)** divide net sales by cost of merchandise sold **(D)** divide cost of merchandise sold by net sales..	D	8.
9. If the departmental margins of Benson Company are 30% of net sales, Benson Company's net income for the fiscal period normally will be **(A)** 30% of net sales **(B)** more than 30% of net sales **(C)** greater than the cost of merchandise sold **(D)** less than 30% of net sales	D	9.
10. Major responsibility for improving a merchandising business' financial condition rests with the **(A)** departmental managers **(B)** advertising manager **(C)** inventory clerk **(D)** accountant...	A	10.
11. Effective company managers of departmentalized merchandising businesses compare percentages of net sales for the current fiscal period with previous periods and with **(A)** gross sales **(B)** future periods **(C)** company goals **(D)** net income...	C	11.
12. A change in departmental margin could occur if **(A)** lower prices are obtained when merchandise is purchased **(B)** the income tax rate is increased **(C)** interest expense increases **(D)** an indirect expense is decreased	A	12.

UNIT B—Identifying Accounting Terms

DIRECTIONS: Select the one term in Column I that best fits each definition in Column II. Print the letter identifying your choice in the Answers column.

Column I	Column II	Answers	For Scoring
A. component percentage analysis	**0.** Comparing the relationship of a component percentage to the total in a financial statement	A	0. ✔
B. departmental margin	**13.** A statement that reports departmental margin for a specific department	C	13.
C. departmental margin statement	**14.** Assigning control of business revenues, costs, and expenses as a responsibility of a specific manager........	F	14.
D. direct expense	**15.** An operating expense chargeable to overall business operations and not identifiable with a specific department..	E	15.
E. indirect expense			
F. responsibility accounting	**16.** The revenue earned by a department less its cost of merchandise sold and direct expenses......................	B	16.
G. responsibility statements	**17.** An operating expense identifiable with and chargeable to the operation of a specific department	D	17.
	18. Financial statements reporting revenue, costs, and direct expenses under a specific department's control............	G	18.

UNIT C—Classifying Items on Departmental Margin and Income Statements

DIRECTIONS: Identify in what statement and in what section of that statement each item below will be reported. Write in the Answers column a letter from the Statement column and a number from the Statement Section column. The company using these statements is a departmentalized sporting goods merchandising business with two departments—clothing and equipment.

		Answers		For Scoring	
		Stmt.	Sec.	Stmt.	Sec.
Statement	*Items*				
A. Departmental Margin Statement	**0–0.** Cash	C	5	0. ✔	0. ✔
	19–20. Insurance Expense—Clothing	A	3	19.	20.
B. Income Statement	**21–22.** Depreciation Expense—Office Equipment	B	4	21.	22.
C. Neither A nor B	**23–24.** Retained Earnings	C	5	23.	24.
	25–26. Rent Expense	B	4	25.	26.
Statement Section	**27–28.** Net purchases	A	2	27.	28.
1. Revenue	**29–30.** Dividends Payable	C	5	29.	30.
2. Cost of Merchandise Sold	**31–32.** Purchases—Clothing....................	A	2	31.	32.
3. Direct Departmental Expenses	**33–34.** Advertising Expense—Equipment.....	A	3	33.	34.
	35–36. Depr. Expense—Store Eq., Clothing .	A	3	35.	36.
4. Indirect Expenses	**37–38.** Salaries Payable	C	5	37.	38.
5. None of the above	**39–40.** Sales Returns and Allowances—Equipment	A	1	39.	40.
41–42. Supplies Expense—Office		B	4	41.	42.
43–44. Utilities Expense		B	4	43.	44.
45–46. Credit Card Fee Expense		B	4	45.	46.
47–48. Merchandise Inventory—Equipment		A	2	47.	48.
49–50. Purchases Returns and Allowances—Equipment		A	2	49.	50.
51–52. Sales—Clothing		A	1	51.	52.
53–54. Salary Expense—Clothing		A	3	53.	54.

Recording direct and indirect expenses

CASH PAYMENTS JOURNAL

PAGE 16

	DATE		ACCOUNT TITLE	CK. NO.	POST. REF.	GENERAL DEBIT	GENERAL CREDIT	ACCOUNTS PAYABLE DEBIT	PURCH. DISCOUNT CR. MACHINERY	PURCH. DISCOUNT CR. SUPPLIES	CASH CREDIT	
1	19— Mar.	1	Rent Expense	334		6 1 4 5 00					6 1 4 5 00	1
2		5	Advertising Expense—Supplies	362		5 4 00					5 4 00	2
3		12	Delivery Expense—Machinery	416		9 3 20					9 3 20	3
4		15	Miscellaneous Expense	431		1 3 2 10					1 3 2 10	4
5		23	Advertising Expense—Machinery	494		8 2 90					8 2 90	5
6		30	Utilities Expense	537		3 0 1 60					3 0 1 60	6
7		31	Salary Expense—Machinery	586		4 7 7 6 53					3 9 1 6 77	7
8			Employees Inc. Tax Pay.—Federal				5 2 5 40					8
9			FICA Tax Payable				3 3 4 36					9
10												10
11												11
12												12
13												13
14												14
15												15
16												16
17												17
18												18
19												19
20												20
21												21
22												22
23												23

Begin Problem 20-2 on page 352. The work sheet prepared in Problem 20-2 is needed to complete this problem. The statements prepared in this problem are needed to complete Problem 20-4. This problem is completed on page 355.

Lone Oak Lumber

Departmental Margin Statement — Hardware

For Month Ended June 30, 19--

				% OF NET SALES
Operating Revenue:				
Sales		27 1 4 8 40		100.5
Less: Sales Ret. & Allow.	4 2 08			0.2
Sales Discount	1 0 1 52	1 4 3 60		0.4
Net Sales			27 0 0 4 80	100.0
Cost of Merchandise Sold:				
Mdse. Inv., June 1, 19--		32 3 6 0 80		119.8
Purchases	16 2 1 8 20			60.1
Less: Purch. Ret. & Allow.	1 4 60			0.1
Purch. Discount	5 8 30	7 2 90		0.2
Net Purchases		16 1 4 5 30		59.8
Total Cost of Mdse. Avail. for Sale		48 5 0 6 10		179.6
Less Mdse. Inv., June 30, 19--		37 8 2 1 30		140.1
Cost of Merchandise Sold			10 6 8 4 80	39.6
Gross Profit on Operations			16 3 2 0 00	60.4
Direct Expenses:				
Advertising Expense		3 1 0 80		1.2
Depr. Expense — Store Equip.		1 8 5 50		0.7
Insurance Expense		6 0 30		0.2
Payroll Taxes Expense		3 2 0 60		1.2
Salary Expense		3 5 6 2 30		13.2
Supplies Expense		2 8 8 40		1.1
Total Direct Expenses			4 7 2 7 90	17.5
Departmental Margin			11 5 9 2 10	42.9

Begin this problem on pages 352 and 353. Use this page with page 354.

Lumber
_____

(continued)

June 30, 19--

	5 Hardware Debit	6 Hardware Credit	7 Lumber Debit	8 Lumber Credit	9 Income Statement Debit	10 Income Statement Credit	11 Balance Sheet Debit	12 Balance Sheet Credit	
	DEPARTMENTAL MARGIN STATEMENTS				INCOME STATEMENT		BALANCE SHEET		
	HARDWARE		LUMBER		DEBIT	CREDIT	DEBIT	CREDIT	
	DEBIT	CREDIT	DEBIT	CREDIT					
40			19 4 8 0 50						40
41				3 6 92					41
42				5 5 38					42
43	3 1 0 80								43
44	1 8 5 50								44
45	6 0 30								45
46	3 2 0 60								46
47	3 5 6 2 30								47
48	2 8 8 40								48
49			5 3 8 20						49
50			1 8 5 20						50
51			1 3 0 4 90						51
52			1 9 8 00						52
53			3 2 00						53
54			1 2 0 60						54
55			3 5 3 30						55
56			3 9 2 6 10						56
57			3 7 0 80						57
58					5 8 6 30				58
59					2 3 00				59
60					2 0 10				60
61					1 2 4 5 20				61
62					4 3 6 10				62
63					4 5 6 0 00				63
64					4 8 4 5 60				64
65					1 6 4 80				65
66					1 8 3 3 30				66
67	21 0 8 9 70	32 6 8 1 80	26 6 9 0 70	38 1 1 7 40					67
68	11 5 9 2 10					11 5 9 2 10			68
69			11 4 2 6 70			11 4 2 6 70			69
70	32 6 8 1 80	32 6 8 1 80	38 1 1 7 40	38 1 1 7 40					70
71					2 5 9 2 52				71
72					16 3 0 6 92	23 0 1 8 80	176 5 3 8 20	169 8 2 6 32	72
73					6 7 1 1 88			6 7 1 1 88	73
74					23 0 1 8 80	23 0 1 8 80	176 5 3 8 20	176 5 3 8 20	74
75									75
76									76
77									77
78									78

The work sheet prepared in Problem 20-2 is needed to complete Problems 20-3 and 20-4. **[1, 2]**

Lone Oak

Work

For Month Ended

	ACCOUNT TITLE	TRIAL BALANCE		ADJUSTMENTS		
		DEBIT	CREDIT	DEBIT	CREDIT	
1	Cash	37 5 1 3 30				1
2	Accounts Receivable	16 9 3 5 70				2
3	Allowance for Uncollectible Accounts		3 3 90		(a) 1 8 5 20	3
4	Merchandise Inventory — Hardware	32 3 6 0 80		(b) 5 4 6 0 50		4
5	Merchandise Inventory — Lumber	48 9 2 1 20		(c) 7 0 5 7 60		5
6	Supplies	1 6 4 9 00			(d) 8 2 4 00	6
7	Prepaid Insurance	6 2 4 30			(e) 2 0 1 00	7
8	Delivery Equip. — Lumber	11 5 3 1 80				8
9	Accum. Depr. — Del. Equip., Lumber		3 5 5 7 00		(f) 1 9 8 00	9
10	Office Equipment	1 3 2 6 00				10
11	Accum. Depr. — Office Equipment		1 8 4 90		(g) 2 3 00	11
12	Store Equipment — Hardware	1 5 8 0 20				12
13	Accum. Depr. — Store Equip., Hardware		5 2 5 40		(h) 1 8 5 50	13
14	Store Equipment, Lumber	7 6 0 2 80				14
15	Accum. Depr. — Store Equip., Lumber		2 6 1 2 30		(i) 3 2 00	15
16	Accounts Payable		20 8 2 3 50			16
17	Employees Income Tax Payable — Federal		1 3 3 8 90			17
18	Federal Income Tax Payable				(j) 2 5 9 2 52	18
19	FICA Tax Payable		1 4 8 0 10			19
20	Salaries Payable					20
21	Sales Tax Payable		1 9 4 0 50			21
22	Unemployment Tax Payable — Federal		7 4 00			22
23	Unemployment Tax Payable — State		2 9 6 20			23
24	Dividends Payable					24
25	Capital Stock		85 0 0 0 00			25
26	Retained Earnings		48 7 4 3 40			26
27	Dividends	5 0 0 0 00				27
28	Income Summary — Hardware				(b) 5 4 6 0 50	28
29	Income Summary — Lumber				(c) 7 0 5 7 60	29
30	Income Summary — General					30
31	Sales — Hardware		27 1 4 8 40			31
32	Sales Returns and Allowances — Hardware	4 2 08				32
33	Sales Discount — Hardware	1 0 1 52				33
34	Sales — Lumber		30 9 6 7 50			34
35	Sales Returns and Allowances — Lumber	9 4 18				35
36	Sales Discount — Lumber	8 6 92				36
37	Purchases — Hardware	16 2 1 8 20				37
38	Purchases Returns and Allowances — Hardware		1 4 60			38
39	Purchases Discount — Hardware		5 8 30			39

Name _____ Date _____ Class _____

Lumber

Sheet

June 30, 19--

| | | HARDWARE | | LUMBER | | INCOME STATEMENT | | BALANCE SHEET | | |
	DEBIT (5)	CREDIT (6)	DEBIT (7)	CREDIT (8)	DEBIT (9)	CREDIT (10)	DEBIT (11)	CREDIT (12)	
1							37 5 1 3 30		1
2							16 9 3 5 70		2
3								2 1 9 10	3
4							37 8 2 1 30		4
5							55 9 7 8 80		5
6							8 2 5 00		6
7							4 2 3 30		7
8							11 5 3 1 80		8
9								3 7 5 5 00	9
10							1 3 2 6 00		10
11								2 0 7 90	11
12							1 5 8 0 20		12
13								7 1 0 90	13
14							7 6 0 2 80		14
15								2 6 4 4 30	15
16								20 8 2 3 50	16
17								1 3 3 8 90	17
18								2 5 9 2 52	18
19								1 4 8 0 10	19
20									20
21								1 9 4 0 50	21
22								7 4 00	22
23								2 9 6 20	23
24									24
25								85 0 0 0 00	25
26								48 7 4 3 40	26
27							5 0 0 0 00		27
28		5 4 6 0 50							28
29				7 0 5 7 60					29
30									30
31		27 1 4 8 40							31
32	4 2 08								32
33	1 0 1 52								33
34				30 9 6 7 50					34
35			9 4 18						35
36			8 6 92						36
37	16 2 1 8 20								37
38		1 4 60							38
39		5 8 30							39

DEPARTMENTAL MARGIN STATEMENTS

Lone Oak

Work Sheet

For Month Ended

	ACCOUNT TITLE	TRIAL BALANCE		ADJUSTMENTS		
		DEBIT	CREDIT	DEBIT	CREDIT	
40	Purchases — Lumber	19 4 8 0 50				40
41	Purchases Returns and Allowances — Lumber		3 6 92			41
42	Purchases Discount — Lumber		5 5 38			42
43	Advertising Expense — Hardware	3 1 0 80				43
44	Depreciation Expense — Store Equip., Hardware			(h) 1 8 5 50		44
45	Insurance Expense — Hardware			(e) 6 0 30		45
46	Payroll Taxes Expense — Hardware	3 2 0 60				46
47	Salary Expense — Hardware	3 5 6 2 30				47
48	Supplies Expense — Hardware			(d) 2 8 8 40		48
49	Advertising Expense — Lumber	5 3 8 20				49
50	Bad Debts Expense — Lumber			(a) 1 8 5 20		50
51	Delivery Expense — Lumber	1 3 0 4 90				51
52	Depreciation Expense — Del. Equip., Lumber			(f) 1 9 8 00		52
53	Depreciation Expense — Store Equip., Lumber			(i) 3 2 00		53
54	Insurance Expense — Lumber			(e) 1 2 0 60		54
55	Payroll Taxes Expense — Lumber	3 5 3 30				55
56	Salary Expense — Lumber	3 9 2 6 10				56
57	Supplies Expense — Lumber			(d) 3 7 0 80		57
58	Credit Card Fee Expense	5 8 6 30				58
59	Depreciation Expense — Office Equipment			(g) 2 3 00		59
60	Insurance Expense — Administrative			(e) 2 0 10		60
61	Miscellaneous Expense	1 2 4 5 20				61
62	Payroll Taxes Expense — Administrative	4 3 6 10				62
63	Rent Expense	4 5 6 0 00				63
64	Salary Expense — Administrative	4 8 4 5 60				64
65	Supplies Expense — Administrative			(d) 1 6 4 80		65
66	Utilities Expense	1 8 3 3 30				66
67						67
68	*Departmental Margin — Hardware*					68
69	*Departmental Margin — Lumber*					69
70						70
71	*Federal Income Tax*			(j) 2 5 9 2 52		71
72		224 8 9 1 20	224 8 9 1 20	16 7 5 9 32	16 7 5 9 32	72
73	*Net Income after Federal Income Tax*					73
74						74
75						75
76						76
77						77
78						78

This problem begins on page 350. The work sheet prepared in Problem 20-2 is needed to complete this problem. The statements prepared in this problem are needed to complete Problem 20-4.

Lone Oak Lumber

Departmental Margin Statement—Lumber

For Month Ended June 30, 19--

					% OF NET SALES
Operating Revenue:					
Sales				30 9 6 7 50	100.6
Less: Sales Ret. & Allow.			9 4 18		0.3
Sales Discount			8 6 92	1 8 1 10	0.3
Net Sales				30 7 8 6 40	100.0
Cost of Merchandise Sold:					
Mdse. Inv., June 1, 19--				48 9 2 1 20	158.9
Purchases		19 4 8 0 50			63.3
Less: Purch. Ret. & Allow.	3 6 92				0.1
Purch. Discount	5 5 38		9 2 30		0.2
Net Purchases			19 3 8 8 20		63.0
Total Cost of Mdse. Avail. for Sale			68 3 0 9 40		221.9
Less Mdse. Inv., June 30, 19--			55 9 7 8 80		181.8
Cost of Merchandise Sold				12 3 3 0 60	40.1
Gross Profit on Operations				18 4 5 5 80	59.9
Direct Expenses:					
Advertising Expense			5 3 8 20		1.7
Bad Debts Expense			1 8 5 20		0.6
Delivery Expense			1 3 0 4 90		4.2
Depr. Exp.—Delivery Equip.			1 9 8 00		0.6
Depr. Expense—Store Equipment			3 2 00		0.1
Insurance Expense			1 2 0 60		0.4
Payroll Taxes Expense			3 5 3 30		1.1
Salary Expense			3 9 2 6 10		12.8
Supplies Expense			3 7 0 80		1.2
Total Direct Expenses				7 0 2 9 10	22.8
Departmental Margin				11 4 2 6 70	37.1

Preparing an income statement with departmental margins

PROBLEM 20-4, p. 461

The work sheet prepared in Problem 20-2 and statements prepared in Problem 20-3 are needed to complete Problem 20-4.

Lone Oak Lumber

Income Statement

For Month Ended June 30, 19--

	DEPARTMENTAL		COMPANY	
	HARDWARE	LUMBER	AMOUNTS	% OF NET SALES
Net Sales	27 0 0 4 80	30 7 8 6 40	57 7 9 1 20	100.0
Cost of Merchandise Sold	10 6 8 4 80	12 3 3 0 60	23 0 1 5 40	39.8
Gross Profit on Operations	16 3 2 0 00	18 4 5 5 80	34 7 7 5 80	60.2
Direct Expenses	4 7 2 7 90	7 0 2 9 10	11 7 5 7 00	20.3
Departmental Margin	11 5 9 2 10	11 4 2 6 70	23 0 1 8 80	39.8
Indirect Expenses:				
Credit Card Fee Expense			5 8 6 30	1.0
Depr. Exp. — Office Equip.			2 3 00	0.0
Insurance Expense — Admin.			2 0 10	0.0
Miscellaneous Expense			1 2 4 5 20	2.2
Payroll Taxes Expense — Admin.			4 3 6 10	0.8
Rent Expense			4 5 6 0 00	7.9
Salary Expense — Admin.			4 8 4 5 60	8.4
Supplies Expense — Admin.			1 6 4 80	0.3
Utilities Expense			1 8 3 3 30	3.2
Total Indirect Expenses			13 7 1 4 40	23.7
Net Income before Fed. Inc. Tax			9 3 0 4 40	16.1
Less Federal Income Tax			2 5 9 2 52	4.5
Net Income after Fed. Inc. Tax			6 7 1 1 88	11.6

Begin this problem on pages 358 and 359. Use this page with page 360. [1, 2]

Inc.
_____

(continued)

December 31, 19--

	CLOTHING DEBIT	CLOTHING CREDIT	TOYS DEBIT	TOYS CREDIT	INCOME STATEMENT DEBIT	INCOME STATEMENT CREDIT	BALANCE SHEET DEBIT	BALANCE SHEET CREDIT	
40				2 77 40					40
41	2 8 38 40								41
42	8 1 60								42
43	2 1 3 1 30								43
44	1 3 95 00								44
45	4 8 14 70								45
46	56 2 4 0 00								46
47	1 4 0 9 00								47
48			7 15 60						48
49			9 81 70						49
50			1 3 95 00						50
51			2 1 79 40						51
52			23 8 9 0 00						52
53			9 86 30						53
54					6 2 55 30				54
55					5 29 50				55
56					3 1 0 00				56
57					8 0 78 90				57
58					2 2 73 10				58
59					15 8 4 0 00				59
60					18 9 2 0 00				60
61					4 22 70				61
62					4 0 16 20				62
63	303 3 66 10	368 6 85 40	113 1 59 70	123 7 42 70					63
64	65 3 19 30					65 3 19 30			64
65			10 5 83 00			10 5 83 00			65
66	368 6 85 40	368 6 85 40	123 7 42 70	123 7 42 70					66
67					2 8 88 49				67
68					59 5 34 19	75 9 0 2 30	255 2 72 10	238 9 0 3 99	68
69					16 3 68 11			16 3 68 11	69
70					75 9 0 2 30	75 9 0 2 30	255 2 72 10	255 2 72 10	70
71									71
72									72
73									73
74									74
75									75
76									76
77									77
78									78

Completing end-of-fiscal-period work for a
merchandising business using departmental margins
MASTERY PROBLEM 20-M, p. 461
[1, 2]

Begin Mastery Problem 20-M on this page.

Playtime,

Work

For Year Ended

#	ACCOUNT TITLE	TRIAL BALANCE DEBIT	TRIAL BALANCE CREDIT	ADJUSTMENTS DEBIT	ADJUSTMENTS CREDIT	#
1	Cash	51 3 2 6 50				1
2	Accounts Receivable	2 7 6 8 40				2
3	Allowance for Uncollectible Accounts		5 4 20		(a) 8 1 60	3
4	Merchandise Inventory — Clothing	103 8 3 6 30		(b) 8 5 1 4 60		4
5	Merchandise Inventory — Toys	35 3 9 4 70		(c) 11 1 4 9 10		5
6	Supplies	3 3 7 8 30			(d) 2 8 1 8 00	6
7	Prepaid Insurance	6 7 1 5 20			(e) 3 1 0 0 00	7
8	Office Equipment	5 4 5 7 00				8
9	Accum. Depr. — Office Equip.		8 6 0 60		(f) 5 2 9 50	9
10	Store Equipment — Clothing	18 7 4 0 00				10
11	Accum. Depr. — Store Equip., Clothing		5 8 3 2 10		(g) 2 1 3 1 30	11
12	Store Equipment — Toys	8 9 1 0 00				12
13	Accum. Depr. — Store Equip., Toys		2 5 6 8 30		(h) 9 8 1 70	13
14	Accounts Payable		26 1 3 1 60			14
15	Employees Income Tax Payable — Federal		9 3 6 90			15
16	Federal Income Tax Payable				(i) 1 5 3 49	16
17	FICA Tax Payable		9 9 0 50			17
18	Salaries Payable					18
19	Sales Tax Payable		2 1 5 6 10			19
20	Unemployment Tax Payable — Federal		4 9 50			20
21	Unemployment Tax Payable — State		1 9 8 10			21
22	Dividends Payable					22
23	Capital Stock		110 0 0 0 00			23
24	Retained Earnings		85 2 4 8 50			24
25	Dividends	5 0 0 0 00				25
26	Income Summary — Clothing				(b) 8 5 1 4 60	26
27	Income Summary — Toys				(c) 11 1 4 9 10	27
28	Income Summary — General					28
29	Sales — Clothing		357 5 7 3 50			29
30	Sales Returns and Allowances — Clothing	8 4 1 30				30
31	Sales Discount — Clothing	8 9 3 20				31
32	Sales — Toys		112 1 9 7 30			32
33	Sales Returns and Allowances — Toys	1 5 9 80				33
34	Sales Discount — Toys	3 7 2 60				34
35	Purchases — Clothing	232 7 2 1 60				35
36	Purchases Returns and Allowances — Clothing		1 0 3 8 90			36
37	Purchases Discount — Clothing		1 5 5 8 40			37
38	Purchases — Toys	82 4 7 9 30				38
39	Purchases Returns and Allowances — Toys		1 1 8 90			39

Use this page with page 358.   [1, 2]

Inc. _____

Sheet _____

December 31, 19--

	Clothing Debit	Clothing Credit	Toys Debit	Toys Credit	Income Statement Debit	Income Statement Credit	Balance Sheet Debit	Balance Sheet Credit	
1							51 3 2 6 50		1
2							2 7 6 8 40		2
3								1 3 5 80	3
4							112 3 5 0 90		4
5							46 5 4 3 80		5
6							5 6 0 30		6
7							3 6 1 5 20		7
8							5 4 5 7 00		8
9								1 3 9 0 10	9
10							18 7 4 0 00		10
11								7 9 6 3 40	11
12							8 9 1 0 00		12
13								3 5 5 0 00	13
14								26 1 3 1 60	14
15								9 3 6 90	15
16								1 5 3 49	16
17								9 9 0 50	17
18									18
19								2 1 5 6 10	19
20								4 9 50	20
21								1 9 8 10	21
22									22
23								110 0 0 0 00	23
24								85 2 4 8 50	24
25							5 0 0 0 00		25
26		8 5 1 4 60							26
27				11 1 4 9 10					27
28									28
29		357 5 7 3 50							29
30	8 4 1 30								30
31	8 9 3 20								31
32				112 1 9 7 30					32
33			1 5 9 80						33
34			3 7 2 60						34
35	232 7 2 1 60								35
36		1 0 3 8 90							36
37		1 5 5 8 40							37
38			82 4 7 9 30						38
39				1 1 8 90					39

Playtime,

Work Sheet

For Year Ended

	ACCOUNT TITLE	TRIAL BALANCE		ADJUSTMENTS		
		DEBIT	CREDIT	DEBIT	CREDIT	
40	Purchases Discount — Toys		2 7 7 40			40
41	Advertising Expense — Clothing	2 8 3 8 40				41
42	Bad Debts Expense — Clothing			(a) 8 1 60		42
43	Depreciation Expense — Store Equip., Clothing			(g) 2 1 3 1 30		43
44	Insurance Expense — Clothing			(e) 1 3 9 5 00		44
45	Payroll Taxes Expense — Clothing	4 8 1 4 70				45
46	Salary Expense — Clothing	56 2 4 0 00				46
47	Supplies Expense — Clothing			(d) 1 4 0 9 00		47
48	Advertising Expense — Toys	7 1 5 60				48
49	Depreciation Expense — Store Equip., Toys			(h) 9 8 1 70		49
50	Insurance Expense — Toys			(e) 1 3 9 5 00		50
51	Payroll Taxes Expense — Toys	2 1 7 9 40				51
52	Salary Expense — Toys	23 8 9 0 00				52
53	Supplies Expense — Toys			(d) 9 8 6 30		53
54	Credit Card Fee Expense	6 2 5 5 30				54
55	Depreciation Expense — Office Equipment			(f) 5 2 9 50		55
56	Insurance Expense — Administrative			(e) 3 1 0 00		56
57	Miscellaneous Expense	8 0 7 8 90				57
58	Payroll Taxes Expense — Administrative	2 2 7 3 10				58
59	Rent Expense	15 8 4 0 00				59
60	Salary Expense — Administrative	18 9 2 0 00				60
61	Supplies Expense — Administrative			(d) 4 2 2 70		61
62	Utilities Expense	4 0 1 6 20				62
63						63
64	*Departmental Margin — Clothing*					64
65	*Departmental Margin — Toys*					65
66						66
67	*Federal Income Tax*	2 7 3 5 00		(i) 1 5 3 49		67
68		707 7 9 0 80	707 7 9 0 80	29 4 5 9 29	29 4 5 9 29	68
69	*Net Income after Federal Income Tax*					69
70						70
71						71
72						72
73						73
74						74
75						75
76						76
77						77
78						78

Playtime, Inc.

Departmental Margin Statement — Clothing

For Year Ended December 31, 19--

					% OF NET SALES
Operating Revenue:					
Sales			357 5 7 3 50		100.5
Less: Sales Ret. & Allow.		8 4 1 30			0.2
Sales Discount		8 9 3 20	1 7 3 4 50		0.3
Net Sales				355 8 3 9 00	100.0
Cost of Merchandise Sold:					
Mdse. Inv., Jan. 1, 19--			103 8 3 6 30		29.2
Purchases		232 7 2 1 60			65.4
Less: Purch. Ret. & Allow.	1 0 3 8 90				0.3
Purch. Discount	1 5 5 8 40	2 5 9 7 30			0.4
Net Purchases			230 1 2 4 30		64.7
Total Cost of Mdse. Avail. for Sale			333 9 6 0 60		93.9
Less Mdse. Inv., Dec. 31, 19--			112 3 5 0 90		31.6
Cost of Merchandise Sold				221 6 0 9 70	62.3
Gross Profit on Operations				134 2 2 9 30	37.7
Direct Expenses:					
Advertising Expense			2 8 3 8 40		0.8
Bad Debts Expense			8 1 60		0.0
Depr. Expense — Store Equip.			2 1 3 1 30		0.6
Insurance Expense			1 3 9 5 00		0.4
Payroll Taxes Expense			4 8 1 4 70		1.4
Salary Expense			56 2 4 0 00		15.8
Supplies Expense			1 4 0 9 00		0.4
Total Direct Expenses				68 9 1 0 00	19.4
Departmental Margin				65 3 1 9 30	18.4

Playtime, Inc.

Departmental Margin Statement — Toys

For Year Ended December 31, 19--

					% OF NET SALES
Operating Revenue:					
Sales			112 19 7 30		100.5
Less: Sales Ret. & Allow.		1 5 9 80			0.1
Sales Discount		3 7 2 60	5 3 2 40		0.3
Net Sales				111 6 6 4 90	100.0
Cost of Merchandise Sold:					
Mdse. Inv., Jan. 1, 19--			35 3 9 4 70		31.7
Purchases		82 4 7 9 30			73.9
Less: Purch. Ret. & Allow.	1 1 8 90				0.1
Purch. Discount	2 7 7 40	3 9 6 30			0.2
Net Purchases			82 0 8 3 00		73.5
Total Cost of Mdse. Avail. for Sale			117 4 7 7 70		105.2
Less Mdse. Inv., Dec. 31, 19--			46 5 4 3 80		41.7
Cost of Merchandise Sold				70 9 3 3 90	63.5
Gross Profit on Operations				40 7 3 1 00	36.5
Direct Expenses:					
Advertising Expense			7 1 5 60		0.6
Depr. Expense — Store Equip.			9 8 1 70		0.9
Insurance Expense			1 3 9 5 00		1.2
Payroll Taxes Expense			2 1 7 9 40		2.0
Salary Expense			23 8 9 0 00		21.4
Supplies Expense			9 8 6 30		0.9
Total Direct Expenses				30 1 4 8 00	27.0
Departmental Margin				10 5 8 3 00	9.5

Playtime, Inc.

Income Statement

For Year Ended December 31, 19--

	DEPARTMENTAL		COMPANY	
	CLOTHING	TOYS	AMOUNTS	% OF NET SALES
Net Sales	355 839 00	111 664 90	467 503 90	100.0
Cost of Merchandise Sold	221 609 70	70 933 90	292 543 60	62.6
Gross Profit on Operations	134 229 30	40 731 00	174 960 30	37.4
Direct Expenses	68 910 00	30 148 00	99 058 00	21.2
Departmental Margin	65 319 30	10 583 00	75 902 30	16.2
Indirect Expenses:				
Credit Card Fee Expense			6 255 30	1.3
Depr. Exp. — Office Equip.			5 29 50	0.1
Insurance Expense — Admin.			3 10 00	0.1
Miscellaneous Expense			8 078 90	1.7
Payroll Taxes Expense — Admin.			2 273 10	0.5
Rent Expense			15 840 00	3.4
Salary Expense — Admin.			18 920 00	4.0
Supplies Expense — Admin.			4 22 70	0.1
Utilities Expense			4 016 20	0.9
Total Indirect Expenses			56 645 70	12.1
Net Income before Fed. Inc. Tax			19 256 60	4.1
Less Federal Income Tax			2 888 49	0.6
Net Income after Fed. Inc. Tax			16 368 11	3.5

						% OF NET SALES

Analyzing a departmental margin statement   [1]

Leathercraft, Inc.
Departmental Margin Statement—Luggage
For Years Ended December 31, 1989 and 1988

	1989			1988		
	Amounts	Amounts	% of Net Sales	Amounts	Amounts	% of Net Sales
Operating Revenue:						
Sales	$431,411.90		*100.4*	$384,805.90		100.4
Less Sales Returns and Allowances	1,718.80		*0.4*	1,533.10		0.4
Net Sales		$429,693.10	*100.0*		$383,272.80	100.0
Cost of Merchandise Sold:						
Merchandise Inventory, January 1	$ 45,566.80		*10.6*	$ 41,010.20		10.7
Purchases	237,204.90		*55.2*	203,901.10		53.2
Total Cost of Mdse. Avail. for Sale	$282,771.70		*65.8*	$244,911.30		63.9
Less Mdse. Inventory, Dec. 31	42,048.50		*9.8*	45,609.50		11.9
Cost of Merchandise Sold		240,723.20	*56.0*		199,301.80	52.0
Gross Profit on Operations		$188,969.90	*44.0*		$183,971.00	48.0
Direct Expenses:						
Advertising Expense	$ 4,325.90		*1.0*	$ 3,449.50		0.9
Bad Debts Expense	4,899.60		*1.1*	3,827.90		1.0
Delivery Expense	10,237.20		*2.4*	8,432.00		2.2
Depr. Expense — Delivery Equipment	5,960.10		*1.4*	4,599.30		1.2
Depr. Expense — Store Equipment	3,901.60		*0.9*	3,432.60		0.9
Insurance Expense	3,398.20		*0.8*	3,023.70		0.8
Payroll Taxes Expense	2,864.30		*0.7*	2,579.40		0.7
Salary Expense	50,243.70		*11.7*	42,960.00		11.2
Supplies Expense	3,922.80		*0.9*	2,981.90		0.8
Total Direct Expenses		89,753.40	*20.9*		75,286.30	19.6
Departmental Margin		$ 99,216.50	*23.1*		$108,684.70	28.4

CHANGE IN % OF NET SALES	
(a) Cost of Merchandise Sold	**+4.0%**
(b) Gross Profit..	**−4.0%**
(c) Total Direct Departmental Expenses..	**+1.3%**
(d) Departmental Margin..	**−5.3%**

[3]

a. Is the departmental margin for the luggage department at a satisfactory percentage of sales? Explain why it is or is not satisfactory.

Not satisfactory. The departmental margin for the luggage department is not at a satisfactory percentage of sales. Specifically, the 23.1% departmental margin for 1989 does not meet the minimum guidelines percentage of 25.0%. This is due primarily to an increase as a percentage of sales of 4.0% in cost of merchandise sold and a 1.3% increase in total direct departmental expenses.

b. Is the trend of the cost of merchandise sold percentage favorable or unfavorable? Explain why it is or is not favorable. Can you suggest some possible reasons for the change in cost of merchandise sold from 1988 to 1989?

Unfavorable. Cost of merchandise sold percentage increased from 52.0% in 1988 to 56.0% in 1989. This increase is directly reflected in the gross profit percentage reduction as well as the departmental margin percentage reduction. Possible reasons for the change in cost of merchandise sold are a higher percentage of purchases and a lower percentage of ending inventory in 1989.

c. Is the trend of the total direct departmental expenses percentage favorable or unfavorable? Explain why the trend is or is not favorable.

Unfavorable. Total departmental expenses percentage has increased from 19.6% in 1988 to 20.9% in 1989, a 1.3% increase. This increase is largely due to a 0.5% increase in salary expense and a 0.2% increase in delivery expense and depreciation expense—delivery equipment.

Perfect Score. 44

Deduct .... —

Your Score .... —

Name _____

Date _____ Class _____

Checked by _____

STUDY
GUIDE
21

UNIT A—Identifying Accounting Terms

DIRECTIONS: Select the one term in Column I that best fits each definition in Column II. Print the letter identifying your choice in the Answers column.

Column I

A. applied overhead
B. cost ledger
C. direct labor
D. direct materials
E. factory overhead
F. finished goods
G. finished goods ledger
H. indirect labor
I. indirect materials
J. materials ledger
K. purchase order
L. work in process

Column II

		Answers	For Scoring
0.	A ledger containing all records of materials................	J	0. ✔
1.	Salaries of factory workers who make a product	C	1.
2.	A ledger containing all cost sheets for products in the process of being manufactured..................................	B	2.
3.	Manufactured products that are fully completed	F	3.
4.	The estimated amount of factory overhead recorded on cost sheets	A	4.
5.	Salaries paid to factory workers who are not actually making products	H	5.
6.	Materials that are of significant value in the cost of and that become an identifiable part of a finished product.....	D	6.
7.	Products that are being manufactured but are not yet complete...	L	7.
8.	All expenses other than direct materials and direct labor that apply to the making of products	E	8.
9.	A ledger containing records of all finished goods on hand................................	G	9.
10.	A completed form authorizing a seller to deliver goods with payment to be made later	K	10.
11.	Materials used in the completion of a product but that are of insignificant value to justify accounting for separately..	I	11.

UNIT B—Examining Manufacturing Cost Accounting

DIRECTIONS: For each item below, select the choice that best completes the sentence. Print the letter identifying your choice in the Answers column.

		Answers	For Scoring
0.	A materials inventory account shows the costs of materials **(A)** that have been used in manufacturing **(B)** that have been ordered but not yet received **(C)** on hand that have not yet been used in manufacturing **(D)** none of these	C	0. ✔
12.	One of the three basic elements of manufacturing cost of any finished product is **(A)** indirect materials **(B)** direct materials **(C)** insurance expense **(D)** none of these	B	12.
13.	A factor considered in estimating factory overhead costs is **(A)** the expected increase in unit costs of factory overhead items **(B)** the applied overhead rate **(C)** the estimated amount of direct labor costs **(D)** none of these....................	A	13.
14.	When a completed product is sold, the cost of the product is recorded in the **(A)** finished goods ledger **(B)** materials ledger **(C)** cost ledger **(D)** none of these	A	14.
15.	One of the three inventories of a manufacturing business is **(A)** prepaid insurance **(B)** direct materials **(C)** direct labor **(D)** none of these	B	15.
16.	When a product is completed, total cost of making that product is recorded in the **(A)** materials ledger **(B)** materials requisition **(C)** finished goods ledger **(D)** none of these	C	16.

UNIT C—Analyzing Manufacturing Cost Accounting Procedures

DIRECTIONS: Place a check mark in the proper Answers column to show whether each of the following statements is true or false.

	Answers		For Scoring
	True	False	
0. A unique feature of a manufacturing business is that it buys materials and by using labor and machines, changes the form of the materials into a finished product	✔		0. ✔
17. Direct labor costs are recorded on cost forms only on the last day of each fiscal period		✔	17.
18. Each materials ledger card should show the quantity of the item of materials that has been ordered	✔		18.
19. One cost sheet is maintained for all manufacturing jobs in a factory		✔	19.
20. Indirect labor is a part of selling expenses		✔	20.
21. A finished goods inventory account shows the cost of completed products still on hand and unsold	✔		21.
22. Direct labor includes only the wages of those working directly on a product	✔		22.
23. Factory overhead includes the wages paid to factory maintenance workers	✔		23.
24. The three inventory accounts related to products manufactured are materials, labor, and finished goods		✔	24.
25. Job-time record amounts are recorded in the Direct Labor column of a cost sheet	✔		25.
26. A purchase order form is used to authorize transfer of items from the storeroom to the factory		✔	26.
27. Most factory overhead expenses occur at the end of a fiscal period		✔	27.
28. Factory overhead expenses should be charged to individual jobs at the time the expenses occur		✔	28.
29. Factory overhead should be distributed among all jobs	✔		29.
30. Each requisition of materials is recorded in the Received columns of an account in the materials ledger		✔	30.
31. Direct materials and direct labor are included in factory overhead		✔	31.
32. Overhead distribution rate is figured by dividing estimated base units by estimated factory overhead costs		✔	32.
33. Applied overhead is recorded on cost sheets during the fiscal period and before actual overhead is known in order to match expenses with revenue	✔		33.
34. Factory overhead should include the amount paid for taxes on the factory building	✔		34.
35. When finished goods are moved to the stock area, summary information from the cost sheet is recorded in the cost ledger		✔	35.
36. At the end of a fiscal period, cost sheets for work in process are totaled to determine ending inventory for the general ledger account Work in Process	✔		36.
37. In figuring a factory overhead distribution rate, a base unit should be selected that most closely relates to actual overhead costs	✔		37.
38. Each materials ledger card should show the quantity on hand of the item	✔		38.
39. Applying factory overhead on cost sheets during the fiscal period and before all factory overhead for the current period is an application of the Historical Cost concept		✔	39.
40. Factory overhead expenses normally are charged to jobs by using an application rate based on a known cost such as direct labor	✔		40.
41. The estimated amount of factory overhead recorded on cost sheets is called Estimated Overhead		✔	41.
42. For purposes of applying factory overhead, base units are usually cost items that can be identified easily	✔		42.
43. A factory overhead base unit could be "total factory overhead costs"		✔	43.
44. The total value for all costs sheets for work still in process equals the work in process balance in the general ledger	✔		44.

Recording entries in a materials ledger

MATERIALS LEDGER CARD

Article ___D14 Coiled Cord___ Acct. No. ___91___
Reorder ___2,500___ Minimum ___200___ Location ___Area B-42___

ORDERED			RECEIVED					ISSUED					BALANCE			
Date	Purchase Order No.	Quantity	Date	Purchase Order No.	Quantity	Unit Price	Value	Date	Requisition No.	Quantity	Unit Price	Value	Date	Quantity	Unit Price	Value
													19-- Aug. 1	340	3.70	1,258.00
19-- Aug. 1	174	2,500						19-- Aug. 2	149	50	3.70	185.00	2	290	3.70	1,073.00
			19-- Aug. 4	174	2,500	3.75	9,375.00						4	290	3.70	}
														2,500	3.75	}10,448.00
								8	157	290	3.70	}	8	2,476	3.75	9,285.00
										24	3.75	}1,163.00				
								16	163	250	3.75	937.50	16	2,226	3.75	8,347.50
								22	178	70	3.75	262.50	22	2,156	3.75	8,085.00
								30	192	320	3.75	1,200.00	30	1,836	3.75	6,885.00

Figuring factory overhead applied rate

Estimated Factory Overhead	÷	*Estimated Direct Labor Costs*	=	*Factory Overhead Applied Rate (as % of Direct Labor Cost)*
$283,500.00	÷	*$405,000.00*	=	*70% of Direct Labor Cost*

COST SHEET

Job. No. _298_

Item _SF52 Smoke Detector_

No. of items _90_

Ordered for _Stock_

Date _August 1, 19--_

Date wanted _August 10, 19--_

Date completed _August 5, 19--_

DIRECT MATERIALS		DIRECT LABOR				SUMMARY	
Req. No.	Amount	Date	Amount	Date	Amount	Item	Amount
321	$427.50	Aug. 1	$ 310.00			Direct Materials	$ 831.50
327	230.00	2	243.00			Direct Labor	1,078.00
336	174.00	3	201.00			Factory Overhead	
	$831.50	4	190.00			(75% of direct	
		5	134.00			labor costs)	808.50
			$1,078.00			Total Cost	$2,718.00
						No. units finished	90
						Cost per unit	$30.20

Recording entries in a finished goods ledger

FINISHED GOODS LEDGER CARD

Description __Telescope__   Stock No. __JK10__
Minimum __80__   Location __Area C-23__

MANUFACTURED/RECEIVED					SHIPPED/ISSUED					BALANCE			
Date	Job No.	Quan-tity	Unit Cost	Total Cost	Date	Sales Invoice No.	Quan-tity	Unit Cost	Total Cost	Date	Quan-tity	Unit Cost	Total Cost
										19-- Aug. 1	170	30.20	5,134.00
					19-- Aug. 1	423	60	30.20	1,812.00	1	110	30.20	3,322.00
					4	436	30	30.20	906.00	4	80	30.20	2,416.00
19-- Aug. 5	298	90	30.20	2,718.00						5	170	30.20	5,134.00
					9	451	40	30.20	1,208.00	9	130	30.20	3,926.00
12	307	100	31.50	3,150.00						12	130	30.20 }	
											100	31.50 }	7,076.00
					19	479	52	30.20	1,570.40	19	78	30.20 }	
											100	31.50 }	5,505.60
23	321	90	31.50	2,835.00						23	78	30.20 }	
											190	31.50 }	8,340.60
					26	482	78	30.20 }					
							58	31.50 }	4,182.60	26	132	31.50	4,158.00
30	335	50	32.00	1,600.00						30	132	31.50 }	
											50	32.00 }	5,758.00

Estimated Factory Overhead Costs	$\div$	*Estimated Direct Labor Costs*	$=$	*Factory Overhead Applied Rate (as % of Direct Labor Cost)*
$423,725.00	$\div$	$498,500.00	$=$	85% of Direct Labor Cost

[2,3]

COST SHEET

Job. No. ___172___   Date ___June 4, 19--___

Item ___48Z Floor Lamp___   Date wanted ___June 14, 19--___

No. of items ___72___   Date completed ___June 13, 19--___

Ordered for ___Stock___

DIRECT MATERIALS		DIRECT LABOR				SUMMARY	
Req. No.	Amount	Date	Amount	Date	Amount	Item	Amount
281	$ 860.00	June 4	$ 129.00			Direct Materials	$1,690.00
288	471.00	5	248.00			Direct Labor	1,480.00
317	359.00	6	175.00			Factory Overhead	
	$1,690.00	7	192.00			(85% of direct	
		8	295.00			labor costs)	1,258.00
		11	165.00			Total Cost	$4,428.00
		12	152.00				
		13	124.00			No. units finished	72
			$1,480.00			Cost per unit	$61.50

[4–6]

FINISHED GOODS LEDGER CARD

Description ___Floor Lamp___   Stock No. ___48Z___

Minimum ___50___   Location ___Area E-40___

MANUFACTURED/RECEIVED					SHIPPED/ISSUED					BALANCE			
Date	Job No.	Quantity	Unit Cost	Total Cost	Date	Sales Invoice No.	Quantity	Unit Cost	Total Cost	Date	Quantity	Unit Cost	Total Cost
										19-- June 1	70	60.90	4,263.00
					19-- June 6	522	30	60.90	1,827.00	6	40	60.90	2,436.00
19-- June 13	172	72	61.50	4,428.00						13	40	60.90 }	
											72	61.50 }	6,864.00
					18	541	15	60.90	913.50	18	25	60.90 }	
											72	61.50 }	5,950.50

Preparing cost records

a. Direct materials cost
   12,500 Units × $75.00 Unit Cost = $937,500.00 Total Direct Materials Cost (estimated)

Estimated Factory Overhead Costs	÷	*Estimated Direct Materials Cost*	=	*Applied rate*
$750,000.00	÷	**$937,500.00**	=	**80% of Direct Materials Cost**

b. Direct labor cost
   12,500 Units × 4.8 Labor Hours/Unit × $10.00/hour = $600,000.00 Total Direct Labor Cost (estimated)

Estimated Factory Overhead Cost	÷	*Estimated Direct Labor Cost*	=	*Applied rate*
$750,000.00	÷	**$600,000.00**	=	**125% of Direct Labor Cost**

c. Direct labor hours
   12,500 Units × 4.8 Labor Hours/Unit = 60,000 hours (estimated)

Estimated Factory Overhead Cost	÷	*Estimated Direct Labor Hours*	=	*Applied rate*
$750,000.00	÷	**60,000**	=	**$12.50 per Direct Labor Hour**

[2, 3]

COST SHEET

Job. No. __254__   Date ___April 8, 19--___

Item ___VC32 Recorder___   Date wanted ___April 18, 19--___

No. of items ___60___   Date completed ___April 17, 19--___

Ordered for ___Stock___

DIRECT MATERIALS		DIRECT LABOR				SUMMARY	
Req. No.	Amount	Date	Amount	Date	Amount	Item	Amount
310	$1,160.00	Apr. 8	$ 275.00			*Direct Materials*	$ 4,500.00
319	2,320.00	9	441.00			*Direct Labor*	2,874.00
327	1,020.00	10	392.00			*Factory Overhead*	
	$4,500.00	11	423.00			*(80% of direct*	
		12	440.00			*material costs)*	3,600.00
		15	370.00			*Total Cost*	$10,974.00
		16	352.00				
		17	181.00			*No. units finished*	60
			$2,874.00			*Cost per unit*	$182.90

FINISHED GOODS LEDGER CARD

Description _Recorder_   Stock No. _VC32_
Minimum _30_   Location _Area B-28_

MANUFACTURED/RECEIVED					SHIPPED/ISSUED					BALANCE			
Date	Job No.	Quantity	Unit Cost	Total Cost	Date	Sales Invoice No.	Quantity	Unit Cost	Total Cost	Date	Quantity	Unit Cost	Total Cost
										Apr. 1	50	181.50	9,075.00
					Apr. 10	339	10	181.50	1,815.00	10	40	181.50	7,260.00
Apr. 17	254	60	182.90	10,974.00						17	40	181.50 }	
											60	182.90 }	18,234.00
					22	383	30	182.90	5,487.00	22	40	181.50 }	
											30	182.90 }	12,747.00
					24	412	25	182.90	4,572.50	24	40	181.50 }	
											5	182.90 }	8,174.50

Perfect Score. 45

Deduct .... —

Your Score .... —

Name _____

Date _____ Class _____

Checked by _____

STUDY
GUIDE
22

UNIT A—Analyzing End-of-Fiscal-Period Work for a Manufacturing Business

DIRECTIONS: Place a check mark in the proper Answers column to show whether each of the following statements is true or false.

		Answers		For Scoring
		True	False	
0.	Two factory accounts, Work in Process and Factory Overhead, are debited when a factory payroll is recorded...	✔		**0.** ✔
1.	Factory Overhead is debited to record actual overhead expenses	✔		**1.**
2.	The balance of the general ledger account Materials equals the sum of all the account balances in the materials ledger..	✔		**2.**
3.	A debit balance in the Factory Overhead account indicates that overhead is overapplied..		✔	**3.**
4.	The materials inventory of a manufacturing business is similar to the merchandise inventory of a merchandising business..............................		✔	**4.**
5.	The Factory Overhead account balance is closed to the Income Summary account...	✔		**5.**
6.	The factory overhead amount that appears on the statement of cost of goods manufactured usually is the same as the actual overhead expenses amount....		✔	**6.**
7.	Overapplied overhead is listed on an income statement as an addition to the cost of goods sold..		✔	**7.**
8.	The Work in Process account balance is listed on the income statement as a current asset..		✔	**8.**
9.	The amount by which applied overhead is less than actual overhead is called underapplied overhead	✔		**9.**
10.	Charging costs to jobs at the time jobs are completed is an application of the Objective Evidence concept...		✔	**10.**
11.	A debit balance in the Factory Overhead account indicates that overhead is underapplied	✔		**11.**
12.	A statement showing details about the cost of finished goods is called a statement of cost of goods manufactured...	✔		**12.**
13.	The amount by which applied overhead is more than actual overhead is called overapplied overhead...	✔		**13.**

UNIT B—Analyzing the Format of a Statement of Cost of Goods Manufactured

DIRECTIONS: For each numbered line of the Statement of Cost of Goods Manufactured, print in the proper Answers column the identifying letter of the correct line name.

Line Name

A. Cost of Direct Materials Placed in Process
B. Cost of Goods Manufactured
C. Direct Labor
D. Direct Materials
E. Factory Overhead Applied
F. Less Materials Inventory, Jan. 31, 19--
G. Less Work in Process Inventory, Jan. 31, 19--
H. Materials Inventory, January 1, 19--
I. Materials Purchased
J. Total Cost of Work in Process During January
K. Total Cost of Work Placed in Process
L. Total Materials Available During January
M. Work in Process Inventory, Jan. 1, 19--

Wok Corporation
Stmt. of Cost of Goods Mfd.
For Month Ended Jan. 31, 19--

		Answers	For Scoring
0. __		D	0. ✔
14. __	$10,000.00	H	14.
15. __	20,000.00	I	15.
16. __	30,000.00	L	16.
17. __	5,000.00	F	17.
18. __	$25,000.00	A	18.
19. __	20,000.00	C	19.
20. __	15,000.00	E	20.
21. __	60,000.00	K	21.
22. __	8,000.00	M	22.
23. __	68,000.00	J	23.
24. __	6,000.00	G	24.
25. __	$62,000.00	B	25.

UNIT C—Analyzing Transactions for a Manufacturing Business

DIRECTIONS: For each transaction below, print in the proper Answers columns the identifying letters of the accounts to be debited and credited.

Account Titles

A. Accounts Payable
B. Accumulated Depr. — Factory Equipment
C. Cash
D. Cost of Goods Sold
E. Depr. Expense — Factory Equipment
F. Employees Income Tax Payable
G. Factory Equipment
H. Factory Overhead
I. Factory Payroll
J. FICA Tax Payable
K. Finished Goods
L. Income Summary
M. Materials
N. miscellaneous factory expense accounts
O. Prepaid Insurance
P. Work in Process

Transactions

Transactions		Answers Debit	Answers Credit	For Scoring Debit	For Scoring Credit
0–0.	Record cash payments journal entry for prepaid insurance bought	O	C	0. ✔	0. ✔
26–27.	Record general journal entry for total of finished goods manufactured during the month	K	P	26.	27.
28–29.	Record general journal entry for month's applied factory overhead	P	H	28.	29.
30–31.	Record general journal entry to close the month's factory expenses to the Factory Overhead account	H	N	30.	31.
32–33.	Record general journal entry for the month's direct materials requisitions	P	M	32.	33.
34–35.	Record general journal entry to close Factory Overhead account when there is overapplied overhead	H	L	34.	35.
36–37.	Record materials purchases journal entry for materials purchased	M	A	36.	37.
38–39.	Record general journal entry for month's cost of goods sold	D	K	38.	39.
40–41.	Record general journal entry to close Factory Overhead account when there is underapplied overhead	L	H	40.	41.
42–43.	Record cash payments journal entry for month's factory payroll	H, P	C, F, J	42.	43.
44–45.	Record general journal end-of-fiscal-period adjusting entry for factory equipment depreciation expense	E	B	44.	45.

Journalizing cost accounting transactions for a manufacturing company

MATERIALS PURCHASES JOURNAL

PAGE 15

[1, 2]

	DATE	ACCOUNT CREDITED	PURCH. NO.	POST. REF.	MATERIALS DR. ACCTS. PAY. CR.	
1	Feb. 19— 6	Cheetah Company	171		3 6 9 4 00	1
2	22	Norte Company	172		1 3 9 4 70	2
3	28	Total			5 0 8 8 70	3
4						4
5						5
6						6
7						7

CASH PAYMENTS JOURNAL

PAGE 15

[1, 3]

	DATE	ACCOUNT TITLE	CHECK NO.	POST. REF.	GENERAL DEBIT	GENERAL CREDIT	ACCOUNTS PAYABLE DEBIT	PURCHASES DISCOUNT CREDIT	CASH CREDIT	
1	Feb. 19— 10	Miscellaneous Expense—Factory	333		1 8 6 90				1 8 6 90	1
2	15	Supplies—Factory	341		4 1 2 90				4 1 2 90	2
3	23	Factory Equipment	352		1 2 6 5 30				1 2 6 5 30	3
4	25	Work in Process	367		5 1 0 0 00				5 7 8 5 90	4
5		Factory Overhead			1 9 5 6 00					5
6		Employees Income Tax Payable				7 7 6 20				6
7		FICA Tax Payable				4 9 3 90				7
8	28	Totals			8 9 2 1 10	1 2 7 0 10			7 6 5 1 00	8
9										9
10										10
11										11

The ledger and journals prepared in Problem 22-2 are needed to complete Problem 22-3.

CASH PAYMENTS JOURNAL

PAGE 11

	DATE	ACCOUNT TITLE	CHECK NO.	POST. REF.	GENERAL DEBIT	GENERAL CREDIT	ACCOUNTS PAYABLE DEBIT	PURCHASES DISCOUNT CREDIT	CASH CREDIT	
1	Apr. 30	Work in Process	371	1130	102 5 7 0 00				100 4 7 5 80	1
2		Factory Overhead		5505	19 9 6 1 50					2
3		Employees Income Tax Payable		2110		13 4 7 8 50				3
4		FICA Tax Payable		2120		8 5 7 7 20				4

GENERAL JOURNAL

PAGE 9

	DATE	ACCOUNT TITLE	POST. REF.	DEBIT	CREDIT	
1	Apr. 30	Work in Process	1130	139 4 1 9 80		1
2		Materials	1125		139 4 1 9 80	2
3		M34				3
4	30	Factory Overhead	5505	45 4 1 4 20		4
5		Depr. Expense — Factory Equipment	5510		7 6 2 8 40	5
6		Depreciation Expense — Building	5515		2 0 8 1 30	6
7		Heat, Light, and Power Expense	5520		5 7 7 8 50	7
8		Insurance Expense — Factory	5525		9 7 3 70	8
9		Miscellaneous Expense — Factory	5530		5 6 0 9 50	9
10		Payroll Taxes Expense — Factory	5535		11 5 1 8 00	10
11		Property Tax Expense — Factory	5540		3 7 8 1 70	11
12		Supplies Expense — Factory	5545		8 0 4 3 10	12
13		M35				13
14	30	Work in Process	1130	64 6 1 9 10		14
15		Factory Overhead	5505		64 6 1 9 10	15
16		M36				16
17	30	Income Summary	3120	7 5 6 60		17
18		Factory Overhead	5505		7 5 6 60	18
19		M37				19
20	30	Finished Goods	1135	289 1 8 5 00		20
21		Work in Process	1130		289 1 8 5 00	21
22		M38				22
23	30	Cost of Goods Sold	5105	388 0 5 0 00		23
24		Finished Goods	1135		388 0 5 0 00	24
25		M39				25
26						26

GENERAL LEDGER

ACCOUNT Materials **ACCOUNT NO.** 1125

DATE		ITEM	POST. REF.	DEBIT	CREDIT	BALANCE DEBIT	BALANCE CREDIT
19-- Apr.	1	Balance	✔			138 4 1 9 00	
	30		MP5	46 5 1 9 00		184 9 3 8 00	
	30		G9		139 4 1 9 80	45 5 1 8 20	

ACCOUNT Work in Process **ACCOUNT NO.** 1130

DATE		ITEM	POST. REF.	DEBIT	CREDIT	BALANCE DEBIT	BALANCE CREDIT
19-- Apr.	1	Balance	✔			17 7 8 1 00	
	30		CP11	102 5 7 0 00		120 3 5 1 00	
	30		G9	139 4 1 9 80		259 7 7 0 80	
	30		G9	64 6 1 9 10		324 3 8 9 90	
	30		G9		289 1 8 5 00	35 2 0 4 90	

ACCOUNT Finished Goods **ACCOUNT NO.** 1135

DATE		ITEM	POST. REF.	DEBIT	CREDIT	BALANCE DEBIT	BALANCE CREDIT
19-- Apr.	1	Balance	✔			156 1 9 6 00	
	30		G9	289 1 8 5 00		445 3 8 1 00	
	30		G9		388 0 5 0 00	57 3 3 1 00	

ACCOUNT Employees Income Tax Payable **ACCOUNT NO.** 2110

DATE	ITEM	POST. REF.	DEBIT	CREDIT	BALANCE DEBIT	BALANCE CREDIT
19-- Apr. 30		CP11		13 4 7 8 50		13 4 7 8 50

ACCOUNT FICA Tax Payable **ACCOUNT NO.** 2120

DATE	ITEM	POST. REF.	DEBIT	CREDIT	BALANCE DEBIT	BALANCE CREDIT
19-- Apr. 30		CP11		8 5 7 7 20		8 5 7 7 20

ACCOUNT Income Summary **ACCOUNT NO.** 3120

DATE	ITEM	POST. REF.	DEBIT	CREDIT	BALANCE DEBIT	BALANCE CREDIT
19-- Apr. 30		G9	7 5 6 60		7 5 6 60	

GENERAL LEDGER

ACCOUNT Cost of Goods Sold **ACCOUNT NO.** 5105

DATE	ITEM	POST. REF.	DEBIT	CREDIT	BALANCE DEBIT	BALANCE CREDIT
19-- Apr. 30		G9	388 0 5 0 00		388 0 5 0 00	

ACCOUNT Factory Overhead **ACCOUNT NO.** 5505

DATE	ITEM	POST. REF.	DEBIT	CREDIT	BALANCE DEBIT	BALANCE CREDIT
19-- Apr. 30		CP11	19 9 6 1 50		19 9 6 1 50	
30		G9	45 4 1 4 20		65 3 7 5 70	
30		G9		64 6 1 9 10	7 5 6 60	
30		G9		7 5 6 60	—	—

ACCOUNT Depreciation Expense — Factory Equipment **ACCOUNT NO.** 5510

DATE	ITEM	POST. REF.	DEBIT	CREDIT	BALANCE DEBIT	BALANCE CREDIT
19-- Apr. 30	Balance	✔			7 6 2 8 40	
30		G9		7 6 2 8 40	—	—

ACCOUNT Depreciation Expense — Building **ACCOUNT NO.** 5515

DATE	ITEM	POST. REF.	DEBIT	CREDIT	BALANCE DEBIT	BALANCE CREDIT
19-- Apr. 30	Balance	✔			2 0 8 1 30	
30		G9		2 0 8 1 30	—	—

ACCOUNT Heat, Light, and Power Expense **ACCOUNT NO.** 5520

DATE	ITEM	POST. REF.	DEBIT	CREDIT	BALANCE DEBIT	BALANCE CREDIT
19-- Apr. 30	Balance	✔			5 7 7 8 50	
30		G9		5 7 7 8 50	—	—

ACCOUNT Insurance Expense — Factory **ACCOUNT NO.** 5525

DATE	ITEM	POST. REF.	DEBIT	CREDIT	BALANCE DEBIT	BALANCE CREDIT
19-- Apr. 30	Balance	✔			9 7 3 70	
30		G9		9 7 3 70	—	—

ACCOUNT Miscellaneous Expense — Factory **ACCOUNT NO.** 5530

DATE	ITEM	POST. REF.	DEBIT	CREDIT	BALANCE DEBIT	BALANCE CREDIT
19-- Apr. 30	Balance	✔			5 6 0 9 50	
30		G9		5 6 0 9 50	—	—

GENERAL LEDGER

ACCOUNT Payroll Taxes Expense — Factory   ACCOUNT NO. 5535

DATE		ITEM	POST. REF.	DEBIT	CREDIT	BALANCE DEBIT	BALANCE CREDIT
19-- Apr.	30	Balance	✔			11 5 1 8 00	
	30		G9		11 5 1 8 00		

ACCOUNT Property Tax Expense — Factory   ACCOUNT NO. 5540

DATE		ITEM	POST. REF.	DEBIT	CREDIT	BALANCE DEBIT	BALANCE CREDIT
19-- Apr.	30	Balance	✔			3 7 8 1 70	
	30		G9		3 7 8 1 70		

ACCOUNT Supplies Expense — Factory   ACCOUNT NO. 5545

DATE		ITEM	POST. REF.	DEBIT	CREDIT	BALANCE DEBIT	BALANCE CREDIT
19-- Apr.	30	Balance	✔			8 0 4 3 10	
	30		G9		8 0 4 3 10		

Preparing a statement of cost of goods manufactured   *PROBLEM 22-3, p. 502*

The ledger and journals prepared in Problem 22-2 are needed to complete Problem 22-3.

Macomber Corporation

Statement of Cost of Goods Manufactured

For Month Ended April 30, 19--

Direct Materials:		
Materials Inventory, April 1, 19--	138 4 1 9 00	
Materials Purchased	46 5 1 9 00	
Total Materials Available During April	184 9 3 8 00	
Less Materials Inventory, April 30, 19--	45 5 1 8 20	
Cost of Direct Materials Placed in Process		139 4 1 9 80
Direct Labor		102 5 7 0 00
Factory Overhead Applied		64 6 1 9 10
Total Cost of Work Placed in Process		306 6 0 8 90
Work in Process Inventory, April 1, 19--		17 7 8 1 00
Total Cost of Work in Process During April		324 3 8 9 90
Less Work in Process Inventory, April 30, 19--		35 2 0 4 90
Cost of Goods Manufactured		289 1 8 5 00

CASH PAYMENTS JOURNAL

PAGE 14

	DATE		ACCOUNT TITLE	CHECK NO.	POST. REF.	GENERAL DEBIT	GENERAL CREDIT	ACCOUNTS PAYABLE DEBIT	PURCHASES DISCOUNT CREDIT	CASH CREDIT	
1	Mar.¹⁹	31	Work in Process	711	1130	58 2 72 00				64 3 1 4 30	1
2			Factory Overhead		5505	20 1 60 00					2
3			Employees Income Tax Payable		2110		8 6 27 50				3
4			FICA Tax Payable		2120		5 4 90 20				4

GENERAL JOURNAL

PAGE 8

	DATE		ACCOUNT TITLE	POST. REF.	DEBIT	CREDIT	
1	Mar.¹⁹	31	Work in Process	1130	64 3 4 4 00		1
2			Materials	1125		64 3 4 4 00	2
3			M211				3
4		31	Factory Overhead	5505	21 5 1 0 00		4
5			Depr. Expense — Factory Equipment	5510		1 4 7 3 60	5
6			Depreciation Expense — Building	5515		7 2 0 00	6
7			Heat, Light, and Power Expense	5520		2 3 1 0 00	7
8			Insurance Expense — Factory	5525		3 8 4 00	8
9			Miscellaneous Expense — Factory	5530		4 3 2 0 00	9
10			Payroll Taxes Expense — Factory	5535		5 8 8 2 40	10
11			Property Tax Expense — Factory	5540		1 8 1 2 00	11
12			Supplies Expense — Factory	5545		4 6 0 8 00	12
13			M212				13
14		31	Work in Process	1130	40 7 9 0 40		14
15			Factory Overhead	5505		40 7 9 0 40	15
16			M213				16
17		31	Income Summary	3120	8 7 9 60		17
18			Factory Overhead	5505		8 7 9 60	18
19			M214				19
20		31	Finished Goods	1135	159 0 0 0 00		20
21			Work in Process	1130		159 0 0 0 00	21
22			M215				22
23		31	Cost of Goods Sold	5105	251 2 8 0 00		23
24			Finished Goods	1135		251 2 8 0 00	24
25			M216				25
26							26

GENERAL LEDGER

ACCOUNT Materials   ACCOUNT NO. 1125

DATE		ITEM	POST. REF.	DEBIT	CREDIT	BALANCE DEBIT	BALANCE CREDIT
19-- Mar.	1	Balance	✓			77 3 1 6 00	
	31		MP7	61 5 8 4 00		138 9 0 0 00	
	31		G8		64 3 4 4 00	74 5 5 6 00	

ACCOUNT Work in Process   ACCOUNT NO. 1130

DATE		ITEM	POST. REF.	DEBIT	CREDIT	BALANCE DEBIT	BALANCE CREDIT
19-- Mar.	1	Balance	✓			48 9 6 0 00	
	31		CP14	58 2 7 2 00		107 2 3 2 00	
	31		G8	64 3 4 4 00		171 5 7 6 00	
	31		G8	40 7 9 0 40		212 3 6 6 40	
	31		G8		159 0 0 0 00	53 3 6 6 40	

ACCOUNT Finished Goods   ACCOUNT NO. 1135

DATE		ITEM	POST. REF.	DEBIT	CREDIT	BALANCE DEBIT	BALANCE CREDIT
19-- Mar.	1	Balance	✓			120 7 5 0 00	
	31		G8	159 0 0 0 00		279 7 5 0 00	
	31		G8		251 2 8 0 00	28 4 7 0 00	

ACCOUNT Employees Income Tax Payable   ACCOUNT NO. 2110

DATE		ITEM	POST. REF.	DEBIT	CREDIT	BALANCE DEBIT	BALANCE CREDIT
19-- Mar.	31		CP14		8 6 2 7 50		8 6 2 7 50

ACCOUNT FICA Tax Payable   ACCOUNT NO. 2120

DATE		ITEM	POST. REF.	DEBIT	CREDIT	BALANCE DEBIT	BALANCE CREDIT
19-- Mar.	31		CP14		5 4 9 0 20		5 4 9 0 20

ACCOUNT Income Summary   ACCOUNT NO. 3120

DATE		ITEM	POST. REF.	DEBIT	CREDIT	BALANCE DEBIT	BALANCE CREDIT
19-- Mar.	31		G8	8 7 9 60		8 7 9 60	

GENERAL LEDGER

ACCOUNT Cost of Goods Sold   **ACCOUNT NO.** 5105

DATE	ITEM	POST. REF.	DEBIT	CREDIT	BALANCE DEBIT	BALANCE CREDIT
19-- Mar. 31		G8	251 2 8 0 00		251 2 8 0 00	

ACCOUNT Factory Overhead   **ACCOUNT NO.** 5505

DATE	ITEM	POST. REF.	DEBIT	CREDIT	BALANCE DEBIT	BALANCE CREDIT
19-- Mar. 31		CP14	20 1 6 0 00		20 1 6 0 00	
31		G8	21 5 1 0 00		41 6 7 0 00	
31		G8		40 7 9 0 40	8 7 9 60	
31		G8		8 7 9 60	—	—

ACCOUNT Depreciation Expense — Factory Equipment   **ACCOUNT NO.** 5510

DATE	ITEM	POST. REF.	DEBIT	CREDIT	BALANCE DEBIT	BALANCE CREDIT
19-- Mar. 31	Balance	✔			1 4 7 3 60	
31		G8		1 4 7 3 60	—	—

ACCOUNT Depreciation Expense — Building   **ACCOUNT NO.** 5515

DATE	ITEM	POST. REF.	DEBIT	CREDIT	BALANCE DEBIT	BALANCE CREDIT
19-- Mar. 31	Balance	✔			7 2 0 00	
31		G8		7 2 0 00	—	—

ACCOUNT Heat, Light, and Power Expense   **ACCOUNT NO.** 5520

DATE	ITEM	POST. REF.	DEBIT	CREDIT	BALANCE DEBIT	BALANCE CREDIT
19-- Mar. 31	Balance	✔			2 3 1 0 00	
31		G8		2 3 1 0 00	—	—

ACCOUNT Insurance Expense — Factory   **ACCOUNT NO.** 5525

DATE	ITEM	POST. REF.	DEBIT	CREDIT	BALANCE DEBIT	BALANCE CREDIT
19-- Mar. 31	Balance	✔			3 8 4 00	
31		G8		3 8 4 00	—	—

ACCOUNT Miscellaneous Expense — Factory   **ACCOUNT NO.** 5530

DATE	ITEM	POST. REF.	DEBIT	CREDIT	BALANCE DEBIT	BALANCE CREDIT
19-- Mar. 31	Balance	✔			4 3 2 0 00	
31		G8		4 3 2 0 00	—	—

GENERAL LEDGER

ACCOUNT Payroll Taxes Expense — Factory   ACCOUNT NO. 5535

DATE		ITEM	POST. REF.	DEBIT	CREDIT	BALANCE DEBIT	BALANCE CREDIT
19-- Mar.	31	Balance	✔			5 8 8 2 40	
	31		G8		5 8 8 2 40		

ACCOUNT Property Tax Expense — Factory   ACCOUNT NO. 5540

DATE		ITEM	POST. REF.	DEBIT	CREDIT	BALANCE DEBIT	BALANCE CREDIT
19-- Mar.	31	Balance	✔			1 8 1 2 00	
	31		G8		1 8 1 2 00		

ACCOUNT Supplies Expense — Factory   ACCOUNT NO. 5545

DATE		ITEM	POST. REF.	DEBIT	CREDIT	BALANCE DEBIT	BALANCE CREDIT
19-- Mar.	31	Balance	✔			4 6 0 8 00	
	31		G8		4 6 0 8 00		

[6]

Tanner Corporation

Statement of Cost of Goods Manufactured

For Month Ended March 31, 19--

Direct Materials:		
Materials Inventory, March 1, 19--	77 3 1 6 00	
Materials Purchased	61 5 8 4 00	
Total Materials Available During March	138 9 0 0 00	
Less Materials Inventory, March 31, 19--	74 5 5 6 00	
Cost of Direct Materials Placed in Process		64 3 4 4 00
Direct Labor		58 2 7 2 00
Factory Overhead Applied		40 7 9 0 40
Total Cost of Work Placed in Process		163 4 0 6 40
Work in Process Inventory, March 1, 19--		48 9 6 0 00
Total Cost of Work in Process During March		212 3 6 6 40
Less Work in Process Inventory, March 31, 19--		53 3 6 6 40
Cost of Goods Manufactured		159 0 0 0 00

CASH PAYMENTS JOURNAL

PAGE 22

	DATE		ACCOUNT TITLE	CHECK NO.	POST. REF.	GENERAL DEBIT	GENERAL CREDIT	ACCOUNTS PAYABLE DEBIT	PURCHASES DISCOUNT CREDIT	CASH CREDIT	
1	19-- May	31	Work in Process	341	1130	46 6 0 4 25				51 7 5 9 40	1
2			Factory Overhead		5505	16 5 1 6 96					2
3			Employees Income Tax Payable		2110		6 9 4 3 33				3
4			FICA Tax Payable		2120		4 4 1 8 48				4

GENERAL JOURNAL

PAGE 19

	DATE		ACCOUNT TITLE	POST. REF.	DEBIT	CREDIT	
1	19-- May	31	Work in Process	1130	74 7 5 0 94		1
2			Materials	1125		74 7 5 0 94	2
3			M698				3
4		31	Factory Overhead	5505	14 4 3 8 17		4
5			Depr. Expense—Factory Equipment	5510		1 1 7 9 34	5
6			Depreciation Expense—Building	5515		6 1 8 75	6
7			Heat, Light, and Power Expense	5520		2 8 2 2 24	7
8			Insurance Expense—Factory	5525		1 0 2 60	8
9			Miscellaneous Expense—Factory	5530		2 2 7 65	9
10			Payroll Taxes Expense—Factory	5535		8 3 3 2 00	10
11			Property Tax Expense—Factory	5540		3 5 5 55	11
12			Supplies Expense—Factory	5545		8 0 0 04	12
13			M699				13
14		31	Work in Process	1130	31 2 2 4 85		14
15			Factory Overhead	5505		31 2 2 4 85	15
16			M700				16
17		31	Factory Overhead	5505	2 6 9 72		17
18			Income Summary	3120		2 6 9 72	18
19			M701				19
20		31	Finished Goods	1135	134 9 3 4 05		20
21			Work in Process	1130		134 9 3 4 05	21
22			M702				22
23		31	Cost of Goods Sold	5105	106 1 2 6 54		23
24			Finished Goods	1135		106 1 2 6 54	24
25			M703				25
26							26

GENERAL LEDGER

ACCOUNT Materials   ACCOUNT NO. 1125

DATE		ITEM	POST. REF.	DEBIT	CREDIT	BALANCE DEBIT	BALANCE CREDIT
19-- May	1	Balance	✔			41 3 2 8 84	
	31		MP5	77 5 3 4 38		118 8 6 3 22	
	31		G19		74 7 5 0 94	44 1 1 2 28	

ACCOUNT Work in Process   ACCOUNT NO. 1130

DATE		ITEM	POST. REF.	DEBIT	CREDIT	BALANCE DEBIT	BALANCE CREDIT
19-- May	1	Balance	✔			20 2 1 4 11	
	31		CP22	46 6 0 4 25		66 8 1 8 36	
	31		G19	74 7 5 0 94		141 5 6 9 30	
	31		G19	31 2 2 4 85		172 7 9 4 15	
	31		G19		134 9 3 4 05	37 8 6 0 10	

ACCOUNT Finished Goods   ACCOUNT NO. 1135

DATE		ITEM	POST. REF.	DEBIT	CREDIT	BALANCE DEBIT	BALANCE CREDIT
19-- May	1	Balance	✔			38 4 0 8 94	
	31		G19	134 9 3 4 05		173 3 4 2 99	
	31		G19		106 1 2 6 54	67 2 1 6 45	

ACCOUNT Employees Income Tax Payable   ACCOUNT NO. 2110

DATE	ITEM	POST. REF.	DEBIT	CREDIT	BALANCE DEBIT	BALANCE CREDIT
19-- May 31		CP22		6 9 4 3 33		6 9 4 3 33

ACCOUNT FICA Tax Payable   ACCOUNT NO. 2120

DATE	ITEM	POST. REF.	DEBIT	CREDIT	BALANCE DEBIT	BALANCE CREDIT
19-- May 31		CP22		4 4 1 8 48		4 4 1 8 48

ACCOUNT Income Summary   ACCOUNT NO. 3120

DATE	ITEM	POST. REF.	DEBIT	CREDIT	BALANCE DEBIT	BALANCE CREDIT
19-- May 31		G19		2 6 9 72		2 6 9 72

GENERAL LEDGER

ACCOUNT Cost of Goods Sold   ACCOUNT NO. 5105

DATE	ITEM	POST. REF.	DEBIT	CREDIT	BALANCE DEBIT	BALANCE CREDIT
19-- May 31		G19	106 1 2 6 54		106 1 2 6 54	

ACCOUNT Factory Overhead   ACCOUNT NO. 5505

DATE	ITEM	POST. REF.	DEBIT	CREDIT	BALANCE DEBIT	BALANCE CREDIT
19-- May 31		CP22	16 5 1 6 96		16 5 1 6 96	
31		G19	14 4 3 8 17		30 9 5 5 13	
31		G19		31 2 2 4 85		2 6 9 72
31		G19	2 6 9 72			

ACCOUNT Depreciation Expense — Factory Equipment   ACCOUNT NO. 5510

DATE	ITEM	POST. REF.	DEBIT	CREDIT	BALANCE DEBIT	BALANCE CREDIT
19-- May 31	Balance	✔			1 1 7 9 34	
31		G19		1 1 7 9 34		

ACCOUNT Depreciation Expense — Building   ACCOUNT NO. 5515

DATE	ITEM	POST. REF.	DEBIT	CREDIT	BALANCE DEBIT	BALANCE CREDIT
19-- May 31	Balance	✔			6 1 8 75	
31		G19		6 1 8 75		

ACCOUNT Heat, Light, and Power Expense   ACCOUNT NO. 5520

DATE	ITEM	POST. REF.	DEBIT	CREDIT	BALANCE DEBIT	BALANCE CREDIT
19-- May 31	Balance	✔			2 8 2 2 24	
31		G19		2 8 2 2 24		

ACCOUNT Insurance Expense — Factory   ACCOUNT NO. 5525

DATE	ITEM	POST. REF.	DEBIT	CREDIT	BALANCE DEBIT	BALANCE CREDIT
19-- May 31	Balance	✔			1 0 2 60	
31		G19		1 0 2 60		

ACCOUNT Miscellaneous Expense — Factory   ACCOUNT NO. 5530

DATE	ITEM	POST. REF.	DEBIT	CREDIT	BALANCE DEBIT	BALANCE CREDIT
19-- May 31	Balance	✔			2 2 7 65	
31		G19		2 2 7 65		

GENERAL LEDGER

ACCOUNT Payroll Taxes Expense — Factory   ACCOUNT NO. 5535

DATE		ITEM	POST. REF.	DEBIT	CREDIT	BALANCE DEBIT	BALANCE CREDIT
19-- May	31	Balance	✔			8 3 3 2 00	
	31		G19		8 3 3 2 00	—	—

ACCOUNT Property Tax Expense — Factory   ACCOUNT NO. 5540

DATE		ITEM	POST. REF.	DEBIT	CREDIT	BALANCE DEBIT	BALANCE CREDIT
19-- May	31	Balance	✔			3 5 5 55	
	31		G19		3 5 5 55	—	—

ACCOUNT Supplies Expense — Factory   ACCOUNT NO. 5545

DATE		ITEM	POST. REF.	DEBIT	CREDIT	BALANCE DEBIT	BALANCE CREDIT
19-- May	31	Balance	✔			8 0 0 04	
	31		G19		8 0 0 04	—	—

[6]

Advant Company

Statement of Cost of Goods Manufactured

For Month Ended May 31, 19--

Direct Materials:		
Materials Inventory, May 1, 19--	41 3 2 8 84	
Materials Purchased	77 5 3 4 38	
Total Materials Available During May	118 8 6 3 22	
Less Materials Inventory, May 31, 19--	44 1 1 2 28	
Cost of Direct Materials Placed in Process		74 7 5 0 94
Direct Labor		46 6 0 4 25
Factory Overhead Applied		31 2 2 4 85
Total Cost of Work Placed in Process		152 5 8 0 04
Work in Process Inventory, May 1, 19--		20 2 1 4 11
Total Cost of Work in Process During May		172 7 9 4 15
Less Work in Process Inventory, May 31, 19--		37 8 6 0 10
Cost of Goods Manufactured		134 9 3 4 05

[7]

Advant Company

Work Sheet

For Month Ended May 31, 19--

	TRIAL BALANCE		ADJUSTMENTS		INCOME STATEMENT		BALANCE SHEET	
ACCOUNT TITLE	DEBIT	CREDIT	DEBIT	CREDIT	DEBIT	CREDIT	DEBIT	CREDIT
Cash	62 26 1 46						62 26 1 46	
Petty Cash	3 75 00						3 75 00	
Accounts Receivable	115 30 0 30						115 30 0 30	
Allowance for Uncollectible Accounts		2 81 9 65		(a) 7 62 75				3 58 2 40
Materials	44 11 2 28						44 11 2 28	
Work in Process	37 86 0 10						37 86 0 10	
Finished Goods	67 21 6 45						67 21 6 45	
Supplies—Factory	2 47 4 55						2 47 4 55	
Supplies—Sales	3 10 7 03			(b) 1 34 4 53			1 76 2 50	
Supplies—Administrative	7 94 20			(c) 2 73 46			5 20 74	
Prepaid Insurance	1 42 2 23			(d) 3 8 93			1 38 3 30	
Factory Equipment	103 00 5 00						103 00 5 00	
Accum. Depr.—Factory Equipment		28 11 6 00						28 11 6 00
Office Equipment	8 61 3 00						8 61 3 00	
Accum. Depr.—Office Equipment		2 76 9 30		(e) 6 8 51				2 83 7 81
Store Equipment	7 77 1 50						7 77 1 50	
Accum. Depr.—Store Equipment		2 88 4 56		(f) 6 1 88				2 94 6 44
Building	237 60 0 00						237 60 0 00	
Accum. Depr.—Building		23 76 0 00						23 76 0 00
Land	99 44 5 89						99 44 5 89	
Accounts Payable		16 53 5 86						16 53 5 86
Employees Income Tax Payable		9 90 3 90						9 90 3 90
Federal Income Tax Payable				(g) 3 02 5 67				3 02 5 67
FICA Tax Payable		12 60 4 97						12 60 4 97
Unemploy. Tax Payable—Federal		5 88 32						5 88 32
Unemploy. Tax Payable—State		3 97 1 14						3 97 1 14
Mortgage Payable		56 25 0 00						56 25 0 00

#	ACCOUNT TITLE	TRIAL BALANCE DEBIT	TRIAL BALANCE CREDIT	ADJUSTMENTS DEBIT	ADJUSTMENTS CREDIT	INCOME STATEMENT DEBIT	INCOME STATEMENT CREDIT	BALANCE SHEET DEBIT	BALANCE SHEET CREDIT
28	Capital Stock		450 0 0 0 00						450 0 0 0 00
29	Retained Earnings		168 3 5 9 21						168 3 5 9 21
30	Income Summary		2 6 9 72				2 6 9 72		
31	Sales		159 8 2 2 56				159 8 2 2 56		
32	Cost of Goods Sold	106 1 2 6 54				106 1 2 6 54			
33	Factory Overhead								
34	Depr. Expense—Factory Equipment								
35	Depr. Expense—Building								
36	Heat, Light, and Power Expense								
37	Insurance Expense—Factory								
38	Miscellaneous Expense—Factory								
39	Payroll Taxes Expense—Factory								
40	Property Tax Expense—Factory								
41	Supplies Expense—Factory								
42	Advertising Expense	2 4 1 6 05				2 4 1 6 05			
43	Delivery Expense	5 8 4 2 24				5 8 4 2 24			
44	Depr. Exp.—Store Equipment			(f) 6 1 88		6 1 88			
45	Miscellaneous Expense—Sales	1 5 0 0 33				1 5 0 0 33			
46	Salary Expense—Sales	11 6 0 4 38				11 6 0 4 38			
47	Supplies Expense—Sales			(b) 1 3 4 4 53		1 3 4 4 53			
48	Bad Debts Expense			(a) 7 6 2 75		7 6 2 75			
49	Depr. Exp.—Office Equipment			(e) 6 8 51		6 8 51			
50	Insurance Expense—Admin.			(d) 3 8 93		3 8 93			
51	Miscellaneous Expense—Admin.	1 5 6 1 41				1 5 6 1 41			
52	Payroll Taxes Expense—Admin.	2 5 2 9 95				2 5 2 9 95			
53	Property Tax Expense—Admin.	9 2 59				9 2 59			
54	Salary Expense—Admin.	15 3 0 9 90				15 3 0 9 90			
55	Supplies Expense—Admin.			(c) 2 7 3 46		2 7 3 46			
56	Gain on Plant Assets		1 5 5 93				1 5 5 93		
57	Miscellaneous Revenue								

	ACCOUNT TITLE	TRIAL BALANCE DEBIT	TRIAL BALANCE CREDIT	ADJUSTMENTS DEBIT	ADJUSTMENTS CREDIT	INCOME STATEMENT DEBIT	INCOME STATEMENT CREDIT	BALANCE SHEET DEBIT	BALANCE SHEET CREDIT	
58	Interest Expense	4 6 8 74				4 6 8 74				58
59	Loss on Plant Assets									59
60	Federal Income Tax			(g)3 0 2 5 67		3 0 2 5 67				60
61		938 8 1 1 12	938 8 1 1 12	5 5 7 5 73	5 5 7 5 73	153 0 2 7 86	160 2 4 8 21	789 7 0 2 07	782 4 8 1 72	61
62	*Net Income after Federal Income Tax*					7 2 2 0 35			7 2 2 0 35	62
63						160 2 4 8 21	160 2 4 8 21	789 7 0 2 07	789 7 0 2 07	63
64										64
65										65
66										66
67										67
68										68
69										69
70										70
71										71
72										72
73										73
74										74
75										75
76										76
77										77
78										78
79										79
80										80
81										81
82										82
83										83
84										84
85										85
86										86
87										87

Advant Company

Income Statement

For Month Ended May 31, 19--

				% OF NET SALES
Operating Revenue:				
Sales			159 82 2 56	100.0
Cost of Goods Sold:				
Finished Goods Inventory, May 1, 19--		38 40 8 94		
Cost of Goods Manufactured		134 93 4 05		
Total Cost of Finished Goods Available for Sale		173 34 2 99		
Less Finished Goods Inv., May 31, 19--		67 21 6 45		
Cost of Goods Sold		106 12 6 54		
Overapplied Overhead		2 6 9 72		
Net Cost of Goods Sold			105 85 6 82	66.2
Gross Profit on Operations			53 96 5 74	33.8
Operating Expenses:				
Selling Expenses:				
Advertising Expense	2 41 6 05			
Delivery Expense	5 84 2 24			
Depreciation Expense—Store Equipment	6 1 88			
Miscellaneous Expense—Sales	1 50 0 33			
Salary Expense—Sales	11 60 4 38			
Supplies Expense—Sales	1 34 4 53			
Total Selling Expenses		22 76 9 41		
Administrative Expenses:				
Bad Debts Expense	7 6 2 75			
Depreciation Expense—Office Equipment	6 8 51			
Insurance Expense—Administrative	3 8 93			
Miscellaneous Expense—Administrative	1 56 1 41			
Payroll Taxes Expense—Administrative	2 52 9 95			
Property Tax Expense—Administrative	9 2 59			
Salary Expense—Administrative	15 30 9 90			
Supplies Expense—Administrative	2 7 3 46			
Total Administrative Expenses		20 63 7 50		

Continue this income statement on the next page.

Advant Company

Income Statement (continued)

For Month Ended May 31, 19--

					% OF NET SALES
Total Operating Expenses				43 4 0 6 91	27.2
Net Income from Operations				10 5 5 8 83	
Other Revenue:					
Gain on Plant Assets			1 5 5 93		
Other Expense:					
Interest Expense			4 6 8 74		
Net Deduction				3 1 2 81	
Net Income before Federal Income Tax				10 2 4 6 02	6.4
Less Federal Income Tax				3 0 2 5 67	1.9
Net Income after Federal Income Tax				7 2 2 0 35	4.5

Advant Company

Balance Sheet

May 31, 19--

Assets											
Current Assets:											
Cash						62	2	6	1	46	
Petty Cash						3	7	5	00	
Accounts Receivable	115	3	0	0	30					
Less Allowance for Uncollectible Accounts	3	5	8	2	40	111	7	1	7	90	
Materials						44	1	1	2	28	
Work in Process						37	8	6	0	10	
Finished Goods						67	2	1	6	45	
Supplies — Factory						2	4	7	4	55	
Supplies — Sales						1	7	6	2	50	
Supplies — Administrative						5	2	0	74	
Prepaid Insurance						1	3	8	3	30	
Total Current Assets											329	6	8	4	28
Plant Assets:											
Factory Equipment	103	0	0	5	00					
Less Accum. Depr. — Factory Equipment	28	1	1	6	00	74	8	8	9	00	
Office Equipment	8	6	1	3	00					
Less Accum. Depr. — Office Equipment	2	8	3	7	81	5	7	7	5	19	
Store Equipment	7	7	7	1	50					
Less Accum. Depr. — Store Equipment	2	9	4	6	44	4	8	2	5	06	
Building	237	6	0	0	00					
Less Accum. Depr. — Building	23	7	6	0	00	213	8	4	0	00	
Land						99	4	4	5	89	
Total Plant Assets											398	7	7	5	14
Total Assets											728	4	5	9	42
Liabilities											
Current Liabilities:											
Accounts Payable						16	5	3	5	86	
Employees Income Tax Payable						9	9	0	3	90	
Federal Income Tax Payable						3	0	2	5	67	
FICA Tax Payable						12	6	0	4	97	

Continue this balance sheet on the next page.

Advant Company

Balance Sheet (continued)

May 31, 19--

Unemployment Tax Payable — Federal	5 88 32		
Unemployment Tax Payable — State	3 9 71 14		
Total Current Liabilities		46 6 2 9 86	
Long-Term Liability:			
Mortgage Payable		56 2 5 0 00	
Total Liabilities		102 8 7 9 86	
Stockholders' Equity			
Capital Stock	450 0 0 0 00		
Retained Earnings	175 5 7 9 56		
Total Stockholders' Equity		625 5 7 9 56	
Total Liabilities and Stockholders' Equity		728 4 5 9 42	

Processing and reporting cost accounting data
for a manufacturing business

Estimated Factory Overhead Costs	÷	Estimated Direct Labor Costs	=	Factory Overhead Applied Rate (as % of Direct Labor Cost)
$100,500.00	÷	$134,000.00 (13,400 hrs. × $10.00/hr.)	=	75%

[2, 4]

MATERIALS PURCHASES JOURNAL   PAGE 10

	DATE		ACCOUNT CREDITED	PURCH. NO.	POST. REF.	MATERIALS DR. ACCTS. PAY. CR.	
1	Jan. 19..	9	Thread Unlimited	631		3 0 0 00	1
2		10	Metals, Inc.	630		5 2 5 0 00	2
3		10	Cloth World	632		1 5 0 0 00	3
4		10	A.J. Moore Company	633		1 6 2 5 00	4
5		20	Plastics, Etc.	635		2 5 0 0 00	5
6		20	Plastics, Etc.	636		7 5 0 00	6
7		24	A.J. Moore Company	634		8 7 5 00	7
8		30	A.J. Moore Company	637		1 6 2 5 00	8
9		30	Sparkle Glass Company	638		1 8 7 5 00	9
10		31	Total			16 3 0 0 00	10
11						(1125) (2105)	11
12							12
13							13
14							14
15							15
16							16
17							17
18							18
19							19
20							20
21							21
22							22
23							23
24							24

GENERAL JOURNAL

PAGE 13

	DATE		ACCOUNT TITLE	POST. REF.	DEBIT	CREDIT	
1	19-- Jan.	15	Payroll Taxes Expense—Factory	5535	1 29 1 49		1
2			FICA Tax Payable	2120		6 84 88	2
3			Unemployment Tax Payable—Federal	2130		78 27	3
4			Unemployment Tax Payable—State	2135		5 28 34	4
5			M417				5
6		31	Payroll Taxes Expense—Factory	5535	1 28 8 98		6
7			FICA Tax Payable	2120		6 83 55	7
8			Unemployment Tax Payable—Federal	2130		78 12	8
9			Unemployment Tax Payable—State	2135		5 27 31	9
10			M432				10
11		31	Work in Process	1130	17 2 80 75		11
12			Materials	1125		17 2 80 75	12
13			M435				13
14		31	Factory Overhead	5505	8 21 4 85		14
15			Depreciation Expense—Factory Equip.	5510		1 0 85 00	15
16			Depreciation Expense—Building	5515		5 70 00	16
17			Heat, Light, and Power Expense	5520		2 5 91 13	17
18			Insurance Expense—Factory	5525		95 00	18
19			Miscellaneous Expense—Factory	5530		2 32 35	19
20			Payroll Taxes Expense—Factory	5535		2 5 80 47	20
21			Property Tax Expense—Factory	5540		3 26 40	21
22			Supplies Expense—Factory	5545		7 34 50	22
23			M436				23
24		31	Work in Process	1130	11 8 23 75		24
25			Factory Overhead	5505		11 8 23 75	25
26			M437				26
27		31	Income Summary	3120	1 75 10		27
28			Factory Overhead	5505		1 75 10	28
29			M438				29
30		31	Finished Goods	1135	41 5 00 75		30
31			Work in Process	1130		41 5 00 75	31
32			M439				32

GENERAL JOURNAL   PAGE 14

	DATE		ACCOUNT TITLE	POST. REF.	DEBIT	CREDIT	
1	19-- Jan.	31	Cost of Goods Sold	5105	34 8 3 9 25		1
2			Finished Goods	1135		34 8 3 9 25	2
3			M440				3
4							4
5							5
6							6
7							7
8							8
9							9
10							10
11							11
12							12
13							13
14							14
15							15
16							16
17							17
18							18
19							19
20							20
21							21
22							22
23							23
24							24
25							25
26							26
27							27
28							28
29							29
30							30
31							31
32							32

CASH PAYMENTS JOURNAL

[2,5]

	DATE	ACCOUNT TITLE	CHECK NO.	POST. REF.	GENERAL DEBIT	GENERAL CREDIT	ACCOUNTS PAYABLE DEBIT	PURCHASES DISCOUNT CREDIT	CASH CREDIT	
1	19— Jan. 15	Work in Process	891	1130	7890 00				8022 90	1
2		Factory Overhead		5505	189 00					2
3		Employees Income Tax Payable		2110		1076 22				3
4		FICA Tax Payable		2120		684 88				4
5	31	Work in Process	965	1130	7875 00				8007 30	5
6		Factory Overhead		5505	189 00					6
7		Employees Income Tax Payable		2110		1074 15				7
8		FICA Tax Payable		2120		683 55				8
9	31	Totals			19549 00	3518 80			16030 20	9
10										10
11										11
12										12
13										13
14										14
15										15
16										16
17										17
18										18
19										19
20										20
21										21
22										22
23										23
24										24

GENERAL LEDGER

ACCOUNT Materials   **ACCOUNT NO.** 1125

DATE	ITEM	POST. REF.	DEBIT	CREDIT	BALANCE DEBIT	BALANCE CREDIT
19-- Jan. 1	Balance	✔			14 4 4 0 00	
31		MP10	16 3 0 0 00		30 7 4 0 00	
31		G13		17 2 8 0 75	13 4 5 9 25	

ACCOUNT Work in Process   **ACCOUNT NO.** 1130

DATE	ITEM	POST. REF.	DEBIT	CREDIT	BALANCE DEBIT	BALANCE CREDIT
19-- Jan. 15		CP24	7 8 9 0 00		7 8 9 0 00	
31		CP24	7 8 7 5 00		15 7 6 5 00	
31		G13	17 2 8 0 75		33 0 4 5 75	
31		G13	11 8 2 3 75		44 8 6 9 50	
31		G13		41 5 0 0 75	3 3 6 8 75	

ACCOUNT Finished Goods   **ACCOUNT NO.** 1135

DATE	ITEM	POST. REF.	DEBIT	CREDIT	BALANCE DEBIT	BALANCE CREDIT
19-- Jan. 1	Balance	✔			19 8 4 0 00	
31		G13	41 5 0 0 75		61 3 4 0 75	
31		G14		34 8 3 9 25	26 5 0 1 50	

ACCOUNT Accounts Payable   **ACCOUNT NO.** 2105

DATE	ITEM	POST. REF.	DEBIT	CREDIT	BALANCE DEBIT	BALANCE CREDIT
19-- Jan. 31	Balance	✔			11 7 7 2 40	
31		MP10		16 3 0 0 00		4 5 2 7 60

ACCOUNT Employees Income Tax Payable   **ACCOUNT NO.** 2110

DATE	ITEM	POST. REF.	DEBIT	CREDIT	BALANCE DEBIT	BALANCE CREDIT
19-- Jan. 31	Balance	✔				1 0 2 4 10
15		CP24		1 0 7 6 22		2 1 0 0 32
31		CP24		1 0 7 4 15		3 1 7 4 47

ACCOUNT FICA Tax Payable   **ACCOUNT NO.** 2120

DATE	ITEM	POST. REF.	DEBIT	CREDIT	BALANCE DEBIT	BALANCE CREDIT
19-- Jan. 31	Balance	✔				1 3 0 3 40
15		CP24		6 8 4 88		1 9 8 8 28
15		G13		6 8 4 88		2 6 7 3 16
31		CP24		6 8 3 55		3 3 5 6 71
31		G13		6 8 3 55		4 0 4 0 26

GENERAL LEDGER

ACCOUNT Unemployment Tax Payable—Federal   **ACCOUNT NO.** 2130

DATE	ITEM	POST. REF.	DEBIT	CREDIT	BALANCE DEBIT	BALANCE CREDIT
19-- Jan. 31	Balance	✔				7 4 48
15		G13		7 8 27		1 5 2 75
31		G13		7 8 12		2 3 0 87

ACCOUNT Unemployment Tax Payable—State   **ACCOUNT NO.** 2135

DATE	ITEM	POST. REF.	DEBIT	CREDIT	BALANCE DEBIT	BALANCE CREDIT
19-- Jan. 31	Balance	✔				5 0 2 74
15		G13		5 2 8 34		1 0 3 1 08
31		G13		5 2 7 31		1 5 5 8 39

ACCOUNT Income Summary   **ACCOUNT NO.** 3120

DATE	ITEM	POST. REF.	DEBIT	CREDIT	BALANCE DEBIT	BALANCE CREDIT
19-- Jan. 31		G13	1 7 5 10		1 7 5 10	

ACCOUNT Cost of Goods Sold   **ACCOUNT NO.** 5105

DATE	ITEM	POST. REF.	DEBIT	CREDIT	BALANCE DEBIT	BALANCE CREDIT
19-- Jan. 31		G14	34 8 3 9 25		34 8 3 9 25	

ACCOUNT Factory Overhead   **ACCOUNT NO.** 5505

DATE	ITEM	POST. REF.	DEBIT	CREDIT	BALANCE DEBIT	BALANCE CREDIT
19-- Jan. 15		CP24	1 8 9 4 00		1 8 9 4 00	
31		CP24	1 8 9 0 00		3 7 8 4 00	
31		G13	8 2 1 4 85		11 9 9 8 85	
31		G13		11 8 2 3 75	1 7 5 10	
31		G13		1 7 5 10	—	

ACCOUNT Depreciation Expense—Factory Equipment   **ACCOUNT NO.** 5510

DATE	ITEM	POST. REF.	DEBIT	CREDIT	BALANCE DEBIT	BALANCE CREDIT
19-- Jan. 31	Balance	✔			1 0 8 5 00	
31		G13		1 0 8 5 00	—	

ACCOUNT Depreciation Expense—Building   **ACCOUNT NO.** 5515

DATE	ITEM	POST. REF.	DEBIT	CREDIT	BALANCE DEBIT	BALANCE CREDIT
19-- Jan. 31	Balance	✔			5 7 0 00	
31		G13		5 7 0 00		

GENERAL LEDGER

ACCOUNT Heat, Light, and Power Expense   ACCOUNT NO. 5520

DATE		ITEM	POST. REF.	DEBIT	CREDIT	BALANCE DEBIT	BALANCE CREDIT
19-- Jan.	31	Balance	✔			2 5 9 1 13	
	31		G13		2 5 9 1 13		

ACCOUNT Insurance Expense — Factory   ACCOUNT NO. 5525

DATE		ITEM	POST. REF.	DEBIT	CREDIT	BALANCE DEBIT	BALANCE CREDIT
19-- Jan.	31	Balance	✔			9 5 00	
	31		G13		9 5 00		

ACCOUNT Miscellaneous Expense — Factory   ACCOUNT NO. 5530

DATE		ITEM	POST. REF.	DEBIT	CREDIT	BALANCE DEBIT	BALANCE CREDIT
19-- Jan.	31	Balance	✔			2 3 2 35	
	31		G13		2 3 2 35		

ACCOUNT Payroll Taxes Expense — Factory   ACCOUNT NO. 5535

DATE		ITEM	POST. REF.	DEBIT	CREDIT	BALANCE DEBIT	BALANCE CREDIT
19-- Jan.	15		G13	1 2 9 1 49		1 2 9 1 49	
	31		G13	1 2 8 8 98		2 5 8 0 47	
	31		G13		2 5 8 0 47		

ACCOUNT Property Tax Expense — Factory   ACCOUNT NO. 5540

DATE		ITEM	POST. REF.	DEBIT	CREDIT	BALANCE DEBIT	BALANCE CREDIT
19-- Jan.	31	Balance	✔			3 2 6 40	
	31		G13		3 2 6 40		

ACCOUNT Supplies Expense — Factory   ACCOUNT NO. 5545

DATE		ITEM	POST. REF.	DEBIT	CREDIT	BALANCE DEBIT	BALANCE CREDIT
19-- Jan.	31	Balance	✔			7 3 4 50	
	31		G13		7 3 4 50		

MATERIALS LEDGER CARD

Article __Tubular Aluminum__   Acct. No. __110__
Reorder __35,000__   Minimum __15,000__   Location __Area A-10__

ORDERED			RECEIVED					ISSUED					BALANCE			
Date	Purchase Order No.	Quantity	Date	Purchase Order No.	Quantity	Unit Price	Value	Date	Requisition No.	Quantity	Unit Price	Value	Date	Quantity	Unit Price	Value
													19-- Jan. 1	24,600	0.15	3,690.00
								19-- Jan. 2	862	6,250	0.15	937.50	2	18,350	0.15	2,752.50
								3	863	6,125	0.15	918.75	3	12,225	0.15	1,833.75
19-- Jan. 3	630	35,000						10	866	1,530	0.15	229.50	10	10,695	0.15	1,604.25
			19-- Jan. 10	630	35,000	0.15	5,250.00						10	45,695	0.15	6,854.25
								11	867	8,500	0.15	1,275.00	11	37,195	0.15	5,579.25
								18	869	7,000	0.15	1,050.00	18	30,195	0.15	4,529.25
								24	872	1,800	0.15	270.00	24	28,395	0.15	4,259.25
								27	874	6,250	0.15	937.50	27	22,145	0.15	3,321.75

MATERIALS LEDGER CARD

Article __Sheet Aluminum__   Acct. No. __120__
Reorder __9,000__   Minimum __3,000__   Location __Area A-20__

ORDERED			RECEIVED					ISSUED					BALANCE			
Date	Purchase Order No.	Quantity	Date	Purchase Order No.	Quantity	Unit Price	Value	Date	Requisition No.	Quantity	Unit Price	Value	Date	Quantity	Unit Price	Value
													19-- Jan. 1	6,500	0.25	1,625.00
								19-- Jan. 10	866	170	0.25	42.50	10	6,330	0.25	1,582.50
								27	873	1,800	0.25	450.00	27	4,530	0.25	1,132.50

MATERIALS LEDGER CARD

Article __Vinyl Strap__ Acct. No. __210__
Reorder __50,000__ Minimum __27,000__ Location __Area B-10__

ORDERED			RECEIVED					ISSUED					BALANCE			
Date	Purchase Order No.	Quantity	Date	Purchase Order No.	Quantity	Unit Price	Value	Date	Requisition No.	Quantity	Unit Price	Value	Date	Quantity	Unit Price	Value
													19-- Jan. 1	48,200	0.05	2,410.00
								19-- Jan. 5	864	15,000	0.05	750.00	5	33,200	0.05	1,660.00
								6	865	7,000	0.05	350.00	6	26,200	0.05	1,310.00
19-- Jan. 6	635	50,000						19	870	8,500	0.05	425.00	19	17,700	0.05	885.00
			19-- Jan. 20	635	50,000	0.05	2,500.00						20	67,700	0.05	3,385.00
								24	871	18,000	0.05	900.00	24	49,700	0.05	2,485.00
								31	875	15,000	0.05	750.00	31	34,700	0.05	1,735.00

MATERIALS LEDGER CARD

Article __Polyester Fabric__ Acct. No. __310__
Reorder __1,500__ Minimum __900__ Location __Area B-20__

ORDERED			RECEIVED					ISSUED					BALANCE			
Date	Purchase Order No.	Quantity	Date	Purchase Order No.	Quantity	Unit Price	Value	Date	Requisition No.	Quantity	Unit Price	Value	Date	Quantity	Unit Price	Value
													19-- Jan. 1	1,800	1.00	1,800.00
								19-- Jan. 3	863	1,050	1.00	1,050.00	3	750	1.00	750.00
19-- Jan. 3	632	1,500	19-- Jan. 10	632	1,500	1.00	1,500.00						10	2,250	1.00	2,250.00
								11	867	1,360	1.00	1,360.00	11	890	1.00	890.00
23	639	1,500														

MATERIALS LEDGER CARD

Article __Cushion 18×18__ Acct. No. __410__
Reorder __650__ Minimum __300__ Location __Area C-10__

ORDERED			RECEIVED					ISSUED					BALANCE			
Date	Purchase Order No.	Quantity	Date	Purchase Order No.	Quantity	Unit Price	Value	Date	Requisition No.	Quantity	Unit Price	Value	Date	Quantity	Unit Price	Value
													19-- Jan. 1	450	2.50	1,125.00
								19-- Jan. 3	863	175	2.50	437.50	3	275	2.50	687.50
19-- Jan. 3	633	650	19-- Jan. 10	633	650	2.50	1,625.00						10	925	2.50	2,312.50
								11	867	680	2.50	1,700.00	11	245	2.50	612.50
16	637	650	30	637	650	2.50	1,625.00						30	895	2.50	2,237.50

MATERIALS LEDGER CARD

Article Cushion 18×42   Acct. No. 420
Reorder 175   Minimum 75   Location Area C-20

ORDERED			RECEIVED					ISSUED					BALANCE			
Date	Purchase Order No.	Quantity	Date	Purchase Order No.	Quantity	Unit Price	Value	Date	Requisition No.	Quantity	Unit Price	Value	Date	Quantity	Unit Price	Value
													19-- Jan. 1	250	5.00	1,250.00
								19-- Jan. 3	863	175	5.00	875.00	3	75	5.00	375.00
19-- Jan. 5	634	175	19-- Jan. 24	634	175	5.00	875.00						24	250	5.00	1,250.00

MATERIALS LEDGER CARD

Article Glide   Acct. No. 510
Reorder 5,000   Minimum 3,500   Location Area D-10

ORDERED			RECEIVED					ISSUED					BALANCE			
Date	Purchase Order No.	Quantity	Date	Purchase Order No.	Quantity	Unit Price	Value	Date	Requisition No.	Quantity	Unit Price	Value	Date	Quantity	Unit Price	Value
													19-- Jan. 1	5,400	0.15	810.00
								19-- Jan. 5	864	1,000	0.15	150.00	5	4,400	0.15	660.00
								6	865	1,050	0.15	157.50	6	3,350	0.15	502.50
19-- Jan. 9	636	5,000						13	868	340	0.15	51.00	13	3,010	0.15	451.50
								19	870	1,360	0.15	204.00	19	1,650	0.15	247.50
			19-- Jan. 20	636	5,000	0.15	750.00						20	6,650	0.15	997.50
								24	871	1,200	0.15	180.00	24	5,450	0.15	817.50
								27	873	400	0.15	60.00	27	5,050	0.15	757.50
								31	875	1,000	0.15	150.00	31	4,050	0.15	607.50

MATERIALS LEDGER CARD

Article Thread _____ Acct. No. _____610_____
Reorder _____600_____ Minimum _____400_____ Location _____Area D-15_____

ORDERED			RECEIVED					ISSUED					BALANCE			
Date	Purchase Order No.	Quantity	Date	Purchase Order No.	Quantity	Unit Price	Value	Date	Requisition No.	Quantity	Unit Price	Value	Date	Quantity	Unit Price	Value
													19-- Jan. 1	460	0.50	230.00
								19-- Jan. 3	863	350	0.50	175.00	3	110	0.50	55.00
19-- Jan. 3	631	600	19-- Jan. 9	631	600	0.50	300.00						9	710	0.50	355.00
								11	867	340	0.50	170.00	11	370	0.50	185.00
23	640	600														

MATERIALS LEDGER CARD

Article Tempered Glass Table Top _____ Acct. No. _____710_____
Reorder _____125_____ Minimum _____50_____ Location _____Area D-30_____

ORDERED			RECEIVED					ISSUED					BALANCE			
Date	Purchase Order No.	Quantity	Date	Purchase Order No.	Quantity	Unit Price	Value	Date	Requisition No.	Quantity	Unit Price	Value	Date	Quantity	Unit Price	Value
													19-- Jan. 1	100	15.00	1,500.00
								19-- Jan. 13	868	85	15.00	1,275.00	13	15	15.00	225.00
19-- Jan. 16	638	125	19-- Jan. 30	638	125	15.00	1,875.00						30	140	15.00	2,100.00

COST SHEET

Job. No. __321__

Item __G110 Chair__

No. of items __250__

Ordered for __Stock__

Date __January 2, 19--__

Date wanted __January 10, 19--__

Date completed __January 10, 19--__

Req. No.	Amount	Date	Amount	Date	Amount	Item	Amount
	DIRECT MATERIALS		DIRECT LABOR			SUMMARY	
862	937.50	Jan. 6	1,250.00			Direct Materials	1,837.50
864	900.00	10	500.00			Direct Labor	1,750.00
	1,837.50		1,750.00			Factory Overhead	
						(75% of direct	
						labor costs)	1,312.50
						Total Cost	4,900.00
						No. units finished	250
						Cost per unit	19.60

COST SHEET

Job. No. __322__

Item __E610 Chaise Lounge__

No. of items __175__

Ordered for __Stock__

Date __January 3, 19--__

Date wanted __January 13, 19--__

Date completed __January 13, 19--__

Req. No.	Amount	Date	Amount	Date	Amount	Item	Amount
	DIRECT MATERIALS		DIRECT LABOR			SUMMARY	
863	3,456.25	Jan. 6	1,710.00			Direct Materials	3,963.75
865	507.50	13	2,140.00			Direct Labor	3,850.00
	3,963.75		3,850.00			Factory Overhead	
						(75% of direct	
						labor costs)	2,887.50
						Total Cost	10,701.25
						No. units finished	175
						Cost per unit	61.15

COST SHEET

Job. No. _____323_____   Date _____January 10, 19--_____

Item _____E710 Table_____   Date wanted _____January 17, 19--_____

No. of items _____85_____   Date completed _____January 17, 19--_____

Ordered for _____Stock_____

Req. No.	DIRECT MATERIALS Amount	Date	DIRECT LABOR Amount	Date	Amount	SUMMARY Item	Amount
866	272.00	Jan. 13	1,020.00			Direct Materials	1,598.00
868	1,326.00	17	510.00			Direct Labor	1,530.00
	1,598.00		1,530.00			Factory Overhead	
						(75% of direct	
						labor costs)	1,147.50
						Total Cost	4,275.50
						No. units finished	85
						Cost per unit	50.30

COST SHEET

Job. No. _____324_____   Date _____January 11, 19--_____

Item _____E510 Chair_____   Date wanted _____January 26, 19--_____

No. of items _____340_____   Date completed _____January 25, 19--_____

Ordered for _____Stock_____

Req. No.	DIRECT MATERIALS Amount	Date	DIRECT LABOR Amount	Date	Amount	SUMMARY Item	Amount
867	4,505.00	Jan. 13	1,270.00			Direct Materials	5,134.00
870	629.00	20	2,165.00			Direct Labor	4,760.00
	5,134.00	25	1,325.00			Factory Overhead	
			4,760.00			(75% of direct	
						labor costs)	3,570.00
						Total Cost	13,464.00
						No. units finished	340
						Cost per unit	39.60

COST SHEET

Job. No. ___325___   Date ___January 18, 19--___

Item ___G210 Chaise Lounge___   Date wanted ___January 28, 19--___

No. of items ___200___   Date completed ___January 27, 19--___

Ordered for ___Stock___

Req. No.	Amount	Date	Amount	Date	Amount	Item	Amount
	DIRECT MATERIALS		DIRECT LABOR			SUMMARY	
869	1,050.00	Jan. 20	750.00			Direct Materials	2,130.00
871	1,080.00	27	1,250.00			Direct Labor	2,000.00
	2,130.00		2,000.00			Factory Overhead	
						(75% of direct	
						labor costs)	1,500.00
						Total Cost	5,630.00
						No. units finished	200
						Cost per unit	28.15

COST SHEET

Job. No. ___326___   Date ___January 24, 19--___

Item ___G310 Table___   Date wanted ___January 31, 19--___

No. of items ___100___   Date completed ___January 31, 19--___

Ordered for ___Stock___

Req. No.	Amount	Date	Amount	Date	Amount	Item	Amount
	DIRECT MATERIALS		DIRECT LABOR			SUMMARY	
872	270.00	Jan. 27	665.00			Direct Materials	780.00
873	510.00	31	335.00			Direct Labor	1,000.00
	780.00		1,000.00			Factory Overhead	
						(75% of direct	
						labor costs)	750.00
						Total Cost	2,530.00
						No. units finished	100
						Cost per unit	25.30

COST SHEET

Job. No. _____327_____

Item _____G110 Chair_____

No. of items _____250_____

Ordered for _____Stock_____

Date _____January 27, 19--_____

Date wanted _____February 7, 19--_____

Date completed _____

DIRECT MATERIALS		DIRECT LABOR				SUMMARY	
Req. No.	Amount	Date	Amount	Date	Amount	Item	Amount
874	937.50	Jan. 27	290.00			*Factory Overhead*	
875	900.00	31	585.00			*for January*	
						(75% of direct	
						labor costs)	656.25

FINISHED GOODS LEDGER CARD

Description __Chair__
Minimum __100__

Stock No. __E510__
Location __Area F-20__

MANUFACTURED/RECEIVED					SHIPPED/ISSUED					BALANCE			
Date	Job No.	Quan-tity	Unit Cost	Total Cost	Date	Sales Invoice No.	Quan-tity	Unit Cost	Total Cost	Date	Quan-tity	Unit Cost	Total Cost
										19-- Jan. 1	200	39.00	7,800.00
19-- Jan. 25	324	340	39.60	13,464.00						25	200	39.00 }	
											340	39.60 }	21,264.00
					19-- Jan. 26	437	200	39.00 }					
							200	39.60 }	15,720.00	26	140	39.60	5,544.00

FINISHED GOODS LEDGER CARD

Description __Chaise Lounge__
Minimum __50__

Stock No. __E610__
Location __Area G-20__

MANUFACTURED/RECEIVED					SHIPPED/ISSUED					BALANCE			
Date	Job No.	Quan-tity	Unit Cost	Total Cost	Date	Sales Invoice No.	Quan-tity	Unit Cost	Total Cost	Date	Quan-tity	Unit Cost	Total Cost
										19-- Jan. 1	50	60.00	3,000.00
19-- Jan. 13	322	175	61.15	10,701.25						13	50	60.00 }	
											175	61.15 }	13,701.25
					19-- Jan. 17	434	50	60.00 }					
							75	61.15 }	7,586.25	17	100	61.15	6,115.00

FINISHED GOODS LEDGER CARD

Description __Table_____ Stock No. __E710_____
Minimum __25_____ Location __Area H-20_____

MANUFACTURED/RECEIVED					SHIPPED/ISSUED					BALANCE			
Date	Job No.	Quantity	Unit Cost	Total Cost	Date	Sales Invoice No.	Quantity	Unit Cost	Total Cost	Date	Quantity	Unit Cost	Total Cost
										19-- Jan. 1	35	51.00	1,785.00
19-- Jan. 17	323	85	50.30	4,275.50						17	35	51.00 ⎫	
											85	50.30 ⎬	6,060.50
					19-- Jan. 25	436	35	51.00 ⎫					
							15	50.30 ⎬	2,539.50	25	70	50.30	3,521.00

FINISHED GOODS LEDGER CARD

Description __Chair_____ Stock No. __G-110_____
Minimum __200_____ Location __Area F-10_____

MANUFACTURED/RECEIVED					SHIPPED/ISSUED					BALANCE			
Date	Job No.	Quantity	Unit Cost	Total Cost	Date	Sales Invoice No.	Quantity	Unit Cost	Total Cost	Date	Quantity	Unit Cost	Total Cost
										19-- Jan. 1	250	18.50	4,625.00
					19-- Jan. 9	433	100	18.50	1,850.00	9	150	18.50	2,775.00
19-- Jan. 10	321	250	19.60	4,900.00						10	150	18.50 ⎫	
											250	19.60 ⎬	7,675.00
					31	439	150	18.50 ⎫					
							50	19.60 ⎬	3,755.00	31	200	19.60	3,920.00

FINISHED GOODS LEDGER CARD

Description __Chaise Lounge__   Stock No. __G210__
Minimum __50__   Location __Area G-10__

MANUFACTURED/RECEIVED					SHIPPED/ISSUED					BALANCE			
Date	Job No.	Quan-tity	Unit Cost	Total Cost	Date	Sales Invoice No.	Quan-tity	Unit Cost	Total Cost	Date	Quan-tity	Unit Cost	Total Cost
										19--Jan. 1	60	27.50	1,650.00
19--Jan. 27	325	200	28.15	5,630.00						27	60	27.50 }	
											200	28.15 }	7,280.00
					19--Jan. 30	438	60	27.50 }					
							40	28.15 }	2,776.00	30	160	28.15	4,504.00

FINISHED GOODS LEDGER CARD

Description __Table__   Stock No. __G310__
Minimum __25__   Location __Area H-10__

MANUFACTURED/RECEIVED					SHIPPED/ISSUED					BALANCE			
Date	Job No.	Quan-tity	Unit Cost	Total Cost	Date	Sales Invoice No.	Quan-tity	Unit Cost	Total Cost	Date	Quan-tity	Unit Cost	Total Cost
										19--Jan. 1	40	24.50	980.00
					19--Jan. 19	435	25	24.50	612.50	19	15	24.50	367.50
19--Jan. 31	326	100	25.30	2,530.00						31	15	24.50 }	
											100	25.30 }	2,897.50

Materials Ledger	Cost Ledger	Finished Goods Ledger
Proof	Proof	Proof
$ 3,321.75	$1,837.50	$ 5,544.00
1,132.50	875.00	6,115.00
1,735.00	656.25	3,521.00
890.00	$3,368.75	3,920.00
2,237.50		4,504.00
1,250.00		2,897.50
607.50		$26,501.50
185.00		
2,100.00		
$13,459.25		

[8]

Leisuretime, Inc.

Statement of Cost of Goods Manufactured

For Month Ended January 31, 19--

Direct Materials:		
Materials Inventory, January 1, 19--	14 4 4 0 00	
Materials Purchased	16 3 0 0 00	
Total Materials Available During January	30 7 4 0 00	
Less Materials Inventory, January 31, 19--	13 4 5 9 25	
Cost of Direct Materials Placed in Process		17 2 8 0 75
Direct Labor		15 7 6 5 00
Factory Overhead Applied		11 8 2 3 75
Total Cost of Work Placed in Process		44 8 6 9 50
Work in Process Inventory, January 1, 19--		0
Total Cost of Work in Process During January		44 8 6 9 50
Less Work in Process Inventory, January 31, 19--		3 3 6 8 75
Cost of Goods Manufactured		41 5 0 0 75

[9, 10]

Leisuretime, Inc.

Work Sheet

For Month Ended January 31, 19--

	ACCOUNT TITLE	TRIAL BALANCE DEBIT	TRIAL BALANCE CREDIT	ADJUSTMENTS DEBIT	ADJUSTMENTS CREDIT	INCOME STATEMENT DEBIT	INCOME STATEMENT CREDIT	BALANCE SHEET DEBIT	BALANCE SHEET CREDIT
1	Cash	31130 73						31130 73	
2	Petty Cash	250 00						250 00	
3	Accounts Receivable	46687 50						46687 50	
4	Allowance for Uncollectible Accounts		806 00		(a) 270 00				1076 00
5	Materials	13459 25						13459 25	
6	Work in Process	3368 75						3368 75	
7	Finished Goods	26501 50						26501 50	
8	Supplies—Factory	1237 25						1237 25	
9	Supplies—Sales	1553 50			(b) 442 15			1111 35	
10	Supplies—Administrative	397 10			(c) 94 63			302 47	
11	Prepaid Insurance	280 80			(d) 23 40			257 40	
12	Factory Equipment	113100 00						113100 00	
13	Accum. Depr.—Factory Equipment		33930 00						33930 00
14	Office Equipment	4320 00						4320 00	
15	Accum. Depr.—Office Equipment		1296 00		(e) 34 25				1330 25
16	Store Equipment	3895 00						3895 00	
17	Accum. Depr.—Store Equipment		1363 00		(f) 31 00				1394 00
18	Building	150000 00						150000 00	
19	Accum. Depr.—Building		22500 00						22500 00
20	Land	50600 00						50600 00	
21	Accounts Payable		4527 60						4527 60
22	Employees Inc. Tax Payable		3174 47						3174 47
23	Federal Income Tax Payable				(g) 2092 76				2092 76
24	FICA Tax Payable		4040 26						4040 26
25	Unemploy. Tax Payable—Federal		230 87						230 87
26	Unemploy. Tax Payable—State		1558 39						1558 39
27	Dividends Payable								

	ACCOUNT TITLE	TRIAL BALANCE DEBIT	TRIAL BALANCE CREDIT	ADJUSTMENTS DEBIT	ADJUSTMENTS CREDIT	INCOME STATEMENT DEBIT	INCOME STATEMENT CREDIT	BALANCE SHEET DEBIT	BALANCE SHEET CREDIT
28	Mortgage Payable		30 000 00						30 000 00
29	Capital Stock		200 000 00						200 000 00
30	Retained Earnings		134 2 5 8 71						134 2 5 8 71
31	Dividends								
32	Income Summary	1 75 10				1 75 10			
33	Sales		58 9 5 5 00				58 9 5 5 00		
34	Cost of Goods Sold	34 8 3 9 25				34 8 3 9 25			
35	Factory Overhead								
36	Depr. Expense — Factory Equipment								
37	Depr. Expense — Building								
38	Heat, Light, and Power Expense								
39	Insurance Expense — Factory								
40	Miscellaneous Expense — Factory								
41	Payroll Taxes Exp. — Factory								
42	Property Tax Expense — Factory								
43	Supplies Expense — Factory								
44	Advertising Expense	8 3 5 95				8 3 5 95			
45	Delivery Expense	2 0 5 3 45				2 0 5 3 45			
46	Depr. Exp. — Store Equipment			(f) 3 1 00		3 1 00			
47	Miscellaneous Expense — Sales	5 1 9 10				5 1 9 10			
48	Salary Expense — Sales	4 0 1 5 00				4 0 1 5 00			
49	Supplies Expense — Sales			(b) 4 4 2 15		4 4 2 15			
50	Bad Debts Expense			(a) 2 7 0 00		2 7 0 00			
51	Depr. Exp. — Office Equipment			(e) 3 4 25		3 4 25			
52	Insurance Expense — Administrative			(d) 2 3 40		2 3 40			
53	Miscellaneous Expense — Admin.	4 4 1 85				4 4 1 85			
54	Payroll Taxes Expense — Admin.	1 2 2 8 92				1 2 2 8 92			
55	Property Tax Exp. — Admin.	5 6 90				5 6 90			
56	Salary Expense — Administrative	5 2 9 5 00				5 2 9 5 00			
57	Supplies Expense — Administrative			(c) 9 4 63		9 4 63			

	ACCOUNT TITLE	TRIAL BALANCE DEBIT	TRIAL BALANCE CREDIT	ADJUSTMENTS DEBIT	ADJUSTMENTS CREDIT	INCOME STATEMENT DEBIT	INCOME STATEMENT CREDIT	BALANCE SHEET DEBIT	BALANCE SHEET CREDIT	
58	Utilities Expense—Administrative	9 8 40				9 8 40				58
59	Gain on Plant Assets									59
60	Miscellaneous Revenue									60
61	Interest Expense	3 0 0 00				3 0 0 00				61
62	Loss on Plant Assets									62
63	Federal Income Tax			(g) 2 0 9 2 76		2 0 9 2 76				63
64		496 6 40 30	496 6 40 30	2 9 8 8 19	2 9 8 8 19	52 8 4 7 11	58 9 5 5 00	446 2 21 20	440 1 13 31	64
65	Net Income after Federal Income Tax					6 1 0 7 89			6 1 0 7 89	65
66						58 9 5 5 00	58 9 5 5 00	446 2 21 20	446 2 21 20	66
67										67
68										68
69										69
70										70
71										71
72										72
73										73
74										74
75										75
76										76
77										77
78										78
79										79
80										80
81										81
82										82
83										83
84										84
85										85
86										86
87										87

Leisuretime, Inc.

Income Statement

For Month Ended January 31, 19--

					% OF NET SALES
Operating Revenue:					
Sales				58 9 5 5 00	100.0
Cost of Goods Sold:					
Finished Goods Inventory, Jan. 1, 19--			19 8 4 0 00		
Cost of Goods Manufactured			41 5 0 0 75		
Total Cost of Finished Goods Available for Sale			61 3 4 0 75		
Less Finished Goods Inv., Jan. 31, 19--			26 5 0 1 50		
Cost of Goods Sold			34 8 3 9 25		
Underapplied Overhead			1 7 5 10		
Net Cost of Goods Sold				35 0 1 4 35	59.4
Gross Profit on Operations				23 9 4 0 65	40.6
Operating Expenses:					
Selling Expenses:					
Advertising Expense		8 3 5 95			
Delivery Expense	2 0 5 3 45				
Depreciation Expense—Store Equip.		3 1 00			
Miscellaneous Expense—Sales		5 1 9 10			
Salary Expense—Sales	4 0 1 5 00				
Supplies Expense—Sales		4 4 2 15			
Total Selling Expenses			7 8 9 6 65		
Administrative Expenses:					
Bad Debts Expense		2 7 0 00			
Depreciation Expense—Office Equip.		3 4 25			
Insurance Expense—Administrative		2 3 40			
Miscellaneous Expense—Admin.		4 4 1 85			
Payroll Taxes Expense—Admin.	1 2 2 8 92				
Property Tax Expense—Admin.		5 6 90			
Salary Expense—Administrative	5 2 9 5 00				
Supplies Expense—Administrative		9 4 63			
Utilities Expense—Administrative		9 8 40			
Total Administrative Expenses			7 5 4 3 35		

Continue this income statement on the next page.

Leisuretime, Inc.

Income Statement (continued)

For Month Ended January 31, 19--

		% OF NET SALES
Total Operating Expenses	15 4 4 0 00	26.2
Net Income from Operations	8 5 0 0 65	
Other Expense:		
Interest Expense	3 0 0 00	
Net Income before Federal Income Tax	8 2 0 0 65	13.9
Less Federal Income Tax	2 0 9 2 76	3.5
Net Income after Federal Income Tax	6 1 0 7 89	10.4

Leisuretime, Inc.

Balance Sheet

January 31, 19--

Assets					
Current Assets:					
Cash			31 1 3 0 73		
Petty Cash			2 5 0 00		
Accounts Receivable	46 6 8 7 50				
Less Allowance for Uncollectible Accounts	1 0 7 6 00		45 6 1 1 50		
Materials			13 4 5 9 25		
Work in Process			3 3 6 8 75		
Finished Goods			26 5 0 1 50		
Supplies — Factory			1 2 3 7 25		
Supplies — Sales			1 1 1 1 35		
Supplies — Administrative			3 0 2 47		
Prepaid Insurance			2 5 7 40		
Total Current Assets				123 2 3 0 20	
Plant Assets:					
Factory Equipment	113 1 0 0 00				
Less Accum. Depr. — Factory Equip.	33 9 3 0 00		79 1 7 0 00		
Office Equipment	4 3 2 0 00				
Less Accum. Depr. — Office Equip.	1 3 3 0 25		2 9 8 9 75		
Store Equipment	3 8 9 5 00				
Less Accum. Depr. — Store Equip.	1 3 9 4 00		2 5 0 1 00		
Building	150 0 0 0 00				
Less Accum. Depr. — Building	22 5 0 0 00		127 5 0 0 00		
Land			50 6 0 0 00		
Total Plant Assets				262 7 6 0 75	
Total Assets				385 9 9 0 95	
Liabilities					
Current Liabilities:					
Accounts Payable			4 5 2 7 60		
Employees Income Tax Payable			3 1 7 4 47		
Federal Income Tax Payable			2 0 9 2 76		
FICA Tax Payable			4 0 4 0 26		

Continue this balance sheet on the next page.

Leisuretime, Inc.

Balance Sheet (continued)

January 31, 19--

Unemployment Tax Payable—Federal		2 30 87		
Unemployment Tax Payable—State		1 5 5 8 39		
Total Current Liabilities			15 6 2 4 35	
Long-Term Liability:				
Mortgage Payable			30 0 0 0 00	
Total Liabilities			45 6 2 4 35	
Stockholders' Equity				
Capital Stock		200 0 0 0 00		
Retained Earnings		140 3 6 6 60		
Total Stockholders' Equity			340 3 6 6 60	
Total Liabilities & Stockholders' Equity			385 9 9 0 95	

Perfect Score. 35

Deduct .... ___

Your Score .... ___

Name _____

Date _____ Class _____

Checked by _____

STUDY GUIDE 23

UNIT A—Analyzing, Forming, and Expanding a Partnership

DIRECTIONS: For each item below, select the choice that best completes the sentence. Print the letter identifying your choice in the Answers column.

	Answers	For Scoring
0. A business in which two or more persons combine their assets and skills is called **(A)** mutual agency **(B)** a partnership **(C)** a corporation **(D)** a partnership agreement...	B	0. ✔
1. Each member of a partnership is called **(A)** a worker **(B)** an incorporator **(C)** a partner **(D)** none of these	C	1.
2. A partner's capital account is located in a general ledger's **(A)** capital division **(B)** asset division **(C)** liabilities division **(D)** revenue division....................	A	2.
3. A partner's drawing account is located in a general ledger's **(A)** asset division **(B)** revenue division **(C)** liabilities division **(D)** capital division	D	3.
4. Goodwill is recorded on a partnership's records **(A)** if the partners agree that a new partner's investment results in goodwill **(B)** if a new partner invests assets with a value less than the share of equity received **(C)** if the partnership is admitting its third partner **(D)** none of these...	A	4.
5. Goodwill is distributed among existing partners according to **(A)** their individual shares of equity **(B)** the partnership agreement **(C)** the amount of cash invested by the new partner **(D)** none of these...	B	5.
6. An entry to show distribution of goodwill is recorded in a partnership's **(A)** general journal **(B)** cash receipts journal **(C)** cash payments journal **(D)** none of these...	A	6.
7. When a new partner is admitted to an existing partnership **(A)** business increases **(B)** the existing partnership is terminated and a new partnership is created **(C)** the new partner must invest cash **(D)** the existing partnership continues and the new partner becomes a part of it	B	7.
8. Partners A and B each have $15,000.00 equity in a partnership and changes in equity are shared equally. A new partner pays each existing partner $15,000.00 personally for a one-third share in the partnership. Partner A, Capital is **(A)** increased by $15,000.00 **(B)** decreased by $5,000.00 **(C)** not changed **(D)** none of these...	B	8.
9. Partners A and B each have $10,000.00 equity in a partnership and changes in equity are shared equally. A new partner invests $10,000.00 for a one-third share in the partnership. Partner B, Capital is **(A)** decreased by $5,000.00 **(B)** increased by $5,000.00 **(C)** not changed **(D)** none of these	C	9.

UNIT B—Analyzing Transactions for Partners' Initial Investments and for Admitting New Partners

Directions: For each transaction below, print in the proper Answers column the identifying letters of the accounts to be debited and credited.

Account Titles

A. Cash
B. Equipment
C. Goodwill
D. Partner A, Capital
E. Partner B, Capital
F. Partner C, Capital
G. Partner D, Capital
H. Partner E, Capital

Transactions

0–0. Received cash from Partner A as initial investment ....

10–11. Accepted cash and equipment from Partner B as initial investment ....

12–13. Partners A and B personally sold one-third equity to Partner C ....

14–15. Partners A and B admitted Partner D with an equity equal to cash investment ....

16–17. Partners A and B admitted Partner E with an equity greater than cash investment.....................................

18–19. Partners A and B admitted Partner C for a cash investment with goodwill involved ....

Answers		For Scoring	
Stmt.	Sec.	Stmt.	Sec.
A	D	0. ✔	0. ✔
A, B	E	10.	11.
D, E	F	12.	13.
A	G	14.	15.
A, D, E	H	16.	17.
A, C	D, E, F	18.	19.

UNIT C—Analyzing Partnership Accounting Practices and Concepts

Directions: Place a check mark in the proper Answers column to show whether each of the following statements is true or false.

0. Each partner is an agent of a partnership..

20. When a partner invests assets and liabilities of an existing business, the information for the journal entry is taken from the existing business' balance sheet..

21. Legally, a partnership must be formed with a written agreement ....

22. Agreeing to the value of assets and liabilities being invested by a partner is an application of the accounting concept Business Entity ....

23. A partnership agreement should state the length of time the partnership is to exist ....

24. When a new partner is admitted to an existing partnership, a new set of accounting records must be prepared..

25. Except for recording owners' equity and income taxes, accounting procedures for a partnership are similar to those for a corporation ....

26. Death of a partner terminates a partnership ....

27. One partner cannot bind a partnership in a contract without the approval of other partners ....

28. A written agreement setting forth the conditions under which a partnership is to operate is known as a partnership agreement.....................................

29. The value of a business in excess of the total investment of owners is called goodwill ....

30. A right of all partners to contract for a partnership is called mutual agency...

31. Assets taken out of a business for the owner's personal use are called withdrawals ....

32. To avoid misunderstanding, a partnership agreement should always be in writing ....

33. The value of assets a partner takes out of a partnership is recorded in an account titled *Capital*..

34. If Partners A and B personally sell part of their equity to Partner C for cash, the total equity of the partnership increases..

35. The account *Goodwill* is located in the Intangible Assets section of a general ledger..

Answers		For
True	False	Scoring
✔		0. ✔
✔		20.
	✔	21.
	✔	22.
✔		23.
	✔	24.
✔		25.
✔		26.
	✔	27.
✔		28.
✔		29.
✔		30.
✔		31.
✔		32.
	✔	33.
	✔	34.
✔		35.

Forming a partnership   PROBLEM 23-1, p. 527

CASH RECEIPTS JOURNAL

PAGE 1

	DATE		ACCOUNT TITLE	DOC. NO.	POST. REF.	GENERAL DEBIT	GENERAL CREDIT	ACCOUNTS RECEIVABLE CREDIT	SALES CREDIT	SALES TAX PAYABLE CREDIT	CASH DEBIT	
1	19-- July	1	Mary Chang, Capital	R1			31 875 00				31 875 00	1
2		1	Accounts Receivable	R2		2 775 16					11 639 44	2
3			Merchandise Inventory			19 480 25						3
4			Supplies			496 73						4
5			Equipment			7 023 04						5
6			Allowance for Uncollectible Accounts				55 49					6
7			Accounts Payable				9 484 13					7
8			Ruth Wilson, Capital				31 875 00					8
9												9
10												10

Admitting a new partner with no change in total equity   PROBLEM 23-2, p. 528

GENERAL JOURNAL

PAGE 2

	DATE		ACCOUNT TITLE	POST. REF.	DEBIT	CREDIT	
1	19-- Oct.	1	Harold Miller, Capital		15 000 00		1
2			Thad Roman, Capital		15 000 00		2
3			Jean Dawson, Capital			30 000 00	3
4			M14				4
5							5
6							6

Admitting a partner with equity equal to investment   PROBLEM 23-3, p. 528

CASH RECEIPTS JOURNAL

PAGE 3

	DATE		ACCOUNT TITLE	DOC. NO.	POST. REF.	GENERAL DEBIT	GENERAL CREDIT	ACCOUNTS RECEIVABLE CREDIT	SALES CREDIT	SALES TAX PAYABLE CREDIT	CASH DEBIT	
1	19-- Mar.	1	Jon Wall, Capital	R100			50 000 00				50 000 00	1
2												2
3												3

Admitting a partner with equity greater than investment   PROBLEM 23-4, p. 529

CASH RECEIPTS JOURNAL

PAGE 5

	DATE		ACCOUNT TITLE	DOC. NO.	POST. REF.	GENERAL DEBIT	GENERAL CREDIT	ACCOUNTS RECEIVABLE CREDIT	SALES CREDIT	SALES TAX PAYABLE CREDIT	CASH DEBIT	
1	19-- Sept.	1	Quint Taylor, Capital	R127			20 000 00				20 000 00	1
2												2
3												3

GENERAL JOURNAL

PAGE 2

	DATE		ACCOUNT TITLE	POST. REF.	DEBIT	CREDIT	
1	19-- Sept.	1	Donald Newsome, Capital		5 000 00		1
2			Teresa Jones, Capital		5 000 00		2
3			Quint Taylor, Capital			10 000 00	3
4			M30				4
5							5

Admitting a partner when goodwill is recognized   *PROBLEM 23-5, p.529*

CASH RECEIPTS JOURNAL

PAGE 9

	DATE	ACCOUNT TITLE	DOC. NO.	POST. REF.	GENERAL DEBIT	GENERAL CREDIT	ACCOUNTS RECEIVABLE CREDIT	SALES CREDIT	SALES TAX PAYABLE CREDIT	CASH DEBIT	
1	Feb. 1	Sean McDowell, Capital	R56			25000 00				25000 00	1

GENERAL JOURNAL

PAGE 2

	DATE		ACCOUNT TITLE	POST. REF.	DEBIT	CREDIT	
1	Feb.	1	Goodwill		8000 00		1
2			Ken Jamison, Capital			4000 00	2
3			Bond Treacher, Capital			4000 00	3
4			M9				4

Forming and expanding a partnership   *MASTERY PROBLEM 23-M, p. 529*

CASH RECEIPTS JOURNAL

PAGE 4

	DATE	ACCOUNT TITLE	DOC. NO.	POST. REF.	GENERAL DEBIT	GENERAL CREDIT	ACCOUNTS RECEIVABLE CREDIT	SALES CREDIT	SALES TAX PAYABLE CREDIT	CASH DEBIT	
1	June 1	Carol Anderson, Capital	R1			9000 00				9000 00	1
2	1	Accounts Receivable	R2		2303 60					3291 23	2
3		Supplies			290 19						3
4		Equipment			3367 14						4
5		Allowance for Uncollectible Accounts				35 79					5
6		Accounts Payable				216 37					6
7		George Heatherton, Capital				9000 00					7
8	Sept. 1	Jose Morales, Capital	R80			6000 00				6000 00	8
9	20	Susan Wires, Capital	R92			5000 00				5000 00	9
10	Nov. 5	Wilma Mason, Capital	R118			6000 00				6000 00	10

GENERAL JOURNAL

PAGE 2

	DATE		ACCOUNT TITLE	POST. REF.	DEBIT	CREDIT	
1	19-- July	1	Carol Anderson, Capital		3 0 0 0 00		1
2			George Heatherton, Capital		3 0 0 0 00		2
3			Allan Bortz, Capital			6 0 0 0 00	3
4			M8				4
5	Sept.	20	Carol Anderson, Capital		2 0 0 00		5
6			George Heatherton, Capital		2 0 0 00		6
7			Allan Bortz, Capital		2 0 0 00		7
8			Jose Morales, Capital		2 0 0 00		8
9			Susan Wires, Capital			8 0 0 00	9
10			M18				10
11	Nov.	5	Goodwill		1 0 0 0 00		11
12			Carol Anderson, Capital			2 0 0 00	12
13			George Heatherton, Capital			2 0 0 00	13
14			Allan Bortz, Capital			2 0 0 00	14
15			Jose Morales, Capital			2 0 0 00	15
16			Susan Wires, Capital			2 0 0 00	16
17			M24				17
18							18
19							19
20							20
21							21
22							22
23							23
24							24
25							25
26							26
27							27
28							28
29							29
30							30
31							31
32							32
33							33

Forming and expanding a partnership

CASH RECEIPTS JOURNAL

PAGE 4

	DATE		ACCOUNT TITLE	DOC. NO.	POST. REF.	GENERAL DEBIT	GENERAL CREDIT	ACCOUNTS RECEIVABLE CREDIT	SALES CREDIT	SALES TAX PAYABLE CREDIT	CASH DEBIT	
1	July	1	Accounts Receivable	R1		2 2 8 0 56					3 2 5 8 32	1
2			Merchandise Inventory			5 2 3 7 29						2
3			Office Equipment			1 9 4 3 49						3
4			Allowance for Uncollectible Accounts				3 5 43					4
5			Accounts Payable				3 6 8 4 23					5
6			Martha Heath, Capital				9 0 0 0 00					6
7		1	Supplies	R2		2 0 7 5 21					3 3 2 3 49	7
8			Merchandise Inventory			5 3 4 2 04						8
9			Office Equipment			1 9 5 9 88						9
10			Accounts Payable				3 7 0 0 62					10
11			James Wood, Capital				9 0 0 0 00					11
12	Sept.	20	Mindy Woke, Capital	R24			1 2 0 0 0 00				1 2 0 0 0 00	12
13	Oct.	5	Merchandise Inventory	R92		7 0 0 0 00					3 0 0 0 00	13
14			Tom Shirer, Capital				1 0 0 0 0 00					14
15												15
16												16
17												17
18												18
19												19
20												20
21												21
22												22
23												23
24												24

GENERAL JOURNAL

PAGE 2

	DATE		ACCOUNT TITLE	POST. REF.	DEBIT	CREDIT	
1	Sept.	1	Merchandise Inventory		9 0 0 0 00		1
2			Richard Oliver, Capital			9 0 0 0 00	2
3			M80				3
4		20	Mindy Woke, Capital		2 2 5 0 00		4
5			Martha Heath, Capital			7 5 0 00	5
6			James Wood, Capital			7 5 0 00	6
7			Richard Oliver, Capital			7 5 0 00	7
8			M85				8
9	Oct.	5	Goodwill		1 0 0 0 00		9
10			Martha Heath, Capital			2 5 0 00	10
11			James Wood, Capital			2 5 0 00	11
12			Richard Oliver, Capital			2 5 0 00	12
13			Mindy Woke, Capital			2 5 0 00	13
14			M90				14
15							15
16							16
17							17
18							18
19							19
20							20
21							21
22							22
23							23
24							24
25							25
26							26
27							27
28							28
29							29
30							30
31							31
32							32
33							33

UNIT A—Identifying Accounting Terms

DIRECTIONS: Select the one term in Column I that best fits each definition in Column II. Print the letter identifying your choice in the Answers column.

Column I	*Column II*	Answers	For Scoring
A. capital statement	**0.** Assets taken out of a business for the owner's personal use..	F	0. ✔
B. deficit	**1.** A partnership financial statement showing distribution of net income or net loss to partners	C	1.
C. distribution of net income statement	**2.** The amount by which allowances to partners exceed net income..	B	2.
D. liquidation of a partnership	**3.** A financial statement that summarizes the changes in capital during a fiscal period	A	3.
E. realization	**4.** The process of paying a partnership's liabilities and distributing remaining assets to the partners	D	4.
F. withdrawals	**5.** Cash received from the sale of assets during liquidation of a business	E	5.

UNIT B—Analyzing Procedures and Concepts Related to Partnership Accounting

DIRECTIONS: Place a check mark in the proper Answers column to show whether each of the following statements is true or false.

	Answers True	False	For Scoring
0. If a partnership agreement includes nothing about how earnings are to be distributed, the partners usually share according to a fixed percentage of 50% and 50%	✔		0. ✔
6. If Partner A has equity of $5,000.00, Partner B has equity of $5,000.00, net income is $20,000.00, and earnings are distributed on a percentage of total equity, each partner will receive $5,000.00		✔	6.
7. Salaries are often paid to partners who devote time to working for the partnership	✔		7.
8. When salaries or interest on equity are allowed, the amounts allowed are credited to partners' capital only if there is sufficient net income		✔	8.
9. Partners may take assets out of a partnership during a fiscal year in anticipation of the net income for the year	✔		9.
10. A partner's drawing account is a contra capital account	✔		10.
11. If a partner takes supplies out of a partnership for personal use, this is an expense of the partnership		✔	11.
12. The adjustments on a partnership work sheet are always the same as those on a corporation work sheet...		✔	12.
13. Partnerships pay federal income taxes on all net income earned by the partnership...		✔	13.
14. A partnership capital statement serves the same purpose as a corporate statement of stockholders' equity	✔		14.
15. The major difference between a partnership balance sheet and a corporate balance sheet is how the owners' equity is reported.............................	✔		15.
16. The Internal Revenue Service considers partners who draw salaries to be employees of the partnership..		✔	16.
17. A partnership submits a report to the Internal Revenue Service showing the amount of earnings distributed to each partner	✔		17.
18. Not recording partners' self-employment taxes on partnership records is an application of the accounting concept Business Entity	✔		18.

UNIT C—Analyzing Partnership Transactions

DIRECTIONS: For each transaction below, print in the proper Answers columns the identifying letters of the accounts to be debited and credited.

Account Titles

A. Cash
B. Loss and Gain on Realization
C. Income Summary
D. Partner A, Capital
E. Partner A, Drawing
F. Partner B, Capital
G. Partner B, Drawing
H. Supplies

Transactions

0–0. Paid cash to Partner A for personal use

19–20. Partner B took supplies for personal use

21–22. Entry to record Partner A's share of net income

23–24. Entry to record Partner B's share of net income

25–26. Entry to close Partner A's drawing account

27–28. Entry to close Partner B's drawing account

29–30. Entry to record sale of supplies for less than book value during liquidation

31–32. Entry to record sale of supplies for more than book value during liquidation

33–34. Entry to distribute credit balance of Loss and Gain on Realization to Partners A and B during liquidation

35–36. Entry to record distribution of remaining cash to Partners A and B during final liquidation

Answers		For Scoring	
Debit	Credit	Debit	Credit
E	A	0. ✔	0. ✔
G	H	19.	20.
C	D	21.	22.
C	F	23.	24.
D	E	25.	26.
F	G	27.	28.
A, B	H	29.	30.
A	B, H	31.	32.
B	D, F	33.	34.
D, F	A	35.	36.

UNIT D—Figuring Distribution of Net Income, Net Loss, or Deficit

DIRECTIONS: Figure each partner's share of the net income, net loss, or deficit in each situation below. Beginning equity is: Partner A, $60,000.00; Partner B, $40,000.00. Net income for the fiscal year is $20,000.00. Write the amounts due each partner in the Answers column.

How much of the net income does each partner receive if the partnership agreement stipulates distribution:

0–0. Using fixed percentage of 50% and 50%

37–38. Using a percentage of each partner's equity to total equity

39–40. Using interest on equity of 10% and remaining divided equally

41–42. Using partners' salaries: Partner A, $8,000.00; Partner B, $4,000.00; remaining divided equally

43–44. Using interest on equity of 5%, salary of $2,000.00 to each partner, and remaining divided equally

45–46. Using interest on equity of 10%, salary of $7,000.00 to each partner, and remaining divided equally

Answers		For Scoring	
Partner A	Partner B		
$10,000.00	$10,000.00	0. ✔	0. ✔
12,000.00	8,000.00	37.	38.
11,000.00	9,000.00	39.	40.
12,000.00	8,000.00	41.	42.
10,500.00	9,500.00	43.	44.
11,000.00	9,000.00	45.	46.

Distributing partnership earnings

a. Fixed percentage only:

	Net Income	×	Fixed %	=	Partner's Share of Net Income
Smith	$35,000.00	×	50%	=	$17,500.00
King	35,000.00	×	50%	=	17,500.00
Total net income					$35,000.00

b. Percentage of each partner's equity to total equity:

	Partner's Equity	÷	Total Equity	=	%	×	Net Income	=	Partner's Share
Smith	$40,000.00	÷	$100,000.00	=	40%	×	$35,000.00	=	$14,000.00
King	60,000.00	÷	100,000.00	=	60%	×	35,000.00	=	21,000.00
Total net income									$35,000.00

c. Interest on equity plus fixed percentage:

	Partner's Equity	×	Interest Rate	=	Partner's Interest
Smith	$40,000.00	×	10%	=	$ 4,000.00
King	60,000.00	×	10%	=	6,000.00
Total interest					$10,000.00

Net income	−	Total Interest	=	Remaining Net Income
$35,000.00	−	$10,000.00	=	$25,000.00

	Remaining Net Income	×	Fixed %	=	Partner's Share
Smith	$25,000.00	×	50%	=	$12,500.00
King	25,000.00	×	50%	=	12,500.00
Total remaining net income					$25,000.00

	Interest	+	Remaining Net Income	=	Partner's Share
Smith	$4,000.00	+	$12,500.00	=	$16,500.00
King	6,000.00	+	12,500.00	=	18,500.00
Total net income					$35,000.00

d. Salary plus fixed percentage:

Salaries for	Smith	+	King	=	Total Salaries
	$10,000.00	+	$15,000.00	=	$25,000.00

Net Income	–	Total Salary	=	Remaining Net Income
$35,000.00	–	$25,000.00	=	$10,000.00

	Remaining Net Income	×	Fixed %	=	Partner's Share	+	Salary	=	Partner's Total Share
Smith	$10,000.00	×	40%	=	$4,000.00	+	$10,000.00	=	$14,000.00
King	10,000.00	×	60%	=	6,000.00	+	15,000.00	=	21,000.00
Total net income									$35,000.00

e. Interest on equity, salary, and fixed percentage:

	Partner's Equity	×	Interest Rate	=	Interest on Equity	+	Salary	=	Total Allowance
Smith	$40,000.00	×	5%	=	$2,000.00	+	$10,000.00	=	$12,000.00
King	60,000.00	×	5%	=	3,000.00	+	15,000.00	=	18,000.00
Total allowance									$30,000.00

Net Income	–	Total Allowance	=	Remaining Net Income
$35,000.00	–	$30,000.00	=	$5,000.00

	Remaining Net Income	×	Fixed %	=	Partner's Share	+	Total Allowance	=	Partner's Total Share
Smith	$5,000.00	×	50%	=	$2,500.00	+	$12,000.00	=	$14,500.00
King	5,000.00	×	50%	=	2,500.00	+	18,000.00	=	20,500.00
Total net income									$35,000.00

f. Interest on equity, salary, and fixed percentage (deficit):

	Partner's Equity	×	Interest Rate	=	Interest on Equity	+	Salary	=	Total Allowance
Smith	$40,000.00	×	10%	=	$4,000.00	+	$12,000.00	=	$16,000.00
King	60,000.00	×	10%	=	6,000.00	+	17,000.00	=	23,000.00
Total allowance									$39,000.00

Net Income	–	Total Allowance	=	Deficit
$35,000.00	–	$39,000.00	=	$4,000.00

		Deficit	×	Fixed %	=	Partner's Share	+	Total Allowance	=	Partner's Total Share
Smith	=	$4,000.00	×	50%	=	$2,000.00	+	$16,000.00	=	$14,000.00
King	=	4,000.00	×	50%	=	2,000.00	+	23,000.00	=	21,000.00
Total net income										$35,000.00

Smith and King

Distribution of Net Income Statement

For Year Ended December 31, 19--

Olive Smith:			
5% Interest on Equity	2 0 0 0 00		
Salary	10 0 0 0 00		
Share of Remaining Net Income	2 5 0 0 00		
Total Share of Net Income		14 5 0 0 00	
George King:			
5% Interest on Equity	3 0 0 0 00		
Salary	15 0 0 0 00		
Share of Remaining Net Income	2 5 0 0 00		
Total Share of Net Income		20 5 0 0 00	
Total Net Income		35 0 0 0 00	

[3]

Smith and King

Distribution of Net Income Statement

For Year Ended December 31, 19--

Olive Smith:			
10% Interest on Equity	4 0 0 0 00		
Salary	12 0 0 0 00	16 0 0 0 00	
Less Share of Deficit		2 0 0 0 00	
Total Share of Net Income			14 0 0 0 00
George King:			
10% Interest on Equity	6 0 0 0 00		
Salary	17 0 0 0 00	23 0 0 0 00	
Less Share of Deficit		2 0 0 0 00	
Total Share of Net Income			21 0 0 0 00
Total Net Income			35 0 0 0 00

Recording partners' withdrawals

PROBLEM 24-2, p. 551

GENERAL JOURNAL
PAGE 5

DATE		ACCOUNT TITLE	POST. REF.	DEBIT	CREDIT	
19-- May	5	Milisa Matthews, Drawing		2 00 00		1
		Supplies — Office			2 00 00	2
		M25				3

CASH PAYMENTS JOURNAL
PAGE 6

DATE		ACCOUNT TITLE	CK. NO.	POST. REF.	GENERAL DEBIT	GENERAL CREDIT	ACCOUNTS PAYABLE DEBIT	CASH CREDIT	
19-- May	26	Bruce Gibson, Drawing	205		4 00 00			4 00 00	1

Completing financial statements for a partnership

PROBLEM 24-3, p. 551

Green Grass Care
Work Sheet
For Year Ended December 31, 19--

	ACCOUNT TITLE	TRIAL BALANCE DEBIT	TRIAL BALANCE CREDIT	ADJUSTMENTS DEBIT	ADJUSTMENTS CREDIT	INCOME STATEMENT DEBIT	INCOME STATEMENT CREDIT	BALANCE SHEET DEBIT	BALANCE SHEET CREDIT	
1	Cash	41 188 63						41 188 63		1
2	Petty Cash	2 00 00						2 00 00		2
3	Accounts Receivable	1 952 66						1 952 66		3
4	Allowance for Uncollectible Accounts		19 52		(a) 1 17 16				1 36 68	4
5	Supplies—Agricultural	9 118 90			(b)7 522 97			1 595 93		5
6	Supplies—Office	1 808 10			(c)1 390 00			4 18 10		6
7	Prepaid Insurance	1 322 71			(d) 490 00			832 71		7
8	Equipment	12 254 00						12 254 00		8
9	Accum. Depr.—Equipment		2 325 00		(e)1 225 00				3 550 00	9
10	Truck	6 000 00						6 000 00		10
11	Accum. Depr.—Truck		1 830 00		(f) 900 00				2 730 00	11
12	Accounts Payable		5 873 29						5 873 29	12
13	Sales Tax Payable		75 23						75 23	13
14	Linda Placer, Capital		23 125 00						23 125 00	14
15	Linda Placer, Drawing	4 400 00						4 400 00		15
16	Tina Dettermeyer, Capital		12 500 00						12 500 00	16
17	Tina Dettermeyer, Drawing	2 600 00						2 600 00		17
18	Income Summary									18
19	Sales		52 255 92				52 255 92			19
20	Advertising Expense	9 60 00				9 60 00				20
21	Bad Debts Expense			(a) 1 17 16		1 17 16				21
22	Depr. Expense—Equipment			(e)1 225 00		1 225 00				22
23	Depr. Expense—Truck			(f) 900 00		900 00				23
24	Insurance Expense			(d) 490 00		490 00				24
25	Miscellaneous Expense	1 738 96				1 738 96				25
26	Rent Expense	7 200 00				7 200 00				26
27	Supp. Exp.—Agricultural			(b)7 522 97		7 522 97				27
28	Supplies Expense—Office			(c)1 390 00		1 390 00				28
29	Truck Expense	5 300 00				5 300 00				29
30	Utilities Expense	1 960 00				1 960 00				30
31		98 003 96	98 003 96	11 645 13	11 645 13	28 804 09	52 255 92	71 442 03	47 990 20	31
32	Net Income					23 451 83			23 451 83	32
33						52 255 92	52 255 92	71 442 03	71 442 03	33

Green Grass Care

Income Statement

For Year Ended December 31, 19--

				% OF NET SALES
Operating Revenue:				
Net Sales			52 2 5 5 92	100.0
Operating Expenses:				
Advertising Expense	9 6 0 00			
Bad Debts Expense	1 1 7 16			
Depreciation Expense—Equipment	1 2 2 5 00			
Depreciation Expense—Truck	9 0 0 00			
Insurance Expense	4 9 0 00			
Miscellaneous Expense	1 7 3 8 96			
Rent Expense	7 2 0 0 00			
Supplies Expense—Agricultural	7 5 2 2 97			
Supplies Expense—Office	1 3 9 0 00			
Truck Expense	5 3 0 0 00			
Utilities Expense	1 9 6 0 00			
Total Operating Expenses			28 8 0 4 09	55.1
Net Income			23 4 5 1 83	44.9

[2]

Green Grass Care

Distribution of Net Income Statement

For Year Ended December 31, 19--

Linda Placer:			
64.9% of Net Income	15 2 2 0 24		
Tina Dettermeyer:			
35.1% of Net Income	8 2 3 1 59		
Total Net Income		23 4 5 1 83	

Green Grass Care

Capital Statement

For Year Ended December 31, 19--

Linda Placer:			
Capital, January 1, 19--		23 1 2 5 00	
Share of Net Income	15 2 2 0 24		
Less Withdrawals	4 4 0 0 00		
Net Increase in Capital		10 8 2 0 24	
Capital, December 31, 19--			33 9 4 5 24
Tina Dettermeyer:			
Capital, January 1, 19--		12 5 0 0 00	
Share of Net Income	8 2 3 1 59		
Less Withdrawals	2 6 0 0 00		
Net Increase in Capital		5 6 3 1 59	
Capital, December 31, 19--			18 1 3 1 59
Total Capital, December 31, 19--			52 0 7 6 83

Green Grass Care

Balance Sheet

December 31, 19--

Assets				
Current Assets:				
Cash			41 1 8 8 63	
Petty Cash			2 0 0 00	
Accounts Receivable	1 9 5 2 66			
Less Allow. for Uncoll. Accounts	1 3 6 68	1 8 1 5 98		
Supplies — Agricultural			1 5 9 5 93	
Supplies — Office			4 1 8 10	
Prepaid Insurance			8 3 2 71	
Total Current Assets				46 0 5 1 35
Plant Assets:				
Equipment	12 2 5 4 00			
Less Accum. Depr. — Equipment	3 5 5 0 00	8 7 0 4 00		
Truck	6 0 0 0 00			
Less Accum. Depr. — Truck	2 7 3 0 00	3 2 7 0 00		
Total Plant Assets				11 9 7 4 00
Total Assets				58 0 2 5 35
Liabilities				
Current Liabilities:				
Accounts Payable			5 8 7 3 29	
Sales Tax Payable			7 5 23	
Total Current Liabilities				5 9 4 8 52
Capital				
Linda Placer, Capital			33 9 4 5 24	
Tina Dettermeyer, Capital			18 1 3 1 59	
Total Capital				52 0 7 6 83
Total Liabilities and Capital				58 0 2 5 35

GENERAL JOURNAL

	DATE		ACCOUNT TITLE	POST. REF.	DEBIT	CREDIT	
1			*Adjusting Entries*				1
2	19-- Dec.	31	Bad Debts Expense		1 1 7 16		2
3			Allowance for Uncollectible Accounts			1 1 7 16	3
4		31	Supplies Expense — Agricultural		7 5 2 2 97		4
5			Supplies — Agricultural			7 5 2 2 97	5
6		31	Supplies Expense — Office		1 3 9 0 00		6
7			Supplies — Office			1 3 9 0 00	7
8		31	Insurance Expense		4 9 0 00		8
9			Prepaid Insurance			4 9 0 00	9
10		31	Depreciation Expense — Equipment		1 2 2 5 00		10
11			Accumulated Depreciation — Equipment			1 2 2 5 00	11
12		31	Depreciation Expense — Truck		9 0 0 00		12
13			Accumulated Depreciation — Truck			9 0 0 00	13
14			*Closing Entries*				14
15		31	Sales		52 2 5 5 92		15
16			Income Summary			52 2 5 5 92	16
17		31	Income Summary		28 8 0 4 09		17
18			Advertising Expense			9 6 0 00	18
19			Bad Debts Expense			1 1 7 16	19
20			Depreciation Expense — Equipment			1 2 2 5 00	20
21			Depreciation Expense — Truck			9 0 0 00	21
22			Insurance Expense			4 9 0 00	22
23			Miscellaneous Expense			1 7 3 8 96	23
24			Rent Expense			7 2 0 0 00	24
25			Supplies Expense — Agricultural			7 5 2 2 97	25
26			Supplies Expense — Office			1 3 9 0 00	26
27			Truck Expense			5 3 0 0 00	27
28			Utilities Expense			1 9 6 0 00	28
29		31	Income Summary		23 4 5 1 83		29
30			Linda Placer, Capital			15 2 2 0 24	30
31			Tina Dettermeyer, Capital			8 2 3 1 59	31
32		31	Linda Placer, Capital		4 4 0 0 00		32
33			Linda Placer, Drawing			4 4 0 0 00	33
34		31	Tina Dettermeyer, Capital		2 6 0 0 00		34
35			Tina Dettermeyer, Drawing			2 6 0 0 00	35

Liquidating a partnership

GENERAL JOURNAL

PAGE 4

DATE		ACCOUNT TITLE	POST. REF.	DEBIT	CREDIT	
19-- July	6	Richard Wilson, Capital		240 00		1
		Michelle Ring, Capital		160 00		2
		Loss and Gain on Realization			400 00	3
		M34				4

CASH RECEIPTS JOURNAL

PAGE 7

DATE		ACCOUNT TITLE	DOC. NO.	POST. REF.	GENERAL DEBIT	GENERAL CREDIT	ACCOUNTS RECEIVABLE CREDIT	SALES CREDIT	SALES TAX PAYABLE CREDIT	CASH DEBIT	
19-- July	1	Loss and Gain on Realization	R102		50000					2000000	1
		Accum. Depr.—Office Equipment			550000						2
		Office Equipment				800000					3
	1	Loss and Gain on Realization	R103		10000					400000	4
		Supplies				50000					5
	3	Accumulated Depreciation—Truck	R104		1220000					300000	6
		Truck				1500000					7
		Loss and Gain on Realization				20000					8

CASH PAYMENTS JOURNAL

PAGE 6

DATE		ACCOUNT TITLE	CK. NO.	POST. REF.	GENERAL DEBIT	GENERAL CREDIT	ACCOUNTS PAYABLE DEBIT	CASH CREDIT	
19-- July	5	Accounts Payable	123		50000			50000	1
	6	Richard Wilson, Capital	124		506000			990000	2
	6	Michelle Ring, Capital	125		484000				3

Completing end-of-fiscal-period work for a partnership

A & D Service

Work Sheet

For Year Ended December 31, 19--

	ACCOUNT TITLE	TRIAL BALANCE		ADJUSTMENTS		INCOME STATEMENT		BALANCE SHEET		
		DEBIT	CREDIT	DEBIT	CREDIT	DEBIT	CREDIT	DEBIT	CREDIT	
1	Cash	27955 32						27955 32		1
2	Petty Cash	300 00						300 00		2
3	Accounts Receivable	1799 38						1799 38		3
4	Allowance for Uncollectible Accounts		27 98		(a) 107 00				134 98	4
5	Supplies — Service	8403 07			(b) 6932 42			1470 65		5
6	Supplies — Office	1600 00			(c) 1280 89			319 11		6
7	Prepaid Insurance	1218 87			(d) 451 55			767 32		7
8	Equipment	13621 00						13621 00		8
9	Accum. Depr. — Equipment		2141 00		(e) 1362 00				3503 00	9
10	Truck	8000 00						8000 00		10
11	Accum. Depr. — Truck		2715 00		(f) 1600 00				4315 00	11
12	Accounts Payable		5418 08						5418 08	12
13	Sales Tax Payable		72 24						72 24	13
14	Alicia Ross, Capital		12000 00						12000 00	14
15	Alicia Ross, Drawing	9000 00						9000 00		15
16	Don Sands, Capital		12000 00						12000 00	16
17	Don Sands, Drawing	9000 00						9000 00		17
18	Income Summary									18
19	Sales		79627 74				79627 74			19
20	Advertising Expense	800 00				800 00				20
21	Bad Debts Expense			(a) 107 00		107 00				21
22	Depr. Expense — Equipment			(e) 1362 00		1362 00				22
23	Depr. Expense — Truck			(f) 1600 00		1600 00				23
24	Insurance Expense			(d) 451 55		451 55				24
25	Miscellaneous Expense	16024 40				16024 40				25
26	Rent Expense	9600 00				9600 00				26
27	Supplies Expense — Service			(b) 6932 42		6932 42				27
28	Supplies Expense — Office			(c) 1280 89		1280 89				28
29	Truck Expense	4880 00				4880 00				29
30	Utilities Expense	1800 00				1800 00				30
31		114002 04	114002 04	11733 86	11733 86	44838 26	79627 74	72232 78	37443 30	31
32	Net Income					34789 48			34789 48	32
33						79627 74	79627 74	72232 78	72232 78	33
34										34
35										35
36										36

[1]

A & D Service

Income Statement

For Year Ended December 31, 19--

			% OF NET SALES
Operating Revenue:			
Net Sales		79 6 2 7 74	100.0
Operating Expenses:			
Advertising Expense	8 0 0 00		
Bad Debts Expense	1 0 7 00		
Depreciation Expense—Equipment	1 3 6 2 00		
Depreciation Expense—Truck	1 6 0 0 00		
Insurance Expense	4 5 1 55		
Miscellaneous Expense	16 0 2 4 40		
Rent Expense	9 6 0 0 00		
Supplies Expense—Service	6 9 3 2 42		
Supplies Expense—Office	1 2 8 0 89		
Truck Expense	4 8 8 0 00		
Utilities Expense	1 8 0 0 00		
Total Operating Expenses		44 8 3 8 26	56.3
Net Income		34 7 8 9 48	43.7

[2]

A & D Service

Distribution of Net Income Statement

For Year Ended December 31, 19--

Alicia Ross:		
5% Interest on Equity	6 0 0 00	
Salary	6 0 0 0 00	
Share of Remaining Net Income	9 7 9 4 74	
Total Share of Net Income		16 3 9 4 74
Don Sands:		
5% Interest on Equity	6 0 0 00	
Salary	8 0 0 0 00	
Share of Remaining Net Income	9 7 9 4 74	
Total Share of Net Income		18 3 9 4 74
Total Net Income		34 7 8 9 48

A & D Service

Capital Statement

For Year Ended December 31, 19--

Alicia Ross:			
Capital, January 1, 19--		12 000 00	
Share of Net Income	16 394 74		
Less Withdrawals	9 000 00		
Net Increase in Capital		7 394 74	
Capital, December 31, 19--			19 394 74
Don Sands:			
Capital, January 1, 19--		12 000 00	
Share of Net Income	18 394 74		
Less Withdrawals	9 000 00		
Net Increase in Capital		9 394 74	
Capital, December 31, 19--			21 394 74
Total Capital, December 31, 19--			40 789 48

A & D Service

Balance Sheet

December 31, 19--

Assets				
Current Assets:				
Cash			27 9 5 5 32	
Petty Cash			3 0 0 00	
Accounts Receivable	1 7 9 9 38			
Less Allow. for Uncoll. Accounts	1 3 4 98		1 6 6 4 40	
Supplies — Service			1 4 7 0 65	
Supplies — Office			3 1 9 11	
Prepaid Insurance			7 6 7 32	
Total Current Assets				32 4 7 6 80
Plant Assets:				
Equipment	13 6 2 1 00			
Less Accum. Depr. — Equipment	3 5 0 3 00	10 1 1 8 00		
Truck	8 0 0 0 00			
Less Accum. Depr. — Truck	4 3 1 5 00	3 6 8 5 00		
Total Plant Assets				13 8 0 3 00
Total Assets				46 2 7 9 80
Liabilities				
Current Liabilities:				
Accounts Payable			5 4 1 8 08	
Sales Tax Payable			7 2 24	
Total Current Liabilities				5 4 9 0 32
Capital				
Alicia Ross, Capital			19 3 9 4 74	
Don Sands, Capital			21 3 9 4 74	
Total Capital				40 7 8 9 48
Total Liabilities and Capital				46 2 7 9 80

GENERAL JOURNAL
PAGE 12

	DATE		ACCOUNT TITLE	POST. REF.	DEBIT	CREDIT	
1			*Adjusting Entries*				1
2	19-- Dec.	31	**Bad Debts Expense**		1 0 7 00		2
3			**Allowance for Uncollectible Accounts**			1 0 7 00	3
4		31	**Supplies Expense — Service**		6 9 3 2 42		4
5			**Supplies — Service**			6 9 3 2 42	5
6		31	**Supplies Expense — Office**		1 2 8 0 89		6
7			**Supplies — Office**			1 2 8 0 89	7
8		31	**Insurance Expense**		4 5 1 55		8
9			**Prepaid Insurance**			4 5 1 55	9
10		31	**Depreciation Expense — Equipment**		1 3 6 2 00		10
11			**Accumulated Depreciation — Equipment**			1 3 6 2 00	11
12		31	**Depreciation Expense — Truck**		1 6 0 0 00		12
13			**Accumulated Depreciation — Truck**			1 6 0 0 00	13
14			*Closing Entries*				14
15		31	**Sales**		79 6 2 7 74		15
16			**Income Summary**			79 6 2 7 74	16
17		31	**Income Summary**		44 8 3 8 26		17
18			**Advertising Expense**			8 0 0 00	18
19			**Bad Debts Expense**			1 0 7 00	19
20			**Depreciation Expense — Equipment**			1 3 6 2 00	20
21			**Depreciation Expense — Truck**			1 6 0 0 00	21
22			**Insurance Expense**			4 5 1 55	22
23			**Miscellaneous Expense**			16 0 2 4 40	23
24			**Rent Expense**			9 6 0 0 00	24
25			**Supplies Expense — Service**			6 9 3 2 42	25
26			**Supplies Expense — Office**			1 2 8 0 89	26
27			**Truck Expense**			4 8 8 0 00	27
28			**Utilities Expense**			1 8 0 0 00	28
29		31	**Income Summary**		34 7 8 9 48		29
30			**Alicia Ross, Capital**			16 3 9 4 74	30
31			**Don Sands, Capital**			18 3 9 4 74	31
32		31	**Alicia Ross, Capital**		9 0 0 0 00		32
33			**Alicia Ross, Drawing**			9 0 0 0 00	33
34		31	**Don Sands, Capital**		9 0 0 0 00		34
35			**Don Sands, Drawing**			9 0 0 0 00	35

Completing end-of-fiscal-period work for a partnership

W & S Sales
Work Sheet
For Year Ended December 31, 19--

	ACCOUNT TITLE	TRIAL BALANCE DEBIT	TRIAL BALANCE CREDIT	ADJUSTMENTS DEBIT	ADJUSTMENTS CREDIT	INCOME STATEMENT DEBIT	INCOME STATEMENT CREDIT	BALANCE SHEET DEBIT	BALANCE SHEET CREDIT	
1	Cash	6 8 6 7 37						6 8 6 7 37		1
2	Petty Cash	4 0 0 00						4 0 0 00		2
3	Accounts Receivable	5 6 0 36						5 6 0 36		3
4	Allowance for Uncollectible Accounts		1 2 33		(a) 3 4 52				4 6 85	4
5	Merchandise Inventory	12 6 4 6 40			(b) 3 5 4 69			12 2 9 1 71		5
6	Supplies—Plumbing	1 2 8 5 46			(c) 6 2 9 88			6 5 5 58		6
7	Supplies—Office	9 1 4 94			(d) 4 1 1 72			5 0 3 22		7
8	Prepaid Insurance	1 2 6 0 72			(e) 6 4 2 97			6 1 7 75		8
9	Equipment	11 5 9 7 00						11 5 9 7 00		9
10	Accum. Depr.—Equipment		2 3 3 1 00		(f) 1 1 5 9 70				3 4 9 0 70	10
11	Truck	7 3 4 0 00						7 3 4 0 00		11
12	Accum. Depr.—Truck		1 5 1 2 04		(g) 7 3 4 00				2 2 4 6 04	12
13	Accounts Payable		4 7 0 8 58						4 7 0 8 58	13
14	Sales Tax Payable		1 3 0 44						1 3 0 44	14
15	Doris Waiser, Capital		24 2 5 0 00						24 2 5 0 00	15
16	Doris Waiser, Drawing	6 0 0 0 00						6 0 0 0 00		16
17	Rolf Schermer, Capital		21 5 0 0 00						21 5 0 0 00	17
18	Rolf Schermer, Drawing	5 0 0 0 00						5 0 0 0 00		18
19	Income Summary			(b) 3 5 4 69		3 5 4 69				19
20	Sales		44 2 3 7 12				44 2 3 7 12			20
21	Purchases	28 8 6 9 38				28 8 6 9 38				21
22	Purch. Ret. & Allowances		3 1 7 56				3 1 7 56			22
23	Advertising Expense	7 5 0 00				7 5 0 00				23
24	Bad Debts Expense			(a) 3 4 52		3 4 52				24
25	Depr. Expense—Equipment			(f) 1 1 5 9 70		1 1 5 9 70				25
26	Depr. Expense—Truck			(g) 7 3 4 00		7 3 4 00				26
27	Insurance Expense			(e) 6 4 2 97		6 4 2 97				27
28	Miscellaneous Expense	9 2 8 00				9 2 8 00				28
29	Rent Expense	8 4 0 0 00				8 4 0 0 00				29
30	Supplies Expense—Plumbing			(c) 6 2 9 88		6 2 9 88				30
31	Supplies Expense—Office			(d) 4 1 1 72		4 1 1 72				31
32	Truck Expense	5 2 2 7 94				5 2 2 7 94				32
33	Utilities Expense	9 5 1 50				9 5 1 50				33
34		98 9 9 9 07	98 9 9 9 07	3 9 6 7 48	3 9 6 7 48	49 0 9 4 30	44 5 5 4 68	51 8 3 2 99	56 3 7 2 61	34
35	Net Loss						4 5 3 9 62	4 5 3 9 62		35
36						49 0 9 4 30	49 0 9 4 30	56 3 7 2 61	56 3 7 2 61	36

W & S Sales

Income Statement

For Year Ended December 31, 19--

				% OF NET SALES
Operating Revenue:				
Net Sales			44 2 3 7 12	100.0
Cost of Merchandise Sold:				
Merchandise Inventory, Jan. 1, 19--		12 6 4 6 40		
Purchases	28 8 6 9 38			
Less Purchases Returns & Allowances	3 1 7 56	28 5 5 1 82		
Total Cost of Mdse. Available for Sale		41 1 9 8 22		
Less Mdse. Inventory, Dec. 31, 19--		12 2 9 1 71		
Cost of Merchandise Sold			28 9 0 6 51	65.3
Gross Profit on Operations			15 3 3 0 61	34.7
Operating Expenses:				
Advertising Expense		7 5 0 00		
Bad Debts Expense		3 4 52		
Depreciation Expense—Equipment		1 1 5 9 70		
Depreciation Expense—Truck		7 3 4 00		
Insurance Expense		6 4 2 97		
Miscellaneous Expense		9 2 8 00		
Rent Expense		8 4 0 0 00		
Supplies Expense—Plumbing		6 2 9 88		
Supplies Expense—Office		4 1 1 72		
Truck Expense		5 2 2 7 94		
Utilities Expense		9 5 1 50		
Total Operating Expenses			19 8 7 0 23	44.9
Net Loss			4 5 3 9 62	−10.3

W & S Sales

Distribution of Net Income Statement

For Year Ended December 31, 19--

Doris Waiser:			
5% Interest on Equity	1 2 1 2 50		
Salary	5 0 0 0 00	6 2 1 2 50	
Less Share of Net Deficit		7 9 1 3 56	
Total Share of Net Loss			1 7 0 1 06
Rolf Schermer:			
5% Interest on Equity	1 0 7 5 00		
Salary	4 0 0 0 00	5 0 7 5 00	
Less Share of Net Deficit		7 9 1 3 56	
Total Share of Net Loss			2 8 3 8 56
Total Net Loss			4 5 3 9 62

Computation of ½ Share of Net Deficit:

($6,212.50 + 5,075.00 + 4,539.62) ÷ 2 = $7,913.56

[3]

W & S Sales

Capital Statement

For Year Ended December 31, 19--

Doris Waiser:			
Capital, January 1, 19--		24 2 5 0 00	
Share of Net Loss	1 7 0 1 06		
Plus Withdrawals	6 0 0 0 00		
Net Decrease in Capital		7 7 0 1 06	
Capital, December 31, 19--			16 5 4 8 94
Rolf Schermer:			
Capital, January 1, 19--		21 5 0 0 00	
Share of Net Loss	2 8 3 8 56		
Plus Withdrawals	5 0 0 0 00		
Net Decrease in Capital		7 8 3 8 56	
Capital, December 31, 19--			13 6 6 1 44
Total Capital, December 31, 19--			30 2 1 0 38

W & S Sales

Balance Sheet

December 31, 19--

Assets				
Current Assets:				
Cash			6 8 6 7 37	
Petty Cash			4 0 0 00	
Accounts Receivable	5 6 0 36			
Less Allow. for Uncoll. Accounts	4 6 85		5 1 3 51	
Merchandise Inventory			12 2 9 1 71	
Supplies—Plumbing			6 5 5 58	
Supplies—Office			5 0 3 22	
Prepaid Insurance			6 1 7 75	
Total Current Assets				21 8 4 9 14
Plant Assets:				
Equipment	11 5 9 7 00			
Less Accum. Depr.—Equipment	3 4 9 0 70		8 1 0 6 30	
Truck	7 3 4 0 00			
Less Accum. Depr.—Truck	2 2 4 6 04		5 0 9 3 96	
Total Plant Assets				13 2 0 0 26
Total Assets				35 0 4 9 40
Liabilities				
Current Liabilities:				
Accounts Payable			4 7 0 8 58	
Sales Tax Payable			1 3 0 44	
Total Current Liabilities				4 8 3 9 02
Capital				
Doris Waiser, Capital			16 5 4 8 94	
Rolf Schermer, Capital			13 6 6 1 44	
Total Capital				30 2 1 0 38
Total Liabilities and Capital				35 0 4 9 40

Name _____

Date _____ Class _____

Checked by _____

STUDY GUIDE 25

UNIT A—Identifying Accounting Terms

DIRECTIONS: Select the one term in Column I that best fits each definition in Column II. Print the letter identifying your choice in the Answers column.

Column I	Column II	Answers	For Scoring
A. appropriations	**0.** An organization providing goods or services with neither a conscious motive nor expectation of earning a profit....	G	0. ✔
B. certificate of deposit	**1.** A plan of current expenditures and the proposed means of financing those expenditures	*H*	1.
C. encumbrance	**2.** Cash disbursements and liabilities incurred for the cost of goods delivered or services rendered.........................	*D*	2.
D. expenditures	**3.** Authorizations to make expenditures for specified purposes	*A*	3.
E. fund	**4.** A commitment to pay for goods or services which have been ordered but not yet provided..........................	*C*	4.
F. general fixed assets	**5.** A document issued by a bank as evidence of money invested with the bank..	*B*	5.
G. not-for-profit organization	**6.** A governmental accounting entity with a set of accounts in which assets always equal equities	*E*	6.
H. operating budget	**7.** Authorized action taken by a governmental organization to collect taxes by legal authority...	*I*	7.
I. tax levy	**8.** Governmental properties that benefit future periods..............	*F*	8.

UNIT B—Analyzing Accounting Practices of a Not-for-Profit Organization

DIRECTIONS: Place a check mark in the proper Answers column to show whether each of the following statements is true or false.

		Answers True	False	For Scoring
0.	Business organizations differ in their kinds of ownership but they have a common objective—to earn a profit	✔		0. ✔
9.	Since a governmental organization does not intend to earn a profit from its operation, success is easy to measure		✔	9.
10.	Both business and governmental organizations apply the accounting equation, assets equal liabilities plus equity..................................	✔		10.
11.	Preparing financial statements for a governmental organization at the end of a fiscal period is an application of the Accounting Period Cycle concept	✔		11.
12.	Revenues for a governmental organization are recorded only when cash is received..		✔	12.
13.	Expenditures for a governmental organization are recorded in the accounting period in which money is spent or liabilities incurred...........................	✔		13.
14.	The fund balance for a governmental organization is reported as assets plus liabilities...		✔	14.
15.	Approval of an annual governmental operating budget by the proper authorities provides legal authorization for expenditures to be made in accordance with the approved budget	✔		15.
16.	In governmental accounting, appropriations are the same as expenditures		✔	16.
17.	In governmental accounting, appropriations should always equal estimated revenues		✔	17.

UNIT C—Analyzing Transactions for a Governmental Organization

DIRECTIONS: For each transaction below, print in the proper Answers columns the identifying letters of the accounts to be debited and credited.

Account Titles

A. Allowance for Uncollectible Taxes — Current
B. Allowance for Uncollectible Taxes — Delinquent
C. Appropriations
D. Budgetary Fund Balance
E. Cash
F. Encumbrance — Supplies, General Government
G. Estimated Revenues
H. Expenditure — Capital Outlays, General Government
I. Expenditure — Other Charges, General Government
J. Expenditure — Personnel, General Government
K. Expenditure — Supplies, General Government
L. Interest Revenue
M. Investments — Short Term
N. Notes Payable
O. Other Revenue
P. Property Tax Revenue
Q. Reserve for Encumbrances — Current Year
R. Taxes Receivable — Current
S. Taxes Receivable — Delinquent

Transactions

Transactions	Debit	Credit	Debit (Scoring)	Credit (Scoring)
0–0. Issued a note payable........	E	N	0. ✔	0. ✔
18–19. Received cash for current taxes receivable...............	E	R	18.	19.
20–21. Recorded current year's approved operating budget..	G	C, D	20.	21.
22–23. Paid cash for property benefiting future periods	H	E	22.	23.
24–25. Encumbered estimated amount for supplies..........	F	Q	24.	25.
26–27. Recorded current year's property tax levy	R	A, P	26.	27.
28–29. Paid note payable plus interest	I, N	E	28.	29.
30–31. Recorded reclassification of current taxes receivable to delinquent status and accompanying allowance accounts........................	A, S	B, R	30.	31.
32–33. Paid cash for supplies previously encumbered......	K, Q	E, F	32.	33.
34–35. Paid cash for gas utility service.........................	I	E	34.	35.
36–37. Received cash for delinquent taxes receivable	E	S	36.	37.
38–39. Paid cash for a certificate of deposit.......................................	M	E	38.	39.
40–41. Received cash for traffic fines	E	O	40.	41.
42–43. Received cash plus interest for certificate of deposit due today	E	L, M	42.	43.

Recording governmental operating budgets

JOURNAL

PAGE 5

	DATE	ACCOUNT TITLE	DOC. NO.	POST. REF.	GENERAL DEBIT	GENERAL CREDIT	CASH DEBIT	CASH CREDIT
1		a. CENTER:						
2	19-- Jan. 1	Estimated Revenues			1056 0 0 0 00			
3		Appropriations				989 0 0 0 00		
4		Budgetary Fund Balance				67 0 0 0 00		
5								
6		b. TOWER:						
7	19-- Jan. 1	Estimated Revenues			793 5 0 0 00			
8		Appropriations				789 2 0 0 00		
9		Budgetary Fund Balance				4 3 0 0 00		
10								
11		c. PARKER:						
12	19-- Jan. 1	Estimated Revenues			1764 0 0 0 00			
13		Appropriations				1722 5 0 0 00		
14		Budgetary Fund Balance				41 5 0 0 00		
15	1	TOTALS			3613 5 0 0 00	3613 5 0 0 00		
16								
17								
18								
19								
20								
21								
22								
23								
24								

NOTE: Totals are not specifically required, but are provided for proofing.

Recording governmental revenue

JOURNAL

PAGE 15

DATE		ACCOUNT TITLE	DOC. NO.	POST. REF.	GENERAL DEBIT	GENERAL CREDIT	CASH DEBIT	CASH CREDIT	
19-- Jan.	1	Taxes Receivable—Current	M78		1250 0 0 0 00				1
		Allowance for Uncoll. Taxes—Current				9 4 0 0 00			2
		Property Tax Revenue				1240 6 0 0 00			3
	8	Taxes Receivable—Current	R124			97 6 0 0 00	97 6 0 0 00		4
	14	Other Revenue	R137			4 6 00	4 6 00		5
Feb.	11	Taxes Receivable—Current	R184			72 3 5 0 00	72 3 5 0 00		6
	16	Other Revenue	R202			1 7 4 50	1 7 4 50		7
Mar.	1	Taxes Receivable—Delinquent	M97		46 8 0 0 00				8
		Allowance for Uncoll. Taxes—Current			9 4 0 0 00				9
		Taxes Receivable—Current				46 8 0 0 00			10
		Allow. for Uncoll. Taxes—Delinquent				9 4 0 0 00			11
	12	Taxes Receivable—Delinquent	R249			9 7 0 0 00	9 7 0 0 00		12
	12	Totals			1306 2 0 0 00	1486 0 7 0 50	179 8 7 0 50		13

NOTE: Totals are not specifically required, but are provided for proofing.

Recording governmental encumbrances, expenditures, and other transactions

JOURNAL

PAGE 21

	DATE	ACCOUNT TITLE	DOC. NO.	POST. REF.	GENERAL DEBIT	GENERAL CREDIT	CASH DEBIT	CASH CREDIT
1	19.. Jan. 11	Expenditure—Other Charges, Public Works	C234		1 8 5 00			1 8 5 00
2	14	Encumbrance—Supplies, Public Safety	M23		1 2 5 00			
3		Reserve for Encumbrances—Current Year				1 2 5 00		
4	15	Notes Payable	NP5			1500 0 0 00	1500 0 0 00	
5	28	Reserve for Encumbrances—Current Year	M30		1 2 5 00			
6		Encumbrance—Supplies, Public Safety				1 2 5 00		
7	28	Expenditure—Supplies, Public Safety	C248		1 2 8 00			1 2 8 00
8	Feb. 5	Expenditure—Capital Outlays, Gen. Gov't.	C257		2 5 5 00			2 5 5 00
9	15	Notes Payable	C269		1500 0 0 00			1512 5 0 00
10		Expenditure—Other Charges, Gen. Gov't.			1 2 5 0 00			
11	28	Encumbrance—Supplies, Public Works	M39		1 7 6 00			
12		Reserve for Encumbrances—Current Year				1 7 6 00		
13	Mar. 15	Investments—Short Term	C286		2000 0 0 00			2000 0 0 00
14	18	Reserve for Encumbrances—Current Year	M48		1 7 6 00			
15		Encumbrance—Supplies, Public Works				1 7 6 00		
16	18	Expenditure—Supplies, Public Works	C305		1 6 9 50			1 6 9 50
17	21	Expenditure—Personnel, Recreation	C312		3 5 0 00			3 5 0 00
18	June 15	Investments—Short Term	R174			2000 0 0 00	203 0 0 0 00	
19		Interest Revenue				3 0 0 0 00		
20	15	Totals			3529 3 9 50	3536 0 2 00	353 0 0 0 00	3523 3 7 50
21								
22								
23								
24								

NOTE: Totals are not specifically required, but are provided for proofing.

Recording governmental transactions

JOURNAL

	DATE	ACCOUNT TITLE	DOC. NO.	POST. REF.	GENERAL DEBIT	GENERAL CREDIT	CASH DEBIT	CASH CREDIT	
1	19-- Jan. 2	Estimated Revenues	M32		1265 0 0 0 00				1
2		Appropriations				1214 0 0 0 00			2
3		Budgetary Fund Balance				51 0 0 0 00			3
4	2	Taxes Receivable—Current	M33		1215 0 0 0 00				4
5		Allowance for Uncoll. Taxes—Current				12 2 0 0 00			5
6		Property Tax Revenue				1202 8 0 0 00			6
7	6	Taxes Receivable—Current	R95			47 3 0 0 00	47 3 0 0 00		7
8	10	Expenditure—Other Charges, Gen. Gov't.	C158		2 2 4 00			2 2 4 00	8
9	12	Notes Payable	NP7			200 0 0 0 00	200 0 0 0 00		9
10	16	Encumbrance—Supplies, Public Works	M44		1 5 5 00				10
11		Reserve for Encumbrances—Current Year				1 5 5 00			11
12	20	Other Revenue	R101			1 2 5 00	1 2 5 00		12
13	30	Expenditure—Capital Outlays, Public Works	C172		3 5 0 00			3 5 0 00	13
14	Feb. 6	Reserve for Encumbrances—Current Year	M48		1 5 5 00				14
15		Encumbrance—Supplies, Public Works				1 5 5 00			15
16	6	Expenditure—Supplies, Public Works	C180		1 6 0 00			1 6 0 00	16
17	24	Encumbrance—Supplies, Recreation	M59		1 2 3 00				17
18		Reserve for Encumbrances—Current Year				1 2 3 00			18
19	Mar. 1	Taxes Receivable—Delinquent	M66		61 4 0 0 00				19
20		Allowance for Uncoll. Taxes—Current			12 2 0 0 00				20
21		Taxes Receivable—Current				61 4 0 0 00			21
22		Allow. for Uncoll. Taxes—Delinquent				12 2 0 0 00			22
23	12	Notes Payable	C212		200 0 0 0 00			203 0 0 0 00	23
24		Expenditure—Other Charges, Gen. Gov't.			3 0 0 0 00				24

JOURNAL

PAGE 21 (cont.)

	DATE	ACCOUNT TITLE	DOC. NO.	POST. REF.	GENERAL DEBIT	GENERAL CREDIT	CASH DEBIT	CASH CREDIT	
25	20	Investments—Short Term	C224		400 0 0 0 00			400 0 0 0 00	25
26	22	Reserve for Encumbrances—Current Year	M78		1 2 3 00				26
27		Encumbrance—Supplies, Recreation				1 2 3 00			27
28	22	Expenditure—Supplies, Recreation	C231		1 2 1 00			1 2 1 00	28
29	Apr. 10	Taxes Receivable—Delinquent	R345			11 0 0 0 00	11 0 0 0 00		29
30	25	Expenditure—Personnel, Recreation	C256		4 0 0 00			4 0 0 00	30
31	July 20	Investments—Short Term	R487			400 0 0 0 00	408 0 0 0 00		31
32		Interest Revenue				8 0 0 0 00			32
33	20	Totals			3158 4 1 1 00	3220 5 8 1 00	666 4 2 5 00	604 2 5 5 00	33
34									34
35									35
36									36
37									37
38									38
39									39
40									40
41									41
42									42
43									43
44									44
45									45
46									46
47									47
48									48

NOTE: Totals are not specifically required, but are provided for proofing.

Recording governmental transactions

JOURNAL

PAGE 32

	DATE		ACCOUNT TITLE	DOC. NO.	POST. REF.	GENERAL DEBIT	GENERAL CREDIT	CASH DEBIT	CASH CREDIT	
1	19--Jan.	2	Estimated Revenues	M78		1518 0 0 0 00				1
2			Budgetary Fund Balance			24 1 0 0 00				2
3			Appropriations				1542 1 0 0 00			3
4		2	Taxes Receivable—Current	M79		1442 0 0 0 00				4
5			Allowance for Uncoll. Taxes—Current				28 8 4 0 00			5
6			Property Tax Revenue				1413 1 6 0 00			6
7		9	Taxes Receivable—Current	R101			54 7 0 0 00	54 7 0 0 00		7
8		17	Expenditure—Other Charges, Public Works	C121		2 7 6 00			2 7 6 00	8
9		20	Notes Payable	NP12			150 0 0 0 00	150 0 0 0 00		9
10		25	Encumbrance—Supplies, Public Safety	M92		1 6 0 00				10
11			Reserve for Encumbrances—Current Year				1 6 0 00			11
12	Feb.	3	Other Revenue	R142			10 5 8 00	10 5 8 00		12
13		10	Reserve for Encumbrances—Current Year	M120		1 6 0 00				13
14			Encumbrance—Supplies, Public Safety				1 6 0 00			14
15		10	Expenditure—Supplies, Public Safety	C178		1 5 2 00			1 5 2 00	15
16		21	Expenditure—Capital Outlays, Recreation	C189		4 7 5 00			4 7 5 00	16
17	Mar.	1	Taxes Receivable—Delinquent	M144		173 1 0 0 00				17
18			Allowance for Uncoll. Taxes—Current			28 8 4 0 00				18
19			Taxes Receivable—Current				173 1 0 0 00			19
20			Allow. for Uncoll. Taxes—Delinquent				28 8 4 0 00			20
21		15	Investments—Short Term	C210		500 0 0 0 00			500 0 0 0 00	21
22		20	Notes Payable	C220		150 0 0 0 00			152 5 0 0 00	22
23			Expenditure—Other Charges, Gen. Gov't.			2 5 0 0 00				23
24		20	Taxes Receivable—Delinquent	R196			12 5 0 0 00	12 5 0 0 00		24

JOURNAL

PAGE 32 (cont.)

	DATE	ACCOUNT TITLE	DOC. NO.	POST. REF.	GENERAL DEBIT (1)	GENERAL CREDIT (2)	CASH DEBIT (3)	CASH CREDIT (4)	
25	Apr. 4	Encumbrance—Capital Outlays, Gen. Gov't.	M168		5 8 0 00				25
26		Reserve for Encumbrances—Current Year				5 8 0 00			26
27	16	Reserve for Encumbrances—Current Year	M180		5 8 0 00				27
28		Encumbrance—Capital Outlays, Gen. Gov't.				5 8 0 00			28
29	16	Expenditure—Capital Outlays, Gen. Gov't.	C257		5 9 8 00			5 9 8 00	29
30	July 15	Investments—Short Term	R279			500 0 0 0 00	510 0 0 0 00		30
31		Interest Revenue				10 0 0 0 00			31
32	15	Totals			3841 5 2 1 00	3915 7 7 8 00	728 2 5 8 00	654 0 0 1 00	32
33									33
34									34
35									35
36									36
37									37
38									38
39									39
40									40
41									41
42									42
43									43
44									44
45									45
46									46
47									47
48									48

NOTE: Totals are not specifically required, but are provided for proofing.

JOURNAL

PAGE

	DATE	ACCOUNT TITLE	DOC. NO.	POST. REF.	GENERAL		CASH	
					1 DEBIT	2 CREDIT	3 DEBIT	4 CREDIT
1								
2								
3								
4								
5								
6								
7								
8								
9								
10								
11								
12								
13								
14								
15								
16								
17								
18								
19								
20								
21								
22								
23								
24								

Perfect Score. 52

Deduct .... —

Your Score .... —

Name _____

Date _____ Class _____

Checked by _____

STUDY
GUIDE
26

UNIT A—Analyzing End-of-Fiscal Period Work for a Governmental Organization

DIRECTIONS: For each item below, select the choice that best completes the sentence. Print the letter identifying your choice in the Answers column.

	Answers	For Scoring
0. Not-for-profit organizations report financial information **(A)** before each election **(B)** when all appropriations have been spent **(C)** by preparing financial statements periodically **(D)** by copying the general ledger accounts	C	0. ✔
1. A not-for-profit organization's performance is measured primarily by **(A)** determining the amount of net income **(B)** determining the efficiency with which resources are used **(C)** evaluating the organization's manager **(D)** figuring the amount of cash accumulated...............................	B	1.
2. Governmental funds do not record or report **(A)** liabilities **(B)** expenditures **(C)** assets **(D)** expenses	D	2.
3. Governmental funds recognize revenues when the revenues **(A)** become measurable and available **(B)** are earned **(C)** are collected **(D)** are budgeted	A	3.
4. When supplies are bought **(A)** an asset account is debited **(B)** an expense account is debited **(C)** an expenditure account is debited **(D)** a fund balance account is debited..	C	4.
5. At the end of a fiscal period, an adjustment is made to record the amount of supplies on hand as **(A)** an asset **(B)** an expense **(C)** an expenditure **(D)** a fund balance	A	5.
6. Before closing the accounts at the end of a fiscal period, the reserve for encumbrances account is considered to be **(A)** an asset account **(B)** a liability account **(C)** a fund equity account **(D)** a budgetary account...........	D	6.
7. The difference between the Revenues/Expenditures Credit column total and the Debit column total of a work sheet is the **(A)** net income **(B)** total cash received **(C)** excess of revenues over expenditures **(D)** unreserved fund balance.............	C	7.
8. One of the sections of a statement of revenues, expenditures, and changes in fund balance — budget and actual is called **(A)** fund equity **(B)** changes in unreserved fund balance **(C)** expenses **(D)** assets...................................	B	8.
9. Expenditures are listed on a statement of revenues, expenditures, and changes in fund balance — budget and actual **(A)** by source **(B)** by type of expenditure **(C)** as totals for each department **(D)** are not listed on this statement...............	C	9.
10. A governmental fund balance sheet has **(A)** one owner's equity section **(B)** two or more owners' equity sections **(C)** a stockholders' equity section **(D)** no owner's equity section	D	10.

UNIT B—Classifying Items on a Governmental Organization's Financial Statements

DIRECTIONS: Identify in what statement and in what section of that statement each item below will be reported. Write in the Answers column a letter from the Statement column and a number from the Statement Section column. The organization using these statements is a town.

Statement

A. Statement of Revenues, Expenditures, and Changes in Fund Balance — Budget and Actual
B. Balance Sheet
C. Neither A nor B

Statement Section

1. Assets
2. Expenditures
3. Fund Equity
4. Liabilities
5. Revenues
6. None of the above

Items

Items	Stmt.	Sec.	Stmt.	Sec.
0–0. Cash	B	1	0. ✔	0. ✔
11–12. Appropriations	C	6	11.	12.
13–14. Encumbrance — Supplies, Public Works	C	6	13.	14.
15–16. Inventory of Supplies	B	1	15.	16.
17–18. Property Tax Revenue	A	5	17.	18.
19–20. Taxes Receivable — Delinquent	B	1	19.	20.
21–22. Expenditures — Public Works	A	2	21.	22.
23–24. Estimated Revenue	C	6	23.	24.
25–26. Accounts Payable	B	4	25.	26.
27–28. Other Revenue	A	5	27.	28.
29–30. Allowance for Uncollectible Taxes — Delinquent	B	1	29.	30.
31–32. Total Fund Equity	B	3	31.	32.
33–34. Reserve for Inventory of Supplies	B	3	33.	34.
35–36. Interest Revenue	A	5	35.	36.
37–38. Notes Payable	B	4	37.	38.
39–40. Interest Receivable	B	1	39.	40.

UNIT C—Analyzing Adjusting and Closing Entries for a Not-for-Profit Organization

DIRECTIONS: For each entry below, print in the proper Answers columns the identifying letters of the accounts to be debited and credited.

Account Titles

A. Allowance for Uncollectible Interest
B. Appropriations
C. Budgetary Fund Balance
D. Encumbrance — Supplies, Recreation
E. Estimated Revenues
F. Expenditure — Personnel, Recreation
G. Interest Receivable
H. Interest Revenue
I. Inventory of Supplies
J. Property Tax Revenue
K. Reserve for Encumbrances — Current Year
L. Reserve for Encumbrances — Prior Year
M. Reserve for Inventory of Supplies
N. Unreserved Fund Balance

Transactions

Transactions	Debit	Credit	Debit	Credit
0–0. Close revenue accounts	H, J	N	0. ✔	0. ✔
41–42. Adjust for unused supplies on hand	I	M	41.	42.
43–44. Close expenditure account	N	F	43.	44.
45–46. Reclassify amount of encumbrances outstanding to prior year status	K	L	45.	46.
47–48. Reverse budget entry	B, C	E	47.	48.
49–50. Adjust for interest revenue due but not collected	G	A, H	49.	50.
51–52. Close outstanding encumbrance account	N	D	51.	52.

Preparing a work sheet for a governmental organization

The work sheet prepared in Problem 26-1 is needed to complete Problems 26-2, 26-3, and 26-4.

Town of Fairview General Fund

Work Sheet

For Year Ended December 31, 19--

	ACCOUNT TITLE	TRIAL BALANCE DEBIT	TRIAL BALANCE CREDIT	ADJUSTMENTS DEBIT	ADJUSTMENTS CREDIT	REVENUES/EXPENDITURES DEBIT	REVENUES/EXPENDITURES CREDIT	BALANCE SHEET DEBIT	BALANCE SHEET CREDIT
1	Cash	72 13 0 00						72 13 0 00	
2	Taxes Receivable—Current								
3	Allow. for Uncoll. Taxes—Cur.								
4	Taxes Receivable—Delinquent	17 70 0 00						17 70 0 00	
5	Allow. for Uncoll. Taxes—Delinq.		7 9 6 0 00						7 9 6 0 00
6	Interest Receivable			(b) 2 7 8 0 00				2 7 8 0 00	
7	Allow. for Uncoll. Interest				(b) 5 5 6 00				5 5 6 00
8	Inventory of Supplies			(a) 3 4 3 0 00				3 4 3 0 00	
9	Investments—Short Term								
10	Accounts Payable		34 3 2 0 00						34 3 2 0 00
11	Notes Payable								
12	Unreserved Fund Balance		39 2 4 4 00						39 2 4 4 00
13	Reserve for Encumb.—Cur. Yr.		1 2 4 0 00	(c) 1 2 4 0 00					
14	Reserve for Encumb.—Prior Yr.				(c) 1 2 4 0 00		1 2 4 0 00		
15	Reserve for Inventory of Supplies				(a) 3 4 3 0 00				3 4 3 0 00
16	Property Tax Revenue		1459 0 0 0 00				1459 0 0 0 00		
17	Interest Revenue		4 7 5 6 00		(b) 2 2 2 4 00		6 9 8 0 00		
18	Other Revenue		9 0 2 0 00				9 0 2 0 00		
19	Expend.—Personnel, Gen. Gov't.	250 0 5 0 00				250 0 5 0 00			
20	Expend.—Supplies, Gen. Gov't.	12 1 0 0 00				12 1 0 0 00			
21	Expend.—Other Chgs., Gen. Gov't.	124 5 1 0 00				124 5 1 0 00			
22	Expend.—Cap. Outlay, Gen. Gov't.	14 5 0 0 00				14 5 0 0 00			
23	Expend.—Personnel, Pub. Saf.	464 7 0 0 00				464 7 8 8 88			
24	Expend.—Supplies, Pub. Saf.	21 8 5 0 00				21 8 5 0 00			
25	Expend.—Other Chgs., Pub. Saf.	168 4 2 0 00				168 4 2 0 00			
26	Expend.—Cap. Outlay, Pub. Saf.	80 9 8 0 00				80 9 8 0 00			
27	Expend.—Personnel, Pub. Wks.	107 7 3 0 00				107 7 3 0 88			

#	ACCOUNT TITLE	TRIAL BALANCE DEBIT	TRIAL BALANCE CREDIT	ADJUSTMENTS DEBIT	ADJUSTMENTS CREDIT	REVENUES/EXPENDITURES DEBIT	REVENUES/EXPENDITURES CREDIT	BALANCE SHEET DEBIT	BALANCE SHEET CREDIT
28	Expend.—Supplies, Pub. Wks.	6 1 5 0 00				6 1 5 0 00			
29	Expend.—Other Chgs., Pub. Wks.	52 1 7 0 00				52 1 7 0 00			
30	Expend.—Cap. Outlay, Pub. Wks.	46 3 0 0 00				46 3 0 0 00			
31	Expend.—Personnel, Rec.	55 2 5 0 00				212 3 5 0 00 / 55 2 5 0 00			
32	Expend.—Supplies, Rec.	21 5 7 0 00				21 5 7 0 00			
33	Expend.—Other Chgs., Rec.	27 7 5 0 00				27 7 5 0 00			
34	Expend.—Cap. Outlay, Rec.	10 4 4 0 00				10 4 4 0 00			
35	Estimated Revenues	1474 9 5 0 00				115 0 1 00 / 1474 9 5 0 00			
36	Appropriations		1447 5 4 0 00				1447 5 4 0 00		
37	Budgetary Fund Balance		27 4 1 0 00				27 4 1 0 00		
38	Encumb.—Supplies, Gen. Gov't.	1 2 4 0 00				1 2 4 0 00			
39		3030 4 9 0 00	3030 4 9 0 00	7 4 5 0 00	7 4 5 0 00	2940 6 6 0 00	2951 1 9 0 00	96 0 4 0 00	85 5 1 0 00
40	*Excess of Rev. Over Expend.*					10 5 3 0 00			10 5 3 0 00
41						2951 1 9 0 00	2951 1 9 0 00	96 0 4 0 00	96 0 4 0 00
42									
43									
44									
45									
46									
47									
48									
49									
50									
51									
52									
53									
54									
55									
56									
57									
58									
59									

Preparing a statement of revenues, expenditures, and changes in fund balance—budget and actual for a governmental organization

The work sheet prepared in Problem 26-1 is needed to complete Problem 26-2. The statement of revenues, expenditures, and changes in fund balance—budget and actual prepared in Problem 26-2 is needed to complete Problem 26-3.

Town of Fairview General Fund

Statement of Revenues, Expenditures, and Changes in Fund Balance—Budget and Actual

For Year Ended December 31, 19--

	BUDGET	ACTUAL	VARIANCE-- FAVORABLE (UNFAVORABLE)
Revenues:			
Property Tax Revenue	1,459 0 0 0 00	1,459 0 0 0 00	—
Interest Revenue	7 2 0 0 00	6 9 8 0 00	(2 2 0 00)
Other Revenue	8 7 5 0 00	9 0 2 0 00	2 7 0 00
Total Revenues	1,474 9 5 0 00	1,475 0 0 0 00	5 0 00
Expenditures:			
General Government	402 8 2 0 00	401 1 6 0 00	1 6 6 0 00
Public Safety	736 4 7 0 00	735 9 5 0 00	5 2 0 00
Public Works	212 4 9 0 00	212 3 5 0 00	1 4 0 00
Recreation	95 7 6 0 00	115 0 1 0 00	(19 2 5 0 00)
Total Expenditures	1,447 5 4 0 00	1,464 4 7 0 00	(16 9 3 0 00)
Excess of Revenues Over Expenditures	27 4 1 0 00	10 5 3 0 00	(16 8 8 0 00)
Less Outstanding Encumbrances, Dec. 31, 19--	—	1 2 4 0 00	(1 2 4 0 00)
Increase in Unreserved Fund Balance for Year	27 4 1 0 00	9 2 9 0 00	(18 1 2 0 00)
Unreserved Fund Balance, Jan. 1, 19--	39 2 4 4 00	39 2 4 4 00	—
Unreserved Fund Balance, Dec. 31, 19--	66 6 5 4 00	48 5 3 4 00	(18 1 2 0 00)

The work sheet and statement of revenues, expenditures, and changes in fund balance—budget and actual, prepared in Problems 26-1 and 26-2, are needed to complete Problem 26-3.

Town of Fairview General Fund

Balance Sheet

December 31, 19--

Assets		
Cash		72 1 3 0 00
Taxes Receivable—Delinquent	17 7 0 0 00	
Less: Allowance for Uncoll. Taxes—Delinquent	7 9 6 0 00	9 7 4 0 00
Interest Receivable	2 7 8 0 00	
Less: Allowance for Uncollectible Interest	5 5 6 00	2 2 2 4 00
Inventory of Supplies		3 4 3 0 00
Total Assets		87 5 2 4 00
Liabilities and Fund Equity		
Liabilities:		
Accounts Payable		34 3 2 0 00
Fund Equity:		
Unreserved Fund Balance	48 5 3 4 00	
Reserve for Encumbrances—Prior Year	1 2 4 0 00	
Reserve for Inventory of Supplies	3 4 3 0 00	
Total Fund Equity		53 2 0 4 00
Total Liabilities and Fund Equity		87 5 2 4 00

Recording adjusting and closing entries for a governmental organization

The work sheet prepared in Problem 26-1 is needed to complete Problem 26-4.

JOURNAL

PAGE 10

	DATE	ACCOUNT TITLE	DOC. NO.	POST. REF.	GENERAL DEBIT	GENERAL CREDIT	CASH DEBIT	CASH CREDIT
1		**Adjusting Entries**						
2	19-- Dec. 31	Inventory of Supplies			3 4 3 0 00			
3		Reserve for Inventory of Supplies				3 4 3 0 00		
4	31	Interest Receivable			2 7 8 0 00			
5		Allowance for Uncollectible Interest				5 5 6 00		
6		Interest Revenue				2 2 2 4 00		
7	31	Reserve for Encumbrances—Current Year			1 2 4 0 00			
8		Reserve for Encumbrances—Prior Year				1 2 4 0 00		
9		**Closing Entries**						
10	31	Property Tax Revenue			1459 0 0 0 00			
11		Interest Revenue			6 9 8 0 00			
12		Other Revenue			9 0 2 0 00			
13		Unreserved Fund Balance				1475 0 0 0 00		
14	31	Unreserved Fund Balance			1464 4 7 0 00			
15		Expenditure—Personnel, Gen. Gov't.				250 0 5 0 00		
16		Expenditure—Supplies, Gen. Gov't.				12 1 0 0 00		
17		Expenditure—Other Charges, Gen. Gov't.				124 5 1 0 00		
18		Expenditure—Capital Outlays, Gen. Gov't.				14 5 0 0 00		
19		Expenditure—Personnel, Public Safety				464 7 0 0 00		
20		Expenditure—Supplies, Public Safety				21 8 5 0 00		
21		Expenditure—Other Charges, Public Safety				168 4 2 0 00		
22		Expenditure—Capital Outlays, Public Safety				80 9 8 0 00		
23		Expenditure—Personnel, Public Works				107 7 3 0 00		
24		Expenditure—Supplies, Public Works				6 1 5 0 00		

JOURNAL

	DATE	ACCOUNT TITLE	DOC. NO.	POST. REF.	GENERAL DEBIT	GENERAL CREDIT	CASH DEBIT	CASH CREDIT	
25		Expenditure—Other Charges, Public Works				52 1 7 0 00			25
26		Expenditure—Capital Outlays, Public Works				46 3 0 0 00			26
27		Expenditure—Personnel, Recreation				55 2 5 0 00			27
28		Expenditure—Supplies, Recreation				21 5 7 0 00			28
29		Expenditure—Other Charges, Recreation				27 7 5 0 00			29
30		Expenditure—Capital Outlays, Recreation				10 4 4 0 00			30
31	31	Appropriations			1447 5 4 0 00				31
32		Budgetary Fund Balance			27 4 1 0 00				32
33		Estimated Revenues				1474 9 5 0 00			33
34	31	Unreserved Fund Balance			1 2 4 0 00				34
35		Encumbrance—Supplies, Gen. Gov't.				1 2 4 0 00			35
36									36
37									37
38									38
39									39
40									40
41									41
42									42
43									43
44									44
45									45
46									46
47									47
48									48

Completing end-of-fiscal-period work for a governmental organization [1]

Town of Belton, General Fund
Work Sheet
For Year Ended December 31, 19--

#	Account Title	Trial Balance Debit	Trial Balance Credit	Adjustments Debit	Adjustments Credit	Revenues/Expenditures Debit	Revenues/Expenditures Credit	Balance Sheet Debit	Balance Sheet Credit
1	Cash	108390 00						108390 00	
2	Taxes Receivable—Current								
3	Allow. for Uncoll. Taxes—Cur.								
4	Taxes Receivable—Delinquent	15430 00						15430 00	
5	Allow. for Uncoll. Taxes—Delinq.		6940 00						6940 00
6	Interest Receivable			(b)2350 00				2350 00	
7	Allow. for Uncoll. Interest				(b)470 00				470 00
8	Inventory of Supplies			(a)2900 00				2900 00	
9	Investments—Short Term								
10	Accounts Payable		29340 00						29340 00
11	Notes Payable								
12	Unreserved Fund Balance		33550 00						33550 00
13	Reserve for Encumb.—Cur. Yr.		870 00	(c)870 00					
14	Reserve for Encumb.—Prior Yr.				(c)870 00		870 00		
15	Reserve for Inventory of Supplies				(a)2900 00				2900 00
16	Property Tax Revenue		1275000 00				1275000 00		
17	Interest Revenue		6680 00		(b)1880 00		8560 00		
18	Other Revenue		8120 00				8120 00		
19	Expend.—Personnel, Gen. Gov't.	213640 00				213640 00			
20	Expend.—Supplies, Gen. Gov't.	10490 00				10490 00			
21	Expend.—Other Chgs., Gen. Gov't.	106550 00				106550 00			
22	Expend.—Cap. Outlay, Gen. Gov't.	12300 00				12300 00			
23	Expend.—Personnel, Pub. Saf.	397540 00				397548 00			
24	Expend.—Supplies, Pub. Saf.	18620 00				18620 00			
25	Expend.—Other Chgs., Pub. Saf.	144150 00				144150 00			
26	Expend.—Cap. Outlay, Pub. Saf.	69300 00				69300 00			
27	Expend.—Personnel, Pub. Wks.	92200 00				92208 00			

| | TRIAL BALANCE | | ADJUSTMENTS | | REVENUES/EXPENDITURES | | BALANCE SHEET | |
ACCOUNT TITLE	DEBIT	CREDIT	DEBIT	CREDIT	DEBIT	CREDIT	DEBIT	CREDIT
28 Expend.—Supplies, Pub. Wks.	5 2 5 0 00				5 2 5 0 00			
29 Expend.—Other Chgs., Pub. Wks.	44 7 5 0 00				44 7 5 0 00			
30 Expend.—Cap. Outlay, Pub. Wks.	39 6 0 0 00				39 6 0 0 00			
31 Expend.—Personnel, Rec.	47 2 2 0 00				^{18}4 2 $_{\,}$ 0 00 / 47 2 2 0 00			
32 Expend.—Supplies, Rec.	1 8 5 0 00				1 8 5 0 00			
33 Expend.—Other Chgs., Rec.	23 4 8 0 00				23 4 8 0 00			
34 Expend.—Cap. Outlay, Rec.	8 8 7 0 00				8 8 7 0 00			
35 Estimated Revenues	1290 0 0 0 00				^{81}1290 0 0 0 00			
36 Appropriations		1238 0 0 0 00				1238 0 0 0 00		
37 Budgetary Fund Balance		52 0 0 0 00				52 0 0 0 00		
38 Encumb.—Supplies, Gen. Gov't.	8 7 0 00				8 7 0 00			
39	2650 5 0 0 00	2650 5 0 0 00	6 1 2 0 00	6 1 2 0 00	2526 6 8 0 00	2582 5 5 0 00	129 0 7 0 00	73 2 0 0 00
40 *Excess of Rev. Over Expend.*					55 8 7 0 00			55 8 7 0 00
41					2582 5 5 0 00	2582 5 5 0 00	129 0 7 0 00	129 0 7 0 00
42								
43								
44								
45								
46								
47								
48								
49								
50								
51								
52								
53								
54								
55								
56								
57								
58								
59								

Town of Belton General Fund

Statement of Revenues, Expenditures, and Changes in Fund Balance—Budget and Actual

For Year Ended December 31, 19--

	BUDGET	ACTUAL	VARIANCE--FAVORABLE (UNFAVORABLE)
Revenues:			
Property Tax Revenue	1,275 000 00	1,275 000 00	
Interest Revenue	7 250 00	8 560 00	1 310 00
Other Revenue	7 750 00	8 120 00	3 70 00
Total Revenues	1,290 000 00	1,291 680 00	1 680 00
Expenditures:			
General Government	344 200 00	342 980 00	1 220 00
Public Safety	630 100 00	629 610 00	4 90 00
Public Works	182 000 00	181 800 00	2 00 00
Recreation	81 700 00	81 420 00	2 80 00
Total Expenditures	1,238 000 00	1,235 810 00	2 190 00
Excess of Revenues Over Expenditures	52 000 00	55 870 00	3 870 00
Less Outstanding Encumbrances, Dec. 31, 19--		8 70 00	(8 70 00)
Increase in Unreserved Fund Balance for Year	52 000 00	55 000 00	3 000 00
Unreserved Fund Balance, Jan. 1, 19--	33 550 00	33 550 00	
Unreserved Fund Balance, Dec. 31, 19--	85 550 00	88 550 00	3 000 00

Town of Belton General Fund

Balance Sheet

December 31, 19--

Assets													
Cash								108	3	9	0	00	
Taxes Receivable—Delinquent	15	4	3	0	00								
Less: Allowance for Uncoll. Taxes—Delinquent	6	9	4	0	00		8	4	9	0	00	
Interest Receivable	2	3	5	0	00								
Less: Allowance for Uncollectible Interest		4	7	0	00		1	8	8	0	00	
Inventory of Supplies								2	9	0	0	00	
Total Assets							121	6	6	0	00	
Liabilities and Fund Equity													
Liabilities:													
Accounts Payable								29	3	4	0	00	
Fund Equity:													
Unreserved Fund Balance	88	5	5	0	00								
Reserve for Encumbrances—Prior Year		8	7	0	00								
Reserve for Inventory of Supplies	2	9	0	0	00								
Total Fund Equity								92	3	2	0	00	
Total Liabilities and Fund Equity							121	6	6	0	00	

JOURNAL

	DATE	ACCOUNT TITLE	DOC. NO.	POST. REF.	GENERAL DEBIT	GENERAL CREDIT	CASH DEBIT	CASH CREDIT	
1		*Adjusting Entries*							1
2	Dec. 31	Inventory of Supplies			2 9 0 0 00				2
3		Reserve for Inventory of Supplies				2 9 0 0 00			3
4	31	Interest Receivable			2 3 5 0 00				4
5		Allowance for Uncollectible Interest				4 7 0 00			5
6		Interest Revenue				1 8 8 0 00			6
7	31	Reserve for Encumbrances—Current Year			8 7 0 00				7
8		Reserve for Encumbrances—Prior Year				8 7 0 00			8
9		*Closing Entries*							9
10	31	Property Tax Revenue			1275 0 0 0 00				10
11		Interest Revenue			8 5 6 0 00				11
12		Other Revenue			8 1 2 0 00				12
13		Unreserved Fund Balance				1291 6 8 0 00			13
14	31	Unreserved Fund Balance			1235 8 1 0 00				14
15		Expenditure—Personnel, Gen. Gov't.				213 6 4 0 00			15
16		Expenditure—Supplies, Gen. Gov't.				10 4 9 0 00			16
17		Expenditure—Other Charges, Gen. Gov't.				106 5 5 0 00			17
18		Expenditure—Capital Outlays, Gen. Gov't.				12 3 0 0 00			18
19		Expenditure—Personnel, Public Safety				397 5 4 0 00			19
20		Expenditure—Supplies, Public Safety				18 6 2 0 00			20
21		Expenditure—Other Charges, Public Safety				144 1 5 0 00			21
22		Expenditure—Capital Outlays, Public Safety				69 3 0 0 00			22
23		Expenditure—Personnel, Public Works				92 2 0 0 00			23
24		Expenditure—Supplies, Public Works				5 2 5 0 00			24

[4]

JOURNAL

PAGE 12 (cont.)

	DATE	ACCOUNT TITLE	DOC. NO.	POST. REF.	GENERAL DEBIT	GENERAL CREDIT	CASH DEBIT	CASH CREDIT	
25		Expenditure—Other Charges, Public Works				44 7 5 0 00			25
26		Expenditure—Capital Outlays, Public Works				39 6 0 0 00			26
27		Expenditure—Personnel, Recreation				47 2 2 0 00			27
28		Expenditure—Supplies, Recreation				1 8 5 0 00			28
29		Expenditure—Other Charges, Recreation				23 4 8 0 00			29
30		Expenditure—Capital Outlays, Recreation				8 8 7 0 00			30
31	31	Appropriations			1238 0 0 0 00				31
32		Budgetary Fund Balance			52 0 0 0 00				32
33		Estimated Revenues				1290 0 0 0 00			33
34	31	Unreserved Fund Balance			8 7 0 00				34
35		Encumbrance—Supplies, Gen. Gov't.				8 7 0 00			35
36									36
37									37
38									38
39									39
40									40
41									41
42									42
43									43
44									44
45									45
46									46
47									47
48									48

Completing end-of-fiscal-period work for a governmental organization   [1]

Town of Copperhill, General Fund

Work Sheet

For Year Ended December 31, 19--

| | TRIAL BALANCE | | ADJUSTMENTS | | REVENUES/EXPENDITURES | | BALANCE SHEET | |
ACCOUNT TITLE	DEBIT	CREDIT	DEBIT	CREDIT	DEBIT	CREDIT	DEBIT	CREDIT
1 Cash	52 148 00						52 148 00	
2 Taxes Receivable—Current								
3 Allow. for Uncoll. Taxes—Cur.								
4 Taxes Receivable—Delinquent	32 074 00						32 074 00	
5 Allow. for Uncoll. Taxes—Delinq.		11 225 00						11 225 00
6 Interest Receivable			(b) 5 080 00				5 080 00	
7 Allow. for Uncoll. Interest				(b) 1 016 00				1 016 00
8 Inventory of Supplies			(a) 3 582 00				3 582 00	
9 Investments—Short Term								
10 Accounts Payable		35 816 00						35 816 00
11 Notes Payable								
12 Unreserved Fund Balance		60 450 00						60 450 00
13 Reserve for Encumb.—Cur. Yr.		1 076 00	(c) 1 076 00					
14 Reserve for Encumb.—Prior Yr.				(c) 1 076 00		1 076 00		
15 Reserve for Inventory of Supplies				(a) 3 582 00				3 582 00
16 Property Tax Revenue		1457 900 00				1457 900 00		
17 Interest Revenue		9 885 00		(b) 4 064 00		13 949 00		
18 Other Revenue		15 973 00				15 973 00		
19 Expend.—Personnel, Gen. Gov't.	260 420 00				260 420 00			
20 Expend.—Supplies, Gen. Gov't.	143 940 00				143 940 00			
21 Expend.—Other Chgs., Gen. Gov't.	129 975 00				129 975 00			
22 Expend.—Cap. Outlay, Gen. Gov't.	15 168 00				15 168 00			
23 Expend.—Personnel, Pub. Saf.	482 590 00				482 590 00			
24 Expend.—Supplies, Pub. Saf.	21 973 00				21 973 00			
25 Expend.—Other Chgs., Pub. Saf.	175 843 00				175 843 00			
26 Expend.—Cap. Outlay, Pub. Saf.	85 245 00				85 245 00			
27 Expend.—Personnel, Pub. Wks.	113 325 00				113 325 00			

	ACCOUNT TITLE	TRIAL BALANCE DEBIT	TRIAL BALANCE CREDIT	ADJUSTMENTS DEBIT	ADJUSTMENTS CREDIT	REVENUES/EXPENDITURES DEBIT	REVENUES/EXPENDITURES CREDIT	BALANCE SHEET DEBIT	BALANCE SHEET CREDIT
28	Expend.—Supplies, Pub. Wks.	6 687 00				6 687 00			
29	Expend.—Other Chgs., Pub. Wks.	52 984 00				52 984 00			
30	Expend.—Cap. Outlay, Pub. Wks.	48 820 00				48 820 00			
31	Expend.—Personnel, Rec.	56 855 00				56 855 00			
32	Expend.—Supplies, Rec.	2 978 00				2 978 00			
33	Expend.—Other Chgs., Rec.	28 910 00				28 910 00			
34	Expend.—Cap. Outlay, Rec.	10 960 00				10 960 00			
35	Estimated Revenues	1487 640 00				1487 640 00			
36	Appropriations		1511 260 00				1511 260 00		
37	Budgetary Fund Balance	23 620 00				23 620 00			
38	Encumb.—Supplies, Pub. Saf.	1 076 00				1 076 00			
39		3103 585 00	3103 585 00	9 738 00	9 738 00	3019 363 00	3000 158 00	92 884 00	112 089 00
40							192 050 0	192 050 0	
41	*Excess of Expend. Over Rev.*					3019 363 00	3019 363 00	112 089 00	112 089 00
42									
43									
44									
45									
46									
47									
48									
49									
50									
51									
52									
53									
54									
55									
56									
57									
58									
59									

Town of Copperhill General Fund

Statement of Revenues, Expenditures, and Changes in Fund Balance—Budget and Actual

For Year Ended December 31, 19--

	BUDGET	ACTUAL	VARIANCE--FAVORABLE (UNFAVORABLE)
Revenues:			
Property Tax Revenue	1,457 9 0 0 00	1,457 9 0 0 00	—
Interest Revenue	13 1 6 0 00	13 9 4 9 00	7 8 9 00
Other Revenue	16 5 8 0 00	15 9 7 3 00	(6 0 7 00)
Total Revenues	1,487 6 4 0 00	1,487 8 2 2 00	1 8 2 00
Expenditures:			
General Government	420 1 3 0 00	419 9 5 7 00	1 7 3 00
Public Safety	769 2 3 0 00	765 6 5 1 00	3 5 7 9 00
Public Works	222 1 5 5 00	221 7 1 6 00	4 3 9 00
Recreation	99 7 4 5 00	99 7 0 3 00	4 2 00
Total Expenditures	1,511 2 6 0 00	1,507 0 2 7 00	4 2 3 3 00
Excess of Expenditures Over Revenues	23 6 2 0 00	19 2 0 5 00	4 4 1 5 00
Plus Outstanding Encumbrances, Dec. 31, 19--	—	1 0 7 6 00	(1 0 7 6 00)
Decrease in Unreserved Fund Balance for Year	23 6 2 0 00	20 2 8 1 00	3 3 3 9 00
Unreserved Fund Balance, Jan. 1, 19--	60 4 5 0 00	60 4 5 0 00	—
Unreserved Fund Balance, Dec. 31, 19--	36 8 3 0 00	40 1 6 9 00	3 3 3 9 00

Town of Copperhill General Fund

Balance Sheet

December 31, 19--

Assets			
Cash			52 1 4 8 00
Taxes Receivable — Delinquent	32 0 7 4 00		
Less: Allowance for Uncoll. Taxes — Delinquent	11 2 2 5 00		20 8 4 9 00
Interest Receivable	5 0 8 0 00		
Less: Allowance for Uncollectible Interest	1 0 1 6 00		4 0 6 4 00
Inventory of Supplies			3 5 8 2 00
Total Assets			80 6 4 3 00
Liabilities and Fund Equity			
Liabilities:			
Accounts Payable			35 8 1 6 00
Fund Equity:			
Unreserved Fund Balance	40 1 6 9 00		
Reserve for Encumbrances — Prior Year	1 0 7 6 00		
Reserve for Inventory of Supplies	3 5 8 2 00		
Total Fund Equity			44 8 2 7 00
Total Liabilities and Fund Equity			80 6 4 3 00

JOURNAL — PAGE 18

DATE	ACCOUNT TITLE	DOC. NO.	POST. REF.	GENERAL DEBIT	GENERAL CREDIT	CASH DEBIT	CASH CREDIT
	Adjusting Entries						
19-- Dec. 31	Inventory of Supplies			3 5 8 2 00			
	Reserve for Inventory of Supplies				3 5 8 2 00		
31	Interest Receivable			5 0 8 0 00			
	Allowance for Uncollectible Interest				1 0 1 6 00		
	Interest Revenue				4 0 6 4 00		
31	Reserve for Encumbrances—Current Year			1 0 7 6 00			
	Reserve for Encumbrances—Prior Year				1 0 7 6 00		
	Closing Entries						
31	Property Tax Revenue			1457 9 0 0 00			
	Interest Revenue			13 9 4 9 00			
	Other Revenue			15 9 7 3 00			
	Unreserved Fund Balance				1487 8 2 2 00		
31	Unreserved Fund Balance			1507 0 2 7 00			
	Expenditure—Personnel, Gen. Gov't.				260 4 2 0 00		
	Expenditure—Supplies, Gen. Gov't.				14 3 9 4 00		
	Expenditure—Other Charges, Gen. Gov't.				129 9 7 5 00		
	Expenditure—Capital Outlays, Gen. Gov't.				15 1 6 8 00		
	Expenditure—Personnel, Public Safety				482 5 9 0 00		
	Expenditure—Supplies, Public Safety				21 9 7 3 00		
	Expenditure—Other Charges, Public Safety				175 8 4 3 00		
	Expenditure—Capital Outlays, Public Safety				85 2 4 5 00		
	Expenditure—Personnel, Public Works				113 2 2 5 00		
	Expenditure—Supplies, Public Works				6 6 8 7 00		

JOURNAL

PAGE 18 (cont.)

	DATE	ACCOUNT TITLE	DOC. NO.	POST. REF.	GENERAL DEBIT	GENERAL CREDIT	CASH DEBIT	CASH CREDIT	
25		Expenditure—Other Charges, Public Works				52 9 8 4 00			25
26		Expenditure—Capital Outlays, Public Works				48 8 2 0 00			26
27		Expenditure—Personnel, Recreation				56 8 5 5 00			27
28		Expenditure—Supplies, Recreation				2 9 7 8 00			28
29		Expenditure—Other Charges, Recreation				28 9 1 0 00			29
30		Expenditure—Capital Outlays, Recreation				10 9 6 0 00			30
31	31	Appropriations			1511 2 6 0 00				31
32		Budgetary Fund Balance				23 6 2 0 00			32
33		Estimated Revenues				1487 6 4 0 00			33
34	31	Unreserved Fund Balance			1 0 7 6 00				34
35		Encumbrance—Supplies, Public Safety				1 0 7 6 00			35
36									36
37									37
38									38
39									39
40									40
41									41
42									42
43									43
44									44
45									45
46									46
47									47
48									48